The Economic Structure of
International Law

The Economic Structure of International Law

✦

JOEL P. TRACHTMAN

HARVARD UNIVERSITY PRESS

Cambridge, Massachusetts

London, England

2008

Library of Congress Cataloging-in-Publication Data

Trachtman, Joel P.
The economic structure of international law / Joel P. Trachtman.
p.   cm.
Includes bibliographical references and index.
ISBN-13: 978-0-674-03098-5 (alk. paper)
1. International law—Economic aspects.   2. International economic
relations.   3. Globalization—Economic aspects.   I. Title.
KZ1252.T73   2008
341—dc22   2008017648

For Lauren

Contents

Preface

THIS BOOK ELABORATES a law and economics–based theoretical understanding of the structure of the international legal system. The need for such a work is clear. Political science has only recently reengaged with international law. Economics has not sought to explain international law broadly, although it has made forays into international trade law, while law and economics has only addressed limited aspects of international law. International legal theory itself has until recently been mired in a stale and equipoised debate between natural law and positive law. Like other legal theory, international legal theory has served more as a statement of position, or a conclusion, than as a social scientific theory. While the debate between natural law and positive law has some important implications, it has suppressed the growth of a social scientific approach to international law. A social scientific approach has also been inhibited by a view of international law that often emphasizes advocacy over analysis. A social scientific approach would use theory, in the tradition of the sciences, as a source of testable hypotheses, not as a source of dogma.

A social science–based account of international law requires great complexity, as it addresses a number of phenomena, including the rise, stability, and efficiency of custom; compliance with treaty; the establishment of international organizations; the use of dispute settlement in international treaty structures; and a host of other topics. While these are varied subjects, the treatment of which requires a variety of tools, it is possible to develop an overarching analytical model of international law. The approach developed in this book is consequentialist: it is based on an attempt to determine the effect of law on behavior. However, this book does not address substantive international law relating to particular fields, such as international environmental law, international trade law, international human rights law, or the laws of war. So it does not examine, for example, how human rights treaties affect the human rights performance of states. Rather, this book provides a systematic framework by which to understand and evaluate the formation and application of law in all of these areas.

At the core of analysis of international law as a system, and permeating to the very periphery, is the question of jurisdiction: the legal manifestation of power, or authority. Even issues of "cooperation," which are the focus of much of international law and international politics scholarship, are just a subset of the problem of allocation of authority. When states cooperate, they agree not to exercise authority that they had *ex ante,* they agree to accept exercise of authority by other states that the other states lacked *ex ante,* or they agree to pool authority in an international organization. We may also assimilate an agreement on substantive law—an agreement to exercise authority in a specified way—to a transfer of authority. These agreements may be implicit or explicit. While this allocation of authority-based understanding of the systemic structure of international law may seem artificial, it is substantively accurate and allows us to develop a parsimonious understanding of the structure of the international legal system.

What sets international law apart from domestic law in unitary states is that international law is concerned, first and foremost, with issues of allocation of authority. Indeed, domestic law is also concerned with issues of allocation of authority, but this theme is much more greatly submerged in domestic legal study. However, allocation comes to the fore in discussions of federal law in a federal system, such as the United States. In international society, there is less substantive international law than there is substantive federal law in the United States, and the allocation of authority is more contestable than in the mature U.S. federal system. Most importantly, every application of substantive law, or primary rules in the H. L. A. Hart sense, depends on a determination of jurisdiction: of the authority to make law applicable.

Of course, international law is also concerned with primary rules: rules regarding subjects such as environmental protection, international trade, human rights, and war. While these are primary rules, international law shows, perhaps more than domestic law, the difficulty of distinguishing clearly between primary rules and secondary rules. After all, primary rules take away the power of individuals to make certain decisions on their own and in that sense allocate authority. Thus, primary rules in the international setting may be understood as simply more specific instantiations of second-ary rules—of rules about the allocation of power. They are more specific in-stantiations insofar as they actually transfer power from one state to another in a specific sense. For example, a human rights rule that allows one state to bring a binding claim against human rights violations in another state may be understood as transferring power from the first state to the second.

This book focuses on secondary rules in the sense used by H. L. A. Hart: on rules whose main purpose is to deal with the formation of law and the allocation of jurisdiction. This book begins with a study of jurisdiction as power, follows its transfer through custom and treaty, and examines the way states share it through organizations. Thus, jurisdiction is the core issue in all of international law. Jurisdiction is the power of states in a legal setting. All international law is concerned with establishing or restraining the power of states.

This book represents the culmination of a number of years of study of the economic analysis of international law. It is not a mere restatement of my study of economic analysis of international law over these years, but an at-tempt to consolidate, integrate, rectify, and extend that study.

A book takes a village, and is a record of an education. I have had the op-portunity to learn from many others in the course of this study, including especially three scholars who coauthored with me papers that formed the basis for important parts of this work. The process of coauthorship with Jef-frey Dunoff, Phil Moremen, and George Norman has been for me a won-derful and challenging exploration, and this process has made it difficult to delineate responsibility. Portions of this work draw on works initially coau-thored with Professors Dunoff (some ideas in Chapters 1 and 4), Moremen (parts of Chapter 7), and Norman (Chapter 3)—and so while I accept full blame for this work, I cannot take full credit. Chapter 2 draws substantially from my 2001 article, *Economic Analysis of Prescriptive Jurisdiction and Choice of Law*, originally published in the VIRGINIA JOURNAL OF INTER-NATIONAL LAW. Chapter 3 draws substantially from my 2005 article with George Norman, *The Customary International Law Game*, originally pub-lished in the AMERICAN JOURNAL OF INTERNATIONAL LAW. Chapter 5 draws some material from my 1996 article, *The Theory of the Firm and the Theory of the International Economic Organization*. Excerpts reprinted by special permission of Northwestern University School of Law, NORTH-WESTERN JOURNAL OF INTERNATIONAL LAW.

Many colleagues have guided and assisted me during this time, in connection with different components of this work, including Anne van Aaken, Kenneth Abbott, José Alvarez, Jeffery Atik, Lucian Bebchuk, David Bederman, Dan Bodansky, William Bratton, Marc Busch, Richard Buxbaum, David Charny, Stanley Cox, Bill Dodge, Jeffrey Dunoff, Daniel Esty, Merritt Fox, Frank Garcia, Damien Geradin, Michael Glennon, Jack Goldsmith, Ryan Goodman, Andrew Guzman, Peter Hammer, Hurst Hannum, Larry Helfer, Robert Hockett, Rob Howse, Robert Hudec, Howell Jackson, John Jackson, Ian Johnstone, Edward Kane, Louis Kaplow, Patrick Kelly, David Kennedy, Michael Klein, Barbara Koremenos, Carsten Kowalczyk, Matthias Kumm, Brian Langille, Rick Mancke, Gabrielle Marceau, Lisa Martin, Joseph McCahery, John McGinnis, Andrew Moravcsik, Sean Murphy, Philip Nichols, Kalypso Nicolaidis, George Norman, Jide Nzelibe, Erin O'Hara, Francesco Parisi, Ernst-Ulrich Petersmann, Sol Picciotto, Eric Posner, Mark Ramseyer, Kal Raustiala, Donald Regan, Eric Reinhardt, Roberta Romano, Alfred Rubin, Jeswald Salacuse, Todd Sandler, Jean Schere, Steven Shavell, Beth Simmons, Anne-Marie Slaughter, Peter Spiro, Richard Steinberg, Paul Stephan, Edward Swaine, Alan Sykes, Paul Vaaler, Detlev Vagts, Joseph Weiler, and Eric White. I also appreciate the valuable suggestions of the anonymous referees consulted by Harvard University Press, and of Michael Aronson, my editor at Harvard University Press.

Components of this book were presented in earlier versions in many fora, at which I was privileged to obtain advice and insights from many additional people. These fora have included the 2005 annual meeting of the American Law and Economics Association, the American Society of International Law, the Berkeley International Law and Politics Seminar, Columbia Law School, Georgetown Law Centre, the European University Institute, several seminars at Harvard Law School, Michigan Law School, the Max Planck Institute for Collective Goods, the Max Planck Institute for Comparative Public Law and International Law, New York University School of Law, UCLA Law School, the Wharton School, and Yale Law School. I thank the hosts and the participants for these valuable opportunities to expose my work to helpful critical review.

Throughout my work on this book, I benefited from able research assistance by many students at the Fletcher School of Law and Diplomacy and Harvard Law School, including Aadeesh Aggarwal, Javier Diaz, Meg Donovan, Alexander Gazis, Jeremy Leong Zhi Jia, Christine Makori, Alfredo Munera, Vijay Palaniswamy, Elisabeth Shapiro, Ekaterina Trizlova, Nirmalaguhan Wigneswaran, and John D. Wood.

The Economic Structure of
International Law

CHAPTER ONE

∴✦∴

Introduction

A Social Scientific Approach to International Law

LAW AND ECONOMICS is the application of economic methods to legal analysis.[1] However, economics itself is not so much a methodology as an epistemology. Economics encompasses a broad range of methods. In this regard, economics is simply another word for rational social scientific analysis—properly applied, it rejects no method that is rational. While it is true that economics is learning to accept the irrational as well, it does not accept irrational theory or methodology, but seeks to apply rational analysis to irrational human behavior.[2] Economics is a strong social science because it is an open system. The only conditions for inclusion in the system are rational analysis (but not necessarily the assumption that people are rational) and methodological individualism.

Therefore, contrary to untutored criticisms, economics requires no assumptions of avarice or even selfishness. Nor does it prescribe any limitations of individuals' preferences to those regarding material goods. Rather, its assumptions are simply (i) methodologically, that individuals seek to maximize the achievement of their preferences; and (ii) normatively, that the only valid source of preferences—of values—is individuals. These are known respectively as methodological individualism and normative individualism. Normative individualism is closely aligned with liberalism. For those who criticize economics as materialistic, it must be pointed out that, properly understood, preferences are completely open to the full range of human aspiration, including not only material goods, but also aesthetic, moral, and altruistic desires.

1

It is therefore important to note that economic methods, properly applied, contain no prejudices in favor of property or against the state. Furthermore, it is simply bad economics—often an ignorant application of the Coase theorem—to assume that the market mode of allocation is always superior to bureaucratic allocation by government. The fundamental theorem of welfare economics, which posits that under perfect competition the market allocates resources efficiently, is qualified by the theory of the second best, which recognizes that in a world without perfect competition we cannot say that a move toward the free market will enhance efficiency.

Properly applied, economic methodologies are simply descriptive of relationships. Good economics helps to reveal relationships between legal rules, institutions, or policies on the one hand, and outcomes on the other hand: it is a consequentialist and self-conscious analytical tool of social life, without its own commitment as to the desirability of particular consequences.

It is also important to note that there is an essential unity to the social sciences, of which economics is only one. Others include political science, sociology, social psychology, and anthropology. They all seek descriptively, or positively, to understand how humanly created institutions (including laws) affect behavior and, normatively, to understand how changes in these institutions would affect behavior to align it more closely with specific preferences. On the other hand, many legal scholars have relinquished any pretensions to autonomy for law as a discipline,[3] and seek theoretical justification in other disciplines, such as economics, politics, and sociology.

Economic methodologies, or social science methodologies, are therefore inclusive in their application to law: they accept all rational ways of knowing about the consequences of social rules.

Economic analysis holds great promise for international law. This promise lies in the ability of economic analysis to suggest useful methods for analyzing the actual or potential consequences of particular legal rules. This approach is consequentialist, and it has everything to do with *lex ferenda*. In determining what the law should be, what else is required than to know what the desired consequences are, and the extent to which the available legal rules achieve these consequences? Of course, we have complex desires. We want both to preserve local prerogatives and to prevent genocide. We want both to promote environmental protection and to increase free trade. We want both predictability and flexibility. Economic analysis cannot tell us how to value these preferences, but it can tell us how to maximize the things we value. Economic analysis is intensely comparative, comparing the achievement of particular preferences under different circumstances. In law and economics, we focus on the consequences of different legal rules. The comparative process may be cross-jurisdictional, historical, or hypothetical in its reference.

On the other hand, economic analysis generally holds little utility for the *lex lata*, strictly understood. It tells us little about how to read or interpret law. In particular fields, of course, such as competition law or trade law, economic analysis may be part of the *lex lata*. That is, legal rules in those areas may refer to, or may be understood to refer to, economic concepts.

Economic analysis does counsel fidelity to process, to the extent that we can rely on legislative processes to be the best structure for identifying the preferences of constituents. Similarly with respect to contract, economic analysis generally counsels fidelity to the transactions that persons make for themselves as the best way to articulate their preferences. This is the learning of the fundamental theorem of welfare economics, which holds that under perfect competition (and absent transaction costs), market allocations produce maximum efficiency. Of course, perfect competition does not exist in the real world, and the real world is filled with transaction costs. However, those who argue that laws should be interpreted with economic efficiency in mind misunderstand the nature of efficiency and misjudge the ability of judges. We are concerned with efficiency to maximize preferences, or utility, not efficiency to maximize wealth, and we cannot easily know the preferences of others. In fact, economists reject the possibility of interpersonal comparison of utility. However, it is important to note that, as discussed below, to the extent that judges are given latitude—to the extent that they are delegated legislative authority—they work in the field of *lex ferenda*.

Furthermore, economic analysis of international law provides an important and interesting conundrum. This work argues that the primary concern in international legal reform is efficiency in the allocation of governmental authority. However, it also recognizes that efficiency in the allocation of governmental authority may be inconsistent with efficiency in the allocation of individual authority: efficiency in the market. So it is important from a political standpoint to recognize that the law and economics of international law may depart from concerns for market efficiency. Cost-benefit analysis would assume that individuals would seek to design governmental institutions, and their powers of intervention, so as to maximize the combined efficiency of market allocations and governmental allocations.

Finally, economic analysis is committed to liberalism, as it comes to law with no preferences of its own, other than the overarching respect for the preferences of individuals. This is the most challenging part of economic analysis for international law. International legal analysis has often allowed itself to become a scholarship of advocacy. While it is often difficult to criticize the consequences sought by the advocate-scholars of international law, and we may share their goals, advocacy is not scholarship. Ideals are the prerogative of each of us as individuals, but the responsibility of scholars is to illuminate, not to promote their own ideals. On the other hand, good scholarship holds great promise for advocacy, for it can clarify causal relationships that are otherwise obscure. Illumination is not neutral.

Theory and Empiricism

There are two main activities in social science, as in science: modeling and empirical testing. A model is based on theory, and sometimes also on empirical testing. It is a source of predictions and hypotheses. Once a model has been validated by empirical testing, it might be appropriate to engage in normative public policy on the basis of the model itself. This type of use would depend on the degree of validation and the extent to which the factual parameters that have been tested accord with the factual parameters in the setting being evaluated without its own empirical testing. However, economics has often been guilty of prescribing on the basis of theory, without sufficient relevant validation.

Economic models begin with price theory, which assumes that, all things being equal, people prefer cheaper goods and services, as well as more efficient means of achieving their nonconsumption goals. This theory, of course, has been powerfully validated in a number of contexts.

An additional level of complexity is added by transaction costs analysis, which simply recognizes, within price theory, that there are costs to engaging in transactions, and that these costs may prevent otherwise efficient transactions or may account for institutional structures.

A third level of complexity is added by game theory, which recognizes that the strategic position of states may prevent or add costs to otherwise efficient agreements. These theories are simply theories, and represent assumptions about behavior—independently of observation, they tell us nothing about the world. As Keynes warned, "The theory of economics does not furnish a body of settled conclusions immediately applicable to policy. It is a method rather than a doctrine, an apparatus of the mind, a technique for thinking, which helps its possessor to draw correct conclusions."[4]

Theory helps us to generate hypotheses. Observation allows us to falsify or to support hypotheses. Once we falsify or support hypotheses, we may find it useful to revise theory. Social scientists use different methods of proof, which usually relate to causal inference: to the causal relationship between an independent variable and a dependent variable.[5] Case studies may provide plausible evidence. Or, especially in cases where there may be multiple independent variables that have a causal effect, we can try to use more sophisticated statistical or regression analysis. The study of statistics includes certain measures of the relative plausibility of an inference—of whether the number of samples and their results are "statistically significant." Regression analysis recognizes that there may be several causal variables, and tries to determine mathematically, in contexts of multiple experiences, which causal variables are having the effect, and the magnitude of the effect. (To be sure, regression analysis, like other statistical analysis, tells us nothing about causation, but only about correlation. It is up to us, using theory, to draw causal inferences from correlations between variables.)

I will now provide some examples of the application of price theory, transaction costs analysis, game theory, and empirical analysis in international law. Recall that the first three are sources of theory and are hypotheses, while the last relates to a method of falsifying or supporting hypotheses.

Price theory is the basis for cost-benefit analysis: in seeking to achieve our preferences, we seek to maximize benefits and minimize costs (benefits and costs are measured in terms of the achievement of our preferences, which are not necessarily monetized or monetizable). Therefore, if my preferences include engagement in ethnic cleansing, I would examine the costs of weapons, of retaliation by my target, or of my reputation. If there exists an international legal rule against ethnic cleansing that is enforced and could result in my punishment, I would examine the discounted costs of punishment. The discount factor would relate to the likelihood of my apprehension and punishment, and the delay until my apprehension and punishment. Therefore, based on the price theory model, we would hypothesize that, mutatis mutandis, a reliably enforceable legal rule with substantial punishment would reduce the likelihood of ethnic cleansing.

Here, it is worth emphasizing that economists work with the marginal case. This legal rule would not prevent every case of ethnic cleansing. Rather, it would place a finger on the scale of the potential perpetrator's cost-benefit analysis, increasing the costs of ethnic cleansing. If in a particular case the costs are still less than the perceived benefits, we would still expect the ethnic cleansing to take place.

Thus, importantly, it is a non sequitur to say that a particular case of noncompliance indicates that there is no legal rule. States, like individuals, construct rules and institutions designed to induce the level of compliance they desire: we can only say that there is no legal rule if there is no behavioral effect. As we will see in Chapter 3, the fact that legal rules can survive some instances of noncompliance, and may be designed to accept some instances of noncompliance, poses a difficult challenge to traditional customary international law theory.

Transaction cost economics addresses the difficulty of identifying partners for the exchange of goods, services, or promises; negotiating exchange; and enforcing the terms of exchange. In international law, we might consider the difficulty of establishing treaties dealing with specific (as opposed to more general) environmental problems. Thus, there may be a smelter in Canada that causes air pollution that, due to prevailing winds, travels to the United States. While it may be useful to deal with some larger environmental issues between the United States and Canada, this particular issue may be too small to merit the devotion of diplomatic energy. Absent transaction costs, this cross-border issue might be resolved, but given transaction costs it goes unresolved. In this case, the cost of the injury would remain with the injured person in the United States. This may be efficient: transaction costs are real costs. However, there may be ways to reduce the transaction costs in this context. For example, it may reduce transaction costs to establish a rule of liability, such as *sic utere tuo,* to the effect that the polluter is responsible for damage to others. Given a rule such as *sic utere tuo,* it may be easier for the parties to negotiate a solution that minimizes the joint costs.

Game theory can help us to understand possible solutions to problems of international cooperation. Political scientists have led the way in modeling international cooperation or coordination problems using a variety of game structures. Although there are many types of games, and each one only essentializes in order to help understand complex real-world problems, the most popular game is the prisoner's dilemma. The prisoner's dilemma, described in detail in Chapter 3, provides a way of understanding the problem of cooperation in circumstances where each individual state can do better by violating a customary international law rule or treaty, but both states will do worse if both violate the rule or treaty. The bilateral prisoner's dilemma, resulting in inefficient violation by both sides, may be escaped by repetition. If you violate the first time, I can retaliate later. If you understand this and value the future sufficiently (i.e., are sufficiently patient), you may determine not to violate the first time. The shadow of the future provides incentives for cooperation. The development of customary international law may be understood this way.

International legal scholarship has in the past provided strong descriptions of particular international legal rules and of behavior. It also has a tradition of prescription: of urging action to enhance the rule of international law, to comply with moral or ethical mandates, to protect the environment, to protect human rights, or to end war. These are often valuable goals, but simply labeling a rule as a human rights rule or an environmental rule does not make it normatively attractive, and does not make it necessarily preemptive of other values. If it did, we would seek every human right, and every environmental protection, to the maximum extent and at all costs. This is clearly not what we do, descriptively, and it is unlikely that we would desire to do it, normatively.

Descriptive or positive economic analysis simply seeks to explain our world: what observable effect do independent variables have on dependent variables? This type of consequentialism is critical to institutional and legal reform—to normative economics: how do we know what changes to prescribe if we have no plausible basis for predicting their effects? If you, or your state, wish greater protection of the global commons, economic analysis would seek data about what mechanisms have been most effective to do so. The answer begins with price theory: how do we make degradation of the global commons more costly? How do we induce actors to take into account the costs of degradation?

Transaction cost economics and property rights theory suggest that as the value of the global commons rises, and as it becomes easier to allocate the global commons, one way to protect it is to establish property rights in the global commons. By allocating to a particular state ownership of a component of the global commons, we induce that state to value that component more highly, as it alone will bear the costs of pollution there.

Where it is more difficult to allocate the commons, other tools may be needed. Perhaps it would be appropriate—less costly in transaction cost terms or more likely to produce a stable and efficient equilibrium in game theory terms—to create an international organization with authority over the common resource.

In order to determine appropriate tools, we need greater empiricism. That is, we need more data about the costs of environmental protection, the costs of environmental degradation, the magnitude of transaction costs in connection with various institutional solutions, how those costs fall on the various parties, and so on. We might use regression analysis to determine whether adherence to a particular environmental treaty has increased protection of the relevant environmental resource. We would seek data about states that signed the treaty and about states that did not sign the treaty, and try to determine, mutatis mutandis, whether the signing of the treaty is correlated with protection of the resource. As mentioned above, regression analysis only tells us about correlation, but we tend to infer some degree of causation from well-tested correlation.

Consequentialism rarely succeeds without empiricism: in order to know what the consequences of a legal rule are, we must examine how similar legal rules have worked in similar circumstances. The trick is in distinguishing between similar and different rules and circumstances. Is there a useful role for theory without empiricism? One might posit that theory can assist with, or can be a form of, institutional imagination. So, while we may not have empirical support for a particular institutional change, the change may be desirable as a conjecture, to be tested through experience. In a sense, much of human institutional development over time has taken place by conjecture and critique. This amounts to a kind of serial gestalt testing, and trial and error, and it may be the best approach to institutional change in particular cases. It is only more recently that we have become self-conscious enough to develop the prospect of more disciplined empirical analysis.

In the absence of this type of data, we may decide to make decisions based on theory—supposition—derived from past experience. After all, we cannot abstain for lack of information: in the real world, not to decide is to decide. Our existential choice is not whether to decide, but whether to obtain more information before we decide. Economic analysis of law provides a framework for determining which information is important, and in what ways. Theory allows us to put information in context. As Kant pointed out, "Experience without theory is blind, but theory without experience is mere intellectual play."[6] Keynes said almost the same thing as Kant's first clause, referring specifically to economics: "Practical men, who believe themselves to be quite exempt from any intellectual influences, are usually the slaves of some defunct economist."[7]

Some international lawyers engage in the "mere intellectual play" of theorizing without empirical validation. Others believe that the main source of prescription is untested theory in the form of natural law. The law and economics of international law calls for the integration of theory and practice. However, it rejects natural law–based prescription as a violation of normative individualism. While any individual may have preferences that accord with the dictates of natural law theory, normative individualism rejects the imposition of those preferences on others. It does not reject the possibility, however, that one individual might have a preference with respect to the preferences of others.

Domestic Society, International Society, and the Fundamental Unit of International Legal Analysis

This book adapts tools of economic analysis of law to the study of international law.[8] This adaptation is suggested, and supported, by the basic analogy between domestic society and international society. At its core, international society, like any society, is a place where individual actors or groups of actors encounter one another and sometimes have occasion to cooperate, to engage in what may broadly be termed "transactions."[9] This view is related to the European Union (and Catholic) doctrine of subsidiarity. One formulation of subsidiarity is that individuals enter into higher levels of relationships only when it allows them to achieve their individual goals more efficiently. Thus, the role of the state is defined by the goals of individuals. Similarly, the role of international law is defined by the goals of individuals. The state acts as agent of its citizens.

The transactional approach to international relations has been developed by, inter alia, Abbott, Keohane, Krasner, and Waltz. In this literature, markets are understood to arise out of the activities of individual persons or firms. These individuals seek to further their self-defined interests through the most efficacious means available. While each individual acts for himself, "from the action of like units emerges a structure that affects and constrains all of them. Once formed, a market becomes a force in itself, and a force that the constitutive units acting singly or in small numbers cannot control."[10] It is important that Kenneth Waltz, known as a realist, suggests here that this "market" exerts behavioral power exogenous to states. The world only starts out anarchic. The theory of international law expounded in this book develops an understanding of the legal form that this market and institutional power can take.

So according to the economic perspective, the international system, like economic markets, is formed by the interactions of self-regarding units—largely, but not exclusively, states.[11] These utilitarian states interact to "overcome the deficiencies that make it impossible to consummate . . . mutually beneficial agreements."[12] Actors in each system are willing—to some extent—to relinquish autonomy in order to obtain certain benefits.[13] Both the international and the domestic systems, then, are seen as individualist in origin, spontaneously generated and unintended products of individual preference-maximizing behavior.[14]

The assets traded in this international "market" are not goods or services per se, but assets peculiar to states: components of power, or jurisdiction. "Jurisdiction" is the word that lawyers use for allocation of authority: the institutionalized exercise of power. In a legal context, power is effective jurisdiction, including jurisdiction to prescribe, jurisdiction to adjudicate, and jurisdiction to enforce. In international society, the equivalent of the market is simply the place where states interact to cooperate on particular issues—to trade in power—in order to maximize their baskets of preferences. Thus, the transaction in jurisdiction is the fundamental unit of analysis in this work. For those who are uncomfortable with the law and economics commitment to private welfare maximization, the model that forms the core of this book looks to *public* welfare maximization, in the sense that it examines maximization of the achievement of regulatory concerns of states.

States enter the market of international relations in order to obtain gains from exchange. For present purposes, we can understand the structure of this market as follows. Beginning from the state of nature, the first level of "trade" is that which establishes constitutional rules: rules about how subsequent and subordinate rules will be made. The next level of trade is that which allows departure from the state of nature: establishment of market-organizing rules of noncoercion, property rights, and contract. These rules facilitate additional transactions among states. Finally, institutions can be established to constrain transaction choices in the future.[15] Of course, in contexts where there are no perceived gains from trade, there should be no trade: no cooperation, no treaty, and no integration. This is implicit in price theory–based neoclassical economics, and contrary to naïve international law advocacy, noncooperation in these areas will be normatively good.

This book is based on the idea that international law is produced in order to allow states to achieve their preferences with greater effectiveness through exchanges of authority: through transactions in jurisdiction. Some of the potential sources of gains from exchange are identified below.

Externalities and Exchange

States may engage in transactions in jurisdiction where a given element of jurisdiction is more valuable to one state than to another.

Actions or inactions of states may have positive or negative "effects" on other states. Thus, for example, the environmental law (or deficiencies therein) in one state may be associated with adverse or beneficial effects (negative or positive externalities) in other states, for example, because the first state's law permits pollution that flows to other states. Domestic environmental laws may also "cause" adverse effects in other states by being too strict regarding the entry of foreign goods into the national market, or too lax with respect to domestic industries, resulting in competitiveness effects (pecuniary externalities). Externalization through regulation that fails to protect foreign interests, pecuniary externalization through strict regulation that has protectionist effects or through lax regulation that may be viewed as a subsidy, and subsidization itself may all be viewed as questions of prescriptive jurisdiction: which state—or international body—will have power to regulate which actions?

The structure of these external effects might be congruent with the structure we often consider in a domestic property rights analysis. In a typical property rights analysis, a farmer and a cattle rancher might be neighbors.[16] The cattle rancher's cattle damage the farmer's crops. Under a legal rule of liability for damages caused by cattle trespass, the cattle rancher will be responsible. Assume that it would cost the cattle rancher $75 to fence his property, while it would cost the farmer $50 to fence his property—either method would eliminate the damage. It is clear that $25 could be saved if the parties can enter into an agreement whereby the farmer erected the fence. The farmer would demand a payment of something more than $50. So the parties may agree, under certain transaction costs and strategic circumstances, to transfer responsibility for erecting the fence. Similarly, one state's emissions of transboundary pollution may damage a second state. The cost of eliminating the pollution might be Euro 75 million, while the cost of remediating the effects in the second state are Euro 50 million. Similarly, an international legal rule allocating responsibility in accordance with the *sic utere tuo* principle might be understood to operate in precisely the same way, with the possibility for reallocation through either implicit or explicit action.

Affected states may thus determine to seek to alter some of the source state's activities, through their own regulation or by seeking changes in the first state's regulation. There are two main ways to do so. The first is bilateral persuasion. The second is through institutionalization. Bilateral persuasion may involve inducement by force, exchange, or implicit reciprocities (either specific or diffuse);[17] it occurs in the "spot market." Institutionalization involves the "wholesale" transfer of power over time through a treaty or an international organization. Both are transactions.

However, externalization cannot be the lone touchstone for determining when local legislation must defer to foreign concerns.[18] First, externalities are notoriously difficult to define. More importantly, the identification of externalities presupposes established property rights. That is, economists take property rights as givens, and define externalities based on the effects of one person's actions on the property rights of another, although the latter may not have any legal recourse.[19] But in the regulatory contexts identified above, it is precisely the scope of each state's power—its jurisdiction—that is at issue. This must be defined before we can properly speak of externalities.[20] We might expect that "property rights develop to internalize externalities only when the gains of internalization become larger than the cost of internalization."[21]

Of course, the creation of such rights—and rules regarding the allocation of jurisdiction to prescribe—raises a host of other issues. Power and wealth are central to this process. Different distributions of power would likely produce different patterns of property rights; and these property rights then become the framework within which wealth is created and distributed.[22] Economic analysis, primarily utilizing the theoretical perspective of the Coase theorem,[23] allows us to examine the possible efficiency or inefficiency of particular allocations. Furthermore, it exposes the distributive ramifications, and inescapably value-laden nature, of the decision to create property rights and to "internalize" externalities. Moreover, to the extent that these property rights represent public goods, we might expect them to be underproduced by the market, acting alone. We return to these issues in greater detail below.

Public Goods

One type of problem of allocation of authority arises from the possibility that international public goods exist.[24] Public goods are goods that are nonexcludable and nonrival in consumption. Examples include the ozone layer or other environmental goods, or perhaps international stability could be understood as a public good. If a particular good is a public good, then because those who invest in its production may not capture all of the benefits, a collective action problem may arise and the public good may be underproduced. This is a problem of a positive externality. Alternatively, a public bad involves adverse effects that are nonexcludable and inexhaustible. Those who produce public bads may not internalize all of the detriments, and the public bad may be overproduced. This is a type of negative externality.

Economies of Scale and Scope, and Network Externalities

Related potential sources of gains from trade are economies of scale and economies of scope, as well as network externalities.[25] Given the increasingly global nature of society, and of problems such as environmental degradation and trade, it seems likely that there would be economies of scale, under some circumstances, in the regulation of these matters.[26] As will be seen in Chapters 3 and 5, there may be institutional economies of scale and scope: development of institutions may make it more likely that more issues will be addressed by those institutions. Network externalities may increase savings with increases in the number of states that are party to an institution or a rule.

Economies of scale have a number of components. First, states may enjoy economies of scale in contexts where they regulate transnational actors. For example, there may be efficiencies gained through coordinated rulemaking, surveillance, and enforcement activities. In the absence of these transactions, states face heightened risks of evasion, detrimental regulatory competition (which can be driven by externalization), and unnecessary regulatory disharmony, all resulting in inefficiencies.[27] Second, there may be technological economies of scale, relating to equipment, acquisition of specialized skills, or organization. Economies of scale may provide a motivation for integration in order to capture these economies, in the sense that the economies of scale tilt the cost-benefit analysis in favor of integration.

Economies of scope are reductions in cost resulting from centralized production of a group of products, especially where the products share a common component.[28] International organizations may share analytical, secretariat, or dispute settlement functions among a group of subject areas. Furthermore, even the ability to include multiple subject matters in a way that makes enforcement of any single commitment easier, such as the inclusion of intellectual property in the World Trade Organization (WTO) in the Uruguay Round, may provide economies. Thus, the existence of the WTO may provide economies of scope that would facilitate the coverage, in the WTO, of additional areas.

Network externalities include efficiencies that arise simply from adoption of the same rule or technology. Harmonization of law can give rise to network externalities. Concentration of international legal transactions in a single institution can also give rise to network externalities.

Finally, economies of scale and scope, and network externalities, may arise from increased frequency of transactions, or from longer duration of transactions. Given greater numbers of transactions in international relations, one would expect greater economies of scale. In addition, learning curve effects may, over time, give rise to economies of experience.[29]

Types and Locations of Transactions in Authority

New institutional economics assumes a dichotomy between transactions and institutions. But between the spot market transaction and the formal organization there exist many types of formal contracts and informal arrangements, and even the formal organization is a nexus of contracts. Thus, the supposed dichotomy is, in fact, a continuum: the boundary between the transaction and the institution is blurred.[30] This book engages in a progression from custom or informal organization to treaty to international organization, recognizing this continuum. One metric of this continuum is the relative scope of retained individual discretion. Where the individual retains greater discretion, she is closer to the pole of the market; where the individual retains less discretion—and assigns more discretion through contract or organization—she is closer to the pole of the firm.[31] However, it is important to point out that this is a generalization: there may be loose rules within firms and tight social norms within markets. This continuum is translated in international relations to the continuum running from intergovernmentalism to integration, where integration denotes a pooling of authority.

Indeed, Coase's dichotomy of firm and market may usefully be compared to Albert Hirschman's dichotomy of voice and exit.[32] The main difference between the market and the firm is in the duration of relations and in how decisions are made. In the (spot) market, decisions are binary: one either enters (buys) or exits (sells). The firm entails longer-term relationships, requiring that one exercise voice. Voice is heterogeneous, including various mechanisms that may amount to selective or partial exit, such as the ability to vote out a government. In the international relations context, the firm may be equivalent to an international organization, or to a less formal "regime."

Maximization

The central theory suggested by the economic approach to international law is that states use and design international transactions (including all rules of international law) or institutions[33] to maximize the participants' net gains, which equal the excess of transaction gains from engaging in intergovernmental transactions, over the sum of transaction losses from engaging in intergovernmental transactions and transaction costs of intergovernmental transactions (including transaction costs of international agreement or of creating and running institutions).[34] Most, if not all, international law may be characterized as involving transactions in jurisdiction, either horizontal or vertical, with this purpose in mind. The maximization of net benefits is by necessity a comparative undertaking: it requires positive evaluation of various forms of transaction or organization, and indicates normative choice of the form that maximizes the positive sum of these factors.[35]

It is necessary to stress that this is a theory suggested by economic analysis of law. It is properly used, not as a normative commitment, and not generally as an assumption, but as a basis for the generation of testable hypotheses.

It may be useful to have in mind a couple of examples. An international legal rule prohibiting the acquisition of territory by use of force may be seen as maximizing net benefits by virtue of the greater security that states enjoy, allowing individual states to spend less on self-defense. They may spend less on self-defense because the threat of aggression is reduced by virtue of the fact that the rewards of aggression are reduced insofar as aggression cannot be the basis for the acquisition of territory. Absent this legal prohibition, each state has the authority to acquire territory by force, but by entering into this rule, each transfers this authority away. It is a transaction in authority.

Similarly, international human rights treaties may be understood as transactions in authority. Although it is sometimes difficult to see the externality when one state abuses the human rights of its own citizens, these externalities may arise in the form of instability, refugees, competitive externalities, or simply feelings of concern. When states enter into these treaties, they are implicitly bartering autonomy to commit human rights abuses. This is also a transaction in authority. Of course, it may be necessary to provide other inducements or side payments in particular cases. But the main point is that we can understand these transactions as transactions in authority. Another word for authority in our context is jurisdiction.

Given problems of definition and quantification, the maximizing theory described above may be too difficult to operationalize in its full form, except in relatively discrete and limited circumstances. Attempts to create predictive models must seek to simplify this theory while retaining some predictive capacity.

Limits of the Domestic-International Analogy

It is not necessary to analogize the world of international relations to a private market in order to apply the tools of law and economics to the international realm. Of course, there are many differences. Recall that we are seeking from domestic law and economics useful theory to generate hypotheses for empirical testing. This testing would allow us to assess the utility of this theory for international law. Indeed, the structural analogy described above has significant limitations when applied to international relations.

The Problem of Nonmonetized Exchange
The international market for power is different from the market for private goods along many dimensions. While there may well be exchange in the

market of international relations, this market is not normally a cash market. Rather, it is most often a barter market, with all the difficulties and transaction costs of barter. For example, agreements within the European Union to engage in mutual recognition of regulation may be understood as a kind of barter. Similarly, all trade negotiations are essentially complex, usually multiparty, barter. The growing liquidity of the market for authority—increasing frequency and scope of exchange—will facilitate, and will be facilitated by, increasing monetization of various types of exercise of state power, including jurisdiction.

The fact that this market for state power is not extensively monetized does not block its economic analysis. Economists have increasingly turned their attention to the analysis of social phenomena where value is exchanged but not valued in money terms.[36] While price theory–based economic analysis is rendered more complicated in nonmonetized contexts, the type of institutional analysis described in this chapter does not rely on monetization, and is very similar in its application to the private firm and to the international organization.

Finally, even preferences that are monetized, and money itself, may not be commensurable or fungible.[37] Again, however, this is much less an argument against the economic analysis suggested here than an expression of a methodological difficulty to be overcome. The theoretical perspective of this book would clearly be incomplete if it failed to take all preferences into account, including both those that are easily monetized and those subject to greater problems of commensurability.[38]

The Problem of State Rationality

Another potential problem with this approach is that it assumes that states are rational utility maximizers.[39] While the assumption of rationality of individuals is under sustained attack, an assumption of rationality may be even less acceptable as applied to states—as suggested by the literature on social choice and public choice. This chapter does not address the assumption of human rationality, and its bounds,[40] but briefly examines the applicability of this assumption to actors in international society, that is, to states. "Much contemporary international relations theory is based on the assumption of state rationality."[41] Of course, the assumption of state rationality is not terribly different from the assumption of corporate rationality, which seems to be a cornerstone of analysis of market behavior.

Bounded rationality involves "the limitations on human mental abilities that prevent people from foreseeing all possible contingencies and calculating their optimal behavior."[42] There are two parts to bounded rationality: limitations on information and limitations on the ability to process information. Assuming rationality, we may view limitations on information as "rational ignorance": the acquisition of more information is too costly in relation to the anticipated benefits. Bounded rationality also implies limitations on the ability to process information already acquired. Processing, like searching, entails an investment of attention, which from the perspective of the decision maker may not be expected to yield a solution that is sufficiently better to make the processing worthwhile. Groups, like individuals, exhibit limitations on information searching and processing, although these problems may be ameliorated and accentuated in different ways by the conjunction of a number of minds.

The literature on social choice and public choice addresses the rationality of group decisions. Arrows's impossibility theorem[43] and Buchanan's methodological individualism[44] indicate that organizations have no rationality of their own but that they intermediate, imperfectly, for individuals. "Even if the collective entity, as such, confronts the alternative, the only genuine choices made are those of the individuals who participate in the decision process."[45] While this theoretical perspective is no doubt correct, institutions are designed by individuals to achieve their purposes.

> Whether it makes pragmatic theoretical sense to impute interests, expectations, and the other paraphernalia of coherent intelligence to an institution is neither more nor less problematic, a priori, than whether it makes sense to impute them to an individual. The pragmatic answer appears to be that the coherence of institutions varies but is sometimes substantial enough to justify viewing a collectivity as acting coherently.[46]

This is no less true of the state than it is of the firm. Rationalist international relations theory assumes that states are rational evaluative maximizers of their own preferences.[47]

The Problem of Endogenous Preferences

A final problem to be acknowledged here is that the structural analogy takes state preferences as exogenous. That is, state preferences are simply "given," and then strategies are developed to maximize these preferences. But preferences depend on context, and in particular on existing political, legal, and institutional arrangements.[48] This suggests a logical difficulty with attempts to explain legal rules or institutions as a simple aggregation of preferences; when preferences are a function of legal rules, these rules cannot, without circularity, be justified by reference to the preferences. It also suggests a dynamic element that is missing from the structural analogy. Since international institutions modify state preferences, the very preferences that might lead, in a particular context, to institutionalization may be changed by the presence of that institution. In Chapter 3, I discuss the competing schools of social norms theory, based respectively on endogenous and exogenous preferences.

The Public Choice Turn

Public choice theory generally assumes that government actors—politicians and bureaucrats—are motivated to maximize their own preferences, rather than those of the citizenry. Often the preferences of these public officials are assumed to be political support, either in the form of votes or in the form of campaign contributions. This assumption seems to generate useful testable hypotheses regarding the behavior of these government actors on behalf of their governments. However, it is critical to bear in mind that this assumption is not a normative position or goal. Furthermore, it is certainly reasonable to assume that the welfare of citizens figures somehow into political support.

While we often assume that states enter the market of international relations in order to maximize the preferences of those who control the international relations mechanism, these actors are subjected to greater or lesser accountability in different circumstances, and therefore act in response to the preferences of constituents in greater or lesser degrees. Furthermore, these actors may have so been educated or socialized as to have internalized the community's preferences as their own.

However, this book generally does not peer inside the billiard ball of the state. This is a result of the limitations of analytical technique, and not of a view that it is unnecessary to examine the internal workings of states. Indeed, one important way of looking at international law is in terms of its effects on domestic politics: in this conception, the role of international law is to strengthen the domestic coalition in favor of a certain type of behavior.

The approach generally taken in this book ignores the possibility that government officials make decisions that maximize their own welfare, without focusing directly on the welfare of citizens. Where used, this is merely a simplifying assumption, and there are certainly circumstances where it would miss important detail. But an analysis of international law that does not attempt itself to evaluate the source or content of state preferences does not require any particular degree of congruence between individual constituent preferences and the preferences expressed by the state. This book's approach is generally applicable regardless of whether the preferences being sought to be maximized are those of individual government operatives or those of citizens.

Normative public choice analysis might develop certain prejudices—normally against international law and organization—based on concerns for reduced accountability of government officials in international fora. On the other hand, some argue in favor of international law and organization as an ally of citizens against the leviathan state.

A Domestic Coalition–Based Theory of Compliance with International Law

As discussed above, for purposes of simplicity, this book will not examine domestic politics of compliance. And yet, domestic politics is the key to compliance with international law. It seems obvious that states will not comply with international law unless they make a political decision to comply. This is no different from saying that domestic laws purporting to bind individuals must cause them to make a decision to comply, if such laws are to cause compliance.

International lawyers have proposed a number of different theories of compliance, including theories based on fairness, on compliance, on technical assistance, and on other factors. However, the most elegant theory of compliance is a domestic coalition–based theory, which asks the question: How does international law interact with domestic coalition politics in order to form, or not to form, a coalition sufficient to decide to comply? This theoretical perspective recognizes first that each state's compliance decision will be different from each other state's decision, and that each state's decision on each instance of compliance in each context will depend on the particular context: human rights has a different dynamic from environmental protection, which has a different dynamic from trade.

This type of domestic coalition–based theory of compliance is rooted in normative individualism, but recognizes that individuals have decided to make their international law compliance decisions largely through the processes of the state. Thus, the state is the partial mediator of individual preferences, and since international law is largely concerned with the behavior of states, it seems perfectly appropriate that international legal compliance would be determined by the domestic political process. This stands in stark contrast to liberal theories of international law that examine the behavior of individuals and assume that national compliance with international law is somehow determined by nongovernmental organizations (NGOs) and private networks. These things generally derive their relevance only from their influence on state politics.

Most importantly, neither the magnitude of remedies, nor the shadow of the future, nor the weight of reputation, alone determines compliance. Rather, these factors are mediated through the prism of domestic politics. If domestic politics is very close to supporting compliance, then international law does little work. If, on the other hand, domestic politics would strongly oppose compliance, then international law must sustain a much greater burden.

Can Law and Economics Learn from International Law?

The international turn is often subversive of assumptions about fundamental features of the domestic sphere, in part because of some of the analogical difficulties discussed above. By seeking to apply settled understandings from law and economics to this new and different landscape, we lay bare the silent assumptions and contingency of these understandings.

To some degree, the international legal system is a primitive legal system, and by examining its rudimentary features and its bare-bones institutions, we may see at a more foundational level some of the substructure of our more highly articulated domestic system.

For example, this work's assimilation of jurisdiction to property, and its analysis of the efficiency of the existing structure for allocation of jurisdiction, challenges our understanding of the naturalness of property rights. Furthermore, we see in Chapter 3 that customary international law has much in common with a nonlegal phenomenon in domestic society: social norms. Thus the very nature of law, and its separation from other social mechanisms, is challenged. We see that there is a relationship between social norms and contract once we examine the relationship between customary international law and treaty.

Similarly, evaluation of the boundary between the spot market for international relations and the international organization raises questions about the boundary between the market and the firm. Furthermore, international law allows us to see even more clearly than domestic law the role of the judge as agent for a collective principal. Finally, the ability of some to deny international law the intrinsic normative force that is often accorded domestic law allows these analysts to approach domestic law also as an ethically indeterminate social tool.

Thus, for those who ask, how is international law binding, or how does international law differ from international politics, the analysis in this book suggests that we turn around and ask the same questions about domestic law. Domestic law arises from a similar anarchy to that we observe in the international system. Despite the national government, individuals remain in a partial state of nature.[49]

In fact, regarding the anarchist, we may ask, how does he or she know that the institutions we have are not the ones that would arise from anarchy? For, at the core of domestic law is a set of individuals, determining how they may work together to achieve their individual preferences more effectively. The fact that they have built an impressive superstructure of institutions sometimes obscures the fact that this superstructure is built on a substructure of individual action. The same theoretical tools, and problems, seem to apply.

Finally, as we consider the "market" among states for regulatory authority, or jurisdiction, which this work proposes as the central study of international law, we recognize that in this market, efficiency means the optimal effectiveness of regulation, where regulation is the expression of state preferences. There may be conflicts between efficiency in the private market for goods and services, and efficiency in the public market for regulatory authority. So, for those who entertain a bias against the economic analysis of law in the private setting because it may at times criticize regulation, a reversal of bias may be appropriate in the international law setting.

Summary of Argument

As noted above, international law, like domestic law, is concerned with the allocation of authority in society. This book is less concerned with the substantive or primary rules of international law themselves than with the core problem of secondary rules: of allocation of authority.[50]

In Chapter 2, I examine the insights gained from transaction cost economics and property rights theory and suggest how these insights might apply to questions regarding the allocation of jurisdiction. This chapter uses transaction cost analysis and the theory of bargaining under asymmetric information. It also recognizes that regulatory competition theory provides some input on how jurisdiction may be allocated. Further, it recognizes that the possibility to transfer jurisdiction is important to evaluate in connection with determining the optimal initial allocation of jurisdiction. Finally, it links property rights theory to the theory of the firm, recognizing that the firm is a contractual arrangement for sharing property and that the international organization is an arrangement for sharing jurisdiction.

Chapter 3 proceeds to examine the capacity for binding transfer of authority through customary international law. It applies the game theory model of the multiplayer prisoner's dilemma to determine the circumstances under which states would be able to reach efficient and stable strategic equilibria of cooperation: of achievement of joint gains where there are temptations to defect. This chapter develops a set of parameters, and a model, for determining when states would be more likely to develop stable multilateral equilibria of compliance with a rule of customary international law. This is a general theory of the binding nature of international law, and more specifically of the capacity of customary international law to affect behavior. It is liberating to examine international law using the lens of price theory. A price theory perspective allows us to recognize that law may have social effects even under circumstances of erratic compliance. We might even recognize, in accordance with theories of efficient breach, that uniform compliance is not necessarily the goal of law, or a priori efficient. Furthermore, a price theory perspective allows international law to be judged by the same standard we apply to domestic law: does it achieve the level of compliance we seek? This chapter develops a game theory–based understanding of the circumstances that would lead to greater or lesser binding force. This is a theory of the binding force—and social purpose—of international law.

Chapter 4 examines treaty. First, it recognizes that the binding force of treaty is derived from the same types of social conditions as the binding force of custom. Second, it recognizes that treaty allows the possibility of (i) a greater specification of obligations, and therefore enhanced ability to discriminate between cooperative and uncooperative behavior, and (ii) the creation of other institutional features that can enhance binding force. Again, this chapter recognizes that under some international legal circumstances, compliance is not efficient, and so this chapter accepts the possibility of efficient breach. However, efficient breach requires certain institutional capacity to determine the proper level of compensation. Chapter 4 also examines the role of the interpreter and adjudicator of treaties, linking this examination to the discussion of adjudication in Chapter 7.

Chapter 5 develops a law and economics perspective on the formation and utility of international organizations by developing the analogy between the theory of the firm and the theory of the international organization. This chapter extends the property rights–based analysis of Chapter 2. International organizations are understood to be worth creating where they are superior means of achieving state cooperative goals compared to alternative devices. These alternative devices include (i) leaving future action to individual state determination, (ii) custom, or (iii) nonorganizational treaty. International organizations may be understood in property rights terms as mechanisms for sharing ownership of a certain bundle of authority. International organizations may alternatively be understood as providing a mechanism for overcoming certain compliance problems, including information problems. Along this strategic line of analysis, the international organization may be understood, like the firm, as a mechanism for aggregating or increasing the number of interactions between particular states, thereby increasing the possibility of compliance.

Chapter 6 examines an emerging issue in international law: the allocation of authority among different functional organizations. This is an important component of the problem of "fragmentation." The international organizational system is different from most domestic systems insofar as most international organizations are responsible only within a particular functional area, such as environment, labor, trade, or security. However, these responsibilities overlap in important ways. This chapter uses some of the analytical techniques developed in earlier chapters to develop an approach to this overlap.

Chapter 7 examines the role of the adjudicator in international law. Adjudicators operate within international organizations and are best understood as a part of the institutional structure of an international organization. Chapter 5 suggests that the utility of an international organization will depend on its internal institutional features. Chapter 3 highlights the information role that adjudicators may serve under the strategic theory of compliance advanced in that chapter. Chapter 7 examines the choice that states may make between specific directions to adjudicators and more general directions: between rules and standards. It examines the circumstances under which member states might be willing to allow individuals direct access to international adjudication. Chapter 7 understands the traditional debate between positivism and natural law as, in important respects, a debate about the scope of agency of adjudicators: have adjudicators been assigned to exercise the moral judgment that a natural law perspective entails, or have treaty writers determined to specify in advance the moral perspective they wish to be applied? Reducing this philosophical conflict to a question about the scope of agency allows international legal analysis to recognize that this is not an issue amenable to philosophical determination by judges, but rather is a choice in the hands of those who delegate authority to judges.

This book does not by any means purport to address every issue in international law. Most importantly, this book does not address at all any particular substantive norms of international law, such as rules against the use of force, human rights laws, or international environmental laws. Rather, this book focuses on the constitution or structure of international law—its secondary rules in the H. L. A. Hart sense. How is authority allocated and transferred? It will be for other works to examine substantive rules of international law in consequentialist terms.

:✦:

CHAPTER TWO

Jurisdiction

JURISDICTION IS THE core issue in all legal analysis. As suggested in Chapter 1, "jurisdiction" is the word lawyers use for questions of the allocation of authority: the institutionalized exercise of power. Politics is not the study of the distribution of goods, as is commonly suggested, but the study of the distribution of authority in society, including but not limited to authority over goods. Thus, any theory of international law must begin with the basic concept of jurisdiction. How is it allocated initially, and why is it reallocated? The latter question—why is it reallocated—is a positive question, but it is related to the normative question of how jurisdiction should be reallocated. This chapter develops a positive theory of why jurisdiction is allocated and reallocated, and on a related normative basis suggests institutional changes that could enhance the quality of allocation and reallocation.

Subsequent chapters in this book are concerned with the reallocation of jurisdiction: of authority. Thus, Chapter 3 is concerned with reallocation through the social norms–like process of creating customary international law rules. Chapter 4 is concerned with the contract-like process of creating treaty rules to reallocate authority. Chapter 5 is concerned with the empowerment of international organizations in order to "share" jurisdiction among states. Chapters 6 and 7 refine these concepts in connection with conflicts among functional organizations and adjudication.

Following the "jurisdiction as property" approach set forth in Chapter 1, we might understand choice of law or prescriptive jurisdiction rules in at least two ways. First, they can be understood as rules of property in the international system. Second, to the extent that these rules of jurisdiction are not broadly agreed, we might understand them as unilateral assertions of "meta-property": as claims that may or may not develop the community recognition that is associated with property rules.

Using the game theoretic approach to customary international law described in Chapter 3, we might examine how these assertions may emerge as efficient or inefficient strategic equilibria. Furthermore, we might understand the modification or new establishment of rules of jurisdiction as transactions in property in a decentralized system. Thus, when one state modifies its claims of jurisdiction in response to incentives offered by another state or group of states, we might understand that modification as a transaction in jurisdiction.

The durable technical legal questions of choice of law and prescriptive jurisdiction resolve into a core normative public policy issue: how should authority be allocated within an interstate or international system?[1] These questions grow increasingly pressing, as greater interstate and international commerce as well as technological advances increase the frequency and scope of conflict over the application of law. Recently, we have seen important international debates regarding the application of national law to the Internet, international mergers, securities regulation, export controls, environmental protection, and taxation. These questions are answered by legislatures, by executive branches, by courts, by treaty writers, and sometimes by international organizations, operating at different vertical levels. This chapter seeks to develop a framework by which to analyze the question of allocation of authority among horizontally related units.

This framework utilizes several tools of economic analysis of law.[2] This chapter generally does not distinguish between the problems of choice of law and those of prescriptive jurisdiction: both address the problem of the horizontal scope of state power.[3] While some have used the private-public distinction as a basis for separating these fields,[4] that distinction has become obsolete and must be replaced by a more subtle metric, resulting in different and more important lines of demarcation, which I develop below. Throughout this chapter, I use the term "prescriptive jurisdiction" generically, to refer to both the question of the scope of application of public law and the choice of law issue in private law.

Several works have applied law and economics to choice of law and prescriptive jurisdiction problems.[5] These works, while extremely useful along a number of dimensions, have failed to establish a complete framework.

Some have exaggerated the importance of regulatory competition and party autonomy, while others have exaggerated the importance of regulatory advantage: the question of which state is a better regulator under the relevant circumstances.

Simply stated, while retaining an allegiance to methodological individualism,[6] this chapter takes state expressions of state preferences seriously:[7] it argues that where states have formulated mandatory law,[8] the decision to make the law mandatory should not lightly be eviscerated through liberal choice of law rules. Both this chapter and Chapter 7 challenge a naïve law and economics understanding that individual choice expressed through the market (in this chapter) or through private litigation (Chapter 7) is necessarily superior to individual choice expressed through government in the form of mandatory laws and in the form of exclusive government control of international litigation.

Of course, international transactions and circumstances challenge mandatory law: under what circumstances should law that is mandatory when all factors are circumscribed within a particular community be made nonmandatory based on foreign connections? When does the public policy that is articulated through the decision to make law mandatory become less compelling due to foreign connections? In fact, however, the mandatory nature of a law is an indicator, and is perhaps the best evidence, that the law addresses externalities in the private sector that would ordinarily be expected to translate into interstate externalities, thereby raising important questions about the value of liberal rules of prescriptive jurisdiction and regulatory competition. Demsetz defines the term "externality" as follows:

> Externality is an ambiguous concept. . . . [T]he concept includes external costs, external benefits, and pecuniary as well as nonpecuniary externalities. No harmful or beneficial effect is external to the world. Some person or persons always suffer or enjoy these effects. What converts a harmful or beneficial effect into an externality is that the cost of bringing the effect to bear on the decisions of one or more of the interacting persons is too high to make it worthwhile, and this is what the term shall mean here. 'Internalizing' such effects refers to a process, usually a change in property rights, that enables these effects to bear (in greater degree) on all interacting persons.[9]

A primary goal of property rights is to match effects with ownership, resulting in the internalization of externalities. A primary function of jurisdictional rules is similarly that of shaping governmental incentives to achieve a greater internalization of externalities among political units: as Demsetz states, "no harmful or beneficial effect is external to the world."[10] On the other hand, transaction cost and strategic considerations may well cause us to decline to internalize in particular cases.

Demsetz addresses a core question of institutional choice. He asks what regime of property rights enables harmful or beneficial effects to bear as greatly as possible on all interacting persons. This raises important concerns. First, what does it mean for an effect to "bear on" someone? This concept raises issues of asymmetric information, interpersonal comparison of utility, and commensurability. The core of this concept lies in preferences: how much are individuals' (or, in our context, states') preferences affected, positively or negatively? Efficiency is enhanced if those who are in a position to decide what to do feel fully the effects of their decisions.

Second, and most importantly, it is not correct to limit evaluation of institutional alternatives to property rights, or entitlements. As Coase showed, a structure of entitlements in a market context is only one institutional alternative: entitlements compete with other institutional structures, such as firms or other organizations.[11] Thus, the question is what institutional structure maximizes the match between preferences and control. This question seems prior, in a constitutional sense, to the question of what institutional structure maximizes satisfaction of preferences.[12] The issue of externality then aligns itself with the question of representativeness of institutions, or revelation of preferences.

This chapter's analytical framework is therefore based, but is not dependent, upon an analogy between legislative or prescriptive jurisdiction—the power to control action through law—on the one hand, and property rights,[13] on the other hand.[14] While these are obviously not the same things, they are sufficiently similar to make it useful to invoke the highly developed body of property rights scholarship as we examine prescriptive jurisdiction.[15] This chapter integrates concerns regarding regulatory competition into this property rights framework.

Further, this chapter links its integrated substantive property rights–based analysis to three literatures that help to suggest appropriate institutional responses. First, it seeks to identify the role of autonomous law in establishing prescriptive jurisdiction regimes, and its relationship to the concept of "comity" in choice of law and prescriptive jurisdiction analysis, as well as the unilateralism-multilateralism dyad in choice of law. This discussion is further advanced by the discussion of customary international law and social norms in Chapter 3. Second, this chapter compares the role of autonomous law to a theory of the firm-based approach to allocating power to centralized entities, such as the European Union or the World Trade Organization (WTO). This discussion is further advanced in the discussion of international organizations in Chapter 5. Finally, this chapter examines how, within a centralized entity, either more specific rules or more general standards might be used to determine allocation of prescriptive jurisdiction.[16] The rules versus standards analysis may be viewed as an extension of the initial property rights analysis, as rules are a more detailed *ex ante* specification of property rights than are standards. This discussion is linked to the discussion of the role of rules and standards in adjudication in international organizations contained in Chapter 7.

There are many possible choice of law or prescriptive jurisdiction rules; each rule must be evaluated in a particular legal or regulatory context. In this chapter, I show how the analytical framework developed here would evaluate two leading examples of rules of prescriptive jurisdiction: the effects test and recognition. I also suggest how this analytical structure might provide insights to assist in addressing prescriptive jurisdiction problems in two regulatory contexts: prescriptive jurisdiction over mergers under competition or antitrust laws and prescriptive jurisdiction over prospectus disclosure regulation under securities laws.

This chapter develops an integrated analytical framework that links the above analytical techniques in the prescriptive jurisdiction context. Like any theory, this framework should not be used alone as an affirmative basis for policy. Rather, it should be used to generate testable hypotheses about choice of law rules. These hypotheses should be tested empirically. However, even without the empiricism necessary to falsify or validate testable hypotheses, a theory that provides a more comprehensive model, or a more plausible model, can be used to suggest that other theories—theories that are also used without empiricism to support normative argument—are deficient.

Thus, if nothing else, this chapter debunks simplistic responses to the prescriptive jurisdiction and choice of law problem both from more traditional perspectives, and from other law and economics literature. As to more traditional perspectives, for example, this chapter shows the weakness of broad assertions (i) that the effects test is improper, (ii) that rules of prescriptive jurisdiction should always be clear, (iii) that courts should exercise little discretion in determining prescriptive jurisdiction, (iv) that unilateralism and multilateralism cannot coexist, (v) that there should be a presumption against "extraterritoriality," and (vi) that in cases of "true conflicts," forum courts should simply apply their own law. As to earlier law and economics–based analyses, this chapter refutes the arguments (i) that jurisdiction should generally be allocated in accordance with "regulatory competence," (ii) that private choice should generally be determinative of governing law, (iii) that clear rules of prescriptive jurisdiction are best, and even (iv) that the most efficient law should govern.

This chapter seeks to describe in social scientific terms the complex and subtle mechanisms of prescriptive jurisdiction. With these explanations as guidance, it is hoped to develop a basis for normative critique and rectification. Note that this chapter establishes a framework for understanding why a state might take unilateral judicial or legislative action to assert jurisdiction. It thus serves as a foundation for the discussion in later chapters of how and why states may cooperate by engaging in different forms of transactions in jurisdiction. The forms of transaction in authority and property in the municipal setting—(i) social norms, (ii) contract, (iii) the firm, and (iv) adjudication—correspond in the international setting, respectively, to (i) customary international law, discussed in Chapter 3, (ii) treaty, discussed in Chapter 4, (iii) international organization, discussed in Chapters 5 and 6, and (iv) international adjudication, discussed in Chapter 7.

The Property Rights Approach, the Value of Prescriptive Jurisdiction, and Regulatory Competition

As noted above, this chapter begins from the fundamental perspective that prescriptive jurisdiction—the right to make a state's law applicable to conduct—is analogous to property in a private context. That is, jurisdiction is the right of a state to control physical assets and the activities of individuals, while "property" is the right of individuals to control physical assets. The analogy becomes more evident when we recognize that both of these rights (jurisdiction and property) involve legally constructed packages of control over things of value. The fundamental unit of analysis in both cases is the transaction: the transaction in property and the transaction in prescriptive jurisdiction.

It is important to recognize that the market for transactions in prescriptive jurisdiction is not yet very liquid. Indeed, the prescriptive jurisdiction scene may be analogized to relatively primitive circumstances in which there has not been much occasion for either the development of property rights or, a fortiori, transactions in property rights.[17] However, this jurisdictional "property" has become more valuable with the rise of the regulatory state and the recognition that the allocation of regulatory power affects important social values. Technology and the rise of trade have also combined to make it more valuable to develop systems for allocation of regulatory power. Consider, for example, the question of whether France can enforce its laws against sales of Nazi memorabilia in the case of offerings by Yahoo on the Internet, or controversies over whether the United States may regulate the way in which Thais fish for shrimp exported to the United States, or over whether the European Union can block a merger between Boeing and McDonnell Douglas, or between General Electric and Honeywell. Thus, this chapter will draw on the literature—both theoretical and empirical—analyzing the rise of property rights in "primitive" circumstances to suggest the conditions under which "property rights"—legal rules allocating prescriptive jurisdiction—will develop in international society.[18]

The Permanent Court of International Justice's 1927 *Lotus*[19] decision marks both the announcement, and the commencement of the unraveling, of the international legal principle that jurisdiction is purely territorial—an analog to a rule of possession in private property.[20] The *Lotus* decision transfers that principle from the positive, descriptive world to the legal, prescriptive world. However, *Lotus* also stands for the proposition that jurisdiction is in important dimensions a *res nullius*, insofar as states may exercise jurisdiction without restraint, as long as they do not interfere with other states' territories or violate rules of positive law that the state exercising jurisdiction has accepted. So, the interesting research questions are why, to what extent, and how has international society moved from a *res nullius* regime to a regime of property rights?[21] A similar question can be asked regarding allocation of authority within the U.S. federal system.

Choice of law scholars have chronicled the chaotic character of conflict of laws jurisprudence.[22] This chaotic character, combined with the inevitable emphases on territoriality on the one hand, and the law of the forum on the other hand, suggests that under this structure, prescriptive jurisdiction has something of a *res nullius* character. Moreover, in many of these private law areas, the "value" of the property involved in choice of law, at least to the state, is low: that is, there are few effects on political operators of a decision to apply or disapply local law.[23] Under circumstances of low value, one would not expect property rights to arise: one would expect a *res nullius* regime.[24] In a *res nullius* regime, as the property becomes more valuable, a common pool resource problem, or tragedy of the commons, may develop.[25] With the rise of public law—herein, simply law that is mandatory—the mandatory character of this law may be taken as an expression of the increasing value to the legislating state of its application.

As property of this type becomes more valuable, given that it is otherwise subject to appropriation, we would expect the rise of property rights: in this context, "property rights" or "entitlements" would be expected to be composed of international laws allocating prescriptive jurisdiction among states.[26]

The Coase theorem suggests beginning with a transaction cost analysis of such laws or legal principles. We may consider external effects of activities, or of laws regulating activities, and determine which allocation maximizes the gains, net of transaction costs. Gains may come from two alternative sources: from creating an allocation that anticipates transactions, and from creating an allocation that facilitates transactions. By anticipating reallocative transactions, the entitlement would initially be allocated to the state to which it is most valuable, while by facilitating transactions, gains would be realized through reallocation of the entitlement to the state in the hands of which it is most valuable. The goal is to maximize the match between ownership and preferences, and thereby to maximize efficiency in the allocation of authority.

We will see below that transaction gains may also be derived from increased beneficial regulatory competition, although transaction losses may be derived from decreased beneficial regulatory competition, or increased adverse regulatory competition. Of course, we must add to the transaction cost perspective a strategic analytical framework, as well as an institutional dimension.

An alternative vision of the international system is that of the "anticommons."[27] The anticommons in our context is a circumstance in which each state has the right to exclude each other state from action. In some respects, due to the lack of clarity of international legal rules, the international system may in different contexts be both a commons and an anticommons. Thus, for example, in particular regulatory contexts the United States may assert jurisdiction, while other states claim the right to exclude the United States from doing so. In the domestic anticommons paradigm, the result is resource underutilization due to holdout problems or overregulation. In the interstate regulatory context, the result of an anticommons would be underregulation.[28]

Favoring Currie: Rehabilitating the Role of State Interests

Just as property rights are based on individual preferences, regulatory jurisdiction is based on state preferences. While states and other social units exist to aggregate preferences, and to express them, we can speak of state preferences only as, and to the extent that, the state reflects the individual preferences of its constituents. As noted in Chapter 1, Arrow and Buchanan suggest that organizations have no rationality of their own, but intermediate, imperfectly, for individuals.[29]

This section shows, based on property rights theory, the potential validity of a focus on state preferences, as opposed to directly expressed individual preferences, in choice of law.[30] While there are substantial public choice critiques of the extent to which state expression of individual preferences is accurate, it is immodest for prescriptive jurisdiction and choice of law rules to take this concern into account. This is because the choice of law situation is serendipitous: it would leave bad law in place when there are no cross-border connections, and eviscerate good law when there are cross-border connections. Thus, this type of public choice critique must be deployed elsewhere. It seems appropriate here to assume, heroically, that legislation incorporates the public interest as well as possible given institutional constraints. That is, for analytical purposes, I assume national laws to be perfect expressions of constituent preferences.

Choice of law involves varied circumstances. Before we can make further analytical progress, it is necessary to begin to develop a way of referring to state preferences. There are two leading parameters:

(i) Whether the law is intended to be facultative[31] or mandatory.[32] This parameter is a very coarse proxy for the degree to which state preferences are engaged.

(ii) The degree of state interest in applying the law in cross-border circumstances. This parameter considers the essential topic of prescriptive jurisdiction: the degree to which state preferences remain engaged as the regulated transaction becomes more and more foreign—as the attributes of the transaction are linked to other states, and/or delinked from the regulating state.

This is simply an interpretation of what Currie intended by "government interests."[33] These parameters substantially affect the design of efficient choice of law rules. Even if a law is mandatory, the degree of state interest[34] in applying the law to particular circumstances may be attenuated to the extent that its violation has adverse effects in other jurisdictions, and lacks adverse effects in the regulating jurisdiction.

For example, it is easy to argue that the U.S. securities laws should not apply to a wholly foreign transaction. The question left open here is the core question of choice of law: assuming that there is a state interest sufficient for a particular legal rule to be mandatory, when is that state interest sufficiently attenuated by virtue of cross-border connections to justify its nonapplication?[35] This question asks whether there remains a true conflict in a fundamental sense, despite some attenuation of state concern due to the cross-border circumstances.

We must recognize that there may be circumstances under which two or more states find that their preferences justify application of their rules, and under which their rules are inconsistent.[36] This is a true conflict. It is not necessarily resolved by application of one state's legal rule to the exclusion of another's. Here Currie suggested that, at least in domestic cases, the simple application of forum law would have to suffice.[37] However, Currie also recognized that in international cases, a court might be required to take a more active role, and decline to apply forum law.[38] There may be contexts in which a compromised or new legal rule would be appropriate to address these true conflicts.[39] Alternatively, perhaps shared governance would increase joint welfare.[40]

There may also be circumstances where all the states involved share a regulatory goal but cannot achieve that goal without coordination. This may involve externalities, public goods, or other reasons why coordination may be useful. Under these circumstances, no state need give up its regulatory or deregulatory goals. These joint gains may arise from new circumstances, including new technologies, that make traditional methods of regulation less effective, or that provide more efficient means of regulation. For example, the rise of the Internet may actually cause regulatory coordination to become more valuable, as it otherwise causes domestic regulation to become less effective.[41]

The reader will note that these parameters resolve to the following question: to what extent are different states' preferences implicated? This is the essential question in prescriptive jurisdiction, for why else do we apply laws than because a state's policies—or preferences—are implicated? The prescriptive jurisdiction question arises, quite simply, because more than one state's preferences are implicated. Of course, mere implication of multiple states' policies does not tell us how to resolve the conflict, but allows us to assess the degree of conflict and therefore begin to understand what types of institutional solutions may be worthy of consideration. We may also avoid the error of trying to deal with public law or mandatory law issues using the same tools that have been acceptable for private law or facultative law issues—these circumstances are recognized to be fundamentally different, to the extent and by virtue of the lack of a significant public policy concern under private decision that controls the applicability of law.

Where government preferences are not implicated substantially, either evidenced by the fact that the law at issue is merely facultative, or because the international setting so attenuates the government preferences, there is no basis for interstate transactions relating to allocation of prescriptive jurisdiction. Under these circumstances, it would seem appropriate to allow private parties to determine the governing law. So, for example, private international law rules relating to contracts for the international sale of goods may be useful as default rules, but would not ordinarily be structured as mandatory international law. The United Nations Convention on Contracts for the International Sale of Goods, which allows private parties to derogate from its terms by agreement, is illustrative.

It will also be apparent that the parameters described above do not directly include private preferences, such as the private interests in justice, efficiency, predictability, or administrability. While these values are extremely important, it is reasonable to assume that they are included in state preferences to the extent appropriate, or at least to the extent possible.[42] That is, when we speak of law, we must be speaking of the expression of state preferences. As Lenin said, all law is public law.[43] The proper distinction to draw is not between private and public law, but by reference to the degree to which law implicates state preferences. Thus, while facultative law may be viewed as embodying a state interest in the provision or application of a default rule, measured by the costs of contracting out of the default rule, mandatory law is viewed as embodying a stronger state preference that it has been determined should not be optional at a price less than the cost of exit from the jurisdiction. In turn, mandatory law may be identified with externalities that, in transaction cost and strategic terms, are appropriate to be internalized through legal rules.

Even an approach based on methodological individualism must recognize that individual preferences are sometimes (in fact, often) expressed through the state. Law is a manifestation of these expressions of individual preferences, but by definition, law is not a direct manifestation of private preferences.[44] It is perhaps this perspective that most sets this book's framework apart from those of some of the other law and economics–based approaches to choice of law and prescriptive jurisdiction. Others focus on the maximization of private preferences without recognizing that individual preferences are also, and importantly, manifested through the mechanism of the state, as state preferences.[45] Indeed, from a normative individualist perspective, the state has no other legitimate purpose. We return to this issue in Chapter 7, where we discuss the extent to which private persons should be accorded rights to litigate in connection with violation of international law.

Having said that the state exists to pursue individuals' preferences, we must recognize that there are two ways that it does so (from a public interest perspective). First, the state protects and facilitates private ownership and exchange: thus, the state is interested in predictability, and more generally efficiency from a private perspective, in choice of law. The state is interested in facilitating the direct revelation of individual preferences. However, second, the state regulates, again by definition, where private ownership and exchange do not produce a satisfactory outcome, measured by the political or bureaucratic decision-making process: at least according to a public interest theory of regulation, regulation protects preferences that are not sufficiently protected through the market, often due to externalities or public goods problems.

Thus, choice of law or prescriptive jurisdiction theory cannot generally be based on the direct preferences of individuals, despite the arguments of most law and economics–based analysis of choice of law.[46] Of course, there will be areas, such as contract interpretation, where states decide to allow individual choice to determine applicable law.

Therefore, it would be odd indeed, having implicitly decided mandatorily to address a particular set of preferences through the state, categorically to back down on those preferences when they engage other states, without further analysis. In fact, in circumstances of mandatory law, where we assume externalities or public goods domestically, it is appropriate to assume the existence or at least the possibility of interstate externalities or public goods. It may be that the international institutional setting changes the calculus of whether to address those externalities through the state or not, but it is by no means clear that this would uniformly, or even predominantly, be the case. Thus, we cannot abandon the search for a more subtle analysis of prescriptive jurisdiction problems.

Efficiency

As discussed in Chapter 1, all international law may be understood in terms of reciprocal restraints on state autonomy, and therefore as transactions in authority. However, traditionally, states do not appear often to have engaged in explicit consensual transactions in prescriptive jurisdiction. Assuming this is true, there may be a variety of explanations.

First, as noted above, prescriptive jurisdiction in the sense discussed here—power to regulate the affairs of private persons—may not have been viewed as a valuable asset in the past, or at least may not have been viewed as an asset valuable in the hands of others. Thus, in an era before substantial cross-border effects or commons issues, territoriality was a relatively complete solution to the problem of allocation of authority, and it would have been strange to depart from it. Furthermore, where multiple states were interested in a particular matter, it may have been viewed as a shared asset: regulation by one state did not preclude regulation by another. The rise of the regulatory state and of international commerce may have contributed to recent recognition of the value of this power.

Second, conceptions of sovereignty, including here expectations of citizens regarding an inalienable core of state power, may have imposed an ideational limit on the political feasibility of overt transactions in prescriptive jurisdiction. In other words, prescriptive jurisdiction might have been viewed as part of an indivisible "bundle" of sovereign rights. With the rise of international law, and the concomitant compromise of sovereignty, these types of transactions seem more common, and state power less inalienable.

In any event, there seem today to be more frequent instances of agreements regarding principles of prescriptive jurisdiction, especially within the economic law arena, broadly speaking. These agreements are transactions in prescriptive jurisdiction. While these agreements often take the form of assertions of seemingly neutral "principles" of jurisdiction, in some cases one side will benefit disproportionately from the adoption of a particular principle, and the parties are certainly aware of this. A simple example, and a relatively early one, is the typical and ubiquitous income tax treaty, wherein the source jurisdiction will often cede fiscal jurisdiction to the jurisdiction of nationality. While in theory, each party is equally capable of being either a source or a nationality jurisdiction, in practice, some countries are capital-exporting countries and others are capital-importing countries. Bilateral investment treaties have similar characteristics.

In a zero transaction cost world, allocation of prescriptive jurisdiction would have no effect on efficiency, although it would have distributive consequences. This is a simple extension from property rights to prescriptive jurisdiction of Coase's *The Problem of Social Cost*.[47] Of course, the world is beset by transaction costs, and so the allocation of jurisdiction has implications for efficiency, as well as for distribution.

Transaction Cost Strategies

Based on the analogy between property rights and jurisdiction, the law and economics approach to property rights may guide the development of international rules of prescriptive jurisdiction. The transaction costs methodology, supplemented to include considerations of strategic behavior under asymmetric information, provides four basic potential strategies. The selection of a particular strategy depends on the context, as explained below. The basic property rights strategies are as follows:

(i) Anticipate transactions. Minimize transaction costs by allocating property rights so as to anticipate, and thereby obviate, transactions. This strategy can be effected by a legislature or a court.

(ii) Clear entitlements. Minimize transaction costs by providing clear and complete property rights, amenable to transfer in the "market" with the least transaction costs.

(iii) Muddy entitlements. Where informal negotiation is the least costly means of reallocation, but will not otherwise occur due to bilateral monopoly, provide unclear and incomplete ("muddy") formal property rights, in order to reduce deadweight losses and encourage reallocative transactions through informal means.

(iv) Organizational solutions. Develop organizations that can make allocative decisions, facilitate negotiations toward reallocative transactions, or override holdouts.

I describe each of the above, and its potential adaptation to prescriptive jurisdiction, below. I also describe competing proposals for allocation based on the "best" or "most efficient" law. I first suggest the varying transaction cost and strategic contexts that would match each of the above strategies. I also add analysis of the role of autonomous law and institutions.[48]

The reason for different strategies is that different circumstances, including different transaction cost profiles, call for different means or combinations of means. The goal of each of the above strategies, and of any efficient combination of strategies, is the same: to maximize the net gains, which equal the transaction gains less transaction losses and less transaction costs.[49]

Furthermore, there are many choice of law or prescriptive jurisdiction rules to be evaluated, in many different legal and regulatory contexts. This chapter can only sample the surface, in an indicative style. Therefore, I review two leading prescriptive jurisdiction regimes: (i) the effects test often associated with U.S. "extraterritoriality," and (ii) recognition. These correspond, in a very rough way, to the transaction cost strategies set forth above, and to transaction cost settings suggesting those strategies (plus organizational solutions), summarized in Table 2.1.

In the following sections, I elaborate on the property rights analysis shown in Table 2.1, supplemented by considerations of regulatory competition, also bringing to bear literatures of autonomous law, the theory of the firm, and rules and standards.

Table 2.1 Transaction cost strategies and jurisdictional rules

Transaction costs of anticipating transactions	Low	High	High	High
Transaction costs of formal reallocative transactions	High	Low	High	High
Transaction cost strategy	Anticipate transactions	Clear allocations	Muddy allocations	Joint ownership organizational solutions
Suggested prescriptive jurisdiction rule	**Effects test**	**Recognition (or territorial conduct)**	**Effects test**	**Organizational solutions**

Internalizing Externalities and the Effects Test:
Anticipating Transactions

"If transaction costs are positive (although presumably low, for otherwise it would be inefficient to create an absolute right), the wealth-maximization principle requires the initial vesting of rights in those who are likely to value them most, so as to minimize transaction costs."[50] The person who is likely to value the rights the most is the one most likely to purchase them.

In the intergovernmental context, this strategy would seek to determine to which governmental jurisdiction the right to regulate would be most valuable. While it is unusual to speak of jurisdiction as having a value, the idea of the effects test asserted by the United States and used by other states is that adverse effects impose a cost on a society. In fact, it is important to ask what basis for jurisdiction would be worth respecting other than effects, broadly viewed. Thus, a government would "value" jurisdiction in proportion to the adverse effects that it can avoid by exercising jurisdiction, or the positive effects it can obtain through regulation, or through avoidance of the application of another state's regulation.[51] Other rules, such as territoriality (generally understood as a reference to territorial conduct, as opposed to territorial effects), can only be validated as proxies for effects, or for other transaction cost reasons.

Following the strategy of anticipating transactions, legislators of international law rules for prescriptive jurisdiction would seek to establish in advance an allocation of prescriptive jurisdiction that market participants—governments—would arrive at themselves in the absence of transaction costs. This is a theoretical exercise that might be subject to empirical testing on the basis of whether the initial allocation of authority is revised through subsequent negotiation.[52]

This analysis leads us to a defense of the effects test, although not necessarily an effects test that is judicially administered. An allocation of authority is likely to be unstable—requiring costly reallocative transactions—if it fails to accord an appropriate measure of authority to a state whose constituents are significantly affected by the circumstance in question. Thus, for example, a rule that allocated all jurisdiction to a state on the basis of territorial conduct, where the territorial effects occurred in another state's territory, would be unstable.[53]

It is important to note that the goal of allocation of property rights in such a way as to obviate transaction costs might call for division of the property right. For example, consider two farmers whose property is divided by a stream (analogous to two states divided by a river). While the right to use the stream may be more valuable to the farmer with more land to irrigate, it is still valuable to the farmer with less land to irrigate. A property rule that allocated the right to use the stream on a basis pro rata to the amount of adjacent irrigable land (rather than in full to the farmer with the greatest amount of adjacent irrigable land) might be the one that best minimizes deadweight losses and, by doing so initially, would also avoid the transaction costs of reallocative transactions.[54] It would, however, incur the transaction costs of measurement and monitoring. If the property right is not so easily divisible, it might be shared, but a sharing arrangement would be more likely to be subject to strategic holdout problems.

Thus, it is important to note that the first strategy—anticipating transactions—would not, like Baxter's "comparative impairment" approach to choice of law,[55] necessarily measure the effects on each state and simply award bundled or plenary authority to the state most affected. Greater complexity must be embraced in order to avoid moral hazard, illegitimacy, and, consequently, instability. Thus, allocation of jurisdiction in accordance with effects could result in the dispersion of jurisdiction among all affected jurisdictions in connection with any particular transaction. This principle would result in overlaps of jurisdiction, and possibly conflicts of regulation. Consider the effects of a Web site that is accessed around the world. Of course, this complexity gives rise to transaction costs and potential holdout problems, which must be taken into account. It would not be surprising if many states that were affected in relatively small measure would simply ignore the effects. However, where shared effects seem large to more than one state, there may be a need for shared authority, or the creation of organizations.

The effects worth considering are not confined to those implicated in any particular case or private transaction: if these effects were considered alone, this strategy would result in instability, not to mention unpredictability. The effects to be considered are not the effects on a particular claimant, nor even the effects of a particular policy or its frustration, but the total social effects on the relevant state on a long-term basis.[56] In addition to considering the positive effects of regulation, it is necessary to consider the negative effects.

This can best be illustrated by the U.S. assertion of so-called extraterritorial application of its law, pursuant to the effects test. Other countries argue that they refrain from such extraterritorial application: that they do not seek to assert the applicability of their policies widely.[57] First, some may not have as highly articulated a policy in fields such as antitrust or securities. Or they may simply be less fearful of certain adversities, such as international terrorism. Second, they may be more reticent to apply their policies to multistate activity—an anticommons effect.[58] Assuming for a moment this disproportionate level of policy and willingness to assert it in the international "market," how can it be fair to allow the United States to, in effect, rule the world? As noted above, we must weigh not only the positive policies of other states but also the negative, or laissez-faire, policies.[59] "We are dealing with a problem of a reciprocal nature."[60] Moreover, these effects should not be considered as limited to narrow monetary loss or gain, but might be considered very broadly to include problems of reciprocity, diminution of the happiness of constituents through disrespect of the rights of nonconstituents, or other concerns that might require consideration of rights.[61]

It is also worth noting that, in accordance with the Calabresi and Melamed analysis, anticipation or mimicry of transactions may be accomplished most accurately through liability-type standards. Importantly, liability-type standards are generally "standards" in the rules versus standards sense, and permit a degree of tailoring by courts.[62] Ayres and Talley argue that "untailored" liability rules (as distinct from standards) also promote efficient transactions, because they provide incentives to reveal private information regarding valuation of entitlements.[63] I discuss this strategy below.

Of course, quantification, including problems of commensurability and interpersonal comparison of utility, is a formidable problem, which is endemic to any nonmarket allocation and cannot be addressed in any detail here. However, it is clear that different persons, or different societies, value different effects in different ways. This is no different from a goods market in which we all value particular goods in different ways. Without a market to provide intersubjective valuations and equilibrium prices, each transaction requires negotiation. This negotiation may lead to holdout or private information problems based on the inability to know the true valuation assigned by the other participant in the transaction.[64] These strategic and information problems may indicate that another assignment of rights would be more efficient. Alternatively, they may be addressed through limited institutions that may be assigned to provide data on valuation.

Here, interestingly, states may be easier to deal with than individuals in terms of interpersonal comparison of utility: there may be an agreed-on or authoritative way to measure effects on states, perhaps performed by an international organization such as the Organization for Economic Cooperation and Development or the United Nations Conference on Trade and Development, which could assist in "valuing" effects. This could be done either bureaucratically, by experts, or judicially, by specially mandated tribunals. So the private information problem might be more tractable in the international setting than in the municipal setting.

Furthermore, it is important to recognize that different legal or regulatory fields will have different transaction cost profiles: this is not a "one allocation fits all" circumstance, although economies of scale or scope may suggest bundling allocations under some circumstances.[65] For example, real estate law might generally be expected to cause effects only in the local jurisdiction. To this extent, it would be relatively cheap in transaction cost terms to make an accurate allocation based on effects: pure territoriality. Securities regulation in current international markets would be expected to have quite different characteristics.

Finally, it is worth mentioning a "substrategy." In circumstances of positive transaction costs, where allocating property rights to the person who values them the most, as prescribed under the analysis above, is not feasible, another approach may be available. This might be occasioned, for example, because it cannot be determined cheaply or accurately enough who most values the rights, or because the transaction costs involved in the dispersion of property rights are high enough to make it less efficient to anticipate transactions.[66] This approach calls for the allocation of property rights to the person who can most cheaply analyze costs and benefits, and initiate appropriate reallocative transactions.[67]

This strategy may be applied to the problem of prescriptive jurisdiction by allocating prescriptive jurisdiction to the government most aware of the regulatory concern, which often would be the government whose constituents are most affected, but might be the government with the greatest regulatory absolute advantage,[68] or perhaps the government subject to the strongest political accountability.[69] This substrategy might allocate bundled jurisdiction to the government most affected, rather than spreading jurisdiction among all affected governments. The government receiving the allocation could then unbundle the prescriptive jurisdiction in various ways. For example, it might, subject again to agency costs, regulate as a kind of trustee or agent for other governments.

It may be that the appropriate person to whom to allocate prescriptive jurisdiction under this strategy is not a national government at all, but is an international or regional organization. If given appropriate resources and powers, an international or regional organization might be able to fulfill these functions better than most governments, and could redelegate authority to the constituent national governments as appropriate.

It should also be noted that sometimes the class of persons to whom prescriptive jurisdiction might be reallocated is that of individuals: there is the possibility that the persons who would value the right most are not states, but some group of individuals, either a nongovernmental organization or the market itself. This perspective may, for example, support an argument for tradable pollution permits.

That is, through internationally tradable pollution permits, governments could allocate quasi-jurisdiction among themselves, and then each government could reallocate pollution permits to private persons operating within their jurisdictions. The private persons, by bidding and establishing a market for these permits, would be in a position to engage in the private sector–level allocation. If pollution permits were permitted to, and did, migrate from one state to another, this activity would serve to reallocate jurisdiction among states. Thus, the migration of "private" property serves to effect a transfer of "public" property, or jurisdiction. To summarize, internationally tradable pollution permits provide a mechanism for globally coordinated allocation of this property. This mechanism would comprise (i) initially bureaucratic or negotiated allocation among states in the first instance; (ii) various initial means of allocation to private persons within states, including auctions, grandfathering, and the like; and (iii) subsequent transnational market-based trading.

Efficiency, Best Law, and Regulatory Competence as Allocative Strategies

Another strategy is to allocate jurisdiction to the state that regulates most efficiently: the state that holds an advantage in regulating the subject matter.[70] Regulatory advantage as a basis for allocation of prescriptive jurisdiction is analogous to a property rights rule that allocates property rights to the person who can use them most efficiently (and, presumably, most valuably). The types of advantage that may apply in the intergovernmental sector may include economies of scale or scope, first-mover advantages,[71] advantages due to greater experience with the type of business or type of regulatory problem, or other advantages in regulating.[72]

The determination of absolute regulatory advantage is reminiscent of the determination of "better law."[73] It raises similar problems of institutional competence and legitimacy. However, if these problems of legitimacy and agency costs could be addressed, regulatory advantage could be an important consideration. Regulatory advantage will also come into play as an argument for possible centralization—there may be circumstances where economies of scale or economies of scope argue for centralized regulatory authority.

It is worth considering why a law and economics approach to choice of law does not simply select the more efficient law. Even if the more efficient law could be identified, this chapter's argument is based on the understanding that conflicts efficiency may override substantive efficiency, just as conflicts justice may override substantive justice.[74] That is, the allocation of authority may be efficient, even where the manner of exercise of the authority is inefficient. In fact, in a contractarian setting, there is little basis for a distinction between these two types of justice. Given this understanding, a better law, or a more efficient law, is not a basis for selection of a legal rule.

More importantly, it is impossible to determine the "better" or more "efficient" law separate from the legislative procedure—the preference revelation device—that produced the law. On this basis, there is no greater justice than conflicts justice or procedural justice—and no necessarily greater efficiency than conflicts efficiency. And the question of what law to apply becomes a fundamental question of justice among overlapping communities, and overlapping substantive goals. The true value of the legal vocation is to manage the procedures that produce justice among overlapping communities and overlapping substantive goals.

Allocation of a bundle of authority on the basis of either a comparative effects test or regulatory advantage presents problems of moral hazard, or agency costs: the regulator may not, in a unilateral (nonreciprocal) mode, without further structuring, have appropriate incentives to safeguard the preferences of other states.

Clear Rules

Posner notes that "unfortunately, assigning the property right to the party to whom it is more valuable is not a panacea. It ignores the costs of administering the property rights system, which might be lower under a simpler criterion for assigning rights . . . and it is difficult to apply in practice."[75] Many practicing lawyers would ask simply that rules of choice of law and prescriptive jurisdiction be made clear. As a blanket strategy, this approach fails to distinguish between different transaction cost circumstances, and fails to deal with circumstances in which clear rules leave substantial externalities unaddressed.

Of course it is true that under zero transaction costs, costless trade will allow efficient reallocation. More relevant in a world mired in transaction costs is the fact that clear and complete rules may reduce transaction costs more than allocations that, although they may often obviate the need for transactions, are complex to formulate and implement, or sometimes fail to obviate the need for transactions, and occasion high transaction costs when transactions become necessary.

Again, the goal is to maximize net gains. Depending on the transaction cost setting, one means to do so may be to formulate and apply clear and complete rules of jurisdiction, in cases where relatively low transaction costs may be obtained by this method.[76] This allows reallocative transactions with the lowest possible transaction costs.[77] Precise and complete specifications of rights work on the transaction costs side of the sum, and may also reduce strategic holdout problems.[78] Open-ended or shared entitlements may reduce the ability to trade, either because it becomes difficult to identify the necessary parties or because there are so many parties that the costs of dealing with all of them become too high.[79]

Thus, rules allocating prescriptive jurisdiction may, by their predictability, administrability, and transparency, facilitate "market" transactions that reallocate authority. In the intergovernmental sector, "market" transactions are agreements allocating authority: treaties, constitutions, uniform laws, practices (such as comity or custom), or other means of circumscribing or validating claims of authority. This is perhaps a basis for support of territoriality as the touchstone for prescriptive jurisdiction: limitation of prescriptive jurisdiction to the territory of the regulating state may provide clarity that can facilitate transactions in international prescriptive jurisdiction.[80] Territoriality refers to a relationship with territory, but any particular legal or natural person, or any particular transaction, may have multiple relationships with one, two, or several separate territories. States often seem to consider territorial conduct the primary reference: it is relatively easy to identify the state where the conduct takes place, and that state is in the best position to apply regulation to that conduct (by virtue of the fact that the actor's assets and personnel are subject to its territorial sovereignty).

Thus, territoriality may, under certain circumstances, be consistent with clear entitlements, but under some circumstances may be associated with muddy entitlements, as conduct or effects may be spread across multiple territories. On the other hand, recognition of home country law is an extremely clear rule, assuming that there is a clear rule identifying the home country (i.e., jurisdiction of incorporation).

Asymmetric Information and the Potential of Imprecise Allocations: Muddy Entitlements and Standards

Where transaction costs for formal transactions are high, some theoreticians argue that less precise, discretionary standards of property rights may be appropriate.[81] Where transaction costs will remain higher, it may be appropriate to decline to specify clear entitlements, either (x) in order to provide incentives for parties to engage in reallocative action without engaging in formal transactions, or (y) in order to leave reallocation to litigation.[82] From this perspective, "muddy" entitlements provide uncertainty that may induce parties to reveal otherwise private information about the way that they value jurisdiction in order to facilitate reallocation. If formal transactions are too costly, we may hope for some kind of transactions, or at least actions, that will allocate assets to their most efficient uses.[83] This principle assumes that the initial assignment is inefficient, and that high transaction costs prevent the enhancement of efficiency through formal reallocative transactions.[84]

Thus, a strategy of providing muddy entitlements indicates that where transaction costs for formal transactions are high, and where it is not possible to formulate an initial allocation that will obviate the need for reallocation, formal property rights should be formulated in muddy terms. Indeed, we might say that muddy property rights are somewhat similar to, or might precede, shared property rights: in order to act, the claimants must either (x) deal with one another, or (y) litigate to clarify ownership.

Litigation may or may not be too costly to consider. Certainly, in many international contexts, litigation is not available. If litigation is unavailable or too costly, muddy property rights raise the holdout problems emphasized by Epstein.[85] In fact, the possibility for litigation is best understood as a kind of generalized institutionalization: the rules are not necessarily clear and the cost of decisions is high, but an external decision maker imposes a solution on the parties. Litigation as a method of allocation is closer to the firm than it is to the market. In this sense, where litigation is available, a strategy of muddy entitlements is related to a strategy of organizational solutions.

The possibility that muddy allocations may be efficient in particular circumstances has important, and perhaps surprising, ramifications when adapted to the prescriptive jurisdiction problem. It would argue that in circumstances of high transaction costs—where transactions in prescriptive jurisdiction are difficult to effect—it may make sense to maintain the current circumstance of relatively imprecise allocations of and limitations on prescriptive jurisdiction, perhaps with improvement by virtue of development of a justiciable standard and assignment of mandatory jurisdiction to a court.[86] This proposition assumes either (i) that litigation is an efficient method of reaching a subtle and efficient allocation, or (ii) that there is a cheaper, informal method for engaging in reallocative transactions, and that by providing unclear or incomplete jurisdictional rules, perhaps in the shadow of litigation, disputants will be guided into a more informal, more relational, and more socially rooted process. In the general public international law context, litigation is unlikely,[87] and informal, negotiated settlement of jurisdictional problems is more common.[88] In fact, comity may be viewed as a type of customary deference, or meta-law, that resolves these types of problems without formal legal obligation.

Muddy rules have another dimension. Not only are they imprecise, but also they allocate authority within a horizontal system in a particular way. As suggested in Chapters 5 and 7, if jurisdiction is pooled in an international organization, the governance of the organization in which it is pooled becomes critical. There are many analytical dimensions of this governance, including, for example, rules of voting in legislatures. A central set of issues involves the choice between establishing more specific rules, perhaps by treaty writing, and more general standards, normally for application by dispute resolution tribunals or courts.[89] In Chapter 7, I discuss the general application to international law of the analytical technique elaborated in the rules and standards literature. Here, I apply that technique to prescriptive jurisdiction issues.

And indeed, in choice of law theory, we observe a debate that cycles endlessly, regarding whether choice of law by courts should be governed by detailed, predictable rules or, instead, by broad standards, such as balancing tests. This is the debate between formalism and anti-formalism. The law and economics literature of rules and standards provides a basis for discriminating between greater and lesser specificity in this context.

Formalism characterizes the First Restatement's[90] approach, calling for clear, formally realizable rules, in theory sharply curtailing the scope of judicial discretion. Currie's attack on the First Restatement approach is characterized by anti-formalism.[91] Choice of law theorists, including some using economic analysis of law, have more recently attacked Currie and the state interest–based approach that he developed. Indeed, today, several law and economics–oriented scholars call for a return to greater formalism.[92]

One interpretation of formalism is that it requires from legislatures specific statements that clearly decide cases: it leaves as little discretion as possible to courts, thereby providing greater predictability for private persons. However, legislatures sometimes explicitly mandate courts to perform balancing tests or other discretionary tests.[93] There is no reason to assume that this delegation, whether explicit or implicit, is not efficient or legitimate. It is not correct to argue that when courts engage in choice of law or prescriptive jurisdiction analysis, even when they adopt a multilateral approach, they are ignoring the commands of their own legislature (presumably to apply local law to every case that comes before the court).[94] Rather, legislators are aware of judicial action and may, implicitly or explicitly, approve it by acquiescence over time.

This chapter, and Chapter 7, taking a more flexible view of the judicial function, seeks to understand this argument in terms of the use of more specific rules and less specific standards to delegate authority to courts, as well as in terms of legislative inaction in the face of judicial activism. We can view courts as agents of legislatures. The question of formalism versus anti-formalism—and of rules versus standards—may be viewed as a debate about the scope of discretion to be granted to courts. This adds another parameter to the rules-standards analysis: are judges or legislatures better, in terms of competence and legitimacy, at informal coordination? One of the leading criticisms of Currie's interest analysis is that it involves judicial weighing of legislative policies, which is argued to be an illegitimate extension of the judicial function.

The rules-standards dichotomy is useful at two phases of our analysis. First, as particular states coordinate autonomously, to what extent are *domestic* courts, applying standards, the best agent of coordination? Second, once states determine to coordinate formally, and establish formal interstate or international organizations to effect their coordination, to what extent should they assign decision-making authority to *international* courts applying standards, as opposed to central legislatures or treaty making? As a definitional matter, we must note that a domestic law might well be viewed in the international setting as contributing to the development of international social norms. Thus, a formal act in the domestic setting may be an informal act as a matter of international law. We discuss this point further in Chapter 3.

The literature of rules and standards is aptly applied to choice of law.[95] In the rules versus standards literature,[96] a law is a "rule" to the extent that it is specified in advance of the conduct to which it is applied. A standard, on the other hand, is a law that is farther toward the other end of the spectrum, in relative terms. It establishes general guidance to both the person governed and the person charged with applying the law, but does not specify in detail in advance the conduct required or proscribed. The relativity of these definitions is critical. Furthermore, each law is composed of a combination of rules and standards. However, it will be useful to speak here generally of rules as separate from standards. I discuss the normative basis for choosing between rules and standards in Chapter 7.

In fact, we may view the rules and standards literature as an extension of the property rights literature. This is so because rules—more specific legal norms in relative terms—may be viewed as more precise allocations of property rights.

Institutional and Organizational Solutions: Autonomous Law, Comity, Joint Ownership, and the Firm

The institutional solution to the problem of allocation of authority recalls for us Coase's other major paper, *The Theory of the Firm*,[97] and its dichotomy between the market and the firm. Institutionalizing control over the disposition of assets responds to a different transaction costs profile.[98] In brief, an organization would be appropriate where the organization can effect internal allocations that result in a better sum of transaction gains, transaction losses, and transaction costs.

Spillovers are always with us. However, it is not correct to suggest, as some do, that interjurisdictional externalities always require centralization.[99] This is the learning of Coase's theory of the firm.[100] Coase's work suggests that we must engage in comparative institutional analysis to determine whether centralization, or a market-type mechanism for exchange, is the most efficient way to internalize externalities. Furthermore, some externalities are not internalized because the attendant transaction costs and strategic costs are greater than the surplus that would be generated thereby. Finally, as discussed below, if regulatory competition is valuable, there may be an added incentive to internalize externalities in order to enhance the results of regulatory competition.

Social Norms and Comity

In Chapter 3, I examine the broad analogy between social norms in a municipal setting and customary international law. Under the theory of the firm, discussed below, autonomous development and use of property rights are compared to more self-conscious and communal development of institutions. The social norms literature suggests an explanation of comity,[101] and also provides some possible limits to comity. I also discuss in Chapter 3 the circumstances under which social norms, including customary international law, may overcome collective action problems and other cooperation problems.

Rational states might be attentive to the interests of other states, even in the absence of formal obligations, in anticipation of reciprocity. One of the traditional core problems in choice of law theory, as applied by domestic courts, is that of unilateralism versus multilateralism:[102] should judicially applied choice of law rules be designed with only the narrower preferences of the forum state in mind, or with the interests of the multilateral system in mind? Stated less abstractly, a unilateral approach suggests that courts faced with choice of law problems determine only whether or not forum law applies. A multilateral approach, on the other hand, examines which body of law, among all those potentially applicable, should be applied.

Robert Ellickson shows that formal property rights might be ignored in certain domestic contexts, in favor of informal "social norms."[103] This analysis invites a comparative institutional analysis, comparing the formal legal system with other, less formal social structures and institutions. We may analogize this kind of informal system with the application of comity in international jurisdictional settings. Comity is a kind of "meta-law," pursuant to which states may defer to one another without formal obligation, but with the backing of reciprocity and other informal incentive structures. In our context, it may best be understood as a precursor to customary international law.

Enter the Theory of the Firm

In the present context, we may look at an absence of interstate laws regarding prescriptive jurisdiction as the "market": a place where states may make ad hoc, individual transactions in jurisdiction. Where they make longer-term arrangements, or establish institutions to allocate jurisdiction in future, they move toward the firm. The distinction between the firm and the market has never been clear.[104] In Chapter 5, I return to the theory of the firm in order to examine the role and structure of international organizations more broadly. Here, I provide a brief discussion to show the relationship of the discussion in Chapter 5 to the problem of horizontal allocation of jurisdiction.

One possible solution to the "property rights" problem is joint ownership through a more formal organization: this is the link between Coase's two seminal articles, *The Problem of Social Cost* and *The Theory of the Firm*.[105] Property rights theory suggests joint ownership where the transaction costs of reallocation within the organization are less than the transaction costs in the market. The literature on the theory of the firm begins with this insight in order to assess the circumstances in which it is efficient to own assets in an organization. We may apply this theory to suggest the circumstances in which it is efficient for prescriptive jurisdiction to be "pooled" in an international organization. The European Union and the WTO are examples of circumstances where prescriptive jurisdiction has been pooled, to varying extents.

Williamson claims that "it is the condition of asset specificity that distinguishes the competitive and governance contracting models. Contract as competition works well where asset specificity is negligible. This being a widespread condition, application of the competitive model is correspondingly broad. Not all investments, however, are highly redeployable."[106]

Williamson sees transaction costs economizing as the main purpose of vertical integration.[107] Vertical integration is seen as a governance response to a particular set of transaction dimensions, including high asset specificity as the principal factor. Williamson assumes that other sources of transaction costs are insignificant, and that transaction gains from economies of scale are significant, making market transaction the obvious choice where asset specificity is low.[108] An extensive literature has followed Williamson's and Coase's work, and I examine some of this literature, and its relationship to international organizations, in Chapter 5. According to this approach, vertical integration becomes attractive where it represents a net transaction cost savings as compared to more contractual or custom-based integration.

The basic learning of the theory of the firm is thus that formal organization will be used where it results in transaction cost economies by comparison to "market"-based transactions. The theory of the firm is not operational in a formal sense, but is indicative as to the types of considerations that might lead to formation of an organization. Organization may be indicated by property rights or transaction cost analysis, but, as suggested below, may also be indicated by regulatory competition theory. While formal organization may be useful to enhance regulatory competition, it also plays an important role in transaction cost economizing.

Application to Selected Issues in Prescriptive Jurisdiction

In this section, I describe two leading approaches to allocation of prescriptive jurisdiction: the effects test and recognition. Using the analytical framework set forth above, I then examine the potential application of these approaches to two international jurisdiction problems: (i) merger control under antitrust or competition law, and (ii) disclosure regulation of prospectuses in international securities offerings. These problems are used as examples to illustrate the considerations indicated by the property rights theory framework established above in this chapter.

The analytical process suggested above first requires an assessment of the value to each involved state of the relevant prescriptive jurisdiction. Thus, facultative law must be treated differently from mandatory law, and there will be many gradations of value. As suggested above, the characterization of a particular rule of law as either facultative or mandatory is simply a gross proxy for the level of government interest.

After the value of the prescriptive jurisdiction is known, it must be discounted or increased, depending on how cross-border circumstances reduce or increase the level of governmental valuation. If the governmental interest is reduced substantially enough, then a rule of party autonomy may be followed. Considerations of regulatory competition may increase or decrease the level of implication of governmental preferences, or may suggest particular institutional features.

Once governmental preferences are evaluated, it is possible to evaluate relative transaction costs and strategic factors, and to evaluate possible institutional responses. Transaction cost economizing is a comparative endeavor: it evaluates particular regulatory contexts, and particular property rights approaches, in order to determine which approach yields the best solution in the particular context.

The Effects Test

I have briefly described the effects test above. The effects test allows the internalization of externalities, but at a potential cost. When sought to be applied by the United States, the effects test has been rejected by its trading partners in the context of antitrust law, export controls, and other areas. The objecting states argue that the effects test results in "extraterritoriality," meaning that the United States is exercising jurisdiction on the basis of something other than territorial conduct. Thus, the objecting states argue that territorial effects is an inappropriate basis for prescriptive jurisdiction. They presumably do so because the application of U.S. regulation imposes costs on them. There are *effects* on both states.

The problem with the effects test is, of course, that actual cases often involve dispersed effects. That is, the antitrust or export control cases that raise concern always involve effects, broadly conceived, both in the United States and in the foreign home country of the entity sought to be regulated. Even foreign constraint of a home country laissez-faire policy may be viewed as adversely affecting the home country.

Perhaps the reason that the effects test has often been rejected is that a rule of jurisdiction based on territorial conduct has served reasonably well in the past. It may only have served well to the extent that conduct and effects occurred in the same state: to the extent that territorial conduct was a good proxy for territorial effects.

Thus, in cases of dispersed, or shared, effects, the effects test does not seem to be a complete response to prescriptive jurisdiction problems. However, in line with the theoretical suggestion that "muddy" allocations may fit circumstances of high formal transaction costs, the effects test may provide incentives for further negotiations toward better allocation. It certainly attracts attention and negotiation, and one would expect that as these issues become more frequent, effects would be a rationally appealing basis for negotiation of other regimes. However, it appears unlikely today that a stable allocation would be based on territorial conduct, as the United States has consistently declined to accept such a limitation, and even the European Union effectively exercises jurisdiction beyond territorial conduct. Most importantly, there is no basis for arguing that the structure of jurisdictional allocation wherein the United States can assert the effects test is, or at least has been, inefficient.

The effects test should also be viewed from the internal perspective of the United States. In this perspective, it is a standard—according to U.S.

courts, the authority to determine whether the requisite quality and quantity of effects (in the antitrust case, direct, substantial, and reasonably foreseeable)[109] are felt within U.S. territory. This standard authorizes courts to engage in the building of social norms by declining to find prescriptive jurisdiction in particular cases. It thereby signals to U.S. trading partners the willingness to establish social norms through reciprocal action. This more deferential interpretation of the effects test is consistent with comity as a strategy to establish international social norms.

It is worth considering the character of possible institutionalization of allocation of jurisdiction pursuant to an effects test. It may be that unilateral effects tests have the result of precipitating negotiations toward more specific rules of prescriptive jurisdiction. On the other hand, one of the problems with an effects test is the concern that some states have that other states predicate assertion of jurisdiction on relatively small local effects. Thus, in order to avoid an anticommons problem, an international tribunal could be assigned to apply a standard along the lines of Baxter's comparative impairment test, allocating authority to the state that is most affected.

Recognition (or Nationality)

Under recognition, a territorial state accepts the regulation of a home state, the home state being defined based on nationality. Recognition is the opposite of territoriality, although, as noted above, recognition is a reallocation subsequent to a presumed initial territorially based allocation. Recognition involves even greater clarity of entitlement, and avoids substantial overlaps. It thus promotes regulatory competition. However, it does so at the expense of substantial possibilities of externalization. Recognition is also a rule, with the characteristics attributable to rules.

We may refer to "rootless recognition" as the acceptance of foreign law to exclusively regulate foreign companies operating in a host jurisdiction, without any predicate—without examination of the extent to which the foreign law satisfies host regulatory concerns, and without "essential harmonization." The expected benefit of recognition includes both lower regulatory costs for the regulated person and enhanced regulatory competition.

"Competition facilitates the control and regulation of the exercise of political power."[110] Recognition of the importance of decentralization for purposes of enhancing regulatory competition is important. The eclectic approach of the current chapter incorporates (but restricts the scope of) consideration of regulatory competition.[111] That is, regulatory competition may add to, or subtract from, the transaction gain that may arise from a particular transaction in regulatory jurisdiction. Regulatory competition confers effects, either adverse or beneficial, on other states, and so is considered as part of the property rights analysis that forms the central focus of this chapter.

Roberta Romano,[112] and Stephen Choi and Andrew Guzman,[113] have argued for modifications of jurisdictional rules in order to promote regulatory competition in the securities law field. They have argued for free issuer choice of the national body of securities regulation that would govern its public offerings of securities. They have done so on the ground that the regulatory competition that would result from this prescriptive jurisdiction regime would result in better securities regulation, or at least in the migration of firms to states with better securities regulation. Importantly, this migration would not involve the costs of physical relocation, but would be facilitated by a rule of respect for the issuer's election. These positions are dependent on an assumption that securities regulation serves no social purpose: that there is no externality worthy of being internalized by regulation. However, the very existence of securities regulation seems to belie this assumption.

In more general terms, Andrew Guzman, Erin O'Hara and Larry Ribstein, Francisco Parisi, and Michael Whincop[114] have advocated revision of choice of law rules to enhance regulatory competition (each to varying degrees and with varying caveats).

The Effect of Spillovers on the Efficiency of Regulatory Competition

Third-party effects—externalities—are critical to the question of whether regulatory competition is beneficial.[115] The question of whether regulatory competition should be increased cannot be answered separately from the broader inquiry into the optimal allocation of regulatory jurisdiction pursued in this chapter. Of course, even within the regulatory competition literature, the utility of regulatory competition is recognized to be dependent on the question of regulatory jurisdiction, in the form of questions of positive and negative externalities that may limit the utility and domain of the Tiebout model.[116]

Just as the determination of property rights serves purposes besides competition per se in the domestic sphere, including efficient incentives for property management and allocation of resources generally, the allocation of regulatory jurisdiction serves purpose beyond regulatory competition.

The question of allocation of regulatory jurisdiction is central to the current analysis based on two considerations. First, the Tiebout model depends on a number of assumptions, including the absence of externalities, and so, in order to assess its applicability, we must evaluate the match between regulatory jurisdiction and effects. Second, even if analysis showed a high level of regulatory competition arising from a particular assignment of regulatory jurisdiction, such as mutual recognition, there could be strong reasons not to adopt that assignment of regulatory jurisdiction. These reasons may be in the nature of externalities, but it might also be that centralization—monopoly—of regulatory jurisdiction provides substantial benefits that outweigh the benefits of the expected competition. These benefits might arise from economies of scale, economies of scope, or network externalities. Thus, there are multiple vectors that must be included in a decision allocating regulatory jurisdiction; competition is only one. However, it seems an important addition to the property law–based analysis that is the focus of this chapter.

Most claims in favor of regulatory competition are based on the Tiebout model, which predicts a Pareto optimal outcome assuming certain parameters are met. The Tiebout model has been described and debated in great detail in many important works.[117] It posits that, subject to the satisfaction of five conditions, competition among small cities for mobile individuals results in the efficient supply of local public goods by those cities.[118]

The five conditions are the following:[119]

(T1) Publicly provided goods and services are produced with a congestible technology (therefore, there is an optimal size of jurisdiction).

(T2) There is a perfectly elastic supply of jurisdictions, each capable of replicating all attractive economic features of its competitors.

(T3) Mobility of households among jurisdictions is costless.

(T4) Households are fully informed about the fiscal attributes of each jurisdiction.

(T5) There are no interjurisdictional externalities.

Of course, these conditions are never satisfied. It is easy to see that T3, T4, and T5 are impossible completely to satisfy in the real world, and that there are likely to be large deviations from T3 and T5 (T1 and T2 may not be met, either). As to T1, there may not today be an optimal size of jurisdiction that is smaller than the entire world for certain matters such as CO_2 emissions, Internet content regulation, or certain areas of finance regulation. T2 requires greater homogeneity of resources than exists in the international setting. As to T3, mobility of firms to other jurisdictions will entail substantial costs, at least of searching and analyzing the relevant laws. As to T4, again, there are serious concerns regarding whether firms or investors are fully informed regarding the attributes of each regulatory jurisdiction.

T4 suggests an important difference between fiscal competition—the original focus of the Tiebout model—and regulatory competition. In the regulatory context, proponents of greater competition in some areas, notably securities regulation, argue that there is a "joint" jurisdictional decision made by producers and consumers. Thus, analysis must examine the degree to which consumers are able to make an informed choice. The economic theory of regulation would suggest that at least some regulation is motivated by the inability of consumers to make an informed choice. It is difficult to imagine that consumers who are unable to make an informed choice regarding the regulated subject matter would be able to make an informed choice regarding the choice of regulatory law governing this subject matter. Given that it is probably more difficult to grapple with issues of applicable law than direct issues of policy, it is unrealistic to say that consumer choice of mandatory regulation is an improvement.

The theory of the second best suggests that, given that all of the conditions of the fundamental theorem of welfare economics are not satisfied, there can be no assurance that increasing the level of satisfaction of any other conditions—such as enhanced mobility of firms—will yield greater efficiency. This theoretical perspective contradicts speculation that greater mobility among firms would necessarily enhance the efficiency of law.

The Strategic Perspective on Interjurisdictional Competition

Furthermore, there are substantial concerns as to whether the Tiebout model can result in a stable equilibrium.[120] The stability of intergovernmental competition is separate from its efficiency: an unstable market for regulation might be characterized by "price wars" or a race to the bottom.[121] Externalities can be a source of instability.[122] Breton points out that centralization may not be the best way to provide stability, but the existence (without necessarily the assertion) of central authority appears necessary to address problems of instability.[123] The central government may set minimum standards of regulation, as has been done in the European Union's essential harmonization technique.

Breton concludes that "in the area of international competition, it would be impossible to prevent an unstable competitive process from degenerating, unless, in the language of international relations 'realists,' a hegemonic power undertook to prevent the debacle."[124] There appears to be no reason in theory why the hegemonic power in this type of context must be a state; we have seen the European Union emerge as just such a power in Europe, and it might be argued that the WTO or functional organizations may play such a role also. Alternatively, perhaps the United States or European Union exercises, or shares, hegemony through these organizations. We may link this analysis with the property rights–based analysis set forth above, and the theory of the firm–based analysis, set forth below.

Perhaps a dynamic governance structure along the lines of "cooperative federalism" or managed mutual recognition may provide a kind of contingent hegemony or centralization that can maintain stability. Within the U.S. federal system, stability is provided by the ability of the federal government to intervene; this is an important distinction between regulatory competition in the U.S. domestic context and regulatory competition in the international context, and may be an important distinction between corporate law, where the federal government has not intervened, and securities law, where it has chosen to intervene.

In the international context, in order to have a similar institutional capability, we would need to build and empower a central authority. Furthermore, Breton argues that horizontal cooperation cannot solve the problem of horizontal instability.[125] Chapter 3 suggests, however, that there may be circumstances in which horizontal cooperation can result in a stable equilibrium. The practical question for the international community is how much authority it must cede to a central "government" in order to develop satisfactory horizontal competition. This question of centralization cannot be answered separately from other questions about the level at which governance should take place or power should be assigned—that is, from questions of subsidiarity. The question of centralization to stabilize regulatory competition may best be joined with the question of subsidiarity raised in the property rights–theory of the firm literature: as we consider the utility of centralization—of institutional ownership of regulatory assets—we must consider the utility of establishing an authority capable of intervening to support regulatory competition.

Competition and Jurisdiction

Thus, while the Tiebout model includes consideration of externalities, it does so only to determine the quality of jurisdictional competition, and as noted above, the relevant parameter is rarely satisfied. Policy makers cannot set jurisdictional rules simply to enhance competition, but must consider other concerns, including those suggested by property rights theory. These concerns include most importantly the match between allocation of authority and internalization of effects, as well as the transaction costs involved in reallocation.

Furthermore, the Tiebout model can only be suggestive in the realm of the second best.[126] However, the Tiebout model contains important insights about the benefits of regulatory competition, which should not be ignored simply because the formal model cannot be applied. Our existential task is to engage in policy analysis even where formal tools come up short. Competition law theory suggests that monopolies reduce welfare, but leaves open the question of what kinds of monopolies will be permitted as welfare enhancing. Long-term (or even short-term) supply contracts, patents, and many other welfare-enhancing devices constitute monopolies. The important question is what temporal, geographic, and subject matter scope these monopolies should be permitted. As noted above, this is importantly related to the question of subsidiarity in international law.

The concerns of these bodies of theory may be used as a guide to analysis, and their insights incorporated in a rough comparative cost-benefit analysis of various jurisdictional rules, although we are a long way from anything approaching a formal model. Comparative institutional analysis must select particular institutions and develop parameters for comparison. The choice of institution, of course, is quite difficult, as all institutions are interconnected, and embedded in broader institutional settings.

The greatest problem with rootless recognition is thus the risk of externalization: these risks must be compared with any benefits expected from greater competition. Moreover, it is worth asking whether there is a structure that would provide the benefits of competition with reduced risks of externalization. Of course, externalization reduces the benefits of competition, and what we are really seeking is a structure that has aggregate benefits greater than those of the other available structures.

Thus, either (i) effects-based regulatory jurisdiction, or (ii) managed recognition (as described in detail below), would allow host states to forestall externalization by imposing their own regulation. More interestingly, managed recognition would provide an opportunity for states to reveal their anti-externalization preferences in negotiation over essential harmonization. This process requires states to revisit—and perhaps to modify—their preferences for regulation. Thus, democratic accountability for harmonization agreements becomes important.

Managed Recognition

A more refined approach to recognition could utilize one or more of the following instruments, all derived from European Union practice, to reduce the risk of externalization:

- Judicial examination of equivalence. "Equivalence," or recognition, could be mandated by a court under a general constitutional free trade provision, based on an examination of the home country regulations to determine that they achieve the host country's purported regulatory goals. Such requirements may be applied pursuant to the "least trade-restrictive alternative" requirements, or pursuant to hortatory provisions, of the WTO Agreement on Technical Barriers to Trade or the WTO Agreement on Sanitary and Phytosanitary Measures, or pursuant to other international mechanisms in other sectors. It is feasible that these disciplines could be extended to other fields. The result would be that recognition would only be required where the host state's regulatory goals are met by the home state regulations, ensuring against externalization.

- Legislative establishment of essential harmonization. International integration organizations such as the European Union or the WTO, or international functional organizations, such as Codex Alimentarius or the International Accounting Standards Board, may engage in efforts that amount to "legislative" establishment of essential harmonization. Unlike in the European Union, the international system does not generally provide for majority voting. The European Union often engages in essential harmonization, as a predicate to mutual recognition, to forge the single market. In negotiating harmonization directives, states recognize that the increased regulatory competition that will result from the proposed mutual recognition will place pressure on their ability to maintain regulation that, by definition, is otherwise desirable from a purely local standpoint, having been legislated through presumptively legitimate processes. Before agreeing to mutual recognition, they agree on a minimum level of regulation that will insulate their home regulation from being reduced in unacceptable ways. Furthermore, they exact a quid pro quo, both in terms of essential harmonization and in terms of other market liberalization in other areas.

- Maintenance of "safeguards" that would allow states to address threats to their public policy. European Union harmonization and mutual recognition initiatives such as the Second Banking Directive of 1989 contain provisions that allow host states to act to protect the "general good." These provisions provide a safeguard against externalization, at least in more egregious cases.

These devices could be used to determine, in more particular cases relating to specific regulatory systems and specific regulatory rules, whether competition or coordination is the superior alternative.

Mergers under Competition or Antitrust Laws: The Boeing–McDonnell Douglas Transaction, the General Electric–Honeywell Transaction, and the Effects Test

In 1997, the European Commission raised "serious doubts" regarding a proposed merger between Boeing and McDonnell Douglas. Boeing and McDonnell Douglas were U.S. companies, and neither had any facilities or assets in the European Union,[127] although they had substantial sales there. Here, the tables were turned, with the United States accusing the European Union of "extraterritoriality."[128] The European Merger Regulation does not require incorporation or assets within the European Union, but focuses instead on sales within the European Union as a basis for prescriptive jurisdiction.[129] This case included the complication that many felt the European position was influenced by concerns regarding the competitiveness of Airbus, and not simply enforcement of the Merger Regulation. However, for purposes of this chapter's analysis, and for purposes of any more general analysis of state preferences, it is appropriate to focus on the preferences incorporated generally in the legislation subject to analysis. Of course, in the market for large commercial jet aircraft, a merger between Boeing and McDonnell Douglas could conceivably have adverse effects in the European Union.

Here, the ostensible regulatory purposes of the relevant U.S. law (the Hart-Scott-Rodino Antitrust Improvements Act) and the Merger Regulation were consistent. However, in this case, the bodies charged with their enforcement, the U.S. Federal Trade Commission (FTC) and the European Commission, respectively, had different perspectives.[130] The FTC approved the merger, while the European Commission opened an investigation and concluded that the proposed merger would strengthen Boeing's dominant position.[131] After certain substantial concessions by Boeing, the European Commission approved the merger. It will readily be understood that here, jurisdiction was extremely valuable to both the United States and the European Union, with weighty political and economic ramifications riding on the allocation of jurisdiction.

In order to apply this chapter's analytical framework, we must first assess factually the possibilities for joint gains from cooperation. Given the high levels of international trade, and particularly transatlantic trade between the European Union and the United States, there are likely to be further instances where the current merger control regimes overlap. As suggested in Chapter 3, repetition may support cooperation. Even putting aside reciprocity, international antitrust problems involve dispersed effects. Indeed, there are real possibilities for gains from regulatory cooperation: "national competition authorities cannot fully protect their citizens from transnational anticompetitive conduct."[132]

There is also a good deal of informal (or semiformal) cooperation among antitrust authorities. This has led to modest progress in international institutionalization, under the title "positive comity."

> Under [positive comity] agreements, the antitrust authority of one country makes a preliminary determination that there are reasonable grounds for an antitrust investigation, typically in a case in which a corporation based in that country appears to have been denied access to the markets of another country. It then refers the matter, along with the preliminary analysis, to the antitrust authority whose home markets are most directly affected by the matter under investigation. After consultation with the foreign antitrust authority, and depending on what conclusions the foreign authority reaches and what action it takes, the referring antitrust authority can accept the foreign authority's conclusions, seek to modify them, or pursue its own action.[133]

While positive comity does not apply directly to merger review, it demonstrates the possibility of examination of cases of domestic conduct linked to foreign effects, at the request of the state experiencing the adverse effects. It also shows the possibility of informal coordination. On the other hand, in the *Empagran* decision, the U.S. Supreme Court found that U.S. antitrust laws do not apply to provide foreign plaintiffs a cause of action based on foreign effects, even when there are also domestic effects on domestic plaintiffs.[134]

What are the likely international policy options in connection with merger review? We can imagine three main options:

- The status quo, leaving international merger relations subject to ad hoc coordination: the market. This seems an acceptable position for now. As they engage in ad hoc coordination, the United States and European Union could each unilaterally engage in exercises of comity, in a tit-for-tat manner. Thus, each jurisdiction could revise its laws, or its interpretations of its laws, to defer to the other in specified circumstances.
- The United States and the European Union could enter into a formal jurisdiction-reallocating agreement, perhaps agreeing to a rule of recognition.
- The United States and the European Union could harmonize their laws and/or create a central enforcement agency.

These are the bilateral options; there are also plurilateral and multilateral options.

The transaction costs of initial allocation seem quite high. The status quo is something of a "standoff," with each party claiming extensive regulatory jurisdiction. Each party has something to gain, and the potential gains seem roughly symmetric. Even if the potential gains were asymmetric, these parties have such extensive relationships that linkage might provide the possibility of a symmetric gains transaction. Under this muddy allocation, we see ad hoc coordination, but as in the Boeing–McDonnell Douglas merger case, it is possible for one state to take action that may be viewed as inappropriately harmful to the other.

The second option raises the possibility of formal agreement, short of harmonization. The parties could agree on a regime of recognition for one another's merger control decisions. This would require agreement on the bases for recognition: nationality, preponderance of assets, preponderance of sales, or a combination of these, and perhaps other, factors. From the property rights perspective, there would be a desire to ensure that recognition does not entail excessive externalization. Thus, some minimal level of protection of the recognizing state's interests should be required as a precondition of recognition. In the European managed recognition technique, essential harmonization serves this purpose. Furthermore, capacity for contingent intervention could be maintained to protect a limited range of important values.

Alternatively, the United States and European Union, and perhaps other states, could establish an organization, or empower an already existing organization, to review mergers on their behalf. Significant asset specificity, especially combined with dispersed effects, might suggest the utility of an organization. An organization could provide information regarding the harm that certain mergers might pose to competition in particular jurisdictions, assisting in overcoming asymmetric information problems that might otherwise hinder bargaining.

One of the problems with setting effects as the leading factor in assigning prescriptive jurisdiction is the fact that valuations of effects (defined as impairment of governmental preferences) are, at least initially, private information in the hands of the affected state. This problem is somewhat less troublesome than it would be in the case of individual preferences, which are truly within each person's private thoughts. In the case of governmental preferences, these can be assessed through various polling or other social science techniques. It may be that international negotiations could be facilitated by the assistance of a third party—an international organization—in assessing effects on particular states. This would provide important input for negotiations on allocation of prescriptive jurisdiction.

Prospectus Disclosure Regulation under Securities Laws: The Daimler-Benz Listing and Recognition versus Harmonization

Daimler-Benz listed its American Depositary Shares on the New York Stock Exchange (NYSE) in 1993. In order to list, Daimler-Benz was required to register with the U.S. Securities and Exchange Commission (SEC) under the Securities Exchange Act of 1934. Daimler-Benz was therefore required to provide a reconciliation of its financial statements to U.S. generally accepted accounting principles (USGAAP). There are many differences between German accounting principles and USGAAP, requiring Daimler-Benz to incur substantial costs and to make disclosure of topics such as hidden reserves. This disclosure was hotly debated among Daimler-

Benz, the NYSE, and the SEC. The SEC was concerned about relaxing its accounting disclosure requirements with respect to foreign registrants—it wished to continue to provide something close to national treatment based on territoriality. Daimler-Benz and the NYSE argued for recognition: that the United States should simply accept financial statements prepared in accordance with German accounting principles.[135] The International Accounting Standards Board has prepared international financial reporting standards. Thus, we have a choice among national treatment, recognition, and harmonization. More recently, similar problems have been raised by the U.S. Sarbanes-Oxley law and European responses.

It is in this field that Romano, and Choi and Guzman, have argued for what I have termed "rootless recognition": recognition of foreign regulation without evaluation or predicate.[136] This approach fails to take into account the state preferences involved. Securities disclosure regulation is motivated by externality or asymmetric information problems, and rootless recognition fails to address those problems. This failure threatens any benefits of regulatory competition and fails to address concerns raised by property rights theory. Thus, the main open question relates to the value to the state of regulatory jurisdiction in this field. If regulatory jurisdiction has no value in terms of state preferences, a regime of private choice should prevail. While there has been an active scholarly debate regarding the utility of securities regulation, there is almost no such debate in the policy community.

Thus, while we may assume that jurisdiction in this context has value to the regulating state—or at least to the United States—what is less clear is the degree to which this value is diminished in the transnational context. For example, to the extent that one argues that the beneficiaries of securities regulation are the citizens of the state in which the regulated issuer does business, there is little need to apply U.S. securities regulation to foreign issuers.[137] On the other hand, to the extent that one focuses on externalities or information asymmetries harming investors, or markets, then there remain significant reasons to apply U.S. securities regulation to foreign issuers offering securities to U.S. persons, or in the United States, respectively.

Within the European Union context, managed recognition has been the rule in securities regulation, as in other areas of financial services. Indeed, in the international context, the work of the International Accounting Standards Board and the International Organization of Securities Commissions seems to suggest that managed recognition will be the rule. Rootless recognition does not seem to have substantial advantages over managed recognition, once one puts aside a generalized suspicion of government action. Indeed, effective in early 2008, after a lengthy negotiation and review process, the SEC adopted rules that would allow foreign issuers to use the International Financial Reporting Standards prepared by the International Accounting Standards Board, without reconciliation to USGAAP.

Assuming that misleading disclosure harms investors and markets in the host country and allocative efficiency in the jurisdiction in which the issuer does business, and that good disclosure imposes costs primarily on the issuer, then effects are somewhat dispersed. Thus, it may be difficult to develop an initial allocation in accordance with effects. However, the transaction costs associated with reallocation may not be substantial. Moreover, gains from reallocative transactions may be symmetrical, at least among states that have active capital markets. Thus, while it may not be possible to decide on an initial allocation, choosing between nationality and effects, it may be relatively simple to agree on reallocation, pursuant to a managed recognition structure.

Conclusions

As noted at the beginning of this chapter, the theoretical structure established herein can be used to rebut other theories, or other principles of choice of law or prescriptive jurisdiction, demonstrating their shortcomings as bases for allocation of prescriptive jurisdiction. Of course, the more satisfying use would be to generate falsifiable hypotheses, in order empirically to test predictions made from this theoretical structure.

The Negative Utility of This Framework

The framework for analysis described in this chapter can serve to show the shortcomings of traditional approaches to prescriptive jurisdiction and choice of law, as well as some of the more recent law and economics literature in this field.

I argue that to the extent that individuals express their preferences through government, governmental preferences are the touchstone of prescriptive jurisdiction analysis. Some law and economics scholars have argued in effect that the occasion of cross-border circumstances is reason enough to abridge the mandatory nature of otherwise mandatory law, in support of private preferences. This argument, however, seems to prove too much. Furthermore, regulatory competition is not appropriate as the leading basis for choosing among approaches to choice of law and prescriptive jurisdiction. Regulatory competition is always with us—the correct question is whether it is useful to increase or otherwise change the structure of regulatory competition.

Clear entitlements may be appropriate in some circumstances, but are not necessarily the best approach to choice of law and prescriptive jurisdiction problems. A prescription from the perspective of a naïve law and economics, and from private legal practice, might simply favor clear entitlements. And indeed, where the entitlement can be designed to encapsulate the effects, clear rules (and high mobility) may well be beneficial, not least because they promote regulatory competition. However, this chapter has suggested that if clear entitlements do not match well with the distribution of effects, then under high transaction cost circumstances, another arrangement may be preferable. Muddy entitlements may promote revelation of private information and informal transfers.

Regulatory competence is only a subsidiary consideration. It is true that, all other things being equal, the state with the greatest absolute advantage in regulation should be allocated prescriptive jurisdiction. However, regulatory advantage is sometimes conflated with an effects-based allocation, and for good reason: the state with the greatest concern is likely to regulate with the greatest efficiency (although other concerned states may find their preferences ignored). Indeed, absolute advantage—regulatory competence—may be based on a number of other things. There may be first-mover advantages, economies of scale, or economies of scope. However, other devices, such as international organization, technical assistance, and contracting, may be used to harness such advantage.

The Positive Utility of This Framework

No assignment of regulatory jurisdiction (or property) is perfect, precisely matching its boundaries with all of the positive and negative consequences of the authority assigned. Property law theory is suggestive as to jurisdictional rules, but also finally refers to a need for judgment, or commensuration and interpersonal comparison of utility. And property law theory does not formally incorporate concerns for interjurisdictional competition. The

Tiebout model can only be suggestive in the realm of the second best.[138] Nor do the more procedural analytical perspectives discussed here provide discrete solutions; rather, the theory of the firm (Chapter 5), social norms (Chapter 3), and rules and standards (Chapter 7) literatures provide important additional considerations.

As noted at the beginning of this chapter, these theoretical perspectives do not by themselves form a basis for affirmative policy making. However, the concerns of these bodies of theory may be used as a guide to analysis, and their insights incorporated in a comparative cost-benefit analysis of various jurisdictional rules, although we are a long way from anything approaching formal analysis. Comparative institutional analysis must select particular institutions and develop parameters for comparison. The choice of institution, of course, is quite difficult, as all institutions are interconnected and embedded in broader institutional settings.

This framework can thus suggest possible testable hypotheses.[139] The European Union may be a useful source of natural experiments. For example, did the move toward essential harmonization and mutual recognition in particular areas, such as bank regulation, result in fewer conflicts over alleged externalization? Did these moves result in greater measures of regulatory competition? There is an active literature on the empirics of regulatory competition, using event studies and other empirical techniques to argue whether regulatory competition yields a race to the "top" or one to the "bottom."

Hypotheses could be tested using historical or comparative data. It would be necessary to develop at least indicative measures of the value of certain types of prescriptive jurisdiction, similar to measures of asset specificity in other institutional economics contexts. It would also be necessary to begin to develop understandings of the types and magnitudes of transaction costs in the market for prescriptive jurisdiction. These efforts would be worthwhile because they would provide strong empirical bases for policy decisions.

This chapter has attempted to suggest an integrated law and economics–based framework for analysis of international and interstate problems of allocation of horizontal prescriptive jurisdiction. It has necessarily painted with a broad brush. Further work will be required to particularize some of the analytical techniques described here to a variety of circumstances, and to begin to hone these theoretical insights through empirical analysis.

This chapter has also established the fundamental units of transactions, and the fundamental motivation for transactions, in the international legal setting. States transact in jurisdiction in international law in order to realize gains from trade. The establishment of rules of jurisdiction, like the establishment of rules of property in a municipal setting, is itself a transaction. But jurisdiction can then be reallocated. In subsequent chapters, we examine mechanisms for reallocation that utilize social norms or customary international law, treaty, organization, and, within organization, adjudication.

✦

Customary International Law

CHAPTERS 1 AND 2 argued that jurisdiction—the allocation of legal authority—is the central concern of international law. They explained the motivation of states to enter into transactions to form rules of jurisdiction, and the variety we observe in rules of jurisdiction. How are rules of jurisdiction formed and changed? How do transactions in jurisdiction take place? Custom, treaty, and organization are the tools available to states to engage in transactions in jurisdiction. This chapter examines the possibility for customary rules of international law to bind states.[1] Chapters 4 and 5 examine the role of treaty and organization as mechanisms to bind states to transactions in jurisdiction.

Customary international law (CIL) is a feat of levitation; it rests not on a rock-solid natural law basis of divine principles, but on a fabric of rational acts, woven through a multiplicity of relations over time. And while there are limits on, and variations in, the effectiveness of CIL, this chapter shows that there are circumstances where it may independently affect the behavior of states. There is no reason in theory, or in data adduced by others, to believe CIL to be generally epiphenomenal. More generally, since certain components of CIL serve as the foundation of all international law, this chapter suggests the circumstances under which we would expect international law to affect state behavior.

The present chapter refines and extends an emerging rationalist understanding of CIL.[2] Pioneering work in this field—notably that of Jack Goldsmith and Eric Posner—has begun to articulate such a rationalist theory. They have argued that CIL does not affect state behavior.[3] This chapter shows why this assertion is incorrect as a matter of theory and, to the extent that it purports to rely on factual observation, is unsupported by the data they present.[4] This chapter provides a richer model that leads to the rejection of Goldsmith and Posner's argument that the multilateral prisoner's dilemma is unlikely to allow CIL to affect state behavior. In fact, this chapter shows that CIL may affect state behavior using exactly the same types of mechanisms by which social norms or law affects individual behavior in the municipal context.

In addition to their game theory–based argument that the multilateral prisoner's dilemma is unlikely to affect state behavior, Goldsmith and Posner argue that states are never motivated by CIL. This latter position arises from a false dichotomy between motivation by self-interest[5] and motivation by law. In a rationalist model, behavior is *assumed* to be motivated by self-interest. If law is artificially separated from self-interest—the Goldsmith-Posner position—then it would logically follow, under a rationalist model, that law has no motivating force. Yet this chapter shows how CIL rules may modify the payoffs associated with relevant behavior and thereby affect behavior through self-interest. CIL may affect behavior, even when it only does so at the margins. While CIL is endogenous to states as a group—meaning that it is not a vertical structure produced outside or above the group of states—it has an independent, exogenous influence on the behavior of each individual state.[6]

Goldsmith and Posner assert that states are not motivated by *opinio juris* to comply with CIL. In their model, not only is there no possibility of multilateral cooperation, but there is also no possibility that CIL would exert any binding force beyond that associated with nonlegal cooperation: CIL is, in their model, epiphenomenal. But under CIL doctrine, if states are not motivated by *opinio juris,* then CIL does not exist. This chapter's analysis provides a plausible basis to assign a discriminating role to *opinio juris,* and therefore to find CIL doctrine internally coherent in at least its core dimension. *Opinio juris* should be understood as a way of referring to the intent of states to propose or accept a rule of law that will serve as the focal point of behavior, implicate an important set of default rules applicable to law but not to other types of social order, and bring into play an important set of linkages among legal rules.

This chapter develops a repeated multilateral prisoner's dilemma model of CIL. Of course, game theory can never capture all real-world detail, including its highly nuanced decision making.[7] The purpose of game-theoretic models is not to predict or prescribe behavior, but to generate testable hypotheses that, once tested, are expected to tell us something useful about the world.[8]

This chapter's analysis focuses on the parameters of the multilateral prisoner's dilemma in the CIL context. These parameters include (i) the relative value of cooperation versus defection; (ii) the number of states effectively involved; (iii) the extent to which increasing the number of states involved increases the value of cooperation or the detriments of defection, including whether the particular issue has characteristics of a commons problem, a public good, or a network good;[9] (iv) the information available to the states involved regarding compliance and defection; (v) the relative patience of states in valuing the benefits of long-term cooperation compared to short-term defection; (vi) the expected duration of interaction; (vii) the frequency of interaction; and (viii) the existence of other bilateral or multilateral relationships among the states involved.

The parameters listed above are incorporated into this chapter's model as independent variables, but from a normative standpoint it is possible for policy initiatives to select or manipulate these parameters. That is, by identifying the parameters for determining whether CIL will affect state behavior, this chapter opens the way to normative institutional design. States may restructure certain institutions in order to facilitate the formation and operation of CIL. There may be circumstances under which it will be normatively attractive to facilitate the development of CIL, rather than to engage in more self-conscious and static treaty making. The institutional dynamism and social immanence that make social norms attractive in the domestic context may also be attractive in at least some international contexts.

Rather than being a mere label for rational cooperation, CIL is a special branch of cooperation that has particular features, including the establishment of a focal point so that states may readily identify what will "count" as cooperation; attention to the motivation of states to offer and accept a rule of law *(opinio juris)*, with certain default rules and prescribed consequences; and the linkage of the particular rule with the broader international legal system.

In this last regard, we might say that by including a particular rule in CIL, states are accepting that the rest of the legal system is now open to being compromised or weakened by noncompliance with that rule. That is, by violating one legal rule, a state may undercut the entire legal system. This connectedness adds strong incentives for compliance. We would expect states to move from non-CIL equilibrium behavior to *opinio juris*–based CIL insofar as the latter makes possible an equilibrium that could not otherwise be achieved, or could not be achieved with such efficiency.[10]

This chapter advances a plausible theory of potential efficient equilibria in the multilateral prisoner's dilemma, and indicates some possible hypotheses and approaches for empirical testing. The chapter is organized as follows. The first section provides a short doctrinal review of CIL and briefly locates this chapter in relation to four literatures: law and economics, social norms, international organization, and industrial organization. The model presented is based largely on earlier work in these other areas. The second section explains the choice of the repeated multilateral prisoner's dilemma as the basis for my model, as well as the choice of an assumed strategy for players within this model. Any game-theoretic model depends on decisions to assume certain game structures and strategies. This section explains why the prisoner's dilemma provides a good fit for the CIL context and explains the choice of an assumed strategy for states to follow. The third section explains the other assumptions and parameters of the model. The fourth section sets forth four illustrative examples of CIL contexts that might be understood in terms of this model. The fifth section elaborates the general structure and implications of the model. The sixth section presents some implications of this model, with concluding remarks in the last section.

In brief, this chapter presents a fully elaborated rationalist model of CIL to describe the parameters that will determine states' compliance with CIL. The analysis has important implications regarding the plausibility of CIL, our understanding of CIL doctrine, the possibility of institutional change to facilitate the development of CIL in particular areas, and future research in CIL.

Customary International Law Doctrine and Social Science Literatures

In order to locate this chapter in its legal and also its broader, social scientific context, I present here a brief description of salient CIL doctrine and of the social science literatures that inform the analysis presented.

Customary International Law Doctrine

As an introductory matter, it is useful to review the fundamental doctrine of CIL. Article 38(1)(b) of the Statute of the International Court of Justice (ICJ) lists the sources of international law applicable by the Court, including "international custom, as evidence of a general practice accepted as law." Section 102 of the American Law Institute's *Restatement (Third) of Foreign Relations Law* states that "customary international law results from a general and consistent practice of states followed by them from a sense of legal obligation."[11] The sense of obligation is referred to in Latin as *opinio juris sive necessitatis*.

As suggested above, for the social scientist studying law, the critical descriptive question relates to the effects of legal rules on behavior. For CIL, this descriptive question is also a doctrinal question, as CIL doctrine requires some level of generality and consistency of practice—some quantum of state behavior. And, at least under the *Restatement* formulation, this behavior must be motivated by *opinio juris*. Under the ICJ Statute, the custom itself may serve as evidence of acceptance as law, of *opinio juris*. Some commentators have suggested that *opinio juris* in a formal sense may not be necessary at all, but that the requirement should be understood in terms of state consent or acceptance.[12]

Not all CIL is created equal; not all law is equally or peremptorily binding. The model developed in this chapter indicates the parameters for discrimination. Simply put, we would expect greater opportunities for the formation of, and compliance with, CIL in some fields than in others. Empiricism would, in this context, require analysis of areas in which CIL has *not* developed—the dog that did not bark. This theoretical approach also accepts the possibility of linkage among diverse fields. This linkage allows for the possible sharing of binding force among diverse fields, integrating and therefore homogenizing the behavioral effects of the legal rules in each field.

Four Literatures

This chapter draws on four semi-autonomous literatures. First, as noted above, there is an emerging rationalist, law and economics–based literature of CIL. The leading work in this area is by Goldsmith and Posner, but there are other important contributions. Second, this chapter draws on a burgeoning literature on social norms in the law, although social norms are studied by all manner of social scientists. Third, the chapter draws on the economics field of industrial organization for game theory–based insights about collusion among competitors in markets. Fourth, the chapter draws on the political science literature of international organization, which has addressed in detail the game-theoretic analysis of cooperation among groups of states.

LAW AND ECONOMICS OF CIL   Goldsmith and Posner suggest that many instances of observed CIL may be understood in terms of bilateral cooperation along the lines of a bilateral prisoner's dilemma game. They then argue that "although game theory does not rule out the possibility of n-state cooperation, the assumptions required for such an outcome are quite strong and usually unrealistic." For this reason, they "doubt the utility of n-player prisoner's dilemmas as an explanation for multilateral or 'universal' behavioral regularities."[13] Their views with respect to coordination games are similar. The present chapter shows, however, that the assumptions for multilateral, or "n-state," cooperation are neither too strong nor unrealistic, and that they are in some cases quite plausible.

SOCIAL NORMS   We might ask, however, whether CIL is different in structure from social norms in a domestic context, and whether, if social norms can affect behavior, CIL can as well. Since the publication of Robert Ellickson's *Order without Law*[14] in 1991, legal scholars have examined the role of informal norms in society and the relationship of those norms to law. Ellickson investigates how cattle farmers in Shasta County, California, manage to establish and apply their own nonlegal rules, with a notable level of compliance, without direct intervention by the state. It is an insightful story about how order can arise without law— or in spite of law.[15]

We may draw a rough, and limited, analogy between the development of social norms in a municipal, or private, setting[16] and the development of CIL in the international public setting. In the international community, CIL is substantively similar to the phenomenon that Ellickson describes.[17] In international political science, regime theorists such as Robert Keohane,[18] Stephen Krasner,[19] and Beth Simmons[20] have told a similar story of the possible rise of order in international society. However, regime theory has generally avoided CIL.[21] While many of the insights of regime theory are relevant in analysis of CIL, the latter has important distinguishing features. Recognition that a rule has become part of CIL may signal its support by, or linkage with, the multisector international legal system, whose accepted and enforced linkage may distinguish legal rules from nonlegal regimes.

Within a municipal setting, the difference between law and social norms is that law alone is the province of the state (setting aside, for the moment, religious law, other nonstate rules, and circumstances in which non-state-made rules are incorporated in the state-enforced law).[22] This distinction is inapposite to the international system, however, which has been characterized as a horizontal, as opposed to vertical, system in which there is no overarching state per se.[23] So, in the international system, there is more overlap, and an indistinct border, between law and social norms. This overlap is perhaps easier to see in the international context than in the domestic context, since in the international context, a significant subset of social norms is termed "law." Ellickson states that the social norms literature defines a "social norm" as "a rule governing an individual's behavior that third parties other than state agents diffusely enforce by means of social sanctions."[24] The focus of this definition on decentralized means of enforcement shows the strong analogy between social norms in the municipal setting and CIL in the international setting. Of course, to the extent that international courts may apply, and institutions of global governance may enforce, CIL, there is a difference. But this application and enforceability are quite limited. There are few circumstances in which CIL rules benefit from mandatory adjudication in *international* tribunals. We would not consider application of CIL by *domestic* courts to amount to the action of "state agents" *at the international level,* although action by domestic courts would certainly be considered action of "state agents" *at the municipal level.* The reason for making this distinction is that, in the international context, *domestic* courts are simply internal deliberative processes of national governments. The application by domestic courts of CIL may thus be understood as a kind of norm internalization.[25]

According to one leading conceptualization of social norms, those norms are preferences that individuals (or, in our case, states) acquire through education, acculturation, or other processes.[26] Consequently, building upon those same processes, it may well be possible to modify the preferences of states through social norms. And the most obvious way to modify those preferences would be by modifying the preferences either of individual government officials or of voters. Indeed, it may be appropriate to consider epistemic communities and networks among government officials as channels of preference modification. Nevertheless, while this constructivist approach may have merit in the CIL setting and includes a potential role for arguments predicated on legitimacy, justice, and morality as bases for preference modification, this chapter will bypass such issues and focus on exogenous explanations of social norms—that is, explanations that look at external influences on actors, rather than at changes brought about through internal processes.[27] Modeling always involves simplification, and the goal of this chapter is to elaborate an exogenous model for future testing. It should be noted, moreover, that testing an exogenous model would help to advance the debate between exogenous and endogenous causes of compliance with CIL.

In connection with exogenous explanations, there are two reasons why the law-based social norms literature has not embraced the repeated multilateral prisoner's dilemma.[28] First, there are concerns that game theory does not capture the nuances of social interaction. The incorporation of multisector contact, repeated interaction, and other parameters will help to address these concerns. Second, there are concerns regarding the credibility of third-party enforcement.[29] Will third parties be properly motivated to join in retaliation against violators? If the threat of retaliation is not credible, there will be strong incentives for violation. I address these concerns below.

INDUSTRIAL ORGANIZATION   Much of our understanding of the utility, structure, and dynamics of the multilateral prisoner's dilemma comes from the economics literature of industrial organization. This literature considers the possibility that firms may enter into cartels or other restrictions of competition that violate U.S. antitrust laws. While firms may find opportunities to communicate, their communications and agreements must be kept secret from the regulatory authorities, and the agreements are not, in any event, enforceable at law. This legal restraint on the enforcement of agreements is analogous to the limitation in the international law setting on enforcement of agreements. In both contexts, there is no vertical state available to enforce contracts. An important concern for industrial organization economists is to identify circumstances under which agreements can be made self-sustaining through the self-interest of the parties to the agreement. For similar reasons, it is worthwhile to examine circumstances under which CIL commitments are self-sustaining.

While the analogy between the antitrust situation and CIL is apparent, we must recognize that there are differences, too. In the CIL setting, public communication is permitted, and there are agreements that at least purport to be binding—namely, treaties. The international legal rule that treaties must be observed *(pacta sunt servanda)* is itself part of CIL.

Another, perhaps more important, distinction is that a cartel has certain characteristics that may differ from those of any particular CIL setting. That is, in a cartel, the more that others adhere to the cartel, the greater the monetary incentives for any particular member to defect. This context is more like a commons problem than a public good or network problem. Later in this chapter, we will discuss some of these distinctions as reflecting variations in payoff structures, with consequent variations in the likelihood of compliance.

INTERNATIONAL ORGANIZATION Political scientists and economists working in the field of international organization have made a good deal of progress in analyzing the problem of international cooperation. Without making reference to CIL, these writers have examined most of the parameters utilized here.[30] In addition to formalizing various considerations that remain informal in much of the political science literature, the model presented here has certain distinctive features described below.

Rather than attempting to structure a model that would capture the dynamics of other international cooperation devices, the model presented here is designed to match most closely the specific context and dynamics of CIL. We must recognize, however, that the question of which international cooperation device to employ or rely on in particular circumstances—treaty, CIL, or some form of nonlegal instrument—itself depends on a set of variables. Furthermore, CIL may be understood as a phase in the formalization of law, or in "legalization."[31] The United Nations' International Law Commission often codifies CIL, and CIL often forms the basis for treaties. This chapter does not present a systematic explanation of the choice among custom, treaty, and other instruments, or of the relationship among these various devices.[32]

The Multilateral Customary International Law Game

Game theory develops models to depict, to abstract, and to formalize various social settings. Given the diversity of social contexts, there is a wide choice of models from which to choose.[33] This section explains the choice of the multilateral prisoner's dilemma as the basic model for understanding CIL, examines the potential strategies that might be played within this game, and explains some of the assumptions made. The repeated multilateral prisoner's dilemma is itself really a family of models, with a number of varying features, including the number of players and their preferences.

Choice of Game

The basic payoff structure assumed in the prisoner's dilemma captures the essential problem of cooperation in a horizontal social setting with externalities. The parties have a choice between compliance and defection, and they can either enrich themselves individually through defection or enrich society—and, in light of the anticipated actions of others, themselves—through compliance.[34] Of course, some CIL contexts might be better modeled using other methods, but by using the prisoner's dilemma, I hope to capture the essence of informal contracting under conditions of divergent interests.[35]

One of the reasons for choosing this game is because it allows us to contextualize a number of insights and concerns that cannot easily be included in other analytical models. For example, the multilateral prisoner's dilemma can take account of a number of the diverse considerations often referred to collectively as "reputation" or "reputational sanctions."[36] The multilateral prisoner's dilemma must be at the core of an exogenous explanation of the effectiveness of social norms. Finally, the multilateral prisoner's dilemma offers parsimony: in the CIL context, the factors that it takes into account seem necessary, and there are no factors that seem superfluous.

The prisoner's dilemma is a noncooperative game—meaning that the players are unable to enter into binding agreements with one another. Although treaties are binding agreements in a formal legal sense, it seems appropriate at the outset to model CIL, including treaties, as a noncooperative game since even treaties bind only through CIL itself. It may be appropriate to relax the assumption that the general international legal context is a noncooperative game, however, once we determine that the CIL rule of *pacta sunt servanda* has binding force, lending binding force to treaties and thereby incorporating an element of cooperation. While *pacta sunt servanda* is critical to *treaty* law, it should be emphasized that it does not affect our analysis of CIL.

On the other hand, we must recognize that CIL itself has two levels. At the foundational level are the CIL rules regarding the formation and binding nature of CIL itself. This rule is the analog to *pacta sunt servanda*, and it plays a similar role: serving as a foundational rule upon which other rules of CIL may be built. For the moment, however, it seems appropriate not to take such a rule into account. However, the conclusion of this chapter suggests that CIL rules may be linked, or in effect networked, in such a way that each rule supports compliance with each other rule, and perhaps results in a foundational rule.

Thus, in a noncooperative, single-play circumstance, with a standard prisoner's dilemma payoff structure, we would expect noncompliance,[37] which is each player's dominant strategy; that is, each player's payoff from defection is superior to its payoff from cooperation, no matter what the other player does. This "strongly dominant" strategy is illustrated in Figure 3.1: no matter what state B does, state A obtains a better payoff by defecting, and vice versa.[38]

Therefore, under the rather restrictive assumptions of the true prisoner's dilemma, each party invariably chooses the strategy that results in reduced individual welfare and reduced aggregate welfare, compared to the cooperative strategy. This outcome is inefficient. By analogy, states

State B

		Cooperate	Defect
State A	Cooperate	A:7/B:7 [sum=14]	A:0/B:10 [sum=10]
	Defect	A:10/B:0 [sum=10]	A:3/B:3 [sum=6]

Figure 3.1 Prisoner's dilemma

playing the CIL game (assuming prisoner's dilemma–type payoffs) in a bilateral single-play setting would fail to form or comply with a CIL rule that increased individual and aggregate welfare. Cooperation is strongly dominated; the resulting equilibrium is for both states to defect.[39] The same is true of a prisoner's dilemma repeated a finite number of times, with that number known in advance to the players. Again, the unique resulting equilibrium is for each player to defect in each period, or round of play.[40]

This conclusion is inescapable in theory, given the constraints of the game: the outcome of the prisoner's dilemma is, by definition, an inefficient equilibrium. This conclusion presents us, in effect, with a normative goal: to modify the real-world circumstances so as to produce stable equilibria that are efficient. That is the major role of CIL—and of international law generally.

Of course, in a world where there was effective third-party enforcement of agreements, the response to the prisoner's dilemma is obvious: the parties would enter into a binding agreement to cooperate, thereby modifying the payoff structure and escaping the prisoner's dilemma. The prisoner's dilemma assumes, however, that its prisoners are held separately and cannot negotiate, reach, or enforce a binding agreement.

In CIL there is no court of general mandatory jurisdiction and no publicly appointed "policeman." While we may draw analogies to the ICJ and the United Nations, these institutions have substantial differences compared to domestic courts and police. Therefore, it is appropriate initially to assume that there is no capacity to make agreements that are binding— which is obviously a simplifying assumption. In fact, the model described here is meant to show that there are substitutes for agreements that are made binding by extrinsic force, and that these substitutes may have binding force. Once the capacity to bind is established, the players are no longer in a prisoner's dilemma.

In the CIL game, there are four additional important distinctions from the assumptions of noncooperative game theory, in general, and from those of the prisoner's dilemma, in particular. First, the players can communicate with one another (and can do so more readily today than during the sixteenth to nineteenth centuries—when some of the fundamental doctrines of CIL originally coalesced). Second, since states play a repeated game with one another with no defined end date, they can respond at an indeterminate future time to something done earlier. Updating of information and punishment are consequently possible. Third, not only is the game (narrowly construed) characterized by a particular CIL rule, such as that of diplomatic immunity, but it is also embedded in a dense fabric of relationships. Fourth, information regarding compliance is often readily accessible; more so today, it would appear, than in the past. These distinctions may transform the game into something quite different from the prisoner's dilemma; while nothing resolves the prisoner's dilemma itself, modifications of the game may result in outcomes that are stable, efficient equilibria. Indeed, given sufficient means by which states may bind one another, it may be useful to use cooperative game theory to analyze some CIL circumstances. I examine this possibility in more detail in Chapter 4.

As will be illustrated below, one of the more difficult problems of multilateral cooperation is a commons problem in which, as in the cartel context, incentives to defect increase with the number of other states that comply. The more that the commons is protected, the greater the benefits of defection are. Where incentives to defect increase with the number of players, we would expect the most severe challenge to cooperation. Not all CIL contexts exhibit this characteristic.

Elinor Ostrom states that a "substantial gap exists between the theoretical prediction that self-interested individuals will have extreme difficulty in coordinating collective action and the reality that such cooperative behavior is widespread, although far from inevitable."[41] She cites considerable evidence regarding the amount and circumstances of cooperation by individuals in multilateral collective action problems. The evidence shows that individuals contribute to the resolution of these problems in substantially greater amounts than the standard prisoner's dilemma model would suggest. Of course, much of the evidence is obtained in circumstances where the assumptions of the prisoner's dilemma are violated—by allowing individuals to communicate, enter into agreements, and repeat play.

Choice of Strategy

The next step in constructing a model of CIL is to postulate a plausible strategy that states might play within the prisoner's dilemma. There are many choices, including tit for tat, grim trigger, and penance. These strategies are stylized assumptions about state behavior, but they are necessary in order to complete the model. The reader will see, however, that these strategies are plausible state responses to defection by others in particular circumstances—in fact the criterion for choosing a strategy in developing a theory is plausibility. There are two ways in which retaliation might occur: the harmed state alone retaliates (bilateral retaliation), or the broader community of states retaliates (multilateral retaliation). The fourth section of this chapter discusses the possibility of bilateral or multilateral retaliation, and how this choice would affect the model.

TIT FOR TAT   Under "tit for tat," states respond to defection with a single defection. Tit for tat is one of the most frequently discussed strategies in connection with repeated prisoner's dilemmas. While tit for tat may win evolutionary games,[42] it is not credible: after a defection, the wronged state will have incentives to accept an undertaking from the defecting state that it will cooperate in future.[43] Even more devastating to tit for tat is that once one state defects, the game cycles endlessly between defection and compliance.[44] Given the implausibility of tit for tat, I reject it and do not evaluate the implications of its use.

GRIM TRIGGER   Second, states may respond to a single defection with defection forever: a "grim trigger" strategy. There are two basic approaches that have been developed in the theory of repeated games. The first assumes that any deviation is met with a response that maximizes the loss that the deviator suffers—even if that course of action imposes costs on the punishers. The second approach assumes that deviation results in reversion to the Nash equilibrium[45] of the prisoner's dilemma: defection. I adopt the latter approach since it appears to be more appealing to players. Essentially, I assume that in the event of deviation, the states revert to the strategies that they would have adopted if no CIL rule had developed in the first place. The grim trigger strategy is credible, as it calls for a reversion to the dominant strategy of defection in response to an initial defection.

The grim trigger strategy is nevertheless unappealing for the same reason that failure to achieve a cooperative solution to the prisoner's dilemma is unappealing: it results in inefficiency. Thus, in his work on treaties relating to environmental commons problems,[46] Barrett rejects the grim trigger strategy because it fails to satisfy the criterion of collective rationality. This criterion is a formal articulation of the intuitive concern that it would be extraordinarily wasteful to abandon an efficient multilateral agreement because of a single defection. While it would be *individually* rational to respond with defection forever—it simply calls for reversion to the Nash equilibrium—that strategy is collectively irrational insofar as rational negotiators have incentives to renegotiate a cooperative arrangement after defection. This renewed effort at cooperation renders the "defection forever," or grim trigger, strategy not credible.

The grim trigger strategy is thus not credible because it is not "renegotiation-proof";[47] that is, after a defection, nondefecting states will have incentives to come together and cooperate with the defector, depriving the grim trigger of credibility and therefore effectiveness. The defector can make an appealing "let bygones be bygones" argument.[48] An obvious counterargument, however, is that renegotiation unravels if states perceive that the defector's argument may be made repeatedly. That is, once the players understand that defection and promises of future compliance will go on indefinitely, would they not decline to renegotiate the first time? Moreover, in the CIL context, we are operating on the assumption that states do not have the possibility of forming binding agreements through renegotiation, preventing this indefinite defection.

Nevertheless, there may be circumstances in which such renegotiation is possible and the offer to renegotiate *and abide by the results* is credible. If so, states will have incentives to defect, and an alternative, "renegotiation-proof" strategy is needed. The penance strategy described below is a "weakly renegotiation-proof" alternative.

With respect to the more empirical question of whether a grim trigger strategy is actually used by states (that is, whether states respond to defection by defection forever), if we think not about the CIL that exists, but about the CIL that does not exist, it is clear that states follow the grim trigger strategy at least in some contexts. In fact, one might argue that the grim trigger is the existing default strategy in CIL. That is, where a CIL rule exists or is proposed for formation, and one state deviates, that may be sufficient provocation to cause others to deviate forever in response: to kill the rule multilaterally. The penance strategy described below is probably a more broadly accurate description of the default strategy in use today.

PENANCE   If renegotiation is possible and credible, states will prefer to renegotiate after a defection, making defection an attractive option.[49] The strategy known as "penance"[50] is both individually credible in that states would individually find it attractive to play it, and collectively credible in the sense that it is likely to be more attractive than renegotiation.[51] Drew

Fudenberg and Jean Tirole show that the following "penance" strategy profile is "weakly renegotiation-proof": begin in the cooperative phase, where both states choose a cooperative play; if state *A* then defects, the other state *B* immediately switches to defect for all subsequent periods until and including the first period in which state *A* reverts to cooperation; after that period, state *B* also reverts to cooperation.[52]

The logic of this strategy in the CIL context is that a state having defected from a rule can have the rule reinstated only by accepting a single period of punishment, in which it cooperates while the other state defects against it. The overall span of punishment (defecting behavior by the state defected against) is equal to the span of defection by the original defecting state, ensuring that there is no net gain from defection. Chapter 4 provides an argument for equal punishment in the context of World Trade Organization (WTO) dispute settlement.

A form of penance seems to be endorsed by the International Law Commission as the CIL rule to be applied in international law generally. Articles 49 to 54 of the Articles on State Responsibility provide that countermeasures may be used only to induce a state to cease a wrongful act *and to make reparations;*[53] the countermeasures must be commensurate with the injury.[54]

Equilibrium Selection, Coordination, and the Role of CIL

One of the problems in a multilateral prisoner's dilemma is identifying the strategy that other players are using, and then coordinating on a single strategy. Fudenberg and Tirole conclude,

> Thus, repeated play with patient players not only makes "cooperation"—meaning efficient payoffs—possible, it also leads to a large set of other equilibrium outcomes. Several methods have been proposed to reduce this multiplicity of equilibria; however, none of them has yet been widely accepted, and the problem remains a topic of research.[55]

Under circumstances of multiple equilibria, "anything that tends to focus the players' attention on one particular equilibrium, in a way that is commonly recognized, tends to make this the equilibrium that the players will expect and thus actually implement."[56] While there is no formal solution to this problem in the literature on game theory, states may coordinate through diplomacy, through other communication, or through their actions advancing particular customary rules. The selection among multiple equilibria may also be understood as a separate coordination game. Here, CIL (as reflected, for example, in the Articles on State Responsibility), the works of publicists, and institutions such as the International Law Commission may also play a role.

Further Parameters and Assumptions

This section develops the more specific parameters and assumptions of the model. It introduces the concepts behind these parameters, explains their salience, and justifies the assumptions made in the model. Recall that the basic model is a repeated prisoner's dilemma, in which repetition of the game in the future, with future payoffs from cooperation, increases the incentives to comply. Under these circumstances, compliance depends on the frequency of future interaction, the patience of states to receive these future payoffs, and the ability of states to identify defection by others.

Payoffs, Efficiency, and Symmetry

By postulating the payoff structure of the prisoner's dilemma, we implicitly assume that failure to reach a cooperative equilibrium—failure to reach an implicit agreement—is inefficient. That is, the payoffs from cooperation, such as transactions in jurisdiction, are greater than the payoffs from mutual defection. Of course, there are many circumstances in which no implicit agreement is needed and in which reaching one would therefore be inefficient. Our present goal, however, is to examine strategic barriers to implicit agreement; reducing these barriers would generally increase efficiency, just as reducing the general barriers to contract between private parties would generally increase efficiency without requiring that parties contract in every circumstance. This perspective is consistent with the first theorem of welfare economics,[57] the Coase theorem,[58] and the "efficiency principle": "If people are able to bargain together effectively and can effectively implement and enforce their decisions, then the outcomes of economic activity will tend to be efficient (at least for the parties to the bargain)."[59] If the barriers to bargaining are eliminated, and parties reach no bargain, we may assume that there was no Pareto-improving bargain available.[60]

As stated above, I assume payoffs along the lines of the classic prisoner's dilemma. Even within this category, however, there is variation. Some circumstances will be more like a commons problem or a cartel, in which the greater the number of players that comply, the greater the incentives to defect. Others will be the opposite, based on network effects, public goods, or economies of scale: the more players that comply, the greater the incentives to comply.[61] In still other cases, the payoffs from defection may not be substantially greater than the payoffs from compliance.

Different players may be affected differently by defection or compliance. In the CIL field, there are notable cases of asymmetry. For example, a state with an extensive diplomatic service will have more at stake in connection with a rule of diplomatic immunity. A landlocked state may have a different perspective on the territorial sea than a state with extensive coastlines. Asymmetry affects each state's incentives to comply.[62]

Identity and Number of Players

Prior work has been skeptical that cooperative multilateral outcomes can be achieved in contexts that do not allow for formally binding agreements. However, as suggested above, the industrial organization literature recognizes important possibilities for cooperative outcomes in multilateral settings—even with a large number of players—and these results would appear to apply to the CIL game.

The number of players in any particular instance of the CIL game will vary. The maximum number of players is the total number of states in the world, although even this assumption may be an oversimplification.

Even limiting our universe to states, there would seem to be—with approximately 200 states in the world—a significant problem in obtaining information about positions and practices, as well as in coordinating actions. However, while states may possess formal sovereign equality, they are not substantively equal, and their participation in the CIL formation process is not homogeneous.[63] It may therefore be necessary to observe the behavior of only the more important states.

Oscar Schachter wrote that

> as a historical fact, the great body of customary international law was made by remarkably few States. Only the States with navies—perhaps 3 or 4— made most of the law of the sea. Military power, exercised on land and sea, shaped the customary law of war and, to a large degree, the customary rules on territorial rights and principles of State responsibility.[64]

Critical theorists and postcolonial theorists of international law emphasize the metropolitan origins of much of existing CIL. While historical circumstances have changed, of course, Schachter's remark is suggestive of a
game in which the number of players varies, depending on the degree to
which their interests are implicated and also on their ability to affect outcomes. In this game, players are heterogeneous across a number of parameters, including interests, power, and, as will be seen below, degree of
patience. In this sense, we may think of powerful states engaging in the
CIL formation-and-maintenance game as exerting power through the articulation, formation, and maintenance of CIL rules. Schachter wrote of
general CIL, but it is also possible to have regional or other plurilateral
CIL.[65]

Some of the leading authors developing rationalist analyses of customary international law are skeptical that multilateral customary processes
can result in stable, efficient strategic equilibria under circumstances other
than pure self-interest or coercion. For example, Goldsmith and Posner
see little possibility for efficient resolution of prisoner's dilemma games in
multilateral settings.[66] While they see possibilities for efficient equilibria in
certain bilateral settings, they assume that "the bilateral prisoner's dilemma
cannot in any event be generalized to the situation of multilateral cooperation, which is such an important part of the traditional account."[67] In this
connection, they follow an established tradition, initiated by Mancur Olson
in 1965: "Unless the number of individuals in a group is quite small, or unless there is coercion or some other special device to make individuals act
in their common interest, rational, self-interested individuals will not act
to achieve their common or group interests."[68]

Olson based his perspective on the assumptions that the benefit of cooperation declines with the number of players, that the costs of monitoring
increase with the number of players, and that the costs of organizing retaliation increase with the number of players.[69] It is obvious, however, that
these assumptions are general conjectures about the world[70] and are not
necessarily true in any particular circumstances. Moreover, these assumptions are only a subset of the parameters worth considering. Finally, technological and social change has made it easier in some circumstances to
monitor and to organize retaliation.[71] My model provides a broader context in which to consider these, and other, parameters.

Kenneth Oye identifies three slightly different ways in which increasing
the number of players reduces the likelihood of cooperation: (i) increased

transaction costs; (ii) decreased credibility of retaliation by third parties, suggesting that players would not retaliate against a defector; and (iii) increased heterogeneity of relative patience.[72] That transaction costs would increase (compared to transaction benefits) is merely a conjecture and, in any event, could readily be counterbalanced by the possibility of economies of scale and scope. As discussed above, the credibility issue may vary with the strategy assumed. Furthermore, as discussed below, it is entirely possible that merely bilateral retaliation could support an efficient equilibrium. With respect to heterogeneous degrees of patience, as discussed in more detail below, it is true that the ability to achieve cooperation would depend on the degree of patience of the least patient state. One implication of this constraint is that patient states may find it useful to exclude impatient states from certain cooperative arrangements, or that cooperative arrangements might survive the self-exclusion of impatient states. Patient states may also be interested in increasing the patience of impatient states.

Information and Bilateral versus Multilateral Retaliation

The relative scale of information costs in the international system is somewhat different from that in a municipal setting. The cost of producing and distributing information regarding state behavior may be a much smaller fraction of the utility of cooperation in the international setting than in municipal, interfirm contexts. Furthermore, there are significant asymmetries among states in terms of the relative cost and value of producing information. Epistemic communities among government officials may play an important role in information transmission.

There are significant differences between bilateral and multilateral games, and between a multilateral game with bilateral retaliation and one with multilateral retaliation. Under bilateral retaliation, information problems are significantly reduced, albeit not eliminated.

An important aspect of the structure of the CIL game pertains to the ability to retaliate in a discriminatory manner. States may have trouble discriminating in the application of sanctions for several reasons. First, they may not be able to obtain information regarding the author of the violation. Such uncertainty might occur, for example, with respect to pollution at sea or a terrorist attack. Second, it may be costly for states to respond in a discriminating way. For example, if the sanction involves trade barriers, the sanctioning state must instruct its customs officers to discriminate among goods by origin. Third, and most important, the relevant good being produced by cooperation may be nonexcludable, as in providing public goods or protecting the international commons. To the extent that states are unable to discriminate, their retaliation, if any, must be multilateral instead of bilateral, which obviously limits the strategies that they are able to play and the relationships into which they may enter. Thus, given that the strategies available to a state are "cooperate" or "defect," there are at least two possibilities that we need to consider in connection with a multilateral game:

Bilateral retaliation: Defection by state *A* against state *B* leads to punishment of *A* only by *B*: bilateral defection leads to bilateral punishment; or

Multilateral retaliation: Defection by state *A* against state *B* leads to punishment of *A* by all states: bilateral defection leads to multilateral punishment.

I focus my analysis on bilateral retaliation for three reasons. First, it makes the analysis simpler without changing any of the qualitative conclusions. Second, multilateral retaliation simply increases the incentives to comply relative to bilateral retaliation. Since bilateral retaliation involves milder punishment of defection than multilateral retaliation, the conditions that support cooperation under bilateral retaliation will certainly support cooperation under multilateral retaliation. In other words, where multilateral retaliation is possible, the conditions that I identify below are sufficient, but not necessary, to support a multilateral rule: any degree of patience that supports a multilateral CIL rule with bilateral retaliation will also support such a rule with multilateral retaliation. Third, there is some force to the argument that bilateral retaliation is a more plausible scenario than multilateral retaliation in most of the situations in which the formulation of CIL is likely to be considered. Articles 42, 48, and 54 of the Articles on State Responsibility generally exclude retaliation by or against third states for truly bilateral injury. These rules seem to limit the formal possibility for multilateral retaliation against bilateral defection, at least *within* a particular CIL rule. But where a CIL rule is not formed, or falls into desuetude, we might understand that there would be implicit multilateral retaliation in the form of noncompliance with the now-defunct rule, as well as retaliation against noninjuring states.

In any event, in the model developed here, I assume that retaliation is applied bilaterally—that if state *A* defects vis-à-vis state *B*, only state *B* will respond, and only against state *A*. If multiple states responded against state *A*, it would simply make cooperation more likely by increasing the punishment for defection.

Thus, assuming bilateral retaliation, we can represent a multilateral prisoner's dilemma game as a set of bilateral games—which is not, as will be seen below, the same as assuming a bilateral game. Rather, it is a multilateral game with bilateral retaliation.

Although as set forth above I assume bilateral retaliation in connection with the basic formal analysis, it is worth discussing the possibility and implications of multilateral retaliation. Under multilateral retaliation, we would be concerned about the ability of players to find out about other players' characteristics or their compliance or defection history. On the one hand, it may be costly for an individual player to find out for itself the history of many other players. On the other hand, the potential responses of many other players may add to the disincentives for defection. There are economies of scale and scope in this type of system, which may counterbalance increased information costs that exist in an n-player setting.[73]

Along these lines, Michihiro Kandori explains that informal enforcement mechanisms fall into two categories: those that use personal enforcement, and those that use community enforcement. These two categories correspond to what I have been referring to as bilateral retaliation and multilateral retaliation. Kandori examines circumstances in which social norms work to support efficient outcomes in infrequent transactions—that is, absent repetition that can allow personal enforcement, but under circumstances where community enforcement may occur.[74] Thus, there may be circumstances in which multilateral retaliation could substitute for repetition. Alternatively, as noted above, multilateral retaliation could result in cooperation in circumstances in which bilateral retaliation would be insufficient. Where members of a community can observe each other's behavior, community enforcement works in much the same way as personal enforcement.[75] Kandori assumes that this is precisely what occurs in small communities. In this context, we might suggest that the global community can itself be understood as a small community. CIL rules often address matters that are public knowledge and are reported in the press. Imagine a municipal community where each individual's behavior is subject to journalistic and intelligence investigation.

Kandori assumes that private information is not shared among community members. When observability is not perfect, obtaining private information regarding compliance with a norm, as well as the distribution of the private information, will be more complicated, and costly. Cooperation may be difficult to sustain because the community may not have defined adequately the social norm, making it difficult to share information or identify defectors. Kandori shows, in theoretical terms, that even where an individual does not have any direct information of other individuals' behavior vis-à-vis other community members, cooperative behavior can sometimes be sustained. In the CIL game, with seemingly greater ability (relative to private society) to observe the treatment of third parties, we would expect a greater basis for cooperation.

Of course, multilateral sanctions are dependent on information regarding defection and on a judgment that the subject has violated the relevant norm. Information may be a trivial problem in certain areas of CIL, but a difficult problem in others. Various institutional responses are possible to provide greater certainty in judging violations. Judgments can depend on individual state determinations, on community views, or on consensus, any of which may follow the lead of a "reputation entrepreneur" or other arbiter or public leader. Such judgments can also be achieved, however, through independent institutions such as courts.

As Milgrom, North, and Weingast argue with respect to the nonstate institutions that enforced compliance among early medieval merchants, "It is the costliness of generating and communicating information—rather than the infrequency of trade in any particular bilateral relationship—that, we argue, is the problem that the system of private enforcement was designed to overcome."[76] In developing this view, the authors argue that third-party dispute settlement can assist in developing cooperation. They argue, in particular, that third-party dispute settlement can solve the following information problem: if two parties have a dispute in which one accuses the other of defection, how can other members of the community determine whether the accusation is true?[77] However, third-party dispute settlement—along the lines of their "law merchant," a private purveyor of information and evaluation—may be more valuable in resolving information problems in the municipal context among traders than in the international context among states. First, there may be fewer states than there are potential traders in the municipal, trading setting. Second, as noted earlier, the cost of information about state compliance may be a smaller proportion of the value of CIL "transactions." Milgrom, North, and Weingast conclude that within the municipal context, given the lack of empirical evidence about the costs of running different kinds of institutions, it is not possible to develop a formal model to show that their proposal for third-party dispute settlement (with the equivalent of a law merchant) minimizes information costs. They opine, however, that such a system seems to incur only the kind of costs that are inevitable, and that it seems well designed to minimize those costs.[78]

Under Milgrom, North, and Weingast's proposal, the players accept the third-party, informational role of the law merchant in order to develop an efficient equilibrium. We might consider the extent to which formal international institutions such as the ICJ, the WTO's dispute settlement process, or its Trade Policy Review Mechanism fill a similar role in connection with states, and whether nongovernmental organizations (NGOs), such as Amnesty International or the World Wildlife Fund, or informal international institutions, such as the Basle Committee (bank regulation) or the Wassenaar Arrangement (export controls on dual-use commodities), can do so in particular niches. Of course, entities such as the WTO, Basle Committee, and Wassenaar Arrangement do not generally deal with CIL; the point is that they may serve an information function that promotes compliance with the treaties or with the informal rules that concern them.

In the model developed here we assume perfect information—which seems reasonable given that we are also assuming only bilateral retaliation. In order for multilateral retaliation to operate, however, information problems must be overcome.

Patience and Discount Factors, Horizon, and the Shadow of the Future

When international lawyers discuss incentives for compliance, they often refer to the possibility of role reversal in the future: of reciprocity and retaliation. They hypothesize a degree of stochastic symmetry. How powerful is the shadow of the future? In repeated prisoner's dilemmas, theorists have shown that the degree to which players value future payoffs will have an effect on players' incentives to comply with a norm. All things being equal, the extent to which a player values future payoffs will determine the extent to which these future payoffs affect the player's behavior.

The model developed here represents the extent of valuation of future payoffs as a discount factor,[79] a factor used to reflect the present value to a particular player of future payoffs. The discount factor reflects the player's preference for payoffs now versus payoffs in the future. It is a central variable that interacts with other variables such as the per-period magnitude of future payoffs, the relative payoffs from defection versus cooperation, the horizon or number of periods predicted, frequency of repetition, the number of other players (under multilateral retaliation), and the degree of linkage to other relationships.

While it might be argued that the CIL game will continue forever, it is useful to assume—in order to emphasize the role of patience in the model—that the game will be finite but that at any given time, it is unknown when it will end. Thus, it makes sense to assume that at any given moment, there will be a long, but finite, horizon.

Public choice considerations would counsel that horizons vary. After all, if the real interaction is not between states, but between governments, we must recognize that governments have varying effective horizons. Governments come and go. The relationship between state and government horizons is to some extent determined by the degree of accountability of the government—the degree to which it represents the interests of its constituents. A democracy may have a shorter horizon than a dictatorship. Some states may have more frequent or more imminent elections at particular moments. Independent of questions concerning the frequency or imminence of elections, we would want to model the relative stability of the ruling party or coalition. Much depends on the prospects for reelection or, in a dictatorship, on its stability or the stability of its policies, including their susceptibility to variation due to corruption. Furthermore, it may be useful to examine whether the real actor is neither the state nor the government, but a more entrenched bureaucracy. Transnational networks, composed of networks of entrenched bureaucrats, may have greater durability than international networks, composed of transient governments. The model presented here combines this question of an individual state's or government's time horizon with "patience."

It is generally understood that a mutually beneficial outcome can exist as a credible equilibrium of the prisoner's dilemma where the game is repeated, subject to conditions relating to the players' discount rates and the time horizon.[80] With repeated play, current actions can be conditioned on past actions, introducing the possibility of rewarding cooperation and punishing defection. Repetition by itself is not sufficient, however, to secure continued cooperation. If the game is repeated a known, finite number of times, both players will have an incentive to defect in the final period, and the game unravels from there to immediate defection.[81] By contrast, if the game is repeated indefinitely, then "all players defecting every period" will remain a credible equilibrium, but there may be additional credible equilibria, depending on the parties' discount factors.[82]

As Fudenberg and Tirole have noted, "if the players are sufficiently patient, then any feasible, individually rational payoffs can be enforced by an equilibrium. Thus, in the limit of extreme patience, repeated play allows virtually any payoff to be an equilibrium outcome."[83] Under circumstances of high discount factors, when players are "patient," the short-term gain from defection in one play is outweighed by the aggregation of even small losses in all future periods. Fudenberg and Maskin show that frequent transactions with the same partner—regardless of the number of players, the number of strategies available, or the size of the payoffs—make it possible to reach an equilibrium with efficient trading.[84]

Multisector Contact

One of the assumptions underlying the prisoner's dilemma is that the game is self-contained. Casual observation of international society suggests that there are many linkages,[85] however, with the result that few issues can be isolated.[86] Players can bind one another in a variety of ways, including by linking the present game to other games in a "supergame." In fact, depending on how we define the game, we can simply term repeated interaction in multiple contexts "repetition," or term it linkage of separate games, depending more on definitional convention than on substance.

Firms—and states—operate in multiple markets and encounter other firms, or states, in multiple contexts: as competitor here, as supplier there, as co-conspirator elsewhere. Industrial organization economists studying the effect of multimarket contact have found that this cross-sectoral activity may support cooperation.[87] For example, Giancarlo Spagnolo has noted that in the case of multimarket contact, collusion—in our context, cooperation—"can be viable in a set of markets even when in the absence of multimarket contact it could not be supported in *any* of these markets."[88] He argues, moreover, that "multimarket contact allows firms to use the threat of a *simultaneous* punishment in more markets" and that this threat "is stronger than the sum of the independent punishments because a firm being punished in one market has a higher marginal valuation of profits, therefore it values more the losses from punishments in other markets."[89]

One important difference between the commercial context and the international relations context is that state relations in the international context almost always cross a number of sectors.[90] States relate to one another in a variety of contexts, with varying roles in each context. Thus, in one context, a particular state may be concerned about the scope of its prescriptive jurisdiction, whereas in another context it may be concerned about the scope of its responsibilities to protect foreign diplomats. As a result, while there may be a "prescriptive jurisdiction game" that is in some dimensions separate from the "diplomatic immunity game," these games may be linked. In fact, states regularly link issues in international relations,[91] with the result that it is not possible to establish precise boundaries for any particular game.

Defection in one area may have consequences in another, with the possibility of cross-sectoral punishment. Thus, it is not enough to examine whether states have sufficient incentives for compliance within a particular sector or arrangement; one must also analyze the effect of activity in other sectors. Hitoshi Matsushima argues that multimarket contact can take the place of perfect information as a basis for a stable equilibrium of implicit cooperation. He shows that with multimarket contact, cooperation can take place even under circumstances of relatively low discount factors.[92] This conclusion suggests that international cooperation in different sectors may be mutually supportive, and that there may be a kind of network effect that makes each additional instance of cooperation more attractive than it would be absent existing instances.[93] This game-theoretic perspective provides support for the early neofunctionalist hypotheses regarding international economic integration.

George Downs and Michael Jones have argued that a particular state may have multiple reputations, within multiple contexts.[94] Without further empirical study, however, it is not possible to know how much segmentation exists in states' reputations. Such research would examine the extent to which different ministries within states, and different "epistemic communities" on a transnational basis, communicate across sectors. Nevertheless, it seems clear in both theory and practice that segmentation is not necessarily complete, so that defection in one context may potentially have consequences within another context. Unfortunately, when the "real" decision maker is a subnational actor,[95] such as a bureaucracy with a defined sectoral mandate, the effectiveness of intragovernmental communication between sectors may be significantly compromised. For this reason, it may be useful to assign broad international relations authority to centralized ministries of foreign affairs. Finally, it may be that segmentation of reputation is efficient from the standpoint of domestic accountability in that it allows different parts of a national government to take responsibility for their own relations and to develop the kind of reputation that maximizes returns within the relevant segment.

It should be noted that Downs and Jones's argument is explicitly about treaties, not custom. In a treaty setting, despite the broad scope of remedies available under the Articles on State Responsibility, states might be understood as implicitly accepting only intratreaty remedies for breach. In the custom context, however, there is no explicit or implicit limitation on responsive or remedial action. Therefore, it may well be that in this more delicate and nuanced context—where there is no implicit consent to limitation—states would consider themselves less constrained when confronted with a breach. In addition, much responsive action in this informal setting is likely to take the form of abstention from future transactions, rather than some form of punishment within the context of the present transaction.

In their study of the behavior of medieval merchants, Milgrom, North, and Weingast explain that "if the relationship itself is a valuable asset that a party could lose by dishonest behavior, then the relationship serves as a *bond*."[96] Thus, the shadow of the future effect is intensified by multimarket contact and perfect information. The broader this effect, the greater the likelihood that individual states will respect particular rules.

Plausible Examples of the CIL Game

Before developing the model and its implications, it is worthwhile for us to stop and suggest how certain actual CIL rules might fit into this framework.

As indicated earlier, the purpose of this chapter is merely to elaborate a model that demonstrates the plausibility of efficient equilibria in a multilateral prisoner's dilemma model of CIL. I did not set out to prove that such efficient equilibria exist in nature, or to prove any of the hypotheses that flow from the model. It is nevertheless useful, by way of illustration rather than proof, to set out some examples of circumstances that might plausibly be characterized as international multilateral prisoner's dilemmas that seem to have reached cooperative equilibria, as opposed to reflecting the outcome of intrinsic self-interest, narrow coercion, bilateral coordination, or a bilateral prisoner's dilemma. My characterization of these examples, like those advanced by others, is dependent upon subjective judgments as to the payoff structure that these circumstances may entail. Without data regarding payoffs, it is not possible to do better.

As suggested in Chapters 1 and 2, much of international law relates to either the allocation of authority or, conversely, the allocation of responsibility for harm. These types of rules may be analogized to rules of property and tort. So, for example, iconic CIL rules—for example, those relating to diplomatic immunity, sovereign immunity, territorial sovereignty, and the territorial sea—may be understood in terms of allocation of authority, which may be assimilated to property. Rules such as responsibility for harm to aliens, or responsibility for environmental harms to other states, may be assimilated to tort. Both types of rules have to do with the allocation and transfer of entitlements.

The strategic context for formation of property or tort rules depends on a number of parameters, including the costs and benefits of the resource, the potential harm, the degree of natural excludability and the cost of artificial exclusion, the degree of rivalry of consumption, the degree of bilateral monopoly, and the transaction costs of negotiation. I outline below four examples that seem to follow the multilateral prisoner's dilemma structure. Of course, any suggestion that a particular game fits a particular context is simply a conjecture, contingent on actual knowledge of the payoffs and other factors.

Restrictive Theory of Sovereign Immunity

Under the traditional, "absolute" theory of sovereign immunity, which was applied by the United States until the 1952 "Tate Letter," states enjoyed jurisdictional immunity from foreign courts whether engaging in "sovereign" acts or "commercial" acts. With the rise of state trading and international commerce, however, more and more private persons discovered that they had no legal recourse in dealing with foreign states.

This state of affairs may be characterized as a multilateral prisoner's dilemma. It is plausible that each state individually would be better off, in terms of its potential responsibility to private persons, maintaining the absolute theory of sovereign immunity. If all states take this position, however, then commercial enterprises may suffer more harm, trade may be diminished, and global welfare may be reduced. Due to differences in utilization of state trading, there may be a degree of asymmetry; the Soviet Union and its satellites favored absolute immunity during the latter half of the twentieth century.

During this same period, the United Kingdom, the United States, and most trading states moved to adopt the "restrictive" theory of sovereign immunity, which holds that states lack immunity for acts of a commercial nature. When states adopted the restrictive theory, they accepted the possibility of lawsuits against them. If a state were to decline to adopt the restrictive theory (or were to renege on its adoption of the restrictive theory) and therefore claimed absolute immunity, it would be required, in turn, to grant absolute immunity to foreign states, reverting to the presumably less efficient status quo (the grim trigger strategy). States therefore had sufficient incentives to "cooperate" in enhancing global welfare by adhering to, and continuing to adhere to, the restrictive theory. They contributed their own acceptance of liability.

When the first state shifted from the absolute to the restrictive theory, it was possible that other states could have claimed a violation of the traditional rule of CIL: absolute immunity. Instead, they gradually accepted the restrictive theory. The model presented here suggests that they may have done so in light of the possible future gains from acceptance of the restrictive theory. With the rise of trade, and especially of state trade, the issue of sovereign immunity has arisen with increased frequency, which, in my model, suggests greater possibility for compliance.

Sovereign immunity is not easy to characterize as a series of bilateral games, but is better characterized as a multilateral game, with the possibility of bilateral retaliation while adhering to the restrictive theory, or multilateral retaliation if the restrictive theory is rejected completely. It is a multilateral game because the uniform acceptance of the restrictive theory has positive effects in terms of both public goods (by increasing world trade) and network externalities (by reducing the need to check which states have adopted the restrictive theory, thereby decreasing the costs of contracting).

Cross-Border Environmental Harm

The rule of *sic utere tuo*, adopted in the *Trail Smelter Arbitration*,[97] is derived from, and remains akin to, the early common law of nuisance.[98] In allocating responsibility to the source state with respect to transboundary pollution, it requires the internalization of externalities. We may understand this rule, like the coordinate domestic law of nuisance, as a response to a collective action problem. Each individual state has incentives to externalize pollution if it fails to take into account harm to downwind or downstream states. The Coase theorem teaches that every externality need not be internalized. There will be transaction cost contexts, however, in which internalization is useful.

The case of transboundary pollution may be understood using the prisoner's dilemma, assuming that global welfare may be increased if each state internalizes externalities in making decisions about pollution. Each state individually has incentives to violate this rule. The CIL rule of *sic utere tuo* arose in order to establish a rule of internalization. It is enforced by the threat of grim trigger, in the form of a "pollute thy neighbor" rule, or by the implicit threat of smaller retaliation along the lines of penance. The *sic utere tuo* rule applies when pollution crosses a single border, as well as when it crosses multiple borders. Furthermore, the transboundary pollution problem, like the nuisance problem, is one where there may be economies of scale in uniformity of arrangements. Therefore, this game is not simply a bilateral one.

The emergence of the *sic utere tuo* rule in international law could plausibly follow a similar path to the emergence of the coordinate rule, or other property rights, in domestic law.[99]

To the extent that a specific type of environmental protection, such as preservation of the ozone layer, is inexhaustible (meaning that one person's enjoyment does not diminish other persons' enjoyment), it may be that the benefits of participation rise with the number of states that participate. Not all environmental goods will have the same payoff structure, so the *sic utere tuo* rule would require extensive analysis. That is, there may be some environmental goods that have characteristics of a commons problem, in which it may be more difficult to support cooperation among larger numbers of players.

Territorial Sovereignty and Prohibition on Acquisition of Territory by Force

The general and specific rules associated with territorial sovereignty may also be modeled, like property rights, as a multilateral prisoner's dilemma.

In particular, during the last century, the CIL rule precluding formal acquisition of territory by force seems to have met with stronger compliance.[100] We may understand this principle as a disincentive for the use of force. If states are restrained by a principle of nonacquisition, they will have weaker incentives to use force. How can we understand the emergence of this principle?

Each state individually has incentives to retain the option to acquire territory through the use of force. However, each state also wishes—defensively—to remove the flexibility of other states to acquire its territory, and perhaps that of others, through the use of force. Although each state has incentives to defect, it refrains from doing so because of fear of retaliation in other areas, or in the narrower area of acquisition of territory. Again, we can see that either grim trigger or penance may serve to maintain the equilibrium of not engaging in acquisition by force.

This problem does not seem to have the characteristics of a commons or a cartel. That is, it does not appear that the incentives to violate would increase with the number of states that comply. If many states had designs on the same territory, as in colonial times, we might see that happening—which is perhaps why a rule against acquisition by force only arose more recently. This rule may have security benefits that rise with the number of states that adhere. That is, the greater the number of states that adhere, the lower the incentives preemptively to attack and therefore the lower each state's defense budget must be. Thus, it is plausible that this rule would result in increasing incentives to comply as the number of adherents increases.

Territorial Jurisdiction

CIL includes the norm of territorial jurisdiction. Each state generally has jurisdiction over conduct within its territory. There is some dispute regarding the scope for "extraterritorial" jurisdiction, specifically with regard to conduct abroad that has adverse effects within the territory of the state seeking to assert jurisdiction. According to Sections 402 and 403 of the American Law Institute's *Restatement (Third) of Foreign Relations Law*, and according to a number of states and scholars, there are substantial limits on a state's right to assert extraterritorial jurisdiction. According to the *Restatement*, states may not exercise jurisdiction when it would be "unreasonable" to do so in light of the various connections and interests involved.

For our purposes, the only important fact is that there is some arguable limit. We can understand this limit within the prisoner's dilemma model. It is noteworthy that, while the United States has on occasion asserted the right to apply its law "extraterritorially," it has often done so at significant diplomatic cost and has accepted some limits on its assertion.

We may assume that each state would prefer to exercise jurisdiction without limit, in order to address circumstances that may impose negative externalities on its citizens. However, each state is restrained by the fear of reciprocation or retaliation, possibly resulting in a stable and efficient equilibrium.

The CIL Game

The discussion in the second and third sections of this chapter indicates that there are many possible assumptions that we might make in developing a CIL game. As noted above, I have chosen to focus on one such game—the repeated prisoner's dilemma—for three principal reasons. First, as discussed above, it is appropriate to assume a setting in which all of the relevant states prefer formation of, and compliance with, a CIL rule to the other possible outcomes. Second, however, I am also assuming, consistent with many real-world situations, that each state can gain from deviating from the cooperative outcome. Third, I am assuming a noncooperative game context in which there are no centralized means to enforce any agreement not to deviate. Interestingly, once the CIL rule of *pacta sunt servanda* comes into being, it may be appropriate to assume a cooperative game. However, in order to examine the structure of CIL, it is more appropriate to assume a noncooperative game.

The games developed below allow us to identify plausible circumstances under which the repeated prisoner's dilemma can result in efficient equilibria both bilaterally and multilaterally. Moreover, they show what types of contexts, including malleable institutional features, may affect the ability of states to reach such equilibria.

Under the payoff assumptions of the prisoner's dilemma, each state prefers unilateral defection to bilateral cooperation, and bilateral cooperation to bilateral defection. The multilateral context of this game is captured by the assumption that some or all of the payoffs in each of the component bilateral games are functions of the number of states in the multilateral context, and of the number of states cooperating. Given the assumptions of the prisoner's dilemma, we have the standard result that all states defect. In other words, no CIL rule will be formed.

Assume, instead, that the bilateral game is repeated indefinitely. To make this assumption more concrete, assume that in any given period, each state believes that, with some probability less than certainty, this game will be played again. Further, suppose that each state has a particular level of patience represented by a discount factor. Now consider whether cooperation can be sustained as an equilibrium when the game is repeated indefinitely. In order to achieve that result, cooperation must be a "subgame-perfect equilibrium," meaning in this case that cooperation induces a set of strategies such that each state's strategy is an optimal response to the other states' strategies at every repetition of play. One such strategy profile that has the potential to support such an equilibrium is the grim trigger strategy:

(i) Cooperate if both states have cooperated in all prior periods.
(ii) Defect in this period and all subsequent ones if either state has defected in any prior period.

As discussed above, an alternative strategy profile, addressing the problem of credibility (collective rationality), is "penance":

(i) Cooperate if both states have cooperated in all prior periods.
(ii) If one state defects in one period, the other state defects in all subsequent periods until the initially defecting state cooperates.
(iii) After the initially defecting state cooperates for one period while the other state defects, the latter state returns to cooperation.

Under either of these strategies, if both states are sufficiently patient—that is, if they sufficiently value future payoffs—both states will cooperate in all periods. The question of the sufficiency of their patience is termed the "patience condition." Stated differently, if both states' actual discount factors exceed a calculated "critical discount factor," cooperation will ensue.[101] The critical discount factor represents the extent to which states value future payoffs.

The patience condition can be interpreted in other ways that are directly relevant to our analysis. First, CIL is more likely to emerge and be sustainable when the returns to cooperation—that is, the payoffs from cooperating—are high relative to those to defection and when the returns to unilateral defection are low. Second, CIL is more likely to be formed between relatively patient states: those with relatively high discount factors. Third, CIL is more likely where the probability of continued interaction between the participating states is high.

The important question to which we now turn is the one raised by Goldsmith and Posner. Does increasing the number of participants make it tougher to sustain cooperation? For that to occur, it is necessary that the critical discount factor becomes higher—more difficult to meet—as the number of states involved increases.

The simplest, but probably least likely, case is that in which none of the payoffs are affected by the number of states involved. In that situation, the multilateral CIL rule is no more than the aggregation of a series of independent, bilateral CIL rules and consequently is no more difficult to sustain than the individual bilateral rules. Goldsmith and Posner accept that at least some bilateral prisoner's dilemmas could be resolved by CIL.

It is more likely, however, that the multilateral context has some relevance in that the number of states that are effectively party to the multilateral CIL rule will affect some of the payoffs.[102] This impact could derive from the public goods or network aspect of the establishment of the CIL rule itself (a point to which we turn below) or, more generally, from the possibility that the greater the number of states that are party to a CIL rule, the greater will be the aggregate benefits that flow from that rule.

The situation that is most often considered, however, has the following characteristics. First, the payoff for each state from cooperation decreases as the number of states party to the CIL rule increases. Second, the payoff for a state from defection is greater when there are more states that continue to abide by the CIL rule. Third, nonformulation of a CIL rule leaves states in an autarkic situation, so that the payoff from nonformulation or total breakdown of a proposed CIL rule is the same— independent of the number of states. In such circumstances, it follows that the critical discount factor is increasing with the number of states involved. The implication is that multilateral CIL is, indeed, harder to sustain than bilateral CIL.

It would be wrong to infer, however, that such CIL rules are *impossible*, or even highly unlikely, to be sustained. First, we are more likely to see multilateral CIL among states that have, and are expected to have, interactions over an extended period. Second, multilateral CIL rules are more likely between "patient" states, meaning states that tend to value future payoffs more highly than others. Third, multilateral CIL rules are more likely to hold when the relevant interactions are frequent.

Moreover, there are three additional countervailing forces that can work to sustain multilateral CIL. The first follows from our analysis above. It is not difficult to imagine circumstances in which the gains from unilateral defection decrease with the number of states while the gains from cooperation increase with the number of states. In such circumstances, the conventional argument is actually reversed. Multilateral CIL rules are *easier* to sustain than bilateral rules.

Under what circumstances might this occur? One possibility[103] is that the rule relates to the investment by each participating state in the provision of a public good.[104] As more states participate, the investment in that public good increases, as does the benefit from cooperation for each individual state. By contrast, the gains from defection can be expected to decrease with the number of states. The same is likely to be true for policies with strong network effects—for example, common international technology standards or common international disclosure standards relating to securities offerings.[105] A single state may gain from going it alone, but the potential gains are likely to be less as the state's position becomes more isolated—that is, as the state remains a single standout while an increasing number of other states adopt a common standard. A third possibility is that there are reputation effects that increase as more states comply with a particular rule. A state gains from defecting on a rule, but the act of defection harms the state's reputation, making it less likely that the state will be able to make agreements with other states.

The second countervailing effect arises when states are involved in a series of international rules (including treaty rules) with overlapping groups of partners. In such a case, defection on one rule has potentially harmful effects for *all* of the rules to which a particular state is party. This situation is similar to one in which the potential for multimarket contact serves to maintain collusion between firms.[106]

In any multilateral context in which states enter into both bilateral and multilateral rules, the critical discount factor—that is, the discount factor required to sustain cooperation—decreases with an increase in the number of bilateral rules to which each state is subject. This result leads to a simple, but compelling, proposition: *a state can use "excess" enforcement power in bilateral cooperation to sustain multilateral cooperation.* This is not airy theory: states generally seek to establish and exploit linkages in order to add to the incentives for compliance by other states.

The third possibility is related to the second. Multilateral cooperation is more easily sustained when it involves frequent interactions among the member states.

The second and third possibilities can, of course, interact. States may be subject to multiple rules—with some involving frequent interactions and some involving infrequent interactions. By the same argument as above, *a state can use "excess" enforcement power available in connection with rules involving frequent transactions to sustain rules involving infrequent transactions.*

Thus, there is a significant set of cases in which it will be possible to form multilateral customary rules of international law. The likelihood of formation in any particular circumstance will depend on a number of factors, including (i) the relative value of cooperation versus defection; (ii) the number of states effectively involved; (iii) the extent to which increasing the number of states involved increases the value of cooperation or the detriments of defection, including whether the particular issue has characteristics of a commons problem, a public good, or a network; (iv) the information available to the states involved regarding compliance and defection; (v) the relative patience of states to realize benefits of long-term cooperation compared to short-term defection; (vi) the expected duration of interaction; (vii) the frequency of interaction; and (viii) the existence of other bilateral or multilateral relationships between the states involved.

Implications

The model presented above suggests that CIL may affect behavior and that its ability to do so will vary with the circumstances. Flat assertions that multilateral CIL cannot produce stable equilibria are false in theory, and can only be proven true in particular circumstances. This model has implications for international legal theory, for CIL doctrine, for policy, and for research.

International Legal Theory: CIL May Affect Behavior

The discussion in this chapter's second and third sections, coupled with the model described in the fifth section, suggests that there is a significant set of cases in which CIL will affect behavior. Since we cannot here assess the actual value of cooperation to states, or their discount rates, or many of the other factors included in the model, it is impossible to say with certainty how often, or by how much, CIL affects behavior. But it is equally impossible to say that it does not affect behavior, that it seldom does so, or even that it has only marginal effects. Therefore, CIL is plausible.

CIL seems no less plausible than social norms in the domestic context. In fact, there are reasons to believe that it may be more plausible—based on economies of scale and scope in the production and distribution of information, and on multisector contact. There are also countervailing factors, however, including the possibility that governments acting in international society may have less sense of permanence and stability than individuals in intrastate contexts or communities—which may make the latter more patient and consequently more likely to adopt and maintain social norms. Interestingly, this analysis suggests that states generally have an interest in the development of domestic political institutions that will instill "patience" in other states. Patience may be associated with accountability, which constrains governments to be responsive to the long-term interests of constituents.

Normative Implications: Institutional Modifications

The prior analysis has a number of potential implications for policy. As Mark Chinen has noted:

> Perhaps game theory's greatest potential for contributing to international law is to provide a rigorous means of describing and articulating important aspects of state interaction and cooperation. The hope is that fully developed game theoretic models will help states design law that creates or enhances the conditions for cooperation, if such cooperation is desirable.[107]

THE ROLE OF REGIONAL OR PLURILATERAL CUSTOM   As demonstrated above, the number of states involved in forming a particular customary rule may have a significant effect on the ability to form and maintain a rule. As we have suggested, this effect will differ in direction, depending on the context. Therefore, states may find that they can develop regional or other plurilateral rules of CIL in circumstances where multilateral rules are more difficult to establish. Regional or other plurilateral intensification of relationships, such as in the European Union or the Organisation for

Economic Co-operation and Development, may establish the conditions for greater use of custom.

NETWORK EFFECTS IN INSTITUTIONALISM   International cooperation in different sectors may be mutually supportive, and there may be a kind of network effect that makes each additional instance of cooperation more attractive than it would be absent existing instances. This game-theoretic perspective provides support for the early neofunctionalist hypotheses regarding international economic integration and suggests the potential rationality of cooperation "for its own sake" or in order to facilitate further cooperation. It also provides theoretical support for strategies of "constructive engagement" outside the CIL context. Network effects may be enhanced in regional or other plurilateral contexts by concentrating and intensifying relationships.

THE INFORMATION ROLE OF NGOS AND INTERNATIONAL COURTS   By disseminating information regarding compliance with particular norms, NGOs or international organizations may play a critical role in improving the availability of information, thereby facilitating the development of CIL. In cases of complex rules or facts—and where, under a regime of autointerpretation, states may argue over compliance—courts or other "independent" third parties may resolve this information problem more definitively.

CUSTOM AND TREATY   This chapter applies the literature of law and social norms in a way that suggests how to bridge the gulf between law and social norms—one that is not as readily apparent in the domestic context. It recognizes that law, on the one hand, and social norms, on the other, are alternative or sometimes complementary means of social control or social cooperation. It thus suggests the utility of comparative institutional analysis[108] between law and social norms.

Custom is a mechanism for international "legislation" that requires only a degree of consensus, not affirmative unanimity. Given the difficulty of establishing global treaties without significant holdouts, and given the need to avoid free riders, we might understand the CIL process as an alternative mechanism for global legislation. A rule of consensus acts as a default rule that promotes compliance and that increases the bureaucratic costs of "persistent objectors." We recognize that this type of strategy would raise concerns regarding democratic legitimacy. This type of legislative technique is not more invasive than majority voting, however, and the "persistent objector" rule allows states to opt out of rules that raise sufficient concern.

There is less of a distinction between CIL and treaty than there is between social norms, on the one hand, and municipal law (including the law supporting enforcement of contracts), on the other. Since treaties are, in legal theory, supported only by CIL and by institutions created by treaty, rather than by an exogenous force, they are something less than contractual. In fact, we may understand treaties as an extension of custom or of social norms. They are, taken together, an important extension, with the capacity to specify required performance in greater detail and to establish more detailed agreement on the content of the relevant norm, thereby overcoming significant information problems relevant to compliance. Moreover, to the extent that treaties specify binding dispute settlement, additional information problems may be overcome.

Since treaties have a greater capacity for concreteness than custom, they lend themselves more to specificity—that is, to rules as opposed to broad standards. Treaties also are more amenable to domestic ratification, which is both a burden in terms of efficiency of agreement and a benefit in terms of accountability. As is anticipated in the literature of rules versus standards,[109] custom may serve as a pathfinder for later established, more specific treaty rules. Conversely, treaty structures, including dispute settlement, may serve as an institutional setting to promote custom.

Doctrinal Implications: A Contractual Approach to *Opinio Juris*

This chapter has not yet directly addressed the argument by Goldsmith and Posner that CIL generally does no work—that state behavior is not motivated by CIL, but only by self-interest.[110] The implication of this argument, not made explicit by Goldsmith and Posner, is that CIL does not exist, because CIL doctrine requires practice motivated by *opinio juris*— by CIL. The Goldsmith-Posner argument is subject to several responses.

CIL RULES MAY AFFECT BEHAVIOR   First, the discussion in the second, third, and fifth sections of this chapter shows that CIL may affect behavior. My refutation of the argument that the multilateral prisoner's dilemma is unlikely to be resolved shows that it is plausible that state behavior is affected by CIL.

A CONTRACTUAL APPROACH TO *OPINIO JURIS*   Under the *Restatement* formulation, CIL does not exist without *opinio juris,* or the sense of legal obligation. As D'Amato suggests,[111] however, it seems that this requirement is circular: the first state that complies "from a sense of legal obligation" must do so erroneously. There may be a solution to this paradox.

Analogizing CIL to social norms, it seems appropriate to suggest that instead of a "sense of legal obligation," the *Restatement* formulation might more correctly refer to an "intent to create or accept a rule of law."[112] As suggested by the formulation contained in Article 38(1)(b) of the ICJ Statute, we may, in addition, refer to a "sense of *incipient* legal obligation."[113] CIL may arise in the international system in just the way that social norms arise in the domestic setting, with the same possible beneficial effects in terms of cooperation and coordination. The social norms analogy suggests, with Myres McDougal, Maurice Mendelson, Edward Swaine, and Hugh Thirlway,[114] that we may understand the initial act of "compliance" not necessarily as an error, but as an offer or as an act of leadership. The offer and acceptance must generally take the form of practice.

Consider the development of social norms in the municipal setting. In Shasta County, at the time that a cattle farmer first returned a lost calf to its owner without charge, despite a lack of legal obligation, there existed no relevant social norm. Yet that action—perhaps recognized by its author as providing efficiencies that would eventually benefit him if multilateralized, or perhaps motivated by something else, but interpreted as a proposal to initiate a rule—began a process that resulted in a new "social norm."

If we understand the "sense of legal obligation" in the *Restatement* not as referring to a fully formed legal rule, but as a perception or assertion that a *legal* rule would be beneficial, the circularity problem is resolved. Thus, custom must be understood not as mere action, but as an initial or continuing proposal for collective action over time, with acceptance evidenced by compliance. A state may test a proposed rule of collective action informally—as, in effect, a trial balloon—without the domestic or international costs that otherwise might attend the proposal.[115] Supporting this approach, a recent report of the International Law Association explained that *opinio juris* requires practice "in circumstances which give rise to a legitimate expectation of similar conduct in the future."[116] This understanding also offers a plausible explanation of changing rules of CIL. In fact, there is no real difference between initiation and change: initiation of a rule is a change from a laissez-faire rule.

Thus, there is a rationale for the *opinio juris* requirement in terms of general state intent: mere regularity of action, or mere action based on motives that do not include the formation of a legal rule, cannot form a rule of CIL. Accordingly, Article 38 of the ICJ Statute specifies "international custom, as evidence of a general practice accepted as law."

CIL RULES MAY BE COTERMINOUS WITH SELF-INTEREST   There is a terminological or doctrinal problem with Goldsmith and Posner's argument, making it seem tautological. Goldsmith and Posner argue that "states do not comply with CIL because of a sense of moral or legal obligation; rather, CIL emerges from the states' pursuit of self-interested policies on the international stage."[117] Unless Goldsmith and Posner mean merely to refute the natural law position that states comply with international law because of its normative appeal or legitimacy, or because it is the right thing to do, this argument involves a non sequitur, as legal obligation and self-interest are not mutually exclusive categories. The field of law and economics has long utilized price theory to understand behavior under legal rules, and there is no question that law can affect behavior *through* self-interest. In the CIL setting, the motivating force is the broader, or potentially longer-term, self-interest that flows from making, and achieving compliance with, a rule or even rules generally—from narrow or diffuse reciprocity, respectively.[118] No one would argue that for domestic law to qualify as law, compliance must be motivated by something other than self-interest.

Goldsmith and Posner's main point here must then be understood simply as the application of an *assumption* of the rationalist model (and one that is subject to at least some contention): that agents care only about their own utility and therefore would not follow a rule of CIL for *intrinsic* reasons, for its own sake. The mistake here is that compliance with international law resulting from a sense of legal obligation is, in fact, consistent with *extrinsic* reasons: there may well be utility in upholding a particular rule, or in upholding the rule of law in general. That is, indeed, precisely what this chapter's model demonstrates.

EVIDENTIARY REQUIREMENTS   Third, CIL may have an effect on behavior at the margins. Accordingly, the evidence presented by Goldsmith and Posner is insufficient to support the argument they present. Their case-based evidence merely suggests that, in a limited range of contexts, there are plausible non-CIL reasons for the behavior observed.[119] Goldsmith and

Posner adduce no data that suggest the relative magnitude of those reasons or that suggest the absence of other reasons. Consequently, they and we have no way of knowing that CIL was not a contributing, or alternative sufficient, cause of behavior.[120] Survey or interview data might be useful to fill this gap.

Of course, to the extent that a particular instance of compliance is fully and exclusively explained by true coincidence of interest or coercion, it cannot be argued that CIL did any work.[121] This chapter's theory of CIL examines the effects of broader self-interest based on reciprocity, and it accepts, as a standard part of the CIL process, the possibility of a different kind of coercion—namely, by punishment for defection. While CIL is endogenous to states in the aggregate, once formed it is at least largely exogenous to any particular state. As explained above, it is also plausible that there are important circumstances in which CIL would have significant effects on state behavior.

VIOLATIONS, OR PROPOSALS FOR CHANGE?   Related to the problem of determining whether a custom has the requisite motivation under CIL doctrine is the question of how to deal with anomalous conduct. Does the anomaly constitute a simple violation, or the initiation of a revised rule of CIL? It is important to recognize that no law, in any system, achieves perfect compliance. Thus we must determine another way to evaluate compliance. The best way is to evaluate the *extent* to which law affects behavior. Thus, the fact that wars occur does not alone mean that the international legal prohibition on the use of force is without effect, just as the fact that murders occur does not mean a domestic proscription of murder is meaningless. Goldsmith and Posner argue that variations in levels of compliance suggest that no multilateral rule exists—or affects state behavior.[122] However, we would expect systematic circumstantial variations in compliance with respect to all laws. Again, no one would say that domestic law does not exist merely because it is violated. Thus, in order to determine that CIL exists or that we as social scientists should pay attention to it, CIL need not in every case *determine* behavior—just as long as it may do so in some set of marginal cases. In game-theoretic terms, even a relatively small cost associated with violating international law could affect the payoffs from compliance, potentially tipping the balance in favor of compliance in marginal cases.

Furthermore, in order to maintain the dynamic, evolutionary character of CIL, it is necessary that any theory of CIL allow for the possibility that some violations of existing rules be understood as proposals to establish new rules.[123] This distinction is both a subtle and difficult one, but it is necessary in any decentralized system. Thus, we should not demand that CIL command absolute compliance or that it be inflexible. In fact, one might argue, as some do about the common law, that one of its great virtues is its dynamism.

Research Implications: An Empirical Research Agenda

Theory alone tells us little about the world. The next step is to develop and test hypotheses based on the theory of CIL elaborated here.

ASSESSING THE PATIENCE AND HORIZON OF STATES   In empirical research, it would be useful to determine parameters or proxies by which to assess the patience (including the horizon) of states and governments, and to compare these parameters against measures of compliance. Is political stability associated with patience, and do we see greater compliance with CIL by states with greater political stability? Are democratic states more patient than nondemocratic ones? Is patience determined by a bell curve, in which strong autocracies and stable democracies are patient, and those in between are not? Are autocratic states more patient because they are not concerned about election cycles? Do we see more violations of law before an election than after? Are states with better-developed financial markets more patient than those without? Are corrupt governments "impatient"? What about more or less independent bureaucracies that may be charged with action that determines compliance with specific rules of CIL? Can these independent bureaucracies exhibit greater patience than their elected governments? These conjectures are linked to the theory of liberal states,[124] as well as to theories of transnational governmental networks.[125] In fact, the correct level of analysis for compliance with certain rules of CIL, in terms both of patience and of information transmission, may be the bureaucratic division rather than the state.

PAYOFFS   Once we have developed empirical methods of measuring patience, it would be necessary to develop empirical measures, or proxies, for payoffs from violation and compliance, in order to determine whether compliance occurs as predicted by the model described here.

PAYOFF STRUCTURE   Is CIL more likely to be formed under circumstances involving public goods or networks—that is, where the value of cooperation may rise with the number of players?

NETWORK EXTERNALITIES IN INTERNATIONAL LAW: MORE RELATIONSHIPS MAKE EACH RELATIONSHIP MORE RELIABLE   Do we see an acceleration of custom, or a tipping point at which sufficient relationships are established to make compliance with CIL more likely? Is there a synergy between the treaty system and CIL? This hypothesis might be tested by examining the relationship between entry into treaties and compliance with CIL. Again, the possibility of network externalities is inconsistent with a disaggregation of the state into independent functional components, because a set of independent components might not be affected across distinct subject areas.

REGIONAL CUSTOM   To what extent can we identify regional or other plurilateral CIL? In terms of compliance, how does it compare to universal CIL?

INFORMATION   Is there a relationship between compliance with CIL and the establishment either of adjudicative bodies or of NGOs that enhance information regarding compliance and defection?

Conclusions

This chapter shows the plausibility of CIL pursuant to rationalist analysis. It therefore serves as a fundamental defense of the international law system. The theory presented here is based on methodological and normative individualism. It thus departs substantially from the airy idealism of natural law theory. It provides a social scientific, theoretical foundation for both international legal positivism and a nuanced rationalism, and sees law as reflecting the actions of states (or their agents) in pursuit of their self-interest, broadly understood.[126] It shows that CIL—and with it, treaty law—is something of a feat of levitation. It rests not on a rock-solid natural law basis of divine (or other) principles, but on a fabric of rational acts, woven through a multiplicity of relations over time.

The goal of this chapter was to develop a model that would generate interesting hypotheses about compliance with CIL. The model described here should be compared to Goldsmith-Posner's approach, which generates no interesting hypotheses about CIL because CIL cannot, on their view, affect behavior. More particularly, Goldsmith and Posner provide no analysis of the circumstances under which either the multilateral or bilateral prisoner's dilemma might yield stable and efficient equilibria. In that sense, this chapter represents a distinct departure and shows the way toward a progressive research program in CIL.

Some may ask: Is this chapter about law, or is it only about social order, labeled "law"? In a sense, all law is social order, labeled law. Therefore, this chapter does not need to distinguish CIL from other forms of cooperation—and, indeed, the basic model is generic, although we make assumptions to accord with the CIL system, such as the general doctrinal rule of bilateral retaliation. This jurisprudential question can be asked about the domestic legal system also. In fact, this chapter contributes to social norms theory by showing that there may be a continuum between social norms and law—that law is different from social norms only in particular enforcement parameters.

While it is true that the basic model described here is one of cooperation—and one that applies to CIL, to treaties, and to other forms of international cooperation—there are some distinctive and important aspects of the CIL game that do not apply to general cooperation. First, CIL rules may serve as equilibrium selection devices that provide a greater possibility for a stable equilibrium. Second, a rule's designation as CIL brings into play a substantial set of default rules within the international legal system, thereby filling in a large portion of the "incomplete contract" regarding states' obligations and expectations under that rule, including the scope of remedies for violation. Third, it may be that designation as CIL serves to link compliance or noncompliance with any particular CIL rule to other rules, thereby extending the possible scope of retaliation to fields that might not otherwise be considered "fair game." With regard to this last point, we might say that designation as CIL, or as international law more broadly, increases the returns to compliance by placing the general sense of international legality at stake. That is, if state A can be a scofflaw in one sector, what prevents state B from being a scofflaw in an area that injures state A? In this sense, there is a possibility for implicit multilateral retaliation, even if formal CIL doctrine does not permit multilateral retaliation. States may be expected to move from non-CIL equilibrium behavior to *opinio juris*–based CIL where the latter either makes equilibrium possible that would not otherwise be possible, or enables that equilibrium to be achieved more efficiently than through other means.

So, designation as "law" certainly has meaning, and social effects. We might assume that legal rules are chosen over other types of rules—rules are designated "law"—when the legal method of cooperation is superior to the other methods. Institutions are chosen for cost and benefit reasons. All institutions are social constructs, and all depend for their power on acceptance, either implicit or explicit.

This chapter serves as a refutation of the central claim of structural realists in political science with respect to international law: that it is epiphenomenal. This chapter shows that international law should best be understood as a social expression of rules that achieve real collective goals, are backed by real sanctions, and have real behavioral effects. It is a strange realism that would ignore such results.

If social norms theory in the domestic sphere finds social norms attractive as a mechanism for production and enforcement of rules, CIL may hold some continuing promise as an alternative to treaty. Perhaps the main distinguishing feature, and potential value, of CIL is systemic. That is, although we have assumed sectoral divisions for modeling purposes, international law may also be understood as a set of linked games, or as one extensive game. Once a particular rule is absorbed into the CIL system, or is established through treaty, it may benefit from linkage to other rules of CIL, and of treaties.[127] The special nature of legal rules may derive simply from their integration into this linked system. It is order and law.

Like all theories in social science, this one has normative implications. CIL has advantages and disadvantages as a process for making rules. As states identify these advantages and disadvantages in particular contexts, they may decide in some contexts to facilitate the development of CIL through institutional modifications.

✦

CHAPTER FOUR

Treaty

TREATY AND CUSTOM are equivalent sources of international law, the main difference being evidentiary: a properly executed and ratified treaty serves ipso facto as evidence of the legal rule expressed in the treaty, while custom requires proof of *opinio juris* and satisfactory practice. Under the jurisdiction-centered approach of this book, treaties exist, like customary international law (CIL), to effect transactions in jurisdiction: to allocate or reallocate authority in legal form. Treaties have the advantage of potential greater specificity and greater self-conscious structuring.

For example, we might easily understand an extradition treaty or a tax treaty as engaging in complex reciprocal—and not-so-reciprocal—transactions in jurisdiction. But it is also possible to understand a human rights treaty or an environmental protection treaty as transferring authority, or jurisdiction. By a human rights treaty, for example, a state relinquishes part of the *domaine reservé*—the sphere of exclusive jurisdiction—in exchange perhaps for reciprocal relinquishments by other states. An environmental protection treaty does the same, or might alternatively be used to convert what was previously a commons, like the ozone layer or the high seas, to regulated use or to transfer authority to an organization. It is also possible that the consideration is not in kind, but in different form, as in the case when execution of a human rights treaty is an implicit condition for foreign aid.

I argued in Chapter 3 that the customary international law method of entering into transactions would be used where it is superior—from a net cost and benefit standpoint—to nonlegal methods of cooperation. In this chapter, I examine treaty from the perspective that states would choose treaty over CIL, and over nonlegal cooperation, where treaty is superior from a net cost and benefit standpoint. I suggested in Chapter 3 that CIL is analogous in some ways to social norms in a domestic setting. Interestingly, treaty may be understood as analogous either to contract or to legislation in a domestic setting.

CIL is foundational to treaty. The CIL rule of *pacta sunt servanda*—treaties are binding—provides infrastructure for the treaty superstructure. Thus, in the most basic doctrinal terms, treaty is no more binding than CIL. And in the most basic social scientific terms, treaty is also no more binding than CIL. Most importantly, the basic theoretical understanding of the capacity of international law to bind that was developed in Chapter 3 with respect to CIL is equally applicable to treaty.

Chapter 3 distinguished among CIL rules. Each CIL rule would have a different binding capacity depending on the parameters developed in Chapter 3. Each of these parameters is equally relevant to analysis of treaty rules. Similarly, each treaty rule would be expected to have a different profile. Yet, as described below in this chapter, there are some systematic differences between custom and treaty.

The first section of this chapter examines the degree to which analytical techniques developed in relation to domestic contract may be applied to international treaty. The second section examines the binding nature of treaty and compares it to CIL. The third section reviews the role of efficient breach in the treaty context. The final section examines the implications of this analysis for treaty interpretation.

Domestic Analogies

There are a number of similarities and differences between treaty and contract, making comparison a useful exercise. This is despite the fact that there is a glaring institutional difference between treaty and contract: treaty lacks the type of normal domestic court of compulsory and universal jurisdiction, with the ability to levy damages or order performance.

However, this chapter suggests that while there is no independent all-powerful umpire, determining rights and making them effective, there are socially immanent—endogenous—mechanisms that may, in particular contexts, serve very roughly the same purpose. Of course, some treaty mechanisms contain surveillance, dispute settlement, and punishment facilities.

The European Union, the World Trade Organization (WTO), the European Convention on Human Rights, and even the United Nations have these types of facilities in some form or to some extent. Although the punishments are not independent of the regulated persons in the same sense that a domestic sheriff would be, they may be applied individually after community approval. The interesting design question is what effect on behavior does this have? Deep analysis of the domestic system would find that the umpire there is also socially immanent. The difference may be more subtle than it first appears.

Attempts at domestic analogy in this field are especially subject to the caveat that there are many different domestic laws of contract. Thus, the similarities and differences depend to an important extent on which domestic law forms the basis for the analogy. As noted in previous chapters, however, it is not the precise legal structures that form the basis for the analogy, but the similarity of concerns. While different domestic legal systems may address concerns differently and with different emphases, the basic concerns of contract law are comparable to the concerns of treaty law.

Some of these concerns include the following:

(i) When should promises or agreements implicate community enforcement?

(ii) What types of promises or agreements should be forbidden?

(iii) When does one person have the capacity to enter into promises on behalf of others?

(iv) What is the right measure of damages for failure to comply with an enforceable agreement?

(v) Under what circumstances should a party be forced to carry out its agreement without an option to pay damages?

(vi) How does an agreement among some parties affect third parties?

(vii) How should independent tribunals interpret agreements?

So, while no one should argue that treaty law would or should operate the same way as any state's domestic contract law, the tools developed in law and economics to analyze the role of contract law are extremely valuable in analyzing the role of treaty law.[1]

International tribunals, and commentators, have long noted the domestic law analogies to treaty.[2] As an agreement intended to be legally binding, a treaty is often considered to be "a form of contract."[3] Like contracts, treaties are intended to serve as a source of rights and obligations between parties. Both are anchored in exchange of promises about future behavior, and, as a general matter, both create "law," or at least obligation, for the contracting parties only.[4] Moreover, treaties are analogized to contract because both "derive their validity from the agreement of the parties."[5] The law of treaties and the law of contracts exhibit a similar structure, as both "establish rules about the making and interpretation of agreements, their observation, modification and termination."[6] Thus, the bodies of law of both treaty and contract address a number of similar questions, including questions about capacity, formation, validity, breach, remedy, and termination. However, the analogy with contract is by no means complete.[7]

As with CIL, it is necessary to have a means to distinguish between legally certified agreements that invoke the default rules, linkages, and other facilities of international law—treaties—and agreements that are not intended to do so. When states sign an international agreement, the default rule is that it is a binding treaty, in accordance with its terms. So, as with domestic contract in a state like the United States, it is up to those who sign the agreement to specify an intent that it not be legally binding in order to avoid the (general) operation of this default rule. The problem of unintended legalization seems much less of a problem among sophisticated governments and their representatives than among individuals.

Treaty and Custom: Binding Effect

The analysis developed in Chapter 3 supports, a fortiori, the proposition that binding force is plausible in connection with treaty law, just as it was seen to be plausible in connection with CIL. Assuming, then, that treaty has some binding effect, at least in some cases, treaty seems amenable to some of the same analytical techniques developed in domestic legal analysis in relation to contract. Goldsmith and Posner have a romantic view of treaty, as they do of CIL: for them, in order for these types of international law to be binding, states must comply with them for intrinsic, rather than extrinsic, reasons. Few would adopt this rather absolute view in the domestic setting—it simply is not true that in order for a rule to be called law, individuals must comply with it for intrinsic, internalized reasons. The Goldsmith-Posner perspective obscures the real social mechanisms that allow these types of international law to bind states. After all, contracts are not binding simply because they are contracts; they are binding because the state adds extrinsic force to them.[8]

As noted above, the formal binding nature of treaty derives from the CIL rule of *pacta sunt servanda*. Therefore, as a matter of formal legal doctrine, no treaty can have greater binding force than CIL. This formal doctrinal perspective is inconsistent with practical perception, and experience, in which it appears that many treaties meet greater compliance than at least some rules of CIL. *Pacta sunt servanda* may be a more binding rule than other rules of CIL, in part because it is systemic and contains an implicit broad set of linkages. The disparity also arises from some of the distinctive features of treaty discussed below.

But the important point is not a matter of doctrine, but of theory: in the "horizontal" international legal system, *both* CIL and treaty must find their binding effect, if any, in the social interaction of states. Therefore, the theoretical perspective expressed as to CIL in Chapter 3 applies, mutatis mutandis, to treaty.

Thus, treaty and CIL are complementary components of the broader framework of international law. As discussed in Chapter 3, CIL may be understood as a method of formation of agreement without express formalities, while treaty by definition requires express formalities. However, the formalities do not necessarily play a decisive role in compliance.

Much of the basic economic analysis of treaty thus parallels that of custom—in fact, at the most basic level, custom is understood in Chapter 3 as informal agreement, while treaty is merely formal agreement. So the greatest difference is in the degree of formality—in the written as opposed to implicit nature of the agreement. Treaty generally depends for its binding effect on the horizontal actions of states, although transnational organizations may be formed to enhance binding effect through adjudication, centralized executive and information functions, and even punishment. Thus, while, at a fundamental level, treaty can be modeled similarly to custom, using the multiperson prisoner's dilemma or other game-theoretic models, each treaty context will differ and there are mechanisms available that may enhance compliance. Most importantly, treaty allows the self-conscious structuring of institutional arrangements that can address cooperation problems.

Therefore, this chapter will examine the binding effect of treaty as it may differ from the binding effect of custom.[9] The reader may wish to review the analytical factors developed in Chapter 3 in order to consider their application in the treaty context. Treaty is different from CIL in several salient respects:

- Treaty requires and permits written specification of the terms, addressing certain information problems relating to the content of the rule. Treaty obligations are therefore less subject to dispute than CIL obligations: "faintest ink over sharpest memory." This depends, of course, on the relative specificity of the rule, and on the consensus among states as to its meaning. In general, however, the written nature of treaty makes it more likely that it will be clear to all.

    - Greater clarity of obligation may make it easier for third states to determine which of two states is breaching, engaging reputational effects or possibly third-party punishment.
    - Treaty may be used by states to create focal points around which equilibrium strategies are more likely to be harmonious.
    - Treaty may be used where greater specification of rules by political as opposed to adjudicative determination is desirable, in accordance with an incomplete contracts or rules-versus-standards analysis. This phenomenon is discussed in detail in Chapter 7.
    - This also suggests that, all other things being equal, treaty can achieve greater binding effect than a comparable CIL rule through its ability to overcome this type of information problem.
    - Furthermore, it suggests the importance of a textual approach to interpretation.

- While CIL may attract judicial and other monitoring and determination of breach, treaty lends itself to self-conscious design and specialized structuring of monitoring and dispute settlement mechanisms. This permits further reduction of information problems, and the self-conscious design of payoff structures: remedies.
- A type of grim trigger strategy in the form of termination of treaty obligations seems doctrinally available in connection with treaty.
- Treaty, like CIL, benefits from a set of default rules. However, these default rules are even more highly articulated in the context of treaty under the Vienna Convention on the Law of Treaties.
- While CIL is often universal, and only exceptionally regional or bilateral, treaty is more readily variable in its coverage. This allows the selection of parties that may be more likely to comply, while it suggests the utility of a rule of effective ejection of states that fail to comply with their treaty obligations. Thus, treaty regimes may exclude

impatient states, or other states less likely to comply. Furthermore, treaty is more heterogeneous in many respects than custom, partly because treaty allows the self-conscious development of various institutional structures. These structures may include surveillance mechanisms, adjudication mechanisms, adjustment or excuse mechanisms, and enforcement mechanisms. As suggested in Chapter 3, depending on the nature of the payoff structure, games with smaller numbers of players may be more or less likely to reach stable and efficient equilibria than broader multilateral games, depending on the type of cooperation problem at hand. Certainly, where impatient players may be excluded, the possibility of compliance is increased.

- In Chapter 3, the customary international law game was modeled using noncooperative game theory. To the extent that treaty is binding—and our analysis of CIL suggests that the CIL rule of *pacta sunt servanda* may achieve a measure of binding effect even under a noncooperative analysis—the game of compliance with treaty may be modeled using cooperative game theory. Once we assume the ability to enter into binding agreements, it is simple to resolve the prisoner's dilemma. While this analysis is somewhat circular, it seems congruent with a systemic, linked approach to compliance with international law. The language of endogeneity and exogeneity seems increasingly imprecise, failing to reflect nuanced and incomplete linkages among subsystems.

- From a public choice standpoint, and depending on the method of ratification of treaty, treaty may avoid some of the concerns regarding unfettered executive action, and a democracy deficit, that may be raised in connection with CIL. Of course, many raise concerns regarding the democracy deficit in connection with treaty, and much depends on the method of ratification.

The above distinctions may suggest why we see greater reliance today on treaty for the formation of new international law. As noted above, theory would suggest that the choice between CIL and treaty is based on the estimation by states of the costs and benefits, including transaction costs, of each device. At particular moments, states have self-consciously shifted from CIL to treaty: many CIL rules have been incorporated in treaty form.

Specificity

Treaties may be specific or vague. In every major treaty regime, we may identify countless examples of ambiguity.[10] The ambiguity may be intentional or unintentional. The choice between greater and lesser specification may be understood using incomplete contracts analysis and rules-versus-standards analysis. I examine this literature, and its implications for the role of adjudicators, in Chapter 7.

Here, we may examine the choice of greater or lesser specificity in terms of the binding nature of treaty, especially as compared to CIL. The international legal system is beset by information problems: it is difficult to know whether a violation has occurred. This information is important for the reasons set out in Chapter 3. In order to cooperate, states must know what behavior counts as cooperation, and what behavior constitutes defection.[11] Treaty may serve, as may other devices, to create a focal point around which cooperation may develop. Information is necessary for retaliation, and therefore for the possibility of binding effect. Information is especially relevant to multilateral retaliation in respect of bilateral violation, which requires third states to make a determination as to whether the violation has indeed occurred. International law is replete with instances of false accusations of violation, often to justify aggression.

Advance specification of detailed obligations, and available exceptions, will allow easier identification of defection, and therefore greater likelihood of punishment. Greater likelihood of punishment increases the likelihood of compliance.

Selection, Ejection, and Number of Players

As noted in Chapter 3, cooperation in a noncooperative game such as the prisoner's dilemma is dependent in part on the patience of states, denoted by their discount factors. One of the problems in universal CIL is the fact that the binding force of the shadow of the future is dependent on the least patient state's discount factor, including all states. Of course, in many legal settings, some noncompliance is acceptable and so it may be that states with low discount factors could participate. On the other hand, cooperative outcomes may be easier to establish where states with low discount factors may be excluded. This can be accomplished *ex ante* or *ex post*.

Ex ante, we might expect states with high discount factors to have more treaty relations, because their treaty obligations would be expected to be more reliable. In order to test this empirically, we would need, as discussed in Chapter 3, to develop direct data or proxies for states' discount rates.

So, one hypothesis that we might derive regarding treaty is that high discount factor states are more likely to be admitted to treaty regimes than low discount factor states. Another, based in part on the possibility of cross-agreement linkages discussed in Chapter 3, is that states that already have many treaty relationships are more likely to comply with each of their treaty obligations, and more likely to form new treaty relationships.

Ex post, we might expect to find that treaties contain mechanisms to eject from the treaty system states that show themselves to be defectors. Thus, Article 60 of the Vienna Convention on the Law of Treaties, and specific provisions of multilateral treaties that allow formal or informal termination of membership of breaching states, may be understood in game-theoretic terms.[12] On the one hand, Article 60 seems to allow a bilateral grim trigger strategy. The rules of state responsibility, which were compared to the penance strategy in Chapter 3, would seem to continue to apply where a treaty relationship is not terminated under Article 60. Thus, states may have a choice of punishments that they may apply.

Cooperative Game Theory

Assuming that treaties may be binding, we may relax the central assumption of the prisoner's dilemma: that the players are unable to enter into binding agreements, and are therefore involved in a noncooperative game.[13] As discussed in Chapter 3, a noncooperative game is one in which negotiation and enforcement of binding contracts are impossible.[14] A cooperative game is one in which players can communicate before each play of the game, and the players may reach binding agreements.[15] Cooperative game theory has been used to analyze nonlegal areas of international relations, such as the formation of alliances.[16]

Bindingness is a matter of degree, and may be a matter of marginal effects on behavior rather than of absolutes. Furthermore, informal or formal mechanisms may serve to "bind." Although the literature does not seem to address circumstances of uncertain or incomplete enforceability, we know that all enforcement in the real world is incomplete. Does treaty

satisfy this requirement of enforceability? The answer cannot be definitively affirmative or negative, although this is true, to a lesser degree, of
municipal law as well, and of contract.

If binding commitments may be established through either CIL or
treaty, cooperative game theory may provide useful analytical tools. To the
extent that we have found in Chapter 3 that CIL may plausibly bind states,
it is possible that the CIL rule of *pacta sunt servanda* would support binding treaty commitments. That is, once we establish a CIL rule of *pacta
sunt servanda* as the result of a noncooperative game, that result may form
the basis for a cooperative treaty game.[17] In this chapter, I will not judge
the basis for a conviction that the other partner will live up to its agreement. I have described the argument for the CIL rule of *pacta sunt servanda* in Chapter 3.

Therefore, in this chapter, I assume that treaties are binding, and evaluate the possibility that states will enter into treaties, and the structure of
remedies for violation. If we made the contrary assumption, a rationalist
analysis of treaty would merely apply the analysis of Chapter 3 to the texts
and institutions of treaty, with the modifications suggested above.

In the cooperative treaty game, any treaty must be such that, at least in
prospective terms, each adherent receives a benefit that is at least as great
as it would receive if it did not join in the treaty. We would not expect rational states to join in the formation of treaty rules that provide them with
lesser payoffs, anticipated *ex ante*, than they would receive by abstention.

Rational states can be expected to abandon treaties, or CIL rules, to the
extent permitted, where their payoff from departure exceeds their payoff
from adherence. However, international law may be sticky: it sometimes
does not allow individual states to abandon rules *ex post* at will. Much depends on the withdrawal provisions of the relevant treaty.

In a multilateral cooperative game, all players or any subset of two or
more players may enter into a binding agreement, termed a "coalition."
The "coalition function" is the sum of payoffs to members of a particular
coalition. Thus, a coalition is any subset drawn from the population of
states, and may be a single state or may be the "grand coalition," composed
of all states.[18] Other coalitions, involving two or more players, are termed
"intermediate coalitions."

There are two types of cooperative games: those in which utility is transferable and those in which utility is nontransferable.[19] In a transferable
utility game, a player within any coalition may transfer utility to another

player in order to keep the second player in the coalition. We can assume for the moment that in the treaty game, utility is transferable among players—that one player in a coalition may compensate another for joining the coalition by making a "side payment."[20] Of course, the degree of transferability of utility is an important question in the real world, given transaction costs, and we might consider the possibilities for package deals and other barter-type compensation. Possibilities for compensation also raise issues of measurement and timing. While there may be high transaction costs in the international law setting, it is possible that transfers of utility may take place, especially when we expand the capacity for transfer through multitransactional and multisectoral contact.

Arce and Sandler point out that in the military alliance setting, there have been instances of explicit cash transfers, such as transfers by Middle East states to the United States during the 1991 Gulf War, and more subtle forms of transfer of utility.[21] Transfers, conditional transfers, and delayed transfers raise the possibility of additional ways to enforce agreements.

The ability to form coalitions depends on whether entry into the coalition is individually rational, and whether the formation of the coalition as a whole is collectively rational. "Individual rationality" in this context is a characteristic of a coalition such that no individual country will leave the coalition, because its payoff within the coalition is greater than its payoff outside. This is consistent with treaty law, in which no state is bound unless it agrees to be bound. This doctrinal characteristic is consistent with Pareto efficiency: we are entitled to assume (excluding for a moment the possibility of coercion or linkage) that a state would not join a treaty unless it is either made better off or at least not made worse off by doing so. "Collective rationality" means that the coalition offers an aggregate payoff that is at least as large as any other rule involving all participating states. Payoffs that are both individually rational and collectively rational are called "imputations."

The "core" is a solution concept: if a particular agreement is "in the core," it will be stable and efficient. Only imputations in the core are stable and efficient. A coalition proposal is in the core if no subcoalition can block the proposal by providing better payoffs to the states that participate. There may be multiple possible agreements within the core. An agreement that cannot be challenged by any subcoalition is called a "core outcome."[22] The core is the set of outcomes that are not dominated by any other outcome.

Cooperative game theory is concerned with agreements within the core. International treaty law will also be concerned with agreements within the core. It is possible that in any given context, the core will be empty. This means that there is no outcome that is not dominated by another outcome. This situation is unstable, as any particular coalition can be dominated by another potential coalition. Instability in this context results in rapid change and arbitrary outcomes. "Quite simply, the core ensures that no coalition can form and do better than what it obtains in aggregate payoffs from the agreement."[23]

How can cooperative game theory be applied to treaty? In order to determine the scope of membership of treaty, it will be necessary to determine whether the treaty is individually rational and collectively rational for its parties. This can be done by examining the payoffs from entry into the treaty for each state.

Entry into Treaty

The assumption of full compliance by treaty adherents under the rule of *pacta sunt servanda,* while obviously counterfactual in a number of real-world contexts, allows us to model a simple two-stage game in which states are assumed capable of making binding commitments, and draw insights from that model.[24] Under this assumption, we need not be concerned with whether the treaty is self-enforcing. Obviously, if the treaty has no enforcement mechanism, it may not be binding. Under these circumstances, we would need to revert to noncooperative game theory analysis. The same type of noncooperative analysis applied to custom in Chapter 3 would be applicable, mutatis mutandis, to treaty.

The stages that are to be analyzed include (i) adherence, and (ii) compliance. Incidentally, as noted in Chapter 3, we could also develop a similar model of customary international law, in which customary international law is understood, consistent with doctrine, to be binding generally, similar to *pacta sunt servanda,* and the decision to accept a custom is analogous to the decision to enter into a treaty.

Under this two-stage game, adapted from Barrett, the players choose in stage 1 whether to enter into the treaty. In stage 2, adherents and nonadherents choose whether to comply or violate, although for an adherent I assume that there is no choice, provided that there are other adherents who are in a position to enforce the initial adherent's obligations. I assume that an agreement is binding, that each player knows what happened at the prior stage, and that each player examines its choices at each subsequent stage when determining what to do at the first stage—whether to enter into the treaty. By this process of backwards induction, we can determine whether states would enter the treaty.

For simplicity, I begin with a two-person prisoner's dilemma game, similar to that analyzed in Chapter 3. I use the prisoner's dilemma here for the same reason it is used in Chapter 3: because it represents a context in which cooperation is tough to achieve. Here, the parties have incentives to defect. In other payoff structures, illustrated by games like the battle of the sexes or stag hunt, the parties do not have similar incentives to defect (although they may not have strong incentives to cooperate).

The following analysis is adapted from Black, Levi, and de Meza, and is structured around a collective good, such as protection of the ozone layer.[25] However, note that this is just one type of payoff structure and by no means exhausts the complexity of real-world types of problems. Assume that the payoff to compliance with a particular norm (not yet part of a treaty) is $rb - c$, where r is the number of states that comply, b is the benefit produced by each complying state's compliance, and c is the cost to each complying state of compliance. Note that in this payoff structure, the aggregate benefits rise in proportion to the number of states that comply. The payoff to a noncomplying state simply equals rb. We assume that b is less than c. Otherwise, there would be no need for a treaty, because each state would have sufficient incentives to comply without the treaty.

For example, with two players that both comply, and assuming $c = 3$ and $b = 2$, the net payoff to compliance to each state is 1. If neither complies, then the payoff to each is 0. If one complies while the other violates, the complying state player gets a payoff of -1, while the noncomplying state gets a payoff of 2. This is indeed a prisoner's dilemma.

Now assume that states may agree to comply through adherence to a treaty. Assume further that this treaty is ineluctably binding, so that it always results in compliance. We know from the discussion above and from the analysis of the prisoner's dilemma provided in Chapter 3 that a nonsignatory will play "violate" at stage 2—this is the dominant solution for a nonsignatory. In this two-player game, assume that one state adheres to the treaty in stage 1. Since it is the only adherent, (assume that) the treaty cannot be enforced against it, and so it plays "violate" in stage 2, as it anticipates that the other state will also play "violate" in stage 2: it understands the other state's dominant solution, and in fact it is acting pursuant to its own dominant solution. The outcome is that both play "violate": the same type of inefficient equilibrium that we expect in a prisoner's dilemma. But here, there is a difference. There is an institutional mechanism for binding agreements.

Anticipating the inefficient solution to the prisoner's dilemma game, both parties examine their choices at stage 1. If one of the parties (A) adheres to the treaty at stage 1, the other party (B) faces the following choice. If B declines to adhere, then A will play violate in stage 2, as discussed in the prior paragraph. B anticipates that it will receive a payoff of 0 if both parties violate. On the other hand, if B adheres, irrevocably binding itself to comply, A will be required to comply, securing a payoff of 1 for B (as well as for A). So, in this setting, B will adhere. A's adherence may be understood as an offer to contract, which B may accept by adherence. Adherence is a (weakly) dominant solution for both players in stage 1.[26]

As suggested by Barrett, this works well for a two-person game, and the two-person prisoner's dilemma when transformed into a cooperative game is easily resolved. This is intuitive and certainly correct. In part, this two-player case is simple for two reasons. First, where only one player adheres, it receives no benefit, but only a detriment. So it is perfectly willing to revert to the Nash solution: noncompliance. Second, under international law doctrine, Barnett and others assume that a single adherent has the right to violate the treaty.

But we are also interested in plurilateral and multilateral treaties. When this two-person model is extended to multiple persons, whether states will adhere to a multilateral agreement will depend on the structure of the payoffs. In a game with n players, at least in the public good context posited above, it may well be that a benefit is created through adherence by a coalition that is less than the grand coalition. So reversion to Nash (reversion to non-compliance) may not be attractive to that group. Second, depending on the nature of the treaty performance, and in particular whether the benefit of compliance is a public good, it may not be possible to either (i) fail to comply or (ii) exclude noncompliant states from the benefit.

Using the same formula provided above, recall that the payoff to a complying state is $rb - c$, while the payoff to a noncomplying state simply equals rb. Assume that the payoff from noncompliance, assuming all others fail to comply, is 0. Therefore, k states will adhere if $kb - c \geq 0$. Therefore, if the number of states $k \geq c/b$, then these states will adhere. Using the values of $c=3$ and $b=2$, if the number of states is greater than or equal to 1.5, they will adhere. So, in this example, two states result (as stated above) in a payoff of 1, and since $1>0$, they will adhere. However, once the number of adherents reaches this level, other states will have no incentive to adhere—they will have an incentive to free ride. Adherence will result in costs incurred by the marginal adherents without affecting the behavior of other states.

The matrix in Table 4.1 depicts this circumstance of a prisoner's dilemma involving five states.[27] For every state that complies, a pure public good is produced, giving all states a benefit of 2, with a cost to the complying state alone of 3. Each state can play either of two strategies: compliance or noncompliance. The dominant strategy is for each state to free ride and play noncompliance, because each of the payoffs for noncompliance in the top row is greater than the payoff for compliance in the bottom row. The Nash equilibrium is an outcome where no state complies.

However, in our two-stage game with the possibility of adherence to a binding treaty, two will be expected to adhere under these assumptions— that is, in equilibrium, the number of adherents is two. This is because the payoff to nonadherents is greater than the payoff to adherents once two have signed. For example, if three states sign, the payoff is 3 to each adherent but 6 to each nonadherent (nonadherents do not bear the cost).

Barrett shows that the gains from cooperation increase with b, and decrease with c. This is intuitive. However, the equilibrium number of state adherents increases with c, and decreases with b. This means that the equilibrium number of states will tend to be small when the gain from cooperation is large, and large when the gain from cooperation is small. Furthermore, in equilibrium, nonadherents can free ride and get a higher payoff than adherents.

Of course, this assumes an isolated treaty adherence game, without the ability to subject states to scrutiny or punishment for "unilateralism." Much depends on the assumed values of the costs and benefits to each state.

Table 4.1 Number of states that comply *besides i*

	0	1	2	3	4
Noncompliance	0	4	6	8	10
Compliance	−1	1	3	5	7

The core challenge to cooperation under these payoffs is free riding: some states may realize the benefit of compliance by others, without incurring any costs themselves. Indeed, each incremental state would prefer to free ride if it could ensure that enough other countries would adhere. This assumes that there is a public goods aspect to the cooperation problem. If, on the other hand, states that fail to comply can be excluded from sharing the benefits, the strategic challenge becomes smaller. To be clear, if there is no public goods aspect to the cooperation problem in the sense that players can be excluded from benefiting from the cooperation of others, all states should then be willing to adhere. By adhering, they achieve a greater payoff than they would receive by failing to adhere.

Even if the cooperation problem is characterized by a public goods–type set of payoffs, there may be a relatively easy solution given the assumption of binding agreements. Under the public goods–type payoffs, assuming binding agreements, the decision to adhere to the (binding) agreement would have the characteristics of a "chicken" game,[28] as described in Figure 4.1.[29] I provide a bilateral illustration for simplicity, but this illustration is readily generalized to multiple-player circumstances.

State B

		Adhere	Refuse
	Adhere	3, 3	2, 4
State A			
	Refuse	4, 2	0, 0

Figure 4.1 A chicken game

Under the payoffs shown in Figure 4.1, each state's best outcome is to abstain from agreement, while others form a stable coalition that will generate the relevant public good. The second-best outcome is to adhere while others adhere. The worst outcome is if no state adheres. In this "chicken" game, neither player has a dominant strategy. In this particular case, there is no unique efficient equilibrium. Each player has two Nash equilibria: refuse to adhere when the other adheres, and adhere when the other refuses.

However, both players wish to avoid the circumstance where they each play "refuse," and the even split in the northwest quadrant seems intuitively attractive, although it is unstable. In order to achieve it, they should each commit to adhere. They may do so through a number of mechanisms. The simplest is a signing conference where each state signs the treaty simultaneously.[30] Only slightly more complex is a specification of a minimum number of adherents prior to entry into force. A further possible arrangement is to specify a cost-sharing obligation.[31]

These settings are comparable to the chicken game, but instead of two wild teenagers hurtling toward a cliff, we have sophisticated diplomats sitting eyeball to eyeball, and thinking about the past and the future. While there may still be incentives to try to avoid contributing, and these incentives may sometimes hold sway, the diplomatic context takes place in a broadly linked setting, where unilateralism may be criticized and subject to punishment. Thus, an assumption of linkage may also help to resolve the chicken game. This chicken game may be illustrated by the United States' refusal to adhere to the Kyoto Protocol. There are many forms of pressure on the United States to adhere—the Kyoto Protocol game is by no means an isolated one.

On the other hand, a large number of players—of states—may make cooperation difficult under certain payoff structures. Sandler shows this in his description of an international public goods problem that has the nature of a stag hunt game.[32]

The stag hunt game, described in Figure 4.2, is derived from a Rousseauvian fable of cooperation among hunters. Unless all hunters are committed to catching the stag, it will escape. Each individual hunter may be tempted by a passing rabbit. Each hunter prefers a share of stag to an individual portion of rabbit, but is uncertain about whether other hunters are sufficiently committed to capturing stag. The analogy to international cooperation in the case of certain types of public goods is as follows: each state prefers its share of the global public good, such as the elimination of terrorist safe havens (stag), but may be distracted by the opportunity to obtain local protection from terrorism (rabbit), especially if it is unsure of the commitment of other states. If the global public good is the elimination of terrorist safe havens, nonparticipation by even a very small number of states can eliminate the gains.[33] Sandler depicts this situation using the stag hunt game, where the cooperative gains are achieved only if a sufficient number of states adhere.

In international legal or organizational terms, a stag hunt context requires a lesser level of international legal inducements to compliance, compared to the prisoner's dilemma, because each player's best strategy is to cooperate. However, there is no dominant strategy because neither player is better off playing either *adhere* or *local protection* regardless of the other player's strategy: for example, if state A adheres, it is only better off if state B also adheres—it is worse off if state B chooses local protection. Note that we are assuming symmetry of preferences: no player actually prefers rabbit. Sandler shows that, assuming the need for self-enforcing agreements, as the number of players increases, depending on the aggregation technology

State B

		Hunt Stag/ Adhere	Chase Rabbit/ Local Protection
State A	Hunt Stag/ Adhere	4, 4	1, 3
	Chase Rabbit/ Local Protection	3, 1	2, 2

Figure 4.2 A stag hunt game

used, coordination can become quite difficult.[34] Aggregation technology is the assumption—or the factual assessment—of the way in which individual contributions determine the overall availability of the public good. For example, some public goods may only be available if every state contributes, while others may become available if just one state acts.

However, assuming enforceable agreements, the situation changes dramatically. This is because the act of treaty adherence, which under the assumption of enforceable agreements ineluctably leads to compliance, is easily observable and susceptible to coordination. At the treaty adherence stage, as opposed to the compliance stage, the facts are wholly unlike the Rousseauvian stag hunt, where hunters are uncertain of the actions of other hunters. As to the compliance stage, once states have adhered to the treaty, only mild incentives are required to ensure that they comply given the stag hunt payoff structure. Reasonable clarity regarding the definition of the cooperative behavior, monitoring to ensure compliance, and modest penalties (formal or informal) should be sufficient.

Remedies for Breach of Treaty, Price Theory, and the Efficient Breach Hypothesis

In the discussion of a cooperative game theory model of treaty, above, we assumed that adherence resulted ineluctably in compliance. Of course, compliance cannot be assumed in the real world. Indeed, treaties may be constructed with flexibility that can allow efficient noncompliance, and appropriate flexibility can help to induce entry into the treaty.

Therefore, we must examine the way that a treaty provides incentives for compliance. The incentives for compliance may be derived from concerns for reputation; from concerns for possible retaliation, including multilateral retaliation; or from formal remedies either under the Articles on State Responsibility or under the treaty itself.

Thus, once a state has entered a binding treaty, the structure of the game is likely to change—the payoffs are likely to be modified. The interesting question is how much. The treaty may specify remedies for violation, or may invoke, explicitly or implicitly, the remedies permitted by CIL, as described in the Articles on State Responsibility.[35] It is important to note that a discussion of remedies only becomes important *after* an acceptance that treaty may exert binding force: that it may actually result in the application of remedies and that the remedies may affect behavior.

A Taxonomy of Remedies

Remedies for violation of law or contract serve a number of functions in society. Remedies may be designed (i) to compel compliance, (ii) to promote compliance, (iii) to promote efficient compliance while avoiding inefficient compliance, and (iv) to punish transgressors separately from the effects on compliance.

At general international law, as reflected in the Articles on State Responsibility, the requirement is cessation and reparation. Reparation takes the forms of restitution, compensation, and satisfaction. General international law fails to distinguish sharply between restitution and compensation as obligations,[36] whereas law and economics theory does so. In law and economics theory, there is an important distinction between property rights, which would require restitution, and liability rules, which merely require compensation.[37] Article 35 of the Articles on State Responsibility provides for restitution only where it is possible and does not impose a wholly disproportionate burden. Depending on how the disproportionate burden criterion is applied, this approach may be understood as a hybridized property and liability rule.

The remedies that may be applied for violation of international law are described by Table 4.2. There are two analytical components: the measure of damages and the period of time for which that measure is calculated.

CESSATION, *LEX SPECIALIS*, AND COUNTERMEASURES   Under the Articles on State Responsibility, a primary obligation of a state that violates its international legal obligations is cessation of the violation.[38] However, obligations require compliance in accordance with their terms. Therefore, if a

Table 4.2 Remedies in international law

	Material Requirement	Temporal Application
Cessation	End violation	Prospective (*ex nunc*)
Restitution	Restore status quo	Retrospective (*ex tunc*)
Compensation	Substitute for restitution or cessation	Retrospective or prospective
Countermeasures	Sufficient to induce compliance	Prospective
Punishment	Sufficient to punish	Retrospective

state has an obligation that is qualified by an alternative performance (e.g., refrain from polluting or clean up the pollution), it cannot be said that there is a strict obligation to refrain from polluting.

Similarly, it is possible for states to specify the remedy that will be available for violation. States are permitted to create lesser or greater remedies than those available at general international law as described in the Articles on State Responsibility. The Articles reflect this in Article 55, which specifically authorizes *lex specialis* arrangements for responsibility. The International Law Commission commentary suggests that certain provisions of WTO law relating to remedies have the character of *lex specialis*.[39]

Interestingly, and in contrast to some of the arguments made regarding strict compliance with WTO law, the International Court of Justice (ICJ) "has generally not made orders for specific performance or for restitution in the absence of express provision for this in an agreement between the parties."[40]

RESTITUTION   As articulated in the *Chorzów Factory* case,[41] restitution is the preferred remedy at international law. In the Articles, "restitution" is defined as reestablishing "the situation which existed before the wrongful act was committed."[42] This may be achieved by returning territory or property. In many contexts, restitution is impossible. In the trade context, restitution could apply in some areas. For example, where an illegal subsidy is paid, it may be that a requirement of disgorgement may be understood as restitution. On the other hand, even disgorgement may not place injured competitors back into the position that they would have enjoyed if the subsidy had never been paid. In many trade contexts, restitution will not be apposite, or will be highly impractical. Thus, this chapter will focus on cessation, compensation, and countermeasures.

COMPENSATION   Under the Articles on State Responsibility, compensation is a "second-best" form of reparation for violation of international law. As the ICJ stated in the *Chorzów Factory* case, "The impossibility, on which the Parties are agreed, of restoring the Chorzów factory could therefore have no other effect but that of substituting payment of the value of the undertaking for restitution." As discussed below, the calculation of the value of the asset taken, or of the performance denied, is complex.

COUNTERMEASURES: INDUCING COMPLIANCE   According to the structure of the Articles on State Responsibility, countermeasures are separate from remedies per se. Countermeasures are unilateral measures by the injured state in response to failure of the injuring state to comply with its obligations to cease the violation and make reparations for the violation.[43] However, countermeasures have a dual character: they are generally designed to induce compliance, but they may also provide some compensation to the injured state.[44]

Under the Articles on State Responsibility, countermeasures are intended to induce compliance by the target state. The Commentary to the Articles understands WTO law to exclude the general international law on countermeasures, by virtue of the WTO Understanding on Rules and Procedures Governing the Settlement of Disputes (DSU)[45] requirement for authorization of measures "in the nature of countermeasures."[46] Therefore, by requiring authorization prior to the use of countermeasures, the WTO restricts a right of states that would otherwise exist at general international law.[47]

PUNISHMENT International law does not sanction punitive action by states. Article 49 of the Articles on State Responsibility requires countermeasures to be "proportionate," which seems to exclude punitive countermeasures. Under Article 47 of the Articles, the purpose of countermeasures is to induce compliance, and does not include punishment. However, retaliation is fungible in a sense: a measure that is intended to induce compliance may also be felt to punish.

While punishment of states in many international law settings seems unappealing, and inconsistent with international law doctrine, there is a rational basis for disproportionately large countermeasures in certain contexts. This basis is the probability of enforcement. Where the probability of enforcement is 50 percent, there is a rationalist argument for doubling the damages in order to induce compliance. Such doubling might be interpreted as punitive.

REPUTATION AND "INTERNATIONAL OBLIGATION" Reputation in this context is best understood not as a formal remedy, but as a parameter that may be valued by states, and may be lost by noncompliance.[48] Reputation, broadly understood, is the reason that there might be a right that has real effects without a formal remedy. The best way to understand reputation is as an informal remedy, and it may easily be understood in rationalist terms. Chapter 3 develops a broad understanding of the effect of informal remedies.

Indeed, we might understand reputation as an additional motivation by states to comply. In this sense, reputation may add an important finger to the scale of compliance. Reputation may help to explain why we observe widespread compliance with WTO law despite existing prospective-only remedies that would seem, considered alone, to provide incentives for breach.[49] Of course, states may not care about reputation per se, but are more likely to care about their ability to induce other states to make concessions in the future, and to comply with existing concessions. This role of reputation may be understood bilaterally, as similar to linkage politics in the political science literature, or as similar to multisector contact in the industrial organization literature.[50] Alternatively, to the extent that information and incentive problems may be overcome, it is possible that multilateral reputational effects could add a much larger finger to the scale of compliance.

Under these circumstances, as discussed in Chapter 3, we might understand dispute settlement as providing a method for discriminating between defection and compliance, in order to provide information necessary for multilateral reputational sanctions to operate. Milgrom, North, and Weingast argue that third-party dispute settlement can assist in developing cooperation.[51] Maggi makes this point in the trade context.[52] Third-party dispute settlement can solve the following information problem. If two parties have a dispute, in which one accuses the other of defection, how can other members of the community determine whether the accusation is true?

Reputation may be a powerful force in promoting compliance, and should be factored into any analysis of remedies. As Kovenock and Thursby, and Mitchell, conclude, formal WTO remedies that seem inadequate to induce compliance on their own seem to be supplemented by reputation, or "international obligation," in order to induce a high level of compliance.[53] While their work does not distinguish sharply among (i) generalized multilateral retaliation and issue linkage, (ii) concern for general respect for international legal rules (which may be the same as (i)), and (iii) a preference for a good reputation, each of these factors may be at work. However, Bown finds "only limited evidence that the costs imposed by 'international obligation' are sufficiently large to" credibly affect behavior.[54]

Article 22.8 of the WTO DSU, specifying that suspension of concessions is a temporary remedy, provides that the WTO Dispute Settlement Body shall continue to keep under surveillance the implementation of adopted recommendations or rulings. This surveillance would help to effectuate the role of reputation.

It may be that reputation has different effects in different types of cases. Perhaps where the violation is clear or flagrant, reputation would have a stronger effect. On the other hand, where the violation is a matter of interpretation, and there are appealing arguments on both sides, reputation may play a weaker role.

Efficient Breach in International Law

No law or legal obligation is peremptorily binding: it does not directly cause human action, but only creates incentives for action, mediated by individual choice. Rather, the main question is the magnitude and type of remedy or penalty for violation. Law and economics begins to approach contract, as it does other law, with price theory. From this perspective, the key to predicting compliance is the price of breach: where the price of a breach is sufficiently high, compliance will result. The price of breach must be measured in terms of both the measure of damages and the extent to which institutions exist mandatorily to require the payment of damages. Among the most influential—and controversial—claims made by law and economics scholars is the theory of efficient breach: positively, that there are circumstances where breach of contract is more efficient than performance, and normatively, that the law ought to facilitate breach in such circumstances.[55]

The idea of the efficient breach hypothesis is that if the obligee can require specific performance of the obligor's promise, the obligee might require such performance even under circumstances where the harm to the obligor from performance exceeds the benefit to the obligee. In bargaining terms, the obligee may hold out for an excessive share of the surplus that would be derived from breach, and this bilateral monopoly might prevent the efficient renegotiated bargain.

Under circumstances of a complete contract, there is no such thing as "efficient breach." This is because under these theoretical circumstances, the parties have already specified the desirable course of action in all states of the world. Thus, under a complete contract, or a complete treaty, it will be efficient to set remedies for noncompliance at coercive levels.[56] Noncoercive levels of remedies are appropriate where the treaty structure is incomplete in terms of its specification of the relationship between, for example, trade and environment or trade and health, as discussed in Chapter 7.

The efficient breach theory presupposes incomplete contracts and effective adjudicatory and enforcement mechanisms that can determine and compel payment of the appropriate level of damages in the event of a breach. That is, where there are no institutions that can provide for payment of damages, a rule of damages is unworkable. But such mechanisms are largely absent from the international context.[57] The theory also presupposes a commensurability between the damages suffered from the breach and a monetary payment or other form of compensation, a presupposition that requires interpersonal (or, in this case, interstate) comparison of utility and is problematic not only in contract but also in the context of arms control, human rights, national security, environmental, and other treaties.

These structural differences may help explain why questions of remedies—which are central to law and economics contract scholarship—occupy a relatively small role in treaty doctrine and scholarship.[58] On the other hand, there is a growing discussion of remedies in the trade context, and in connection with the International Law Commission's Articles on State Responsibility. Remedies are also relevant to the discussion, above, of the relationship between property and liability rules protecting entitlements.

The efficient breach hypothesis would turn a contract damages rule into, in the language of Calabresi and Melamed, a liability rule.[59] But liability rules have certain drawbacks that are especially pertinent in the international realm. First, liability rules impose on the wider community the collective expense of determining an "objective" cost of a breach.[60] While domestic societies typically provide the "public good" of well-functioning, compulsory dispute resolution systems (at least in developed countries), the international community has often declined to do so. Second, liability rules represent only an approximation of the value of the breach to the promisee. Even assuming such monetization is objectively possible for the types of "goods" exchanged by treaty—and it often is not—states may be more reluctant than individuals to subordinate their subjective valuations to the judgments of others.[61]

Some international lawyers will reject the concept of efficient breach on a normative basis.[62] They might argue that accepting the efficient breach hypothesis would threaten precisely the feature that renders treaties the "major instrument of international cooperation in international relations,"[63] the belief that treaties will be obeyed, even when contrary to a state's immediate, short-term interest. Condoning "efficient" breaches of these treaties would undermine the fundamental rule of *pacta sunt servanda,* and likely render more difficult the possibility of sustained cooperation in an international community through treaty regimes.

Of course, the same objection may be raised in the domestic context. Contract is important because of the belief that contracts will be obeyed, but it is still efficient to allow breach under certain circumstances. In fact, entry into contract may be facilitated by the understanding of parties that breach may be permitted under certain circumstances.[64] Sykes has made a similar argument regarding the General Agreement on Tariffs and Trade (GATT) escape clause.[65]

This analysis suggests that, where effective dispute resolution exists and damages can be relatively easily monetized, states are more likely to adopt an "efficient breach" rule. One context in which mandatory dispute resolution now exists, and in which something akin to efficient breach is de facto (if not de jure) permitted, is the GATT-WTO system.[66]

Under the current WTO DSU, when a WTO dispute settlement panel or the Appellate Body concludes that a measure is WTO inconsistent, "it shall recommend" that the measure be brought into conformity with WTO law. Once this determination is adopted by the WTO Dispute Settlement Body, the respondent state can, and should, comply with the ruling by amending or withdrawing the offending measure. Alternatively, the state may retain the offending measure and, instead, provide compensatory benefits to restore the balance of negotiated concessions disturbed by the noncomplying measure. Finally, the state may choose not to change its law or provide compensation, and, instead, suffer likely retaliation against its exports authorized by the WTO for the purpose of restoring the balance of negotiated concessions. Thus, we might usefully understand the WTO system as authorizing a member to choose to breach an obligation, and pay compensation to the injured party.[67]

Public Interest Remedies and Public Choice Remedies

As we consider remedies in the international system, among states, as compared with remedies in the domestic system, among individuals and firms, we must recognize that states are imperfect mediators of individual preferences.[68] Therefore, a remedy that appears on its face to be consistent with public interest—with welfare economics—may not yield efficient incentives in a world of states.

Indeed, if the goal were simply to induce compliance through the actions of government operatives, then penalties calculated to induce action by these operatives would be appropriate. But the goal is not necessarily to induce compliance in all cases. Rather, the goal in a number of international legal settings, including most economic areas, seems to be to induce compliance when compliance is efficient, and breach when it is not.

The normative goal of public choice analysis must be to enhance the alignment between the behavior of governmental operatives and public welfare. So, there is no normative argument that remedies in international disputes *should* be designed to maximize the welfare of government operatives. Rather, the normative goal is to suggest methods in which remedies could be redesigned in order to provide optimal incentives for welfare maximization. Of course, without great knowledge of the problems of alignment between governmental operative welfare and public welfare, it is impossible to be certain that any particular pattern of incentives will result in public welfare–oriented behavior by government operatives.

For those who would argue that governments require special penalties that are calculated to induce welfare-consistent behavior by governmental operatives but are not themselves congruent with welfare, we might ask why similar special penalties are not applied to corporations. Surely we understand that corporate governance may be inconsistent with welfare-maximizing behavior by the firm, and yet we do not have special penalties designed to induce welfare-maximizing behavior in light of our understanding of corporate governance.

Finally on this point, it appears clear that public choice analysis, powerful as it is in a descriptive vein, comes up short in the normative domain. That is, while public choice analysis can tell us about governmental response to incentives, it generally has avoided telling us how to match incentives with welfare. In the present context, public choice analysis tells us nothing about which remedies would maximize public welfare.

And yet, public choice sheds critical light on the problem of compliance with international law. An examination of the domestic political landscape in the bound state is necessary in order to predict compliance or violation of international law. Furthermore, where remedies are intended purely to induce compliance, avoiding the complicating possibility of efficient breach, they must be sufficient to induce the establishment of domestic political coalitions necessary to cause compliance.

If international law is to do any work, the domestic political coalitions must otherwise be in favor of violation, while the addition of an international legal rule modifies the domestic coalitions in favor of compliance. The international legal rule may do so through remedies, as discussed above, or it may do so in addition by virtue of the domestic politics of compliance with international law. That is, where compliance with international law has political support, as for example in the United States through the operation of the American Society of International Law or other nongovernmental organization activities, or through a generalized sense that it is valuable to support the integrity of international legal rules, then this political support for compliance with international law *in general* will add to the incentives to comply in any particular case.

Treaty Interpretation

The contract analogy described above suggests that law and economics' first impulse in interpretation should be for text-based interpretation of treaties, even ahead of a purported efficiency-based interpretation. This is because text-based interpretation preserves the bargain actually struck by the parties to the treaty and—when the "markets" for treaty-effected transactions are well functioning—such bargains are presumptively efficient. Such a "market-based" (analogizing the interaction of states to enter into treaties to a market) determination of preferences is likely to be more highly respected than a court's third-party interpretation.

Of course, Article 31 of the Vienna Convention on the Law of Treaties, requiring interpretation in accordance with the ordinary meaning of the terms contained in the text, seems broadly consistent with a text-based approach to interpretation, as opposed to a more teleological or natural law–based interpretation.[69]

Richard Posner famously claimed (positively) that common law courts seek economic efficiency in their decisions,[70] and many law and economics advocates claim (normatively) that this is what they should do. However, no individual can determine "efficiency" for another, if efficiency is defined as maximization of preferences, because no individual knows another's utility function. Just as Chapter 2 suggested that courts cannot determine the "efficient" law for purposes of conflicts of law analysis, courts cannot determine the efficient interpretation of contract or treaty. Rather, societies structure legislatures, courts, and markets to enable constituents to maximize their subjectively determined preferences, subject to institutional constraints. There is no reason to expect that any of these institutions could, a priori, identify and aggregate these preferences in the abstract.

On the other hand, there is some basis for respecting private contracts as written, given that they presumptively reflect the preferences of their parties. This presumption is subject to a public choice qualification in connection with treaty interpretation. Treaty interpretation is more like statutory interpretation than like contract interpretation[71] from an efficiency standpoint. That is, there may be concerns, based on public choice analysis, that certain treaties do not reflect welfare-enhancing transactions, just as some statutes do not reflect welfare-enhancing transactions. Under these circumstances, some may suggest that it would be useful for a court or other interpreter or enforcer to engage in some review of the terms of the treaty.[72] On the other hand, treaties have a dual dimension: domestically they can be analogized to statute, while internationally they have the character of a contract. Thus, it may be that an efficiency analysis is ambivalent: suspicious of the domestic efficiency of treaty based on the analogy to statute, and hospitable to the international efficiency of treaty based on the analogy to contract.

In order to enhance the binding effect of treaty, the ability to refer disputes regarding interpretation of the terms of the treaty to binding settlement may resolve certain information problems, as discussed in Chapter 3. In a bilateral setting, it may make it easier for a victim of defection to determine not to forgive a clear breach. In a multilateral setting, it may facilitate multilateral punishment or other reputational consequences.

Furthermore, even if a judge could determine the efficient interpretation in a particular case, this would be a limited, static approach to efficiency, rather than a broader, dynamic approach. That is, it may be broadly efficient to allow parties to enter into, and to enforce, contracts that would have inefficient outcomes under some circumstances, especially given time inconsistency. Respect for text promotes additional transactions: if authoritative interpreters respect the original texts, states will be encouraged to enter into treaties. This includes respect for loopholes and gaps in enforcement left in the text. The analysis in Chapter 2 suggests that under certain conditions, muddy allocations may be intentional and efficient.

There are difficulties with this argument. One, mentioned above, is that interpreting texts is inevitably a creative, not mechanical, exercise. In fact, those charged with interpretation may be delegated a degree of flexibility, or independent authority, in order to fill gaps or remedy "problems." More importantly, this argument presupposes that the bargains reached through interstate transactions accurately reflect underlying preferences.

But law and economics also identifies many situations in which market failure occurs and bargains do not necessarily maximize preferences. For example, as noted above, public choice theory suggests that treaties may advance the interests of the political elites that negotiate the treaties, rather than the broader interests of the constituents they purportedly represent.[73] Other law and economics methods identify a variety of other factors—including transaction costs, externalities, imperfect information, coordination difficulties, and strategic behavior—that cause states to fail to conclude mutually beneficial bargains. Thus, much of law and economics analysis is devoted to exploring whether, in any particular factual context, the market for international transactions is well functioning—and therefore producing presumptively efficient outcomes—and proposing ways to improve imperfect markets.

Perhaps a more important criticism of the argument for strict fidelity to text is that it may be that the drafters of the text—the principals—would actually prefer, either *ex ante* or *ex post*, a more teleologically based or natural law–based interpretation. The parties may specifically wish to delegate to judges the task of adjusting or revising their bargain in response to stochastic developments, or even in response to the judge's vision of justice or morality. Examples of implicit delegation of discretion to the judge in the domestic context are doctrines of impossibility and impracticability in contract, and in international law the somewhat analogous doctrine of *rebus sic stantibus.* In Chapter 7, I discuss the law and economics literature of rules and standards. Broader standards may be understood as implicitly delegating authority to judges to apply these standards.

Here, the judge should seek to adhere to whatever defines his or her agency. So there can be no general statement about the role of the judge and the scope for application of justice, morality, or the perceived intent of the parties. Rather, the role of the judge must depend on the mandate to the judge. Even this becomes difficult, as the mandate to the judge may be subject to implicit change. There is no doubt that the judges of the U.S. Supreme Court, or of the European Court of Justice, in the early years of those tribunals, exceeded the ambit originally intended by the authors of their mandates. But perhaps the authors of their mandates, in granting them effective *competenz-competenz* in a variety of ways, implicitly authorized them to determine their own mandate. This is also true of international commercial arbitration, in which tribunals must comply with their mandate, but are accorded *competenz-competenz* to determine the scope of their mandate.

Conclusion

While there are substantial differences between treaty and contract, the law and economics techniques that have been developed to analyze the dynamics of contract are useful in analyzing the dynamics of treaty. We see that treaty is an extension—in fact, a special case—of the model developed in Chapter 3 to deal with CIL. Treaty is analogous to explicit contract, while CIL is analogous to implicit contract.

✦

CHAPTER FIVE

International Organization

CHAPTER 2 EXAMINED the allocation of authority in the market of international relations, noting that there would be circumstances in which it would be useful to share authority through international organizations. Chapter 3 examined the development of customary rules for allocation of authority—transactions in the market, without explicit contract or organization—but noted that these types of transactions could be facilitated by organizations that provided information or other relevant services. Chapter 4 examined treaty as a formal, but one-off, form of transaction. This chapter examines the creation of organizations to facilitate transactions in authority, and to serve as repositories of authority themselves. The focus in this chapter is on the costs of transactions, and the comparison of institutional alternatives.

Debates regarding the competences and governance of international organizations such as the United Nations, the World Trade Organization (WTO), the European Union, and the North American Free Trade Agreement (NAFTA) seem to grow more polarized. To what extent and how shall these organizations be designed to discipline the activities of states? What kinds of legislative authority, if any, should reside within these organizations? Should judges in these organizations be permitted to strike down national regulatory measures? These are some of the central questions of globalization. After developing a theoretical perspective on international organizations, this chapter suggests how this theoretical perspective would encompass two important examples: the move to majority voting in the European Community (now part of the European Union) in the late

1980s, and the move to mandatory dispute settlement in the WTO in the mid-1990s. In Chapter 6, I examine the relationship among different functional international organizations, and in Chapter 7, I examine how dispute settlement functions as a governance mechanism within international organizations.

This chapter returns to the transaction cost economizing first introduced in Chapter 2, which discussed jurisdiction in property rights terms. Here, the focus is on the institutional response to transaction costs. The purpose of this chapter is to examine the theory of the firm and related transaction cost–based literatures of the new institutional economics,[1] law and economics, and industrial organization,[2] and the application of their analytical techniques to the linked problems of competence and governance of international organizations.

In addition, the multiple-person prisoner's dilemma model developed in Chapter 3 may help to shed light on the purpose of the international organization, as well as the business firm. By funneling transactions into a firm or international organization, and linking transactions within a firm or international organization, it may be possible more easily to resolve the multiple-player prisoner's dilemma. Furthermore, the possibility for third-party adjudication presented by an international organization may assist in resolving one of the most difficult information problems in the multiple-player prisoner's dilemma. Under multilateral punishment, how do third states know that a breach has occurred?

"Hierarchical arrangements are being examined by economic theorists studying the organization of firms, but for less cosmic purposes than would be served by political and economic organization of the production of international public goods."[3] In this chapter, I ask the same initial question about the international organization that Coase asked in 1937 about the business firm and that Keohane asked in 1982[4] about the international regime: why does it exist, and if its existence is justified, why is there not just one big one? New institutional economics, industrial organization, and law and economics owe great intellectual debts in the relevant areas to Coase's two seminal papers, *The Theory of the Firm* and *The Problem of Social Cost.*[5] Coase explains that these articles are related. "In order to explain why firms exist and what activities they undertake, I found it necessary to introduce . . . the concept that has come to be known as 'transaction costs.' "[6]

"While the kind of close comparative institutional analysis which Coase called for in The Nature of the Firm was once completely outside the

universe of mainstream economists, and remains still a foreign, if potentially productive enterprise for many, close comparative analysis of institutions is home turf for law professors."[7] As we determine why the
international organization exists, and how big it should be, we must analyze
the internal governance of international organizations, including voting
rules and other rules about how decisions are made. Within U.S. federalism, and within the European Union, this question includes that of "horizontal federalism": how do the different branches of government,
including for example in the United States the executive, legislature, and
judiciary, combine to exercise centralized power? This question includes
the question, addressed in Chapter 7, of the role of dispute settlement.
The structure of horizontal federalism is critically related to the question
of vertical federalism: what powers should be at the center, and what powers should remain at the periphery?

And of course the question of governance "inside the box" is inextricably
linked to the question of how big the box should be and what functions it
should have.[8] In addition, the mechanism inside the box remains dependent upon, and is constantly affected by, the institutional structure outside
the box. Together they constitute a system. No component of the system
operates in isolation from the rest of the system.

Beginning with Coase, the new institutional economics has developed
analytical tools to address similar questions to those raised above, within
the context of the business firm.[9] This chapter is premised on the proposition that business firms and international organizations have some characteristics in common, and that this admittedly limited commonality makes
comparison worthwhile.

Law and economics has drawn on, and is related to, industrial organization and new institutional economics in this field.[10] These three schools of
thought have been concerned, primarily in the context of the firm, with
the two questions discussed above: why does the firm exist, and how
should it be governed? These schools of thought have in common a recep-
tivity to, and in new institutional economics a focus on, transaction cost
economizing rather than (or, more properly, in addition to) the price theory common in neoclassical economics. "The discriminating alignment
hypothesis to which transaction cost economics owes much of its predictive content holds that transactions, which differ in their attributes, are
aligned with governance structures, which differ in their costs and competencies, in a discriminating (mainly, transaction cost economizing) way."[11]

This theoretical perspective has become the dominant approach to analysis of the corporate firm;[12] this chapter asks whether it may be a useful approach to the analysis of international organizations. This type of adaptation has been performed in connection with other types of nonfirm organizations, including application of "positive political theory"[13] to governmental organizations,[14] but has only been performed in a limited sphere in connection with international organizations.[15]

This analytical and critical theory, and its methodology, would reject both reflexive world federalism and reflexive autarchy. Less obviously, this theory rejects blanket calls for "strong" international institutions. Rather, it calls for a method that requires that each question be answered within its particular context. It is thus a prescription for further theoretical and empirical work.[16]

While Coase's ideas stimulated a thick literature seeking to address the theory of the business firm, international organizations have received much less attention in the theoretical literatures of law, economics, and politics.

Much of the legal literature of international organizations was written prior to the mid-1990s when legal scholars began to engage other social sciences, and has continued in a largely descriptive positivist project, or has embraced utopian ideals. Much of the more recent literature is analytical, realistic, and informed by the perspective of other disciplines. Modern scholarship of European Union law is also significantly analytical, realistic, and interdisciplinary.

An economic theory of international organizations would focus on welfare. Welfare may take many forms. In the trade context, from the standpoint of neoclassical international trade economics, welfare can be increased by free trade. Economics has made significant strides toward analyzing data to assess some of the trade benefits of integration, and to compare regional integration to multilateral integration in these terms. It has not addressed in an organized way the opportunity costs of integration: what does a state lose when it gives up a part of its autonomy to regulate, for example, food quality or banking services? These opportunity costs must be analyzed in institutional "trade" terms: how much autonomy is foregone, and what is it worth; and how much compensating influence over centralized decisions is obtained, and what is it worth?[17] These are the central issues in debates about globalization.

I argued in Chapter 1 that there are circumstances where there are gains to be derived by exchanging autonomy for integration in particular areas—for transactions in authority. However, economics has spent little time assessing the institutional constraints on the ability to make exchanges in this field. Yet this question is analogous in important ways to a question that economics has addressed in detail: the question of the transaction cost motivations for organization in the form of the firm versus the market.

The international organizations literature of political science has considered the theory of the firm, industrial organization,[18] the new institutional economics,[19] and public choice. However, this literature has until relatively recently deemphasized the role of formal institutions[20] in favor of greater emphasis on power, regimes, and informal institutions.[21] As recently as 1986, it was possible to make the following statement:

> One pattern that can be discerned throughout the maturation of the international organization field in the postwar era has been the steady disengagement of international organization scholars from the study of organizations, to the point that one must question whether such a field even exists any longer except in name.[22]

However, by 1996, Duncan Snidal was able to write that "international institutions are once again at the center of the substantive and intellectual agendas of international politics."[23] The study of international organizations began in the early part of the twentieth century, with the kind of technical, institutions- and law-oriented perspective that is attractive to lawyers,[24] although it was often motivated by utopianism. It was diverted from its formal institutional focus by a consensus between the two main competing theoretical perspectives in international relations. These perspectives reject the utopian perspective, and until recently seemed to neglect its formal institutional concerns. These two main theoretical perspectives are sometimes referred to as neorealism and neoliberalism, although these labels conceal an important degree of convergence, as well as significant internal diversity.

The neorealist perspective tends to ignore formal institutions and law as ineffective, and to consider policy as determined by the confluence of power and interest of states.[25] Neorealism provides a positive account of state behavior based on national interest and national power.

Neoliberalism, despite its interest in institutions, is only slightly different for our purposes.[26] Neoliberal institutionalism, led by Robert Keohane,[27] looks to the institutionalization of power through regimes, sometimes led by powerful "hegemons."[28] However, despite the fact that this body of literature professes interest in both informal and formal institutions, its research program has until recently focused largely on informal regimes, as opposed to formal legal or institutional mechanisms.[29] "Regime theory does not recognize anything distinctively 'lawlike' about international rules."[30] Thus, neorealism and neoliberal institutionalism[31] are united by a common focus on national interest and national power, and by a tendency to relegate formal institutions and legal constraints to irrelevance.[32]

The basic building blocks of modern political theory, "the distribution of preferences (interests) among political actors, the distribution of resources (powers), and the constraints imposed by the rules of the game (constitutions),"[33] are in fact quite comparable to the basic building blocks of institutional economics: preferences, wealth, and institutions. States transact in power to maximize the achievement of their particular interests.[34]

This chapter argues that formal institutions are relevant in the international sphere, as in the domestic sphere, although the degree of relevance may differ, and may change over time. In both spheres, they constrain the naked exercise of power, serve as a conduit for power from an initial time to a later time, and result in states sacrificing later-held interests in order to comply. The assumption of rational preference maximization is retained, and accepted as the sole motivating force of individuals and states. These sacrificed later-held interests are presumably anticipated to be smaller than the benefits to be obtained from entry into the institution. At the time when compliance occurs, the sacrificed later-held interests are presumably smaller than the payoffs from compliance, including, inter alia, the kinds of factors that support compliance with CIL or treaty, and the value of maintaining the integrity of the specific institution. The institution itself becomes a "bond" or hostage to support compliance. The model developed in Chapter 3 to analyze customary international law was seen to be adaptable to treaty-based law, and is also adaptable to institutions. The constraint is not complete in any context,[35] nor would we necessarily want it to be: the concept of efficient breach shows that strict compliance is not always the best outcome.[36]

In the context of this realistic approach, it is not correct to say that the international sphere is anarchic, while the domestic sphere is ordered.[37] While the international sphere may have "weaker" institutions (in terms of their ability to make decisions and coerce compliance), as compared to an orderly domestic society, the difference is only one of degree, and while some portions of international society are extremely orderly (like interbank correspondent relations for trade letters of credit), some segments of domestic society seem anarchic.

Finally, as indicated above, "weakness" of institutions is a design characteristic, and not necessarily a fault. States may be willing to take on greater substantive obligations if there is more procedural "give" in the system. States may be unwilling to take on "strong" obligations that are not supported by democratic legitimation. It may be optimal for other reasons for states to take on only weaker obligations. Again, this is based on a model of states motivated only by self-interest.

Most international organizations literature focuses more on analyzing behavior outside and around the box than inside the box, using "the box" to refer to the formal international organization.[38] This focus is consistent with a neorealist[39] or neoliberal[40] theoretical perspective, which would agree that the products of formal organizations are determined not by the formal mechanics of those organizations, but for the realist by the external power relationships that they mimic[41] and for the regime theorist by the less formal regime dynamics that they mimic.[42] These perspectives may be substantially dependent on the empirical phenomena observed: while the United Nations has not constrained war (at least not completely), the International Postal Union has brought a satisfactory level of order to international mail.

The focus of much recent international organizations literature outside the box and around the box, as opposed to inside the box, is comparable to the pre-1980s focus of neoclassical economists on markets, avoiding examination of corporate governance structures and other economic institutions.[43] These pre-1980s economists saw the corporation as a black box, as a production function, and did not analyze how its internal structure might affect the decision to organize production within the firm or the relative efficiency of such organization.[44] Similarly, with important exceptions, international organizations literature has often seemed to regard international organizations either as production functions or as trivial structures that serve as vessels for the real activity based on unconstrained power and interest. Thus, there was a remarkable parallel development between political science and economics: both have emphasized the market (the world of spontaneous governance, in Williamson's terms)[45] at the expense of attention to the firm (the world of intentional governance; again, Williamson's term for hierarchical organization).

Of course, informal institutions are important,[46] both independently and in synergy with formal institutions, and the boundary between informal and formal is unclear. In fact, Chapter 3 shows that a method of production of "formal" law in the international system is comparable to the method of production of social norms in domestic systems. Furthermore, formal law often has its greatest social effect outside of formal legal fora.[47] However, given the growth of formal institutions, both in numbers and in competences, in recent years, it seems appropriate to refocus on them. In addition, formal institutions are more susceptible to self-conscious design, and are thus a useful focus for considering the design of institutions.

As noted above, until the 1990s, international organization scholars had all but abandoned the field of formal structure—of formal governance—of international organizations. The new institutional economics, industrial organization, and law and economics literatures paid little attention to international organizations.[48] Although a public choice literature of international organizations developed, applying economic theory to activities of international organizations,[49] this literature did not apply the theory of the firm to the analysis of formal international organizations.[50]

Keohane has applied the theory of the firm to regimes, but instead of responding to his question of why regimes exist, as Coase would, with "transaction costs," Keohane responds with a related, but less general, concept: market failure. "In situations of market failure, economic activities uncoordinated by hierarchical authority lead to inefficient results, rather than to the efficient outcomes expected under conditions of perfect competition."[51] This perspective is exactly the one Coase sought to debunk in his attack on Pigou. "Both the concept of 'market failure' and of 'government failure' are rejected as they correspond to a 'Nirwana' view. There exists in general no ideal market and no ideal government which could remedy the shortcomings of the other decision-making mechanisms in a perfect way."[52] A Coasean perspective would demand to know whether regimes or institutions are affirmatively better than the "market," and would particularize this inquiry by examining specific issues and institutions.

The Market of International Relations Revisited

As discussed above, there is no nirvana, and so neither market failure nor government failure[53] alone has policy ramifications; rather, it is necessary to engage in comparative institutional analysis. Nor is there, in truth, a default option: an institution that should retain power unless it is affirmatively shown that another institution is more efficient. Neither the market nor the state can claim this advantage. Rather, they are each on an equal footing with the firm and international organizations: candidates for allocations of authority.

Having said this, path dependence, network externalities, economies of scale, and economies of scope may argue for concentrating certain types of authority in certain institutions; this is a potential argument for sovereignty of states as we know it.[54] Recall the discussion in Chapter 1 of the source of gains that may motivate exchange in this market and the motivations of states in seeking such gains. This section continues by addressing the issue of the transaction costs occasioned by exchange and the related theory of the firm. It then further explores the market of international relations by examining the extent to which some of the characteristics of private goods markets and private firms are replicated in the market of international relations.

The Costs of Exchange: Transaction Costs

Recall the discussion in Chapter 2 of the transaction cost analysis of jurisdiction. The initial allocation of jurisdiction matters for efficiency purposes because international society, like any other society, is beset by transaction costs. It is costly for states to identify appropriate counterparties, to negotiate with them, to write complete contracts with them, and to enforce those contracts. Whether these transaction costs are disproportionately great in international society, as compared to any particular domestic society, is not clear.

It is worthwhile to relate transaction costs to agency costs.[55] Agency costs may be viewed as the costs of organization within an institution, while transaction costs are the costs of organization in the market. Alternatively, agency costs may be viewed as a type of transaction cost that occurs within an institutional setting; this is the definitional convention used in this chapter (except where agency costs are referenced specifically), in order to facilitate discussion of comparative transaction costs, comparing costs within an institution to costs outside an institution.

The central insight of Coase's two seminal papers involves the importance of transaction costs in economic organization.[56] In fact, the transaction cost focus of Coase's two papers explains institutionalization in the form of the firm as well as in the form of government regulation: it frames the problem as one of comparative institutional analysis, considering all alternative institutions. Coase posited that people use the market or the firm to organize their productive activities, depending on which is the best mechanism, under the circumstances. By "best" in this context, we mean the method that maximizes the positive sum of transaction gains, transaction losses, and transaction costs.

Comparative Institutional Analysis

Thus, Coase's theory of the firm is not exclusively about transaction costs: in fact, the lowest transaction cost solution is not always to be preferred.[57] Rather, the point is that in a zero transaction cost world, infinite exchange would allow perfectly efficient allocation. In a positive transaction cost world (the world as it is),[58] a decision maker might accept some transaction costs in order to enhance gains from trade, or accept reduced gains from trade in order to reduce transaction costs even more. The actual decision depends on the magnitude of each. Komesar[59] calls for a cost-benefit analysis methodology that compares a number of available institutional alternatives to seek the maximum gains from trade net of transaction costs. "Comparative economic organization never examines organization forms separately but always in relation to alternatives."[60]

Using Coase's and Williamson's comparative institutional perspective, and combining it with the public choice analysis of government, Komesar develops a legal methodology of comparative institutional analysis.[61] Komesar expands the domain of comparative institutional analysis to compare market organization to governmental organization. Thus, transaction cost economizing can be used to attack the seemingly impenetrable thicket of arguments between laissez-faire and regulation. This moves our institutional choice question one step up from that addressed by Coase and Williamson. Viewing the market (here inclusive of firms) as a discrete institution, Komesar compares this institution with the institution of domestic government: with regulation. This move up the vertical institutional hierarchy provides a platform from which this chapter may take a further step, to begin to compare national autonomy with international organization along similar lines. Komesar also compares particular types of governmental activity, including adjudication and regulation, using transaction cost analysis.

The Coase Theorem and the Prisoner's Dilemma

The Coase theorem,[62] which has been extensively elaborated and critiqued, though never explicitly articulated as such by Coase himself, indicates that, absent transaction costs, the initial allocation of property rights, including regulation, would not affect efficiency.[63] The reason that this initial allocation would, assuming zero transaction costs, not affect efficiency is that market participants would engage in costless reallocative transactions that would result in an efficient outcome, and all externalities would thus be internalized: no decision maker would fail to take into account all of the costs of his or her decision.[64] Thus, in a zero transaction cost world, an externality, standing alone, would not justify regulation. In our context, an externality, standing alone, justifies neither international law nor international organization.

Assume for a moment an efficient set of international law rules; that is, a structure of laws that satisfies the aggregate preferences of all countries (or their citizens) better than the alternatives. This set of rules maximizes the value of all social resources available to states (it does not necessarily affect private sector efficiency), consistent with value relativity; that is, it accepts each actor's preferences as given, and seeks to maximize their satisfaction. In a zero transaction cost world (without problems of holdouts), this set of entitlements would occur regardless of the initial set of international law rules (if any): actors would costlessly reallocate to the efficient position.[65] Coase's insight applied to international law is that, given that transaction costs exist and are indeed inescapable, the initial set of international law rules specified has important consequences. It is necessary to compare legal and institutional frameworks, including reliance on market mechanisms, to determine which is best. Transaction costs in the market resulting in externalities are not a sufficient reason for regulation; transaction costs in the international relations "market" is not a sufficient reason for regimes or formal organizations.[66] Regulation carries with it transaction costs as well, and both the market and regulation suffer from imperfect allocation. In fact, Coase's insight requires us to compare institutional structures in every case.

An important critique of the Coase theorem asks whether states will ever be able to agree on the distribution of the gains from exchange of authority, or whether they will become mired in endless cycling of negotiation, especially under a zero transaction cost assumption. This is the problem of "holdouts."[67]

Much of the political science literature is skeptical of the possibility for cooperative solutions.[68] Garrett argues that "in situations in which there are numerous potential solutions to collective action problems that cannot easily be distinguished in terms of their consequences for aggregate welfare—and the [EU] internal market is one—the 'new economics of organization' lexicon conceals the fundamental political issue of bargaining over institutional design."[69]

Brennan and Buchanan respond to this criticism by explaining that bargaining over institutional design is cooperative in nature, and that the aggregate increased value will provide incentives for agreement.[70] They compare such constitutional bargaining with "ordinary politics." First, they agree with Garrett and Krasner regarding ordinary politics: "the Pareto-optimal set would be exceedingly large."[71] They continue as follows: "this prospect is dramatically modified, however, when the choice alternatives are not those of ordinary politics but are, instead, rules or institutions within which patterns of outcomes are generated by various nonunanimous decision-making procedures."[72]

The indirectness and broadly reciprocal nature of the distributional consequences of constitutional bargaining erect a Harsanyian veil of uncertainty that provides incentives for agreement on efficient institutions. This veil of uncertainty is limited because those who negotiate constitutions can predict some of the distributive consequences of constitutional-type bargains. This argument suggests that bargaining problems can be overcome in connection with the decision to form an international organization, which can then make decisions in "ordinary politics" terms.

States versus People as Constituents

The central questions in considering whether the theory of the firm may be useful in considering international organizations are twofold. First, are the citizens of the member states the real parties in interest? Second, assuming that the citizens of the member states are the real parties in interest, how does the intermediation of their national governments affect the applicability of the theory of the firm? Both of these questions have to do with the accountability of international organizations.

With respect to the question of whether the citizens of the member states are the real parties in interest, certainly from a normative contractarian, liberal, or cosmopolitan standpoint the answer is an emphatic yes.[73] From a positive standpoint, and from a traditional realist or a modern public choice standpoint, the answer may be no. Much depends on the responsiveness of the relevant state government. Thus, from a positive standpoint, states are neither billiard balls nor simple conduits but, like other institutions, are complex mediating prisms that transmit the interests of individuals at varying speeds, with varying intensities, and with varying degrees of distortion.

From the standpoint of individuals, in addition to their direct functions, states serve as agents for entering into international relations. From the standpoint of the international organization, states may be seen as units of decentralized organization. The cosmopolitan individual-centered perspective, based as it is on contractarian individual choice, raises a perplexing theoretical question about the structure of international organizations. Are international organizations dependent on the consent of all individuals who are citizens of the member states? This question is only different in scale, however, from the question of whether the government of a particular member is dependent on the consent of each individual citizen.[74] Our working assumption is that nations do not themselves have preferences, but simply represent individuals that do.[75]

Accepting the fact that states intermediate, and that state governments generally control the exercise of states' rights, in international organizations (subject to successful claims of a democracy deficit), then the values maximized through transactions are not directly those of individuals, but are the values aggregated through state governments. This chapter does not address the extent of congruence between the values of governments and the values of their citizens. Stated another way, this chapter seeks to address the institutional issues in international organizations; I leave for public choice theorists who address national governments the analysis of institutional issues in states.

Thus, while corporations certainly have structures that differ from those of most international organizations, the structures are at least comparable, allocating competences and rights to make decisions in various ways. There is an extensive corporate governance literature concerning the problem of agency costs and conflicts of interest, attempting to ensure the fidelity of corporate managers to shareholder welfare.[76] The public choice perspective on international organizations exhibits similar concerns regarding the pursuit by (i) national governments, and (ii) their delegates to international organizations, of their own respective interests, rather than citizen interests.

It is important to recall, however, that we are using a comparative institutional analysis. Thus, of course we would like to reduce these agency-type costs, but we must be mindful of the transaction costs of their reduction, and of the availability of institutional substitutes. Thus, while the corporation carries with it agency costs, Coase posited that corporations exist, where they do, because the agency costs are smaller than the alternative transaction costs of the same allocation through the market. The same may well be true of the state as intermediary, on the one hand, and of the international organization, on the other.

Frey and Gygi cite some examples of the types of rules that public choice theory would suggest delegates to international organizations may prefer, which may be inconsistent with the interests of the citizens of their countries. These include rules that require more meetings and travel, rules that allocate quotas of employees to member states, rules that provide the particular international organization with a monopoly in its function, rules that constrain exit from the international organization, and rules that provide financial autonomy to the international organization.[77]

On the other hand, according to Frey and Gygi, citizens want competition among international organizations, with limitations on exclusive jurisdiction—monopoly authority—accorded particular international organizations (see Chapter 6). Similarly, citizens want to ensure ease of exit from the international organization; exit fortifies and serves as a substitute for voice. In order to avoid "mutual assured destruction," citizens want to ensure possibilities for partial exit through rules that allow the unbundling of the public goods provided by the international organization. Citizens are interested in obtaining "fiscal equivalence" by virtue of rules allowing voting in proportion to national contribution: this avoids problems of moral hazard. Finally, citizens prefer election of the governing body of the international organization by a popular vote, enhancing direct accountability.

No one would argue that international organizations and business firms exist for the same purposes. Obviously an international organization does not have profit maximization as a goal.[78] However, this chapter simply argues that they exist as organizations for the same reasons: they are presumed to be more efficient means of achieving their respective purposes than the alternatives.[79] Under Coase's theory of the firm, the purpose of the business firm is to establish a set of relationships more efficiently—in terms of transaction gains net of transaction costs—than operations in the market could. There seems little to distinguish the international organization: this theoretical perspective predicts that international organizations are formed to establish a set of relationships more efficiently than the equivalent of the market in international society. Each member state government maximizes its basket of preferences.

Efficiency

In organizational terms, "an organization is considered to be efficient if the members unanimously accept the general rules under which it operates."[80] This test is comparable to, and derived from, the Pareto efficiency criterion. However,

> Only if individuals' preferences are revealed in markets is the outcome oriented approach consistent with the economic approach because prices and quantities consumed reflect the individuals' voluntary decisions. If the results of voluntary decisions fulfill the commonly accepted Pareto conditions, then the situation is considered to be efficient; Pareto-efficiency thus coincides with efficiency in the constitutional perspective . . . However, international organizations' activities are not valued in markets.[81]

We observe what seems like a critical difference between international organizations and firms: as discussed in Chapter 1, the output of international organizations is not monetized, and the utilities sought through international organizations cannot be aggregated. There is no monetized market that may reveal valuation of particular goods. Thus, the only available test of the Pareto efficiency of the rules of an international organization is whether these rules are accepted by the constituents.[82] In order to be consistent with normative individualism, in fact, the reference should be to individual constituents, rather than states. From a policy perspective, comparative institutional analysis may, given an articulated set of preferences and priorities, indicate the institutional structure that can satisfy those preferences best, as among those institutional structures compared. Thus, the comparative institutional analysis suggested here is designed to inform political discourse, with the ultimate test of efficiency being simply the (tautological) fact of political acceptance of a particular set of rules.

It is important to keep in mind that each institutional solution must fit into a wider institutional structure, including the structure of states themselves, the general international legal system, and the structure of other international organizations. "Although the Paretian approach is piecemeal, over time all the laws may be modified or replaced, just as a ship's carpenter may eventually replace all the planks in the hull while it remains afloat."[83] Indeed, each plank must be checked, and it is likely that a change in one will commend change in others. The magnitude and complexity of this project must give rise to considerations of optimal processes and coordination mechanisms.

Furthermore, what is efficient today depends on what was done in the past. However, bygones are still bygones. What was done in the past is only important for the institutional and technological infrastructure it has left behind. Change must be evaluated in context. The costs of changing to a new system must be worthwhile before an otherwise more efficient structure is substituted for an otherwise less efficient structure.[84] However, the larger point is that a static model of efficiency can and must incorporate path dependency and all other context sensitivities. In this sense, history, to the extent that its effects persist, is no more than another part of the wider existing institutional structure that is the essential reference for determining the efficiency of any particular component institutional structure.[85]

Competitors and Monopoly Power

The competitive environment of international organizations is certainly different from that of business firms. However, international organizations exist in a competitive environment. On a relatively horizontal axis, they compete against other international organizations, against non-governmental organizations (NGOs), and against transnational entities like multinational corporations. On a more vertical axis, they compete against states themselves. They compete not so much for profits, but for responsibility, or authority. Just as a business firm gets more profits when it does well (and, if it wishes, can expand its business), an international organization may receive more authority when it does well. Of course, it may need and demand more funding to fulfill additional responsibilities. Finally, as noted above, the absence of a price system hinders the competitive process and reduces the directness of its discipline. It may not be significant in a substantive sense that an international organization is financially bankrupt or solvent: its mission may be nonpecuniary, and it may therefore be designed to lose money. But it is significant whether an international organization is shirking or abusing its responsibility or carrying out its responsibility inefficiently.

Interestingly, while international organizations may be thought to compete with states for responsibility, they are also vehicles of collusion among states.[86] Chapter 3 utilizes industrial organization research regarding collusion among private persons to analyze the possibility of cooperation among states. However, it is necessary to recognize that cooperation among states—or its pejoratively named twin, collusion—may be efficiency enhancing or efficiency reducing. Under circumstances of beneficial regulatory competition, cooperation among states would reduce efficiency in the provision of public goods.

While cooperation among accountable national executive branches would presumably avoid inefficiency, collusion among executive branches, to the disadvantage of the legislatures and the citizens, might increase inefficiency.[87] This type of potential collusion is a reason for particular concern regarding "democracy deficits." Indeed, international organizations may raise information costs for taxpayers, allowing politicians to favor interest groups more easily.[88] Some have argued that the control of executives over dispute resolution in the WTO, combined with the relative opacity of the WTO dispute resolution process, permits a degree of unconstrained control by the executive that would not be acceptable in the domestic sphere. See Chapter 7.

There is wide scope for competition between international organizations, on the one hand, and substate entities and NGOs, on the other hand, as well as among international organizations. I examine the issue of allocation of authority among international organizations, and competition among international organizations, in Chapter 6. Among international organizations, there are bilateral, regional, multilateral, and functional organizations,[89] and in each of these categories there may be multiple organizations competing for responsibility, or for gain.

Operationalizing the Transaction Cost Theory: Hierarchy in International Relations

This section seeks to examine attempts to operationalize the transaction cost theory, as it applies to institutions. The major problem with generating testable hypotheses is that it is often difficult to measure transaction gains,[90] transaction losses, and transaction costs on a comparative basis. Analysts have developed two basic kinds of responses. First, they have often decided to ignore transaction gains and losses, concentrating their study on transaction costs.[91] For the reasons set out above, this raises serious questions.

Second, they have tried to identify particular transaction profiles associated with particular transaction cost magnitudes, and to associate institutional responses with those transaction cost profiles.[92] For the reasons set forth below, such simplification, too, seems problematic. Rather, this chapter proposes a more particularistic approach, identifying particular institutional components in particular institutional settings, hypothesizing substitute components, and evaluating prospective comparative transaction gains, losses, and costs.

Williamsonian Asset Specificity Applied to International Relations

Williamson focuses on asset specificity as a basis for problems of opportunism and, in turn, as a basis for integration within a firm. This type of problem arises after economic relations are entered, and arises from the fact that one party makes an investment in transaction-specific assets. The classic and perhaps apocryphal example of Fisher Body and General Motors is used to illustrate the utility of vertical integration to safeguard the party required to make the asset-specific investment from opportunistic behavior on the part of the other party.[93] In this example, an asset-specific investment is one that can only realize its full value in the context of continued relations with another party.

Williamson claims that "it is the condition of asset specificity that distinguishes the competitive and governance contracting models. Contract as competition works well where asset specificity is negligible. This being a widespread condition, application of the competitive model is correspondingly broad. Not all investments, however, are highly redeployable."[94]

What makes a particular transaction in international relations "asset specific"? Any transaction where one state advances consideration at a particular point in time, and must rely on one or more other states to carry out their end of the bargain at a later point in time, or experience a significant loss in its expected value, is "asset specific." For example, a state might reduce its trade barriers, including tariff and nontariff barriers. While it might be argued that this is the kind of self-enforcing transaction in which the consideration can be withdrawn, it is often difficult to reestablish trade barriers, and doing so involves political and economic costs. Often the domestic political costs of reducing trade barriers are incurred at the time they are reduced, and perhaps cannot be fully recouped later by reestablishment of the barriers. Second, to the extent that the barriers are reduced on a multilateral basis, under conditions of most favored nation treatment,[95] withdrawal may be made more difficult, as a matter of both international law and domestic politics, not to mention customs administration. In addition, the entry into an international organization itself may have high political costs, again at the outset. It may not be fully possible to be reimbursed for these costs.

Finally, recent attempts to harmonize regulation present a more compelling case of asset specificity. Where a state modifies its domestic regulatory system in pursuit of an internationally agreed plan of harmonization, it is difficult to reverse this course due to defection by another state. On the other hand, it is relatively easy for another state to defect, and it may be difficult to identify and evaluate defection.

Williamson's model does not satisfactorily distinguish among various types of institutionalization, from contract to hierarchy. Here, it becomes important to recognize, as Williamson does, that between market and hierarchy is a broad continuum of "hybrid" structures, including, for example, long-term contracts. Williamson does not, however, establish a predictive relationship between degree of asset specificity, on the one hand, and type of institutionalization, on the other.

As Williamson points out, the obligor can be bound by any of three general categories of structure.

- First, there can be a contractual obligation to make a payment upon failure to give value later ("explicit contract"). The discussion of treaty in Chapter 4 addresses this possibility in the international context.
- Second, where it may be difficult to write an explicit contract, or where only an incomplete and unspecific contract can be justified to be written, an alternative "is to create and employ a specialized governance structure to which to refer and resolve disputes" ("incomplete contract and hierarchy"). "Incomplete contract and hierarchy" may include, or incorporate, firms, common law rules of property or tort, regulation, state action, and international organization. This chapter and Chapter 7 are concerned with this type of governance.
- "Third is to introduce trading regularities that support and signal continuity intentions"[96] ("informal reciprocity").[97] Here, one might add complementarity of transactions: regularities may arise even if the specifics of the transaction differ. One might also add the concept

that institutions may be used to support informal reciprocity, by assisting in the dissemination of information, by defining the requirements of reciprocity, and by more direct action. Chapter 3 is concerned with this type of governance.

These three types of binding mechanism may all be referred to as types of governance or institutionalization: these are simply categories of institutions. "Explicit contract" institutionalizes in very discrete ways, with the presumed use of courts as gap fillers where the contract turns out to be incomplete. "Incomplete contract and hierarchy" is more like a traditional institution or firm, where only broad guidelines are set in advance, and a decision-making procedure is established to complete the contract. Finally, "informal reciprocity" may be specific or diffuse, but is outside of what is typically considered law or contract. As suggested in Chapter 3, it is *implicit* agreement, and it may or may not be designed to take advantage of the default rules and other characteristics of CIL.

Any of these structures may be used to deal with the need to bind others over time. At least the first two, and probably often the third, depend upon a framework of law, including property rights and contract enforcement. The important inquiry is, assuming that surplus arises from a relationship, what is the best mechanism to use to establish the relationship—to maximize the surplus at the lowest transaction cost? There is a rich diversity of binding mechanisms that have been described, including the use of hostages, collateral, hands tying, union, self-enforcing agreements, and regulation.[98] The core issue, of course, is modifying the payoffs from defection.

In order to attempt to develop a predictive theory of economic organization, Williamson identifies and explicates factors responsible for differences among transactions, responsible for different transaction cost profiles, and in turn, responsible for uses of different binding mechanisms.[99] Williamson suggests three main transaction dimensions that may be used to develop a predictive theory of economic organization: asset specificity, uncertainty, and frequency.[100] It is worth noting that asset specificity does not directly give rise to transaction costs, but to potential opportunism. The potential opportunism, in turn, gives rise to the need for binding mechanisms or institutions, which involve transaction costs. However, the greater the asset specificity, the greater will be the incentives for and costs of opportunism, requiring and justifying the expenditure of greater transaction costs and more reliable binding mechanisms. Williamson argues that market transaction is the obvious choice where asset specificity is low.[101] According to this approach, vertical integration becomes attractive where it represents a net transaction cost savings compared to individual transactions in the market.

The choice of binding mechanism depends also on the degree of uncertainty involved: the lesser the uncertainty, the greater the ability to write specific or relatively "complete" contracts to address any uncertainty. The level of complexity of a relationship, and the degree of uncertainty about the future—about the relative future value of the various commitments—combine with the "asset specificity" that characterizes the transaction *ex ante,* to make it increasingly difficult to write complete contracts. Thus, it might be said that complexity and uncertainty amplify asset specificity in this sense. In addition, the more frequent the instances of a particular type of transaction, the greater economies of scale there will be in creating governance structures that address its governance needs. Complementary transactions that have different purposes or terms may have similar effects.

Williamson adds a critical dimension to this model: change. Change in the environment accentuates uncertainty and the incompleteness of contracts. Williamson distinguishes price-based adaptability in the market from coordination-based adaptability in the firm. He links adaptability to asset specificity, finding that in circumstances where there is both frequent need for modification of relationships, especially where prices are not expected to serve as sufficient coordinating statistics, and high levels of asset specificity, hierarchy (firm) may be more responsive than market (contract) forms of relationship.[102]

Uncertainty and complexity make it necessary to do more than simply establish formally realizable rules to govern future situations: they give rise to the need to establish standards to be applied by third parties to particular contexts. Further dimensions of the choice between rules and standards are addressed in Chapter 7. However, as uncertainty and complexity increase, the need to define and delegate categories of authority to bureaucratic, legislative, or dispute resolution type bodies, namely, to establish hierarchy, also increases. These institutional mechanisms are needed in order to determine how standards established by the parties should be applied in future when particular issues arise. In other words, greater integration in the sense of delegation of authority is necessary.

Williamson thus sees transaction cost economizing as the main purpose of vertical integration.[103] Vertical integration is seen as a governance response to a particular set of transaction dimensions, including high asset specificity as the principal factor. With high asset specificity, the value of contracting is increased, but the type of contract—and institution— depends on other factors.

Complete Contracts, Constitutive Documents, and Dispute Resolution

Williamson seeks to link the study of the institutional environment (meaning the general legal context external to particular organizations) to the study of the internal institutions of governance.[104] Perhaps the most salient difference, from a lawyer's perspective, between firms and international organizations is the general legal context in which they exist. Corporations exist in a thick context of domestic law, including contract law and corporate law, but also including all of the law that gives rights to noncontractual stakeholders, like employees, consumers, tort claimants, and statutory claimants under environmental laws. This thick domestic legal context is highly articulated and performs three functions that are critical for our purposes. As described in more detail in the following three paragraphs, it prohibits many forms of coercion, it supplies a reliable and predictable mechanism to complete contracts, and it regulates private relations for the purported general good. More generally, it is a source of rules that are, either mandatorily or facultatively, incorporated in any corporation's set of constitutive rules.

First, this thick domestic legal context prohibits most forms of physical coercion and certain forms of economic coercion, while permitting certain types of economic and psychological influence, such as quantity discounts, or advertising. Compare this with the problem of coercion in the international system.

Second, this body of law may specify the terms of a relationship where the parties have not done so: it may complete contracts. Take the example of a commercial contract governed by New York or English law. In the event of a dispute, the parties would have an extremely detailed body of statutory and common law that has responded to an enormous history of commercial disputes: this body of law performs the function of a set of terms automatically incorporated by reference in the contract. The likelihood that the dispute is not governed by statute or precedent is small, and consequently, the likelihood of proceeding to full litigation is also small. The domestic institutional setting is thick with experience and legislation;

it reflects the choices of a complex and relatively comprehensive society. The international institutional setting is thin by comparison. The international setting is thin both in substance and in procedure, meaning that in the event of a dispute, there will be many uncertainties, regarding both the relationship among different potentially applicable norms, and the procedural issues that can have an outcome-determinative effect.

The role of general law in completing contracts reminds us that no institution is an island: each exists in a broader institutional setting. The broader institutional setting penetrates the institutions at various points, to complete contracts and to supply broader institutional rules where appropriate. Thus, each particular institutional setting is really a complex of interacting institutional settings.

By comparison to firms in a domestic context, international organizations exist in a comparatively thin context of relatively laissez-faire international law with two main types of "law." The first is treaty, which corresponds for our purposes to contract in domestic law. That is, we do not even think of contracts as law emanating from a vertical government in domestic law, but as "private" promises that government will enforce. The second is customary international law (including the customary international law of treaty), which contains little regarding the rights and duties of parties to international organizations and of international organizations themselves: there is no significant body of "corporate law" of international organizations.[105]

Thus, international law is often subject to the problem of incompleteness in a way that domestic contracts are not. Domestic contract disputes always have an answer: "the common law abhors a vacuum." Courts interpret, construct, or leave the loss where it falls. In international treaties, especially those without compromissory clauses,[106] the loss more often stays where it falls, and autointerpretation would be expected to intensify this effect.

An example of an incomplete contract in international relations is the WTO agreement (including the General Agreement on Tariffs and Trade [GATT]). Among other things, WTO law binds tariff levels, prohibits quotas, and establishes national treatment and most favored nation rules of nondiscrimination. However, it does not completely exclude from its operation actions that member states may take to protect the global commons. Thus, when the United States banned Mexican tuna because Mexico did not comply with unilaterally imposed U.S. requirements regarding dolphin-safe fishing, the provisions of GATT that provide exceptions to GATT rules for values like the protection of animal life required interpretation, inter alia, as to whether these provisions could extend to animal life outside the regulating state. The unadopted 1991 dispute resolution panel decision[107] held that they did not, while the unadopted 1994 decision[108] on the same substantive issues was more equivocal. The point is that there were no international environmental rules available effectively to supplement the GATT contract.[109] This has been addressed, to a limited extent, in dispute settlement and treaty writing in the WTO period.

Furthermore, as there was no mandatory dispute resolution process in GATT prior to the 1994 establishment of the WTO, this dispute could have been left entirely to autointerpretation, and would have been decided in the court of power politics and reputation—in the market. Finally, the "weakness" of GATT dispute resolution prior to the establishment of the WTO in 1994 (including Mexico's reluctance to press these issues during NAFTA negotiations) left these respective panel reports unadopted, and ultimately without legal effect.

In a domestic legal system, dispute resolution processes can be relied upon to complete contracts, to the extent that the parties find that either litigation or arbitration is a cost-effective means to implement their rights. In the international legal system, similar reliability can be constructed, but is generally not available. This is not simply another way of referring to the fact that the international legal system is more horizontal than vertical. Rather, it emphasizes the limited array of institutions available in the international legal system. Milgrom, North, and Weingast point out that the medieval law merchant enforcement system "succeeds even though there is no state with police power and authority over a wide geographic realm to enforce contracts. Instead, the system works by making the reputation system of enforcement work better."[110] The system uses formal institutions to supplement an informal mechanism, as described in more detail in Chapter 3.

In the international legal system, public international law serves the function that a constitution serves in the domestic legal system: it is a main component, and governs the production of the remainder, of the institutional environment for international organizations and for states. It provides a limited set of rules regarding the formation of law and its interpretation, application, and enforcement. Thus, it serves as a set of background norms for treaties and other less "constitutional" varieties of customary international law.

To summarize, in international law, there are fewer institutional and legal structures to complete contracts. First, in international law, there is not a very complete body of law that can be applied to supply missing terms to incomplete treaties. Second, in international law, there is generally no dispute resolution tribunal with mandatory jurisdiction. Thus, it is often difficult to rely on the ability to complete contracts through dispute resolution mechanisms. The alternative, of course, is to write comprehensive contracts. Even if this were efficient to do (and presumably it would be more efficient with large international relations issues than with smaller business issues), there is still a problem of enforcement. These problems can be resolved in part through relational contracting, through the multiplication of relationships either in number or over time in order to reduce, through a portfolio technique, the risk of asset specificity in a single relationship. This type of resolution can be expanded by linking transactions with multiple parties.

Summary: Market and Hierarchy

Assuming asset specificity, it may be useful to establish devices to constrain opportunism in order to realize gains from trade, depending on the costs and benefits of these devices. Institutions may be used to constrain opportunism. Institutions entail transaction costs, as do market transactions. Institutions may specify discrete rules, but are, under positive transaction costs, always incomplete. Even the discrete rules are incomplete in their interpretation, application, and enforcement, as well as their relation to one another.

In addition, it is necessary to specify bureaucratic, legislative, or dispute resolution methods of completing incomplete contracts in order to avoid opportunism: to complete the contemplated transaction as "intended." The higher the magnitude of asset specificity, the greater the incentives for opportunism and the greater the need for institutional integration: for the transfer of authority to bureaucratic, legislative, or dispute resolution mechanisms.

Governance in the Market and Governance in Hierarchy: Toward a Dynamic Model of the Relationship between Vertical Federalism and Horizontal Federalism in International Relations

Does it really make a difference whether human activities are organized within a hierarchical environment? It is important to recognize that the boundary between the inside of the box and the outside of the box is quite porous, and the labels "market," "transaction," "firm," and "hierarchy" are gross generalizations. Alchian and Demsetz point out that the firm "has no power of fiat, no authority, no disciplinary action any different in the slightest degree from ordinary market contracting."[111] Indeed, the firm is a "nexus of contracts."[112] We may argue, similarly, that the international organization is a nexus of international legal rules.

Herbert Simon states that "the possibility of using internal division-by-division balance sheets, and internal pricing in negotiation between components of an organization further blurs the boundary between organizations and markets."[113] "The wide range of organizational arrangements observable in the world suggests that the equilibrium between these two alternatives may often be almost neutral, with the level highly contingent on a system's history."[114] On the other hand, Simon recognizes that the existence and effectiveness of large organizations depend on "some adequate set of powerful coordinating mechanisms."[115]

A lawyer can corroborate Simon's perspective by showing that any set of contractual relationships that can be established within a corporation can also be established by various contractual devices, and vice versa: any market structure can be recreated, with some difficulty, within the firm. The Coasean theory of the firm does not address the internal governance of the firm, but transaction cost economics does. "The coordination problem is not solved by merely putting a nonmarket form of organization in place. . . . Instead, it is transformed into a problem of management."[116] Similarly, the problem of international transactions in authority is not solved merely by putting an international organization in place.

Thus, it makes little sense to consider the market versus hierarchy decision in isolated terms; rather, within this broad and densely overlapping organizational structure, particular points must be evaluated to determine what type of relationship fits best at that point. As noted above, there is a theoretical fungibility between market contract relations and internal relations within a hierarchical structure. In fact, these things are theoretically indistinct.

Furthermore, transaction costs outside the firm and "agency costs" within the firm are indistinct, and, of course, will exist concurrently in many circumstances. The important question is how to minimize these costs of relationship. While no device is the presumptive winner, it is possible for network externalities, path dependence, and economies of scope to support some degree of uniformity of outcome.

Subsidiarity: Intrafirm Centralization and Decentralization

Thus far, this chapter has been concerned largely with the delegation of responsibilities to international organizations from the perspective of a sovereign state that, until such delegation, retains plenary power. There appears to be little difference in theory between this question and the question of subsidiarity: once an international organization exists, and has plenary power (albeit cabined within limited authorizations), what powers should it exercise at the center, and what powers should it devolve to decentralized units? All other things being equal, the question remains, where should responsibility be lodged?

Thus, the transaction cost approach described above is applicable to the question of centralization or decentralization within an international organization. The industrial organization literature perspective on decentralization is similar to the perspective associated with the principle of subsidiarity: "Adapting well to changing local circumstances, using local information well, saving on the costs of information transfer, and making effective use of scarce central management time and attention all argue for pushing decision-making power and responsibility as far down in the organization as possible."[117] The ability of an international organization to decentralize appropriately will be a factor in its ability to compete for responsibility.[118]

Indeed, the question of centralization versus decentralization must be answered in synergy with the question of intergovernmentalism versus integration. That is, as a state delegates responsibility to an international organization, it must consider how the international organization will carry out that responsibility, in terms of centralization or decentralization. "In a system with both centralized and decentralized decisions, the centralized decisions serve to define the parameters of the decentralized ones and to put constraints on the local decision makers."[119]

Therefore, when authority is delegated to an international organization, it is necessary to ask how that authority will be exercised: what is the decision-making process within the international organization? International organizations may be delegated authority, but the internal decision-making process may recreate the "market" of international relations, for example by requiring unanimity prior to action. Thus, there are two types of intergovernmentalism: intergovernmentalism outside the walls of an institution and intergovernmentalism within an institution. Why bring intergovernmentalism within an institution? The institutional context may bring various benefits in terms of facilitation, commitment, and legitimation.

In a more complex way, the possibility for various internal decision processes makes the choice between integration and intergovernmentalism a choice along a continuum, instead of a stark binary choice. Thus, an international organization may be accorded responsibility for a particular issue area as a whole, while the decision-making structure preserves intergovernmentalism in some respects,[120] and allows greater integration in other respects. In this sense, the structure of horizontal federalism—relations between legislatures, executives, and judiciaries—may replicate or complement vertical federalism, that is, relations between the center and the components.[121]

As mentioned above, the "firm" is a gross way of referring to a number of specific characteristics of organization. This perspective describes the corporation as a nexus of contracts. At any given point in time, each of these contracts is an incomplete contract. To the extent that they are incomplete, they may be completed with respect to particular issues by four possible means: (i) exercise of residual control (to the extent residual control has been assigned), (ii) renegotiation by consensus, (iii) decision by majority voting, and (iv) dispute resolution. It is worthwhile here briefly to distinguish these different means.

Exercise of residual control is the means emphasized by Hart and Grossman for "completing" incomplete contracts. Yet in some cases and to specified extents, residual control is shared. Thus, to the extent of retained state sovereignty, each state holds residual control. To the extent of delegated responsibility to an organization, residual control may be assigned to the legislative organs of the organization. In the event of ambiguity or lack of specification, residual control is either (i) back in the hands of the states, subject to text-based arguments by other states under a rule of autointerpretation; or (ii) in the hands of such dispute resolution tribunal as may be created and assigned jurisdiction.

Renegotiation by consensus is equivalent to voting under a rule of unanimity. Assuming two parties, they are in a position of bilateral monopoly.[122] Another way of describing a rule of unanimity is that it requires Pareto-efficient action,[123] and makes it more difficult to move to potential Pareto improvements, unless actual compensation arrangements may be made. See the discussion in Chapter 4 of problems of formation of coalitions to produce public goods. Rules of unanimity may still allow potential Pareto improvements under circumstances where multiple issues are covered, so that there is room for creation of "basket deals."[124] This requires multiple issues and issue linkage, which involve transaction costs. The question before us is how do these transaction costs compare with those raised by majority voting, and how do the respective deadweight losses compare?

Majority voting, including qualified majority voting,[125] is associated with a derogation of sovereignty, as it entails a willingness to accept a resolution of a future issue without consent of each state.[126] Majority voting is thus also associated with integration, while rules of unanimity are associated with intergovernmentalism.

In corporate law, Easterbrook and Fischel suggest that voting rights generally flow to the constituencies that comprise the main residual claimants: generally shareholders, but at times of financial distress, perhaps bondholders or preferred stockholders.[127] This would align residual control with residual financial responsibility.[128] In the international organization context, this is an argument for maintaining residual control in the member states, or in their citizens. It is an argument for assigning residual control to the member states because the member state governments are generally viewed as having full responsibility for the welfare of their constituents, and therefore experience residual responsibility.

Finally, dispute resolution entails derogation of sovereignty of a different type. It assumes that the contract has specified some standards, explicitly or implicitly, for reference in determining particular issues that arise. As discussed above, dispute resolution is a central means for completing incomplete contracts, on an *ex post* basis.

Williamson points out that while integration may result in the ability to resolve disputes by fiat, the ability to resolve disputes by fiat gives rise to uncertainty regarding the possibilities for intervention, diminishing "high-powered incentives."[129] While "high-powered incentives" may not translate well from corporate affairs to international law, one possible interpretation may be in terms of a chill over appropriate national regulation. In international dispute settlement, the development over time of a set of jurisprudential principles may reduce this type of uncertainty. For example, in the field of foreign investment law under NAFTA, the possibility of intervention in domestic environmental prerogatives by a dispute settlement tribunal pursuant to Chapter 11 of NAFTA may have loomed large early in NAFTA's life, and may in some instances have caused legislators to tread too warily, but this risk was substantially reduced by a set of decisions over time that showed that these tribunals would not intervene excessively. Dispute resolution may also serve to provide neutral interpretations of obligations that can feed the process of reputation-based relations.[130]

Methodology

Given the difficulties in operationalizing the theory of the firm described above, this chapter must be modest in its approach to methodology. From a positive standpoint, the theory suggested here would indicate a full methodology that calculates, on a comparative basis, the sum of the following factors for particular institutional structures: (i) gains from the transaction; (ii) losses from the transaction, including losses of flexibility or autonomy; and (iii) transaction costs. From a normative standpoint, as suggested earlier in this work, it would seek to maximize the present value of net gains.

The most direct methodology would choose a particular institutional context, establish a comparative foil, and calculate each of the factors listed above. If substituting the comparative foil for the status quo would increase net gains, a normative perspective would recommend change.

This methodology requires the quantification, or at least the estimation of magnitudes, of these difficult factors that, especially in the international intergovernmental sector, would generally not be monetized. Further theoretical and empirical work will be required in order to determine whether a simplified or truncated analysis, perhaps focusing only on transaction costs, would yield useful results.

Empirical work might be used to determine whether there are general categories of high asset specificity or high transaction cost transactions, and whether it is possible empirically to associate particular institutional solutions with those transactions. A pattern of such association might be instructive. In particular, it would be useful to test whether transactions characterized by a high degree of asset specificity are associated with higher degrees of transfer of authority to international organizations. "The basic strategy for deriving refutable implications . . . is this: Transactions, which differ in their attributes, are assigned to governance structures, which differ in their organizational costs and competencies, so as to effect a discriminating (mainly transaction cost economizing) match."[131]

Of course, as a practical matter, all policy decisions should be comparative, so the only real question is how formal and how precise each comparison shall be. Perhaps the problem of operationalization may be resolved through narrow definition of the institutions evaluated. Given sufficiently narrow definition, a full transaction cost and transaction benefits analysis, and comparison, may be performed. The next question, of course, is how will a narrow perspective be used to make policy: how will a series of narrow perspectives be combined to form a policy regarding a broader institution?

Thus, the method indicated by the above theory is comparative institutional analysis.[132] In most social science, and in law in particular, there is no laboratory—no place in which all other factors can be held constant, and a particular regulatory device evaluated. Rather, the laboratory most available to law is the comparative or historical method.[133] This laboratory provides historical or comparative settings for evaluation of law or regulation. Cappelletti, Seccombe, and Weiler describe the utility of the comparative method as follows.

> Comparative legal analysis will then be brought to "evaluate" laws, institutions and techniques in relation to that particular problem and need. This approach represents, in a real way, a "Third School" of legal thinking, different both from mere positivism, for which law is a pure datum not subject to evaluation, and from evaluation of such datum based on abstract, airy, inevitably subjective criteria such as "natural law" principles.[134]

Thus, the methodology is necessarily inductive, rather than deductive. Of course, this does not mean that every possible institutional matrix must be subjected to evaluation. Rather, the social scientist's art is deductively to choose institutional structures for evaluation that are likely to yield useful results, to engage in a type of triage of evaluation. Such selective evaluation is a type of rational ignorance, based on the presumption that it economizes on search and evaluation costs.

As we engage in selective evaluation, we must recognize that the range of possible comparative foils is infinite. There are three types of comparative foil. The first is cross-jurisdictional, as in horizontal comparative law.[135] This type of comparison could include, for example, evaluation of particular European Union institutions for use in NAFTA, or the WTO. The cross-jurisdictional category might also include domestic law foils for international law evaluation. For example, is the U.S. Commerce Clause a good model for application to regulatory nontariff barriers in the international setting?[136]

A second category of comparative foil is historical, or diachronic.[137] For example, does the organization of the Roman Empire hold lessons for current efforts toward European economic integration?[138] The historical and cross-jurisdictional may be combined: should NAFTA use some of the institutional devices that have been successful within the European Union? Finally, and most flexibly, the comparative foil may be constructed. While there is little that is new under the sun, a particular device may, and often should, be a hybrid, custom designed for a particular use.

It is worth noting that comparison may be either qualitative or quantitative. It may utilize case studies and juxtapose them, or it may utilize regression analysis that has the capability to juxtapose numerous cases. There is an extensive and growing literature using regression analysis to compare a variety of features of domestic law, and one of its signal characteristics is that lawyers have not participated: it is comparative law without the lawyers.[139]

The first, and perhaps most difficult, problem of measurement relates to the assessment of transaction gains. Some types of gains will be more amenable to measurement than others. Any cost-benefit methodology would obviously be incomplete without considering all costs, as well as all benefits. In connection with analysis of international institutions, it is necessary to consider both the benefits of greater control over the autonomy of other states, and the costs of giving up autonomy.

The Matrix of Choice

In the context of international relations, we might begin to categorize the available choices of institutions, as depicted in Table 5.1.

Of course, each of the categories listed in Table 5.1 contains great diversity; the true matrix for institutional choice is infinite. All sorts of combinations and hybrids are possible, and adaptation from other institutional settings is possible. "Because comparison necessarily involves a common metric, it suggests the interchangeability of techniques that are now associated with a specific institution."[140]

There are multiple types of international action. Unilateralism amounts to operations in the "market," which may grow to development of customary rules or comity, based on reciprocity. Bilateralism allows for development of contract-type rules, but not third-party-type legitimation or supervision, except where dispute resolution or other institutions are created in order to fulfill this function. Regionalism allows greater commitment, and may engender the development of institutions, like those of the European Union,

Table 5.1 Institutional choice

Degree of Legal Integration	Private Sector	Domestic Government	International Government
Competition (absence of cooperation)	Competition	Regulatory competition and externalization; failure to produce public goods	Regulatory competition and externalization; failure to produce public goods
Spontaneous cooperation	Spot market	Uninstitutionalized transactions in power among decentralized units of government	Uninstitutionalized transactions in power among states, perhaps including customary international law
Contractual (including firms and organizations as nexus of contracts)	Contract	Regulatory agreements or federal action	International agreements or centralized action
Judicial (assumes contractual relation)	Arbitration—private interest litigation	Judicial—public interest litigation	Dispute resolution
Legislative (assumes contractual relation)	Firm governance	Legislative	Majority voting

with independent power. Regionalism also includes as a potential sanction the ability to exclude. Multilateralism also allows greater commitment, through the power of potential multilateral responses to breach.

Within each of these branches, the choice of the more integrationist approach entails additional choices of (i) the degree of centralization or decentralization, and (ii) rules versus standards applied by institutions.

Finally,

> Williamson's demonstration that the firm/transaction choice is highly complex impacts the institutional choice between market and regulation by raising the cost of regulation. . . . The relevance of any of these insights, however, can only be determined by integrating them into an institutional choice different than the intra-market institutional choice upon which Williamson focused.[141]

This is an argument for functionalism and against idealism. It argues that the choice of integration is a difficult one, and that integration from above, without the full political process endorsing integration from below (analogous to regulation in this context), will require a costly analysis.

Constitutional Moments

Constitutional economics brings a positive analytical perspective to constitutions, including the constitutions of international organizations. Under this approach, constitutions are simply instruments of human interaction: mechanisms by which to share authority in order to facilitate the establishment of rules. Constitutional rules are not natural law; instead, they are political settlements designed to maximize the achievement of individual citizens' preferences. In a transaction cost or strategic model, constitutions are designed to overcome transaction costs or strategic barriers to Pareto-superior outcomes.

Thus, from this perspective, if there were no potential value to be obtained from cooperation, constitutions would be unimportant, and would not exist. Constitutions exist to resolve transaction costs and strategic problems that would otherwise prevent the achievement of efficient exchanges of authority. Where there is value to be obtained by agreement, constitutions may be used to facilitate the realization of this value by reducing transaction costs and strategic costs, such as the problem of states holding out or defecting from their commitments.

Constitutional economics recognizes the possibility of constitutional moments. A "constitutional moment" in the Buchanan and Tullock[142] sense is an historical moment at which a Harsanyian "veil of uncertainty" allows individuals, or in our case states, to agree on constitutional change even though they are uncertain of the possible future implications. In fact, it is the uncertainty that facilitates agreement. Constitutional moments generally result from a shift in the concerns, or perception of concerns, of constituents. This perspective explains agreement to secondary rules: rules such as majority voting regimes, or allocations of authority, that determine the ability to make primary rules that actually govern behavior. In this theoretical perspective, states would agree on new secondary rules where they are certain enough that they will be benefited in the aggregate, but uncertain about how much of the benefit they may capture.

Constitutional change would be expected to occur when there are shifts in state preferences, shifts in the technological or institutional means to achieve those preferences, or shifts in states' perceptions of these things. What types of shifts might result in a future constitutional moment at the WTO? It is difficult to say, but issues such as increasing public awareness and concern about the WTO, and pressures from other global interests including environmental protection, human rights and health, increasing concern regarding global poverty and the role of trade, and fear of terrorism, could contribute to a tectonic movement at the WTO.

To summarize, constitutional economics sees constitutions as devices to enhance achievement of preferences. The task of framers of constitutions, and of analysts, is to engage in comparative institutional analysis—even if the reference is historical or hypothetical—in order to determine which institutional features will maximize the net achievement of preferences. So, each of the other components of constitutionalization is harnessed to this same task.

Constitutional Bargains I: Legislative Jurisdiction and Voting Rules in the Single European Act

One of the two most significant constitutional changes in European Union history is the Single European Act (SEA) of 1986, which facilitated the "completion" of the single-market project.[143] The major constitutional change made by the SEA[144] was to permit qualified majority voting in cases that, despite language in the original Treaty of Rome to the contrary, had been addressed by voting according to what amounted to a requirement for unanimity.[145] I consider only voting in the Council, and do not consider here the important collateral effects of the cooperation procedure established in the SEA and the co-decision procedure enacted under the 1992 Treaty on European Union (TEU), or of judicial review.[146]

How does the SEA fit into this chapter's theory? In this case, at least one goal was clearly to reduce deadweight losses due to barriers to trade at the private level, which were viewed as deadweight losses at the public level. The Cecchini Report attested to the potential reduction of private deadweight losses that creating the internal market was expected to achieve.[147] Of course, the Cecchini Report only considered one dimension of deadweight losses: those from lost trade in goods and services because of regulatory and other barriers to trade and investment ("private sector deadweight losses"). However, private sector deadweight losses flow only indirectly into the analysis suggested in this chapter, which considers gain and loss to the state. We may call the losses from failure to enter into otherwise useful intergovernmental agreements "public sector deadweight losses." From the state's standpoint, private sector deadweight losses are partially reflected in public sector deadweight losses.

The Cecchini Report did not consider a potential countervailing source of deadweight losses: deadweight losses in the domestic public sector arising from restrictions on the ability of member states to regulate so as to maximize local preferences ("regulatory losses"). However, member states were certainly wary that the move to majority voting necessary to achieve the single market would bring about some measure of regulatory deadweight losses.

Thus, one formulation of a hypothesis would be the following: the voting provisions of the SEA were designed to reduce transaction costs associated with voting for single-market measures, in order to facilitate transactions in governmental authority in Europe, and thereby diminish public sector deadweight losses, in an amount greater than the concomitant regulatory deadweight losses. This hypothesis raises difficult issues of quantification, especially in connection with regulatory losses. However, we will not seek to quantify these values. In order to evaluate this hypothesis in an indicative sense, we will examine the history of the SEA to determine if it was motivated by reduction of transaction costs in order to diminish public sector deadweight losses.

It is worth noting that the modification we are considering—the move to majority voting—occurred within a complex context. One reading of the Luxembourg Compromise, which the SEA was thought to "reverse," would read it simply as an informal waiver of a treaty provision, at a time when states were unlikely to comply in any event: it sometimes makes sense to change agreements. It is an "order despite law"[148] story. The Luxembourg Compromise shows the resilience of the problem of allocation of power, and the use of multiple temporizing and adjusting devices to manage the problem, for the Luxembourg Compromise is part of a package of tools with then Article 100A(4) (now Article 95(4)) of the Treaty of Rome added by the SEA, with the principle of subsidiarity added in Article 3b (now Article 5) by the TEU, and with other legal and political devices. Some commentators have pointed out that when the SEA was implemented, facilitating legislative action, the European Court of Justice backed away from its previously powerful integrationist tilt.[149]

These tools, together or in series, as the case may be, show an exceedingly complex vertical allocation of power. They also illustrate how residual control may be divided in subtle and ambiguous terms. A picture of institutional flow and autonomous adaptation begins to emerge. This adaptability makes static formal institutional analysis suspect, and requires a subtle evaluation of the actual use of institutions in context, as well as the process of institutional change.

Historical Background

The original 1957 Treaty of Rome was, given its monumental function, a brief document, a *traité cadre*. It is an intentionally and in some cases unintentionally incomplete contract, with several potential completion devices. First, the European Court of Justice is assigned various types of limited jurisdiction to interpret and apply the treaty.[150] Second, various kinds of amendments and substantive legislation are authorized.[151] In this chapter, I will concentrate on legislation. The Treaty of Rome permits legislation by "directives," which emerged as the principal legislative tool of the builders of the single market. Not only was the original Treaty of Rome intended to grow by interpretation and legislation, but it also had provisions for phased integration. The example relevant here is the several provisions that provided for majority voting to commence on January 1, 1966, on certain issues.

This is not the place to write the history of the 1966 Luxembourg Compromise.[152] President Charles de Gaulle of France refused to accept the agreed transition at January 1, 1966, to majority voting under several provisions, including Article 101, of the Treaty of Rome, arguing that France's power and interests had changed.[153] The crisis over this refusal abated on January 29, 1966, when the Luxembourg Compromise was adopted.[154] As a result, majority voting was not adopted as planned, and was not in effect until the passage of the SEA.

The Luxembourg Compromise recorded the French view that a member state could invoke "vital national interests" as a basis for declining to proceed to a vote (by majority). Of course, what was accepted as available to the French had to be available to all. Until 1982, it was also accepted that "vital national interests" was to be defined by the dissenting state: *competenz-competenz*, in this legislative sense, was in the hands of the member states individually.[155]

Under a rule of unanimous voting, it is still possible to make compromises: to persuade another not to exercise its veto, or to construct a package deal. In order to do so, of course, it is necessary to provide a bribe of some valuable concession. Often in this context, the bribe would be in the form of a countervailing agreement not to veto, in a vote of similar importance, or possibly in some combination of matters. Cobbling together such barter transactions entails significant transaction costs: (i) the cost of searching for a partner, (ii) the cost of identifying appropriate "bribe" issues, (iii) the cost of negotiating the transaction, and (iv) the cost of enforcing the transaction.[156]

In addition, under a rule of unanimous voting, a national government gets no political cover for European Union decisions, and in Abbott and Snidal's terms, no ability to "launder"[157] national policy through European Union decisions. The national government cannot claim to have been outvoted. Where the national government might like to barter away an issue, a rule of unanimity requires it to do so explicitly: it must tell its domestic constituents that it "sold them out." Under a rule of majority voting, on the other hand, it can report credibly that the issue was beyond its control, and blame its partners and the Brussels bureaucrats. "Laundering" entails the ability to effect at the international political level what is otherwise too costly in political terms at the national level.[158]

Finally, unanimous voting restricts the subject areas that may be addressed: the fact that a particular state would veto action in that subject area is a complete bar to action.

The SEA as a New Constitutional Bargain

The voting reforms of the SEA were seen as an "improvement" in the European Union's capacity to legislate. "One way to view 1992 is as a move to reduce costs associated with self-enforcing agreements based on linkages and hostages by replacing bilateralism with an alternate governance structure: minilateralism."[159] Certainly history has shown a great acceleration of legislation after the implementation of the SEA, although this acceleration could have been caused by political factors that would have existed without the SEA. In other words, it is at least possible to view the SEA as simply mimicking "underlying" political realities: the need to complete the internal market. This chapter will not show the causal link between the voting reforms and the legislation, but will seek to show that the causal link was expected by those who negotiated the SEA.[160]

Of course, the development of the SEA itself was largely intergovernmental, with the power and interests of states as the determinants of its shape and success. Moravcsik refers to the SEA as "intergovernmental institutionalism."[161] The institutionalism referred to here is the role of the centralized institutions, including the Commission and its then president, Jacques Delors. After "France moved into the German and Benelux camp in arguing for more majority voting to allow the completion of the Single Market," Delors jumped on this bandwagon.[162]

Thus, states and the existing transnational mechanism militated toward majority voting, recognizing that this would facilitate further substantive agreement. In part as a response to economic and political "eurosclerosis," the member states developed a consensus toward majority voting. "At their Milan session in mid-1985, the European Community heads of government agreed to a negotiating conference to amend the Treaty for this and other purposes."[163]

> The revival of a supranational style of decision making and the strengthening of European institutions in the Single Act resulted most immediately from decisions by governments to press, in their own interests, for a removal of internal economic barriers and for institutional changes that would permit such a policy to be carried out.[164]

As noted above, the change made by the SEA was intricate, especially in light of then Article 100A(4) of the Treaty of Rome, which tempered the increased integration otherwise provided by the SEA, but in a different institutional dynamic that constrains state discretion procedurally.[165] Thus, the agreement to Article 100A(4) in the SEA, and the persistence of the Luxembourg Compromise, might be viewed as capping the cost to states of regulatory deadweight losses: these institutional features were designed to provide an escape clause in case the cost of regulatory deadweight losses became too high. The TEU provisions on subsidiarity and the post-Maastricht revulsion from centralized control may be viewed also as reactions to the centralizing impetus of the SEA.

The Maximizing Calculus

We might begin to summarize, in a very rough and tentative way, the comparative gains from the SEA, as described in Table 5.2.

The point of this section is that states appear, roughly, to have made this type of calculus in their decision to move to majority voting in the SEA. The persistence of the Luxembourg Compromise may be understood as a contingent limit on centralized decision making, protecting member states from excessive intervention.

Table 5.2 Comparative analysis of gains from SEA transaction

	Pre-SEA	Post-SEA
Gains from transaction (from international agreement)	Public sector deadweight losses due to inability to engage in transactions in authority due to transaction costs: failure to achieve gains from trade	Significant: Cecchini Report
Losses from transaction (production costs or opportunity costs)	n/a	Regulatory deadweight losses capped by Article 100A(4) and by the persistent Luxembourg Compromise
Transaction costs	High transaction costs of barter and problems of enforcement of political agreements	Reduced on a per-transaction basis due to ability to bind dissenters; reduced holdout problems and increased ability to make exchange
Net gains from transaction	Zero—status quo	Positive

Constitutional Bargains II: Defection, Dispute Resolution, and New Issues in the World Trade Organization

A persistent problem in the GATT-WTO system has been the fear of defection.[166] Fear of defection may provide disincentives for agreement *ex ante*, and may provide incentives for preemptive defection *ex post*. Inability to bind the other leaves trade partners in the prisoner's dilemma, unable to resolve the dilemma through cooperation. Often the result has been unilateralism, especially as exercised by the United States through Section 301 of the Trade Act of 1974. Unilateralism is combined with autointerpretation, allowing might to make right in international relations.

Enhanced dispute resolution may increase the willingness of states to accept rules as concessions, because it reduces the costs of enforcement.[167] The extension of dispute resolution also can result in greater completion of contracts: contracts that benefit from effective dispute resolution mechanisms implicitly leave less room for opportunism or holdout strategies by virtue of incompleteness. Furthermore, as seen in the Uruguay Round, enhanced dispute resolution provides incentives for states to renounce, at least in part, unilateralism and autointerpretation. On the other hand, enhanced dispute resolution may cause states to feel that they lose control of outcomes—so there is an agency cost associated with enhanced dispute resolution.

How might this example of change be explained by the theoretical perspective advanced in this chapter? As with the SEA, at least one goal of the Uruguay Round was to reduce deadweight losses due to barriers to trade at the private level, which were viewed as deadweight losses at the public level.[168]

Here, theory would predict that states would design institutions that are expected to facilitate the entry into and enforcement of agreements. The pre-WTO dispute settlement arrangement might have been expected to deter further agreements, based on apprehension on the part of states that the commitments of others are not reliable, and thus do not justify their own investment in compliance. This is a problem of high asset specificity without congruent institutions to enforce agreements. It is also a problem of incomplete contracts, especially in regard to "new" issues, such as trade and intellectual property rights and trade and environment. It is a problem of transaction costs insofar as the cost of designing unilateral or bilateral arrangements for enforcement may be more costly than the potential gains from trade. Thus, "stronger" dispute resolution arrangements can address asset specificity, can complete contracts, and can reduce the transaction costs of entry into and enforcement of commitments. On the other hand, stronger dispute resolution might make states more cautious about the commitments they undertake. Finally, as mentioned in Chapter 4, enhanced dispute resolution, combined with a requirement of exclusivity of use, may reduce the scope of unilateralism.

Historical Background

As is now well understood and the subject of much commentary, the Uruguay Round brought a dramatic shift in the structure of dispute settlement in international trade.[169] Prior to the establishment of the WTO, and its Understanding on Rules and Procedures Governing the Settlement of Disputes (DSU), GATT dispute settlement suffered from many significant weaknesses. Chief among the perceived weaknesses was the fact that consensus among the members of the GATT Council (the full membership) was required in order for the report of a dispute resolution panel to be accorded legal effect.[170] Thus, the loser had the ability to block consensus adoption of a panel report, and often did so or temporized sufficiently to undermine the effectiveness of the process. This problem, combined with others, made GATT dispute resolution less attractive, and less reliable, as a method of interpreting or completing the incomplete contract of GATT, or simply of enforcing relatively clear obligations. It encouraged members like the United States to "go unilateral" using Section 301 of the Trade Act of 1974 and other authorization of unilateral action under domestic law to "take the law into their own hands." After a comprehensive study of GATT dispute resolution from 1948 to 1989, Robert Hudec concludes as follows:

> The record of positive results in almost nine out of ten cases has obviously been high enough to induce governments to use the dispute settlement system extensively, and to invest considerable political capital in trying to strengthen it further. At the same time, however, the failure rate of 12 percent has served as a vivid warning that it is a new and primitive legal order, one that is still some distance away from being able to impose its order on all major problems.[171]

The change made in the 1994 DSU was to reverse the consensus rule: panel decisions are now adopted automatically unless rejected by consensus.[172] On the other side, Article 23 of the DSU forbids unilateral action in dispute resolution, at least where the complaint is for violation or nullification or impairment of benefits under a WTO agreement.

During the earlier stages of the Uruguay Round negotiations, the United States and Canada staked out a position that panel reports should be adopted automatically.[173] The European Union and Japan favored the status quo.[174] On the other hand, the United States resisted a commitment not to take unilateral action, while the European Union, Canada, and Japan sought such a commitment. "The issue would boil down to whether a greatly strengthened and broadened GATT dispute settlement procedure would be sufficient to induce the United States to back off or at least greatly restrain its unilateral approach for dealing with unfair trade practices."[175] The cost of autointerpretation and unilateralism, of course, is the possibility that unilateral action is used as a vehicle for defection, or that it is seen as such. On the other hand, the United States and other countries were concerned regarding the possible threat to sovereignty that effective dispute resolution might pose. As with the SEA, the strengthened WTO dispute resolution system required some substitute safeguards in order to be acceptable, including a new appellate review process.[176]

The Maximizing Calculus

We might begin to summarize, in a very rough and tentative way, the comparative gains expected from the WTO DSU, as described in Table 5.3.

Again, the point of this section is that states appear to have made this calculus in connection with the move to enhanced dispute resolution in the WTO. This chapter lacks a substantial empirical foundation, and the examples provided above are mere sketches of plausible accounts.

Toward a Progressive Research Program
in International Integration

The foregoing analysis incorporates the following hypotheses regarding transactions between states and institutional choice:

(i) Cooperation (trade in power) will occur when the gains from trade in power exceed the sum of the losses from trade plus transaction costs: when net gains are positive. This formula, of course, applies to all international transactions, including those effected by custom and treaty.

Table 5.3 Comparative analysis of gains from DSU transaction

	Pre-DSU	Post-DSU
Gains from transaction (from international agreement)	Deadweight losses due to problems with binding commitments; diminished willingness to comply and to enter into new commitments; unilateralism provides possibilities for defection or perceptions of defection	Positive: permitted acceptance of Uruguay Round package, with significant coverage of new areas, and reduction of possibilities for defection
Losses from transaction (production costs or opportunity costs)	n/a	Opportunity costs arising from more enforceable restrictions on national action, although these costs are capped by lack of direct effect of WTO law in many states, and ability to accept retaliation; diminished by establishment of procedure for appellate review
Transaction costs	High transaction costs of enforcing agreements	Reduced transaction costs due to use of mandatory multilateral interpretation and legitimation of enforcement
Net gains from transaction	Zero—status quo	Positive

(ii) States design international institutions to maximize net gains, subject to information and strategic constraints.

(iii) High magnitudes of asset specificity suggest high levels of institutionalization.

Maximization of gains is by necessity a comparative institutional analytic process. A progressive research program would operationalize these hypotheses in specific factual settings, developing falsifiable hypotheses in those settings, and then testing them. There are significant theoretical issues to be addressed, as well as an infinite number of institutions to be evaluated.

The transaction cost methodology has a number of limitations.[177] First, it is often by necessity crude and indeterminate. Its analytical approach requires that pieces of intricately interconnected structures be hived off for separate comparative analysis. Not only must institutional components be separated from one another, but they also must be separated for analytical purposes from the noninstitutional components of the phenomenon: the preferences and production cost structure. "Observed situations represent a combination of underlying circumstances and institutional responses."[178]

Finally, there is the difficulty of measurement of transaction costs and benefits. It may be possible to use (and to measure) transaction cost proxies, such as asset specificity, uncertainty, and frequency, but only further empirical research will tell us whether these types of proxies can be reliable. Is monetization useful, and should it be pursued as a policy objective? Tradeable permits in pollution or other international public goods might begin to develop greater monetization. Greater monetization might also reduce transaction costs by reducing the need for barter, or for complex barter, and by allowing value to be stored and transported from one time to another. Similarly, it might be useful to develop measures of integration, as in corporate analysis.[179] Once measures of integration are in place, it may be possible to evaluate the relationship between different levels of integration and particular governance structures.

Conclusion

This chapter has added an institutional dimension to the discussion of allocation of jurisdiction in Chapter 2, and has added a transaction cost dimension to the discussion of customary international law and treaty in Chapters 3 and 4, respectively. It provides a framework for understanding when international organizations might appear, and how the internal mechanisms of organizations might be determined. In Chapter 6, I discuss the relationships among different international organizations, and how these "horizontal relationships" relate to the more "vertical" analysis provided so far.

The maximization approach described in this chapter—maximizing gains from trade in power or authority, net of losses from trade and transaction costs—encounters significant problems of operationalization. However, two routes appear promising. First, it appears that the selection of institutional features for analysis should seek relatively discrete and limited institutional features, amenable to calculation of gains from trade, losses from trade, and transaction costs. Second, it seems appropriate to analyze further, and test empirically, the relationship between high asset specificity and depth of integration.

This chapter has suggested that international organizations, and less articulated institutions, may, under appropriate transaction cost circumstances, provide the means to capture greater gains from intergovernmental "trade": from transactions in power. From a positive standpoint, it has hypothesized that states design institutions to maximize the results of these transactions. From a normative standpoint, it has argued that this is indeed the measure of an institution's effectiveness, and the metric for designing efficient institutions.

Here, for purposes of simplicity, efficiency is defined in terms of maximization of state government preferences, without regard directly to the preferences of individual constituents. This separation must be recognized to be artificial, but arises from the need to analyze discrete institutions. Once discrete institutions are analyzed, perhaps analyses may be stitched together. In this regard, it seems that the design of international organizations would have significant effects on the design of states, and vice versa. A staged programmatic research program must be structured to perform this work in the optimal order.

Finally, while integration may provide benefits, it is clear that integration has costs. A normative theory of integration would suggest integration when, but only when, the maximization formula described here indicates positive net gain.

✦

Interfunctional Linkage and Fragmentation

INCREASING GLOBALIZATION links the world territorially. This is the reason for international law. However, the world is also linked interfunctionally: it is clear that trade and environment, health and security, finance and human rights, and so on are all connected concerns. Writing a treaty or law about one inevitably engages others. This is one important dimension in which all of our laws are incomplete. These varying topics are substantively linked, in the sense that a decision in one area has effects in another functional area. They can also be artificially linked in order to provide bargaining power or enforcement power, as was discussed in Chapter 3.

Linkage is endemic to international politics, as states seek linkages that will allow them to obtain concessions from other states. This chapter builds on Chapter 5 to examine the organizational aspects of linkage, focusing on the trade context. In fact, the linkage phenomenon is simply a subcase, involving the issue of diverse values, of the analysis of the reasons for institutionalization, and the options for governance within the organization, presented in Chapters 5 and 7. Chapter 3 showed that the possibility of linkage may actually permit international legal rules to enjoy greater binding force. Diverse values may be integrated within an organization, or in the market of international relations. This phenomenon is by no means unique to the international context: domestic political institutions are constantly called upon to integrate diverse values within domestic political institutions. The trade context provides a useful example, but is by no means the exclusive forum for linkages.

For example, "trade and . . ." linkages arise when nontrade issues are linked to trade. Thus, if the United States declines to trade with Burma until it complies with certain human rights or democracy standards, this is a "trade and . . ." linkage. All "trade and . . ." linkages are constructed, in the sense that the decision to link trade to other issues is always a political decision, and is not otherwise determined by the nature of things. Governments link trade concessions to the satisfaction of other, nontrade policy interests, either politically or legally, whenever they find such linkage useful to the achievement of their goals.

Linkages may be unilateral ad hoc (or "market") policies limited to a particular situation or type of situation. For example, the United States may impose a human rights–based embargo on Burma. On the other hand, states may develop institutions, political or legal, to effect or constrain linkage in the future: these may be bilateral or multilateral. Particular linkages may be, and are, articulated through international law, including World Trade Organization (WTO) law. Particular linkages may be, and are, constrained by international law, including WTO law. These rules of international law have been established and validated through the normal, and presumptively legitimate, processes of international legislation. However, they are neither complete nor immutable. Our continuing choice is institutional: what institutions, if any, will best allow states to manage linkage so as to maximize their preferences?

The general issue raised by most linkage claims is whether trade rules and environmental, labor, human rights, or other nontrade rules should somehow be combined at the WTO in a different way than they now are.[1] The fundamental basis for responding to such a question is welfare, broadly understood: does it make individuals, in the aggregate, better off to do so? The tools of economic analysis cannot respond definitively to the question of whether a particular response to linkage claims increases or decreases welfare. Economic analysis points to the market as the best determinant of welfare, assuming no transaction costs. In the final analysis, individuals, and states acting for them, must address the issue of welfare consequences for themselves, and express their preferences through the political process or through the market process. When they express their preferences through the political process, lawyers, economists, and other social scientists may assist by showing the possibilities, the varying costs and benefits, and the distributive consequences provided by each.

This chapter is intended to indicate a particular way of arraying possible institutional responses to linkage claims, and a particular way of categorizing their costs and benefits. This chapter uses the tools of law and economics and of the new institutional economics described in other chapters—specifically, literatures of property rights (Chapter 2), the theory of the firm (Chapter 5), and rules versus standards (Chapter 7)—to suggest the range of institutional possibilities available and to suggest how states should discriminate among them. This chapter provides a theoretical structure that, like all theories, should not be used alone as a basis for policy, but as a structure for determining which data are relevant and for analyzing those data. Therefore, this chapter does not take a position on particular linkage claims. However, it is hoped that by showing how analysis should proceed, this chapter will help decision makers to resist arguments based on incomplete analysis.

Political Linkage and Institutional Linkage

Linkage, as a political fact, is pervasive. States bargaining with one another in the international relations market use whatever tools are at hand: security matters are linked to trade, finance is linked to environmental protection, and membership in regional organizations is linked to human rights. This is a natural, and a presumptively efficient, phenomenon. In these contexts, states find themselves in a barter economy, trying to make deals by seeking to identify "bilateral coincidences of wants." Until the days of greater use of techniques such as internationally tradeable pollution permits, or more direct monetization of jurisdiction, barter will continue. In barter economies, the greater the breadth of subject matters available, the greater the possibilities for making a deal.

As an example of linkage as a political fact, consider the linkage between trade and intellectual property rights. This political linkage evolved into an institutional linkage. Beginning in the mid-1980s, at the urging of U.S. pharmaceutical and other intellectual property–dependent companies, the United States began to link trade to intellectual property protection. The U.S. policy was later incorporated in a number of unilateral U.S. policy instruments, including conditionality for application of zero-tariff treatment for imports from developing countries under the Generalized System of Preferences (GSP)[2] and so-called Special 301 trade sanctions.

What did the United States seek? The explicit goal was to influence domestic regulation of other states in terms of the level of intellectual property protection, an area that had traditionally been understood as largely within domestic jurisdiction. The United States sought enhanced protection under domestic intellectual property laws of other states for its intellectual property–dependent exporters. In fact, it sought to exercise, indirectly through diplomacy, authority over intellectual property protection in other countries. Thus, it sought a transaction in authority.

This story reached an interim conclusion in 1994, with the end of the Uruguay Round of trade negotiations and the signing of the Agreement on Trade-Related Aspects of Intellectual Property Rights (TRIPS). This agreement was the product of political linkage: in the famous so-called Grand Bargain, the United States, the European Union, and others exchanged concessions in agriculture and textiles for concessions in intellectual property protection and services trade. Political linkage was transformed into institutional linkage in the form of TRIPS, within the broader context of the WTO.

This agreement accorded the United States (and other parties) enforceable rights to require enhanced intellectual property protection in other states: it transferred a measure of authority over domestic intellectual property law to other WTO members, or perhaps one might say to the WTO itself. Other WTO members may bring dispute settlement cases to enforce these rights, and the WTO may decide whether these rights have been breached. In fact, the WTO agreements carry forward in time and in institutional form the political linkage that existed at the moment of conclusion of the Uruguay Round. They do so by providing for so-called cross-retaliation: in the case of a breach of TRIPS, if the complaining state cannot satisfactorily retaliate by withdrawing TRIPS concessions, it may be permitted to withdraw concessions in other areas, such as in market access for agricultural products.

TRIPS is an archetypical, and advanced, case history of linkage. We may view TRIPS as an exercise in contention over the allocation of jurisdiction, and we may view other linkage issues as also being concerned with the allocation of jurisdiction.

This chapter begins by further explaining its basic premise: that linkage is a problem of allocating jurisdiction. As suggested in earlier chapters, there are two basic, and related, types of allocation of jurisdiction: (i) horizontal allocation of jurisdiction among states (Chapter 2), and (ii) vertical allocation of jurisdiction between states and international organizations (Chapter 5). This chapter examines (iii) horizontal allocation of jurisdiction among international organizations. These three types of allocation are related.

As explained in Chapter 2, vertical allocation of jurisdiction between states and international organizations is a means of addressing contention over horizontal allocation of jurisdiction among states. Horizontal allocation of jurisdiction among international organizations is an emerging area of concern, in which the allocation of jurisdiction to a particular functional organization can have substantive effects on the horizontal allocation of jurisdiction between states.

That is, if a particular issue of concern, such as the issue of turtle-safe fishing for shrimp in the waters around South and Southeast Asia, is definitively allocated to the WTO to determine in accordance only with WTO law, then the states that preferred to have trade concerns dominate environmental concerns will be more likely to see their interests vindicated. On the other hand, to the extent that environmental organizations or law prevails, the opposite horizontal effect will result. The reader will immediately see that this type of problem presents itself as a kind of choice of law and choice of forum problem: an interfunctional one, rather than an international one.

As suggested in Chapter 1, horizontal allocation of authority among states is the core issue in international law in general, and in linkage problems in particular. We may understand "trade and . . ." problems as problems about allocation of jurisdiction. As suggested by the analysis in Chapter 5, issues of linkage, like other issues, may be addressed either *within* a particular international organization or in terms of the relationship *among* multiple international organizations. This chapter is concerned with relationships among multiple international organizations. Chapter 7, examining dispute settlement, examines how linkage issues may be addressed within a single international organization.

The Law and Economics of Allocation of Jurisdiction among International Organizations

The question of linkage is, first, a question of allocation of jurisdiction horizontally among states; and, second, a question of allocation of jurisdiction vertically between states and international organizations, of subsidiarity. Third, and of growing importance, is the question of allocation of jurisdiction horizontally among international organizations. The question of linkage must continually be traced back to disputes regarding horizontal allocation of authority between states because the outcome of a linkage dispute will have distributive consequences horizontally between states. As indicated in Chapters 2 and 5, these horizontal disputes over authority may be resolved through the establishment of an international organization. Hence, horizontal disputes are linked to vertical disputes. But then, another level of dispute is added when different international organizations assert authority over the same issue. This second-level horizontal dispute may indeed replicate the horizontal dispute between states.

Today, because of the relative softness of their law and the weakness of their dispute resolution, as well as the imbalance between adjudicative capacity and legislative capacity in the international system as a whole, the WTO's competitors do not seem to be contesting strongly the WTO's authority, at least in formal terms. Informally, and in the world of nongovernmental organizations and public opinion, of course, the WTO's authority is strenuously debated. And the WTO itself recognizes that it might be more successful, or at least less vulnerable, if other organizations took on a greater role. Other organizations could take on a greater role in legislation—in establishing treaty norms, or in adjudication, thereby raising either choice of law or choice of forum issues between themselves and the WTO. In either instance, they cannot do so without encountering the WTO. These encounters raise questions of institutional devices for allocation of jurisdiction between international organizations.

The WTO dispute settlement system generally does not directly admit other treaty norms for application as law.[3] Of course, the WTO treaty system could be amended to admit other norms directly. Whether it should be so amended depends on the particular context, and the parameters discussed throughout this chapter. For example, if states wish to make an arrangement permitting, permanently, compliance with the Montreal Protocol on Transboundary Movement of Hazardous Waste, even where such compliance may violate the General Agreement on Tariffs and Trade (GATT), the most effective way to do so is to include in GATT a specific reference to, and exception for, compliance with the Montreal Protocol. The effect of such an amendment would be to establish a particular kind of response to linkage claims: one of integration of the relevant environmental norms with the relevant trade norms. Obviously, as discussed in Chapter 5, this type of amendment would be facilitated by a regime of majority voting. The North American Free Trade Agreement's (NAFTA) provision stating that certain multilateral environmental agreements trump NAFTA's norms provides a precedent for a specific "carveout."[4]

The initial comparison for states is whether this approach would be less costly in transaction cost terms, and distributively satisfactory, compared with other approaches. I mention two alternatives. First, the potential inconsistency between the Montreal Protocol and GATT could be ignored on an *ex ante* basis, and addressed when particular conflicts arise, through negotiations between states. This would be something like a market mechanism for allocating authority. Second, and this is the actual circumstance today under WTO law, this type of conflict could be addressed through WTO dispute settlement, with a focus on the eligibility of the respondent state for an exception under Article XX of GATT. This is an institutional mechanism, applying a somewhat "muddy" standard, within one international organization. In choice of law terms, it is a unilateral, as opposed to a multilateral, approach.

Furthermore, it is not impossible that the Appellate Body would interpret WTO law to allow bilateral or multilateral "waivers" outside of the formal provisions therefor, which could have a similar effect. While the positive interpretive argument for this is quite weak, the normative argument is stronger, especially considering the difficulty of achieving greater flexibility and order through treaty amendments. I use the term "flexibility" pointedly, to refer to its use in European Union parlance, where it means having an organization with a core of shared norms, but allowing varying groups of members to share additional norms without requiring other members to go along. Flexibility is the opposite of the "single undertaking" approach that was followed in the Uruguay Round. It is also inconsistent with the understanding of the WTO legal system as conferring community-wide benefits, and not just as a network of bilateral deals subject to bilateral restructuring at will.

Assuming that there exists an international organization that serves as an interlocutor for the WTO in a particular field, such as the International Labor Organization (ILO) in labor, the United Nations Environmental Program (UNEP) or a possible "World Environmental Organization" in environment, or the International Monetary Fund (IMF) in finance, we encounter a second horizontal allocation of prescriptive jurisdiction problem: which of these organizations has jurisdiction over a particular issue? For, while, as discussed below, there is room for creative ambiguity, at certain junctures it will be necessary for one organization's norms to trump another's. Having said this, it is clear that there is no a priori reason why the WTO's norms should generally trump those derived from organizations that focus on labor, environmental, or other concerns (or vice versa).

It is appropriate to think of international organizations, whether multilateral, functional, or regional, in the same way that we thought of states: as representatives of individual constituents. Of course, international organizations, like states, aggregate individual preferences imperfectly and are subject to a host of public choice critiques. Thus, the same analytical techniques as developed in Chapters 2 and 5, based on property rights theory, the theory of the firm, and regulatory competition theory, are applicable to the relationship among international organizations. We can understand the degree of implication of the preferences of an international organization as a basis for its assertion of jurisdiction. However, if other international organizations' preferences are implicated, a conflict may arise.

Of course, there are multiple institutional options for allocating jurisdiction among international organizations. The default option, of course, which might be described as rather primitive, is simply to leave these organizations in a state of nature, or at least under the general public international law system. Under these circumstances, they would negotiate with one another regarding particular instances of conflict, and negotiations would take place among their constituent states, reaching varying degrees of resolution. The second option, not necessarily prior in any sense to the third, is to use specific rules in treaties to allocate jurisdiction. The third option is to use standards in treaties as a basis for allocation by a tribunal. It may even be that the theoretical perspective provided in Chapter 5 would serve as a guide to determining whether an overarching organizational structure—superior to all other international organizations—is appropriate.

We may consider the allocational options in ways analogous to those available in the interstate setting discussed above. It is not the same for the United States and Malaysia to dispute jurisdiction over Malaysian shrimp trawlers as it is for the WTO and a possible World Environmental Organization to contend over the same thing, but these two types of contention have some dynamics in common. Both sets of organizations, after all, represent people seeking to achieve certain trade and environmental goals, albeit at different vertical levels.

Of course, the allocational options are somewhat different from those in the case of interstate conflict. For example, in the context of functional, as opposed to regional, international organizations, there is no "territoriality." Furthermore, an analysis of "effects" would be somewhat different from that anticipated in the interstate setting. However, as with states, we might evaluate effects in terms of the impairment or facilitation of the entity's ability to achieve the preferences sought to be achieved (by people) through that entity: of its mission.

Recall that in connection with allocating jurisdiction to states, territoriality is only valid as a rough proxy for the degree to which the achievement of state preferences is impaired. Similarly, a concept of "primary coverage" might be useful as a basis for allocating jurisdiction among international organizations to the extent that primary coverage is a proxy for effects on the achievement of an organization's mission. Thus, a concept of primary coverage could be an analog to territoriality. By primary coverage, we mean that the responsibilities allocated to the particular functional organization are very strongly implicated. That is, for "core" trade issues such as tariffs, we might say that the WTO has primary coverage. While, of course, there is no discrete "core," we must recognize that there are varying degrees of implication of particular policies. This makes sense in terms of respect for the intent of the states', and their citizens', desire to allocate certain authority to particular international organizations.

This primary coverage or core analysis should be predicated on the ability of the relevant organization to reflect individual or state-expressed preferences. Thus, we might find that an international organization that fails to reflect preferences better than its alternatives might lose its primary coverage or core role, and be supplanted by another organization. While this seems appealing in theory, it is difficult to specify a mechanism for change.

We might also postulate that recognition could be applied in interorganizational allocation: one organization may recognize a norm or status developed by another, within the other's field of "primary coverage." The GATT-WTO system has informally deferred on occasion to the ILO and to the World Health Organization,[5] and has relationships of limited formal deference to the IMF.[6] The WTO Agreement on the Application of Sanitary and Phytosanitary Measures specifically allocates a measure of jurisdiction to Codex Alimentarius, the International Office of Epizootics, and the International Plant Protection Convention. Also, using Article XX of GATT as a vehicle, the *Shrimp/Turtle* Appellate Body Report suggested that WTO law could take account of multilateral environmental agreements. Finally, recall that NAFTA provides for formal deference to certain multilateral environmental agreements. These are more subtle and variegated mechanisms than across-the-board deference or across-the-board ignorance.

Assuming a progressive view of international relations, we would expect functional integration to take on increasing subtlety and complexity. While there would, of course, be practical difficulties of integrating the work of varying organizations with varying expertise, epistemic communities, and formal rules, the value of functional integration will grow with the value of horizontal regional or multilateral economic integration. That is, horizontal regional or multilateral economic integration grows in utility with the rise of technology, transportation, and communications.

As these forms of economic integration grow in the context of trade and finance, they seem to increase the value of functional integration in the international context, emulating the functional integration that exists in the domestic context. For example, we have found it useful within particular countries to integrate our approach to the relationship between the free market in goods and services—trade—and environmental protection: to recognize that these are both values that we as a domestic society seek, but that they are not always consistent with one another.

The Size of International Organizations

In Chapter 5, we asked the same initial question about the international organization that Ronald Coase asked in 1937 about the business firm: why does it exist, and if its existence is justified, why is there not just one big one? In this chapter, we ask, in transaction cost and strategic terms, is it better to include additional issues within a single organization, or to have multiple organizations "contract" with one another in the market? Recognizing the utility of making trade-offs among different issue areas,[7] we ask what institutional structure best facilitates these trade-offs.

Broader organizations may offer economies of scale and scope. On the other hand, broader organizations could reduce the domain of interorganizational competition. As noted in Chapter 5, the Herbert Simon perspective recognizes the essential fungibility between internal organizational arrangements and contractual arrangements in a market. In the present context, this means that it does not necessarily matter whether functions are separated in function-specific international organizations or are integrated within a single organization, such as the United Nations or perhaps the WTO. Within a single organization, the critical question will be how these different concerns or functions are integrated. We live in a world of path dependence: given that the WTO exists, and no World Environmental Organization yet exists, there may be actions, such as adding functional responsibility to the WTO, that make sense in this given situation yet would not make sense were the starting point different.

Negotiations in the WTO context may provide an advantage over negotiations in a multilateral environmental agreement, in the UNEP, in the ILO, or in another functional context: the greater possibility of linked package deals. While institutional linkages may be made between discrete functional organizations, under some circumstances doing so within a single organization may enhance administration and legitimacy.[8] The WTO already contains much scope for package deals: for side payments. "With all side payments prohibited, there is no assurance that collective action will be taken in the most productive way."[9] However, it is worth noting that the WTO system, with its effective requirements of unanimity for amendment, results in greater requirements for "package deals" than a system that relies on majority voting for new "legislative" rules.

The Role of Interorganizational Competition

Surely, it is appropriate at least in some circumstances for international organizations to be subjected to competitive pressure,[10] but international organizations must also cooperate with one another in appropriate circumstances. Moreover, international organizations exist in a context of both horizontal and vertical competition. That is, international organizations like the European Union compete for political or regulatory authority not only with organizations like the North Atlantic Treaty Organization, the Basle Committee on Banking Regulation, or the WTO, but also with their member states. The European Union also cooperates with these other organizations in various ways. In aspirational theoretical terms, this competition and cooperation constitute a search for the optimal jurisdictional area: what vertical and horizontal governance satisfies the constituents' preferences most?[11]

As suggested above, in order to allow regulatory competition to develop a stable and efficient equilibrium, it is, inter alia, necessary to develop a structure that can reduce interjurisdictional externalities. In the interstate setting, we think of a "hegemon" or a central government that can intervene as necessary to require the internalization of externalities. What structure would play this role in interorganizational competition? Perhaps the United Nations, or perhaps the International Court of Justice (ICJ), if granted appropriate jurisdiction, could fulfill this role. In order to induce states to provide the United Nations or the ICJ with this power, it would be necessary to convince states that they would individually benefit. It would take a "constitutional moment" to do so. It appears that such a constitutional moment would require greater historical experience of the need for this role to be fulfilled than exists today.

Conclusion

Issues of linkage exist as a factual matter, regardless of our institutional response. If we must rely only on existing single-issue institutions, then the scope of our institutional choice—of our available responses to international problems—will be constrained. It is therefore useful, as an exercise in institutional imagination, to explore the establishment of other institutional devices. To the extent there is a community of interests, there will be reasons to consider what institutional devices may improve the ability of states to realize joint gains. The next step is to develop a matrix of institutional devices, and to evaluate those institutional devices using some of the tools developed in this chapter and in Chapter 5.

This chapter has viewed fragmentation problems as institutional problems associated with the allocation of jurisdiction along horizontal, vertical, and functional dimensions. Surely these problems exist regardless of our perception of them, or the consensus definition of particular issue areas. This chapter has tried to suggest a method of analysis of these problems that understands them first as issues of horizontal allocation of jurisdiction, second as issues of vertical allocation of jurisdiction, and third as issues of horizontal allocation of jurisdiction among international organizations. Under some circumstances, it may be appropriate to consider a fourth type of allocation of jurisdiction: vertically between inferior international organizations and a superior international organization charged with addressing conflicts among inferior international organizations.

✦

International Adjudication

THIS CHAPTER extends the analysis developed in previous chapters by examining the role of international adjudication in international allocation of authority. Obviously, adjudication is a part of the internal governance of international organizations, or at least is a feature of a treaty structure. As suggested in earlier chapters, adjudication is a nuanced mechanism for determining (i) allocation of authority between states (horizontal state to state), (ii) allocation of authority between states and international organizations (vertical), and (iii) allocation of authority among international organizations (horizontal international organization to international organization). This chapter examines the possible effects of variations in instructions that can be given to judges—variations in legal rules that delegate authority to judges—on these allocations.

Much international legal analysis focuses on the role of judges and adjudication. Much of this analysis considers the scope of a judge's authority: whether or not the judge is engaging in "judicial legislation," or remaining within the scope of his or her authority. From a law and economics standpoint, judges can be understood as agents of multiple principals: of the parties to the agreement, statute, or constitution that gives them authority. From this perspective, the issue of scope of judicial authority is understood as an agency question: how to authorize and monitor agents, given the fact that they have independent preferences that may conflict with those of the principals.

It is common, especially among those who utilize social science methodologies, to dismiss the idealism and imprecision of natural law theory.

While these concerns have appeal, natural law–based argumentation may also be understood in terms of the agency role of the judge, insofar as the judge is explicitly—or, more likely, implicitly—authorized to apply a vision of morality. Indeed, it is possible to understand arguments from natural law or morality in a judicial setting as arguments to the quasi-legislative discretion allocated to judges. This type of implicit or explicit agency to apply a vision of morality may be more appealing in the international legal setting, lacking an effective day-to-day legislative capacity, than in many domestic systems.

Pursuant to this understanding, the extent to which judges are authorized to apply natural law—principles that are not contained in positive legislation—is a question of the scope of their agency: whether they are authorized to consider these principles external to the positive law that comprises their explicit instructions. That judges are not explicitly authorized to exercise moral judgment does not mean that they are not authorized to do so, or that it is not useful and efficient for them to do so. Rather, we may understand the incessant debate about "judicial legislation" as a nuanced discipline on the scope of judicial agency.

The liberal model that forms the basis for this book can accommodate the use of natural law as a basis for judicial moralizing. In a society in which moral values are not universal, but are shared to variable extents, it is still useful to moderate the application of law through morality. Legislators may plan explicitly on this, avoiding the direct political costs of a moral stand, or the bureaucratic costs of anticipating how moral dilemmas may arise. Alternatively, they may simply accept the possibility of moral intervention as part of the general background of their legislative activity. In any event, there is no reason to assume that all desirable moral contribution to public policy takes place in the legislature, or not at all. It is perfectly plausible that judges or others would be delegated some measure of authority to exercise their own moral judgment, or even to sense and reflect a collective moral judgment. Of course, one person's moral judgment is another's bitter constraint on freedom. So there must be nuanced limits on the scope of judicial authority.

Moreover, the judge's existential burden is to serve as guardian of procedural justice values, and therefore to reject, at times, valid claims of substantive justice. In a liberal society, it is an affirmation of each person's humanity to respect their views, and therefore the legislative results of democratic process. This is what we mean by procedural justice. In particular cases, the results of the democratic process may be so clear that the judge's agency will not permit him to make a determination in accordance with his view of substantive justice. This conflict between procedural justice and substantive justice is a conflict between moral relativism and moral absolutism. It is the genius of a legal system that it can compromise between these poles.

The Agency Role of Judges: the Judge as Manager under the Theory of the Firm

It is clear that dispute resolution arrangements—and, more generally, *ex post* enforceability—affect the willingness of states to enter into agreements, including those for organizations, *ex ante*.[1] After all, what would be the purpose of entering into an unenforceable agreement?[2] Dispute resolution arrangements are intended to provide some degree of formal enforceability.

Before we analyze the relationship between dispute resolution and discrete treaty language, it is useful to review the role of dispute resolution in governance. Dispute resolution plays two roles. First, as noted above, dispute resolution is necessary to the application of legislation, and in this regard is not important for its own sake, but as the place where legislation becomes binding and effective.[3] Legislation without adjudication at least raises greater concerns regarding the application and effectiveness of the legislation.[4] Even if there are no formal enforcement mechanisms, adjudication can overcome information problems and assist in inducing compliance, as discussed in Chapter 3. Second, dispute resolution inevitably interprets and expands upon legislation. In a common law system, indeed, dispute resolution amounts unabashedly to a type of legislation. Even in a civil law system,[5] or one such as the World Trade Organization (WTO) that formally rejects stare decisis, dispute resolution may be a source of persuasive or helpful precedent: of less binding legislation.

The Choice between Treaty Specification and Delegation to Dispute Resolution

When treaty negotiators negotiate the language of a particular provision, in addition to determining, with whatever detail they deem appropriate, the substantive treatment of an issue, they determine the extent to which subsequent specification is delegated to dispute resolution or other processes. Of course, this is only a very important option under circumstances where dispute resolution is likely to be invoked. Most international treaties do not provide for mandatory dispute settlement.

To the extent that dispute resolution establishes precedents that are either formally binding or informally persuasive in order to maintain consistency, the decision regarding the postlegislative role of dispute resolution is not different, in abstract theoretical terms, from the decision by a legislature to delegate rule-making or interpretative functions to an administrative agency. Recognizing that dispute resolution tribunals engage in interpretation and construction, how and why do particular provisions operate to authorize interpretation and construction?

Not only do treaty writers delegate authority to dispute resolution tribunals, they also maintain complex relationships with the dispute resolution process, both formal and informal. These relationships may be understood in principal-agent terms.

One avenue of influence is the ability to establish new treaties or treaty provisions,[6] and thereby "legislatively" to reverse the outcome of a dispute resolution determination. This is obviously quite difficult under a rule of unanimity. Another is arguably to specify the "standard of review," which can establish a particular level of deference to member state interpretations of international law. Third, and relatively unusual in general international law, is a formal "political filter" device. This political filter was important in the WTO context prior to the 1994 changes to WTO dispute resolution, and there has been some discussion of bringing it back in attenuated form.[7] Finally, informal forms of control may be influential in constraining judges' decisions.[8]

Thus, dispute resolution should be seen in context as a hybrid, or a confluence of adjudicative and legislative authority. Positive political theory would analyze the interaction of adjudicative and legislative authority in game-theoretic and perhaps other terms, examining how the structure of the relationship between these two bodies affects outcomes.[9]

In this section, I examine the mechanisms by which competences to address important issues are assigned to dispute resolution. We may view the indeterminacy, incompleteness, or standard-like nature of these treaty provisions as a form of implicit delegation to dispute resolution. In other words, we can increasingly view the decision to draft these provisions as they are, or as time goes by, to leave them as they are, as legislative decisions, and as delegations.

This and the following section develop two linked analytical techniques, for application to dispute resolution. The first, the incomplete contracts analysis, is largely consistent with the second, rules versus standards.

Professor Hadfield applies an incomplete contracts analysis to statutes in the domestic setting, which can be applied in turn to treaties and customary international law (CIL) in the international setting.[10] She thus extends Williamson's approach, discussed in Chapter 5, to incomplete contracts. Treaties may be optimally incomplete with appropriate instructions to decision makers to complete the "contract" in particular cases. The parameters to consider include (i) the costs of advance specification, (ii) the degree of stochasticity, (iii) the ability to customize to particular facts in specific cases, and (iv) the potential value of diversity of compliance techniques. This literature tends to treat the legislature as a unitary actor. It will be exceedingly important for us to recognize that the legislature in our case (as in Hadfield's) is a group of actors, each subject to strategic and social choice limitations on its ability to act.

As discussed in Chapter 5, there are fewer institutional and legal structures to complete contracts in international law than in many domestic legal systems. First, in international law, there is not a very complete body of customary or other general law that can be applied to supply missing terms to incomplete treaties. Second, in general international law, there is usually no dispute resolution tribunal with mandatory jurisdiction. Thus, it is often difficult to rely on the ability to complete contracts through dispute resolution mechanisms.

Rules versus Standards

A related literature examines the economics of rules and standards—instead of dealing with incomplete contracts, this literature deals more directly with different types of law. This literature addresses the fact that laws are sometimes established more specifically in advance, as rules, or less specifically in advance, as standards. Importantly, for standards, it assumes that there is an independent person to interpret and apply the standard. This is not necessarily a court, but we can see the rules-versus-standards literature as an extension of the incomplete contracts literature.

Defining Rules and Standards
In the rules-versus-standards literature, a law is a "rule" *to the extent that* it is specified in advance of the conduct to which it is applied. Thus, a law against littering is a rule to the extent that "littering" is well defined. Must

there be intent not to pick up the discarded item, are organic or readily biodegradable substances covered, is littering on private property covered, and is the distribution of leaflets by air covered? Any lawyer knows that there are always questions to ask, so that every law is incompletely specified in advance, and therefore incompletely a rule.

A standard, on the other hand, is a law that is farther toward the other end of the spectrum, in relative terms. It establishes general guidance to both the person governed and the person charged with applying the law, but does not specify in detail in advance the conduct required or proscribed. The relativity of these definitions is critical. It is more apparently and intentionally incompletely specified in advance. Familiar constitutional standards in the U.S. legal system include requirements like "due process," prohibitions on uncompensated "takings," or prohibitions on barriers to interstate commerce. A well-known statutory standard in U.S. law is "restraint of trade" under the Sherman Act. It is worth noting that the distinction between a rule and a standard is not necessarily grammatical or determined by the number of words used to express the norm; rather, the distinction relates to how much work remains to be done to determine the applicability of the norm to a particular circumstance. Furthermore, this distinction assumes, with H. L. A. Hart, and contrary to certain tenets of critical legal theory, that language may be formulated to have core meanings, penumbral influence, and limits of application.[11] If all language were equally indeterminate, there would be no distinction between a rule and a standard.

Incompleteness of specification may not simply be a result of conservation of resources. It may be a more explicitly political decision to either agree to disagree for the moment, to avoid the political price that may arise from immediate hard decisions, or to cloak the hard decisions in the false inevitability of judicial interpretation. It is important also to recognize that the incompleteness of specification may represent a failure to decide how the policy expressed relates to other policies. This is critical in the trade area, where often the incompleteness of a trade rule relates to its failure to address, or incorporate, nontrade policies.

Obviously, each law is composed of a combination of rules and standards. However, it will be useful to speak here generally of rules as separate from standards.

The Costs and Benefits of Rules and Standards

Rules are more expensive to develop than standards, *ex ante*, because rules entail specification costs, including drafting costs and negotiation costs, as well as the strategic costs involved in *ex ante* specification. In order to reach agreement on specification—in order to legislate specifically—there may be greater costs in public choice terms.[12] This is particularly interesting in the trade context, where treaty making would be subjected to intense domestic scrutiny, while application of a standard by a dispute resolution process would be subjected to reduced scrutiny. On the other hand, nongovernmental organizations (NGOs) have sought in this connection to enhance transparency in dispute resolution. Finally, rules require clear decision; standards may serve as an agreement to disagree or to temporize, or may help to mask or mystify a decision made.[13] Under standards, both sides in the legislative process may claim victory, at least initially.

Rules are generally thought to provide greater predictability. There are two moments at which to consider predictability. First is the ability of persons subject to the law to be able to plan and conform their conduct *ex ante*, sometimes known as "primary predictability."[14] The second moment in which predictability is important is *ex post*, after the relevant conduct has taken place. Where the parties can predict the outcome of dispute resolution—where they can predict the tribunal's determination of their respective rights and duties—they will spend less money on litigation. This type of predictability is "secondary predictability." Both types of predictability can reduce costs. While rules appear to provide primary and secondary predictability, tribunals may construct exceptions in order to do what is, by their lights, substantial justice, and thereby reduce predictability. It may be difficult to constrain the ability of tribunals to do this.

Furthermore, as noted in Chapter 2, game theory predicts that some degree of uncertainty—of unpredictability—may enhance the ability of the parties in some transaction cost contexts to bargain to a lower cost solution. Thus, simple predictability is not the only measure of a legal norm; rather, we must also be concerned with the ability of the legal norm to provide satisfactory outcomes under particular circumstances, including strategic settings. In economic terms, we must be concerned with the allocative efficiency of the outcome.

As we consider the relative allocative efficiency of potential outcomes, it is important to recognize that there is a temporal distinction between rules and standards. Standards may be used earlier in the development of a field of law, before sufficient experience to form a basis for more complete specification is acquired. In many areas of law, courts develop a jurisprudence that forms the basis for codification—or even rejection—by legislatures. With this in mind, legislatures (or adjudicators) may set standards at an early point in time, and determine to establish rules at a later point in time.[15] It is clear that a rule of stare decisis is not necessary to the development by a court or dispute resolution tribunal of a body of jurisprudence. It is also worth noting that in a common law setting, or any setting where tribunals refer to precedents, the tribunal may announce a standard in a particular case, and then elaborate that standard in subsequent cases until it has built a rule for its own application.

As noted above, where instances of the relevant behavior are more frequent, economies of scale will indicate that rules become relatively more efficient. For circumstances that arise only infrequently, it is more difficult to justify promulgation of specific rules. In addition, rules provide compliance benefits: they are cheaper to obey, because the cost of determining the required behavior is lower. Rules are also cheaper to apply by a court: the court must only determine the facts and compare them to the rule.

The Institutional Dimension of Rules and Standards

Another distinction between rules and standards, often deemphasized in this literature, is the institutional distinction: with rules, the legislature often "makes" the decision, while with standards, the adjudicator determines the application of the standard, thereby "making" the decision. Again, it is obvious that these terms are used in a relative sense (this caveat will not be repeated). Economists and even lawyer-economists seem to assume that the tribunal simply "finds" the law, and does not make it. Of course, courts can make rules pursuant to explicit or implicit statutory or constitutional authority: the hallmark of a rule is that it is specified *ex ante,* not that it is specified by a legislature. However, at least in the international law system, rules are largely made by treaty, and standards are largely applied by tribunals.

But the difference between legislators and courts is an important one, and may affect the outcome. The choice of legislators or courts to make particular decisions should be made using cost-benefit analysis. Such a cost-benefit analysis would include, as a critical factor, the degree of representativeness of constituents: which institution will most accurately reflect citizens' desires? There are good reasons why such cost-benefit analysis does not always select legislatures. First, there is a public choice critique of legislatures. Second, even under a public interest analysis, legislatures may not be efficient at specifying *ex ante* all of the details of treatment of particular cases. Third, the rate of change of circumstances over time may favor the ability of courts to adjust. Finally, we must analyze the strategic relationship between legislators and courts. Thus, in order fully to understand the relationship between rules and standards, the tools of public choice or positive political theory[16] should be brought to bear to analyze the relationship between legislative and judicial decision making.[17]

The Strategic Dimension of Rules and Standards

It is not possible to consider the costs and benefits of rules and standards separately from the strategic considerations that would cause states to select a rule as opposed to a standard. Johnston analyzes rules and standards from a strategic perspective, finding that, under a standard, bargaining may yield immediate efficient agreement, whereas under a rule, this condition may not obtain.[18] This understanding is an extension of the property rights–based analysis elaborated in Chapter 2. Johnston considers a rule a "definite, ex ante entitlement" and a standard a "contingent, ex post entitlement." Like Kaplow, he does not here consider the source of the rule, whether legislature or tribunal.

Johnston notes the

> standard supposition in the law and economics literature . . . that private bargaining between [two parties] over the allocation of [a] legal entitlement is most likely to be efficient if the entitlement is clearly defined and assigned ex ante according to a rule, rather than made contingent upon a judge's ex post balancing of relative value and harm.[19]

Johnston suggests this supposition may be incorrect:[20] "when the parties bargain over the entitlement when there is private information about value and harm, bargaining may be more efficient under a blurry balancing test than under a certain rule."[21] This is because under a certain rule, the holder of the entitlement will have incentives to "hold out" and decline to provide information about the value to him of the entitlement. Under a standard, where presumably it cannot be known with certainty *ex ante* who owns the entitlement, the person not possessing the entitlement may credibly threaten to take it, providing incentives for the other person to bargain. Johnston points out that this result obtains only when the *ex post* balancing test is imperfect, because if the balancing were perfect, the threat would not be credible. This provides a counterintuitive argument, in particular contexts, for inaccuracy of application of standards.[22]

Applying Incomplete Contracts and Standards and Rules Analysis

The following discussion examines the problem in the WTO of relating trade to other values as an example of the relationship between rules and standards in international law. This discussion extends the discussion of linkage in Chapter 6, as well as the broader discussion of international organizations in Chapter 5. It compares case-based decision making by the WTO dispute settlement system with the possibility of decision making by the more political processes of, for example, the WTO Committee on Trade and Environment, or more immediate decision making or treaty making by the WTO.

Table 7.1 summarizes the factors to be considered, as derived from the analysis set forth above, and their general application to rules and standards, respectively.

As the WTO continues to address the problem of the intersection between international environmental law or domestic health regulation, on the one hand, and international trade law, on the other hand, it will be interesting to observe the extent to which adjudication resulting in reports from the Appellate Body determines this intersection. For now, the Appellate Body has retained jurisdiction to address these relationships, and has read WTO law to provide itself wide standard-like flexibility in responding to these problems. In the *Asbestos* case,[23] the Appellate Body left room to

Table 7.1 Costs and benefits of rules and standards

	Rules	Standards
Administrative cost of formulation	Higher cost	Lower cost
Public choice costs of specification, including costs of transparency	Higher cost	Lower cost
Perceived legitimacy; democracy deficit	Lower cost	Higher cost
Primary predictability—predictability for actors *ex ante*	Lower cost	Higher cost
Secondary predictability—ease of application by dispute resolution tribunal	Lower cost	Higher cost
Gaining experience prior to specification	Decreased benefit	Increased benefit
Economies of scale with greater frequency	Increased benefit	Decreased benefit
Minimizing strategic costs—promotion of bargaining toward efficient agreement	Decreased benefit	Increased benefit

examine rather impressionistically whether the importing state conferred "less favourable treatment" on goods from the exporting state, in violation of the General Agreement on Tariffs and Trade (GATT), Article III. In the *Shrimp* case,[24] it found that the *chapeau* of Article XX of GATT, providing exceptions for certain categories of domestic measure, requires it to establish a "line of equilibrium" between trade values and nontrade values. And in *Asbestos* and *Korea-Beef*,[25] in connection with the subsections of Article XX that require the domestic measure to be "necessary" to achieve the listed goal, the Appellate Body explicitly stated that it would engage in a balancing test in order to determine necessity. Thus, the Appellate Body understands its role as guardian of a set of standards, not as a mere transmitter of rules.

In 1994, the trade ministers who approved the results of the Uruguay Round also approved a Decision on Trade and Environment.[26] This decision called for the formation of the WTO Committee on Trade and the Environment (CTE) with a mandate to make recommendations regarding the modifications of the multilateral trading system needed to "enhance positive interaction between trade and environmental measures." The CTE issued a report at the Singapore Ministerial in 1996.[27] This report did not constitute legislation, and its "approval" at the Singapore Ministerial[28] was not a legislative or treaty-making act. In fact, as set forth in more detail below, the CTE has remained a "talking shop," with no direct legislative impact thus far. However, the lack of direct legislative impact does not mean that the CTE has had no impact on the context of WTO dispute resolution.

Explaining the Relative Dominance of Dispute Resolution

What plausible explanations can we posit for the dominance thus far of WTO dispute resolution in addressing the relationship between trade concerns and environmental concerns?

Some WTO members have provided an explanation that is consistent with a rules and standards analysis:

> When account is taken of the limited number of MEAs that contain trade provisions, and the fact that no trade dispute has arisen over the use of those measures to date, some feel that there is no evidence of a real conflict between the WTO and MEAs; existing WTO rules already provide sufficient scope to allow trade measures to be applied pursuant to MEAs, and it

is neither necessary nor desirable to exceed that scope. According to this view, the proper course of action to resolve any underlying conflict which may be felt to exist in this area is for WTO Members to avoid using trade measures in MEAs which are inconsistent with their WTO obligations. Any clarification in that respect can be provided, as necessary, ex post through the WTO dispute settlement mechanism.[29]

This excerpt refers to the relative infrequency, indeed the speculative nature, of possible conflict between multilateral environmental agreement (MEA) obligations and WTO law. Of course, there has been somewhat more frequent conflict between unilateral environmental measures and WTO law. As additional disputes occur, the Appellate Body will have opportunities to articulate a jurisprudence that will be influenced by the scope of MEAs, as well as by decisions of the CTE and the WTO generally. In turn, the Appellate Body's jurisprudence may stimulate a codification or a negative codification—a legislative reversal.

If we fill in the table of costs and benefits in the trade and environment context, the distribution described in Table 7.2 might be the result. Of course, Table 7.2 is speculative: much more empirical and analytical work would be required to fill it in with greater certainty. In addition, it is difficult to quantify and commensurate among the various costs and benefits. This kind of analysis is merely meant as a guide to political discourse, which would presumably evaluate each of the categories of costs and benefits.

Table 7.2 suggests that with more experience, and as more trade-environment conflicts arise (perhaps due to the increase of trade law, the increase of environmental law, or both), one might expect a shift from standards to rules. This type of analysis can play an important role in validating the decision of the international community *not* to develop rules in this area as yet.

Disciplining Domestic Regulation

As shown in the prior section, states may delegate to tribunals the task of applying general disciplines to domestic measures. Perhaps the most active multilateral context in which states have done this is in the field of regulatory trade barriers. These regulatory barriers have a real or purported regulatory goal, and often the task of the tribunal is implicitly to determine whether to accept or reject the ostensible regulatory justification. This type

Table 7.2 Costs and benefits in trade/environment context

	Rules	Standards
Administrative cost of formulation	Higher cost	Lower cost—status quo
Public choice costs of specification, including costs of transparency	Very high cost, given extreme diversity of perspectives	Lower cost—status quo
Perceived legitimacy; democracy deficit	Lower cost	Higher cost
Primary predictability—predictability for actors *ex ante*	Lower cost, but depends on avoiding development of substantial exceptions through dispute resolution	Higher cost
Secondary predictability—ease of application by dispute resolution tribunal	Lower cost, but depends on avoiding development of substantial exceptions through dispute resolution	Higher cost
Gaining experience prior to specification	Reduced benefit, although the magnitude of reduction declines as experience is already gained	Increased benefit, especially as dispute resolution decisions raise opportunities for dialog
Economies of scale with greater frequency	Increased benefit—and likely to grow as more intersections between trade and environment arise	Decreased benefit, but may serve as casuist legislature over time, reaping similar economies of scale
Minimizing strategic costs—promotion of bargaining toward efficient agreement	Reduced benefit, although the magnitude of reductionmay decline as uncertainty of result of rules rises with development of exceptions	Increased benefit given uncertainty of outcome

of linkage or "trade and . . ." problem manifests itself in particular circumstances, and each circumstance must be addressed separately, except to the extent that benefits arise from analyzing similar problems together. This problem is one of synthesizing and maximizing complex preferences in the context of multiple overlapping communities. A similar task could be assigned to a human rights tribunal, or to a tribunal charged with determining the legality of military action: to what extent is national autonomy to violate a particular rule permitted under exceptional circumstances?

As described in Chapter 6, the "trade and . . ." problem is a problem of intersecting jurisdictions, on both horizontal and vertical axes, each with varying interests. If the conflict between the market and regulation is a chess game, then the conflict between trade values, or more generally, international values, and other social values is a three-dimensional chess game, with geometrically increased complexity. In addition to choosing between laissez-faire and intervention, the level of intervention must also be chosen. Importantly, as suggested in Chapters 2 and 5, the upward vertical move to empower an organization must also be understood as a method of horizontal accommodation, and as a structure for allocating authority horizontally.

Thus, institutional choice has multiple parameters. The first parameter to be addressed is the vertical level of society at which choice takes place. Second is the type of institution—for example, legislative versus adjudicative—to be assigned the task of choice. Third is the standard that the selected institution will follow. The following section focuses on this last parameter as a device, applied at a central adjudicative level, to select between the assignment of power to local legislatures and the denial of power to local legislatures. However, the rule or standard applied at the central adjudicative level may also determine the choice between central adjudication and legislation as the institutional setting for decision.

A Taxonomy of Trade-Off Devices

This section examines the trade-off devices used by the European Court of Justice (ECJ), WTO dispute resolution panels or the WTO Appellate Body, and the U.S. Supreme Court, in connection with "trade and . . ." problems within the European Union, WTO, and U.S. systems, respectively. The major categories of trade-off devices are listed and briefly defined below. In each of the jurisdictions studied, these trade-off devices appear in combination, rather than alone, and each category of trade-off device conceals considerable latitude for heterogeneity. Thus, despite the list of only six categories, far more combinations and variations are possible.

(i) *National treatment rules.* A national treatment rule is a type of anti-discrimination rule that examines whether different legal standards are applied to comparable cases, as between the domestic and the foreign. National treatment rules entail surprising complexity. In order to deal with more difficult cases, they sometimes incorporate some of the tests set forth below in this list.

(ii) *Simple means-ends rationality tests.* These tests consider whether the means chosen is indeed a rational means to a purported end. Simple means-ends rationality testing is often combined with limitations on ends. Analytically, simple means-ends rationality testing is included in all of the tests described below in this list, and is sometimes used as a proxy to detect discrimination. As it imposes little real discipline, and is often included in other tests, we do not analyze the use of simple means-ends rationality testing in detail below.

(iii) *Necessity or least trade-restrictive alternative tests.* This type of test goes a significant step beyond simple means-ends rationality testing. It inquires whether there is a less trade-restrictive means to accomplish the same end. The definition of the end is often outcome determinative. In some cases, necessity testing is qualified by requiring that the means be the least trade-restrictive alternative that is *reasonably available.* In addition, necessity testing is sometimes combined with limitations on the categories of ends permitted.

(iv) *Proportionality.* Proportionality sensu stricto[30] inquires whether the means are "proportionate" to the ends: whether the costs are excessive in relation to the benefits. It might be viewed as cost-benefit analysis with a margin of appreciation, as it does not require that the costs be less than the benefits. Proportionality may be either static or comparative, in the same way as cost-benefit analysis. A comparative approach to proportionality testing would include in its calculus the costs and benefits of alternative rules.

(v) *Balancing tests.* Balancing tests purport to decide whether a measure that impedes trade is acceptable, balancing all of the factors.

Balancing may be viewed as a kind of amorphous or imprecise cost-benefit analysis.[31] More charitably, and perhaps more correctly, it may be viewed as a kind of cost-benefit analysis that recognizes the difficulty of formalizing the analysis, and seeks to achieve similar results informally.[32]

(vi) *Cost-benefit analysis.* Static cost-benefit analysis in the context at hand[33] juxtaposes the regulatory benefits of regulation with the trade costs of regulation, as well as other costs of regulation, and would strike down regulation where the costs exceed the benefits. Cost-benefit analysis in this context may be viewed as stricter scrutiny than the domestic cost-benefit analysis that has recently become popular, as it adds a cost dimension not normally included: detriments to trade. Adding trade detriments to the calculation would presumably have the marginal effect of causing some regulation to fail a cost-benefit analysis test. It is worth comparing static cost-benefit analysis, simply juxtaposing the costs and benefits of a single rule, with a more dynamic comparative cost-benefit analysis, comparing the net benefits of multiple rules, and recommending the rule with the greatest net benefits.

Toward Comparative Institutional Analysis

This section examines strategies for judicial management of the relationship—the trade-off—between trade and other values. These strategies have been established pursuant to constitutional or treaty language, and used in dispute resolution fora in the European Union's common market, in the multilateral trade system under the WTO, and in the United States' internal common market. While these strategies for management are based on legislative or constitutional texts, the texts are consistently indeterminate—perhaps more than most laws—and thus the task of constructing strategies for management has often fallen on dispute resolution bodies.

Within this comparative analysis, it is important to keep in mind the two leading alternatives to the trade-off exercise as a means to moderate between trade values and other social values: (i) *laissez-régler* (used here to denote a permissive attitude taken by the international system, allowing local governments freedom to regulate in the domestic sphere) and (ii) international regulation (a decision to moderate between these values in a more specific, and in a positive,[34] international legislative manner).

The first alternative—*laissez-régler*—may allow the erosion of international commitments in ways that may be unacceptable in at least some international law settings, but may be acceptable in other settings where few externalities exist, or where states may make ad hoc bargains at low transaction costs. In fact, mechanisms for managing the conflict between trade values and other social values have the effect of constraining state intervention, either in favor of laissez-faire or, where combined with international legislative devices, in favor of international regulation. "The modern regulatory state inevitably produces burdens on trade, if only because of the unavoidable lack of regulatory uniformity."[35] Petersmann argues in favor of international disciplines on national regulation—against *laissez-régler*—in order to protect laissez-faire.[36]

A *laissez-régler* approach to local regulation is a decision to decentralize decisions about regulation. Kitch explains why decentralization is not *necessarily* the enemy of free trade: that centralized supervision or control is only one way that local units can cooperate to achieve their goals.

> The fact that there is decentralized authority over the laws and government practices affecting commerce does not mean that there will not be free trade. Free trade among decentralized authorities will result from voluntary cooperation, motivated by the fact that free trade will produce greater wealth for all to share. In the short run, this approach to free trade may cause significant bargaining instability, as each jurisdiction tries to establish a bargaining position through bluff, threat, and implemented threat. But in the long run, this system may provide more free trade than centralized authority because it places stronger incentives on each jurisdiction to promulgate efficient rules for both its internal and external commerce.[37]

Kitch is implicitly comparing two different centralizing structures: one mandatory, and the other voluntary; one based on treaty or organization, and the other based on autonomous cooperation. As North has pointed out, Kitch's perspective seems to be based on an assumption that it is cheaper in transaction cost terms for states within the U.S. federal system to get together on an informal basis to cooperate, than it is for this cooperation to be imposed by the federal government: Kitch is making an assumption as to which is the more efficient instrument of cooperation.[38] North responds that we do not "know that decentralized authority would promote more efficient rules than would centralized authority."[39]

Furthermore, as suggested in Chapters 2 and 5, there are a number of rationales for centralization, as well as a number of potential rules for allocating authority among states under decentralization. The variety of rationales makes it difficult to choose between centralization and decentralization. The trade-off devices examined herein may be viewed as heuristics for determining, in particular settings, whether decentralized authority or centralized authority is more satisfactory. They may be viewed as instruments for effecting a dynamic and variable type of subsidiarity analysis. In the sense discussed in Chapter 2, these trade-off devices may be viewed as heuristics for contingent intervention by a centralized hegemon, ensuring stable and efficient regulatory competition.

As instruments of negative integration, the trade-off devices discussed in this section may serve another dynamic purpose, by providing incentives for positive international regulation where they strike down domestic regulation. Furthermore, these trade-off devices clarify and cull the appropriate topics of and scope for international regulation, by indicating what domestic regulation is acceptable. Once domestic regulation is identified as acceptable pursuant to the rules applied by courts, it is for the legislative process to determine whether the international values are great enough to justify superseding domestic law by international regulation. In this respect, these trade-off devices may serve to allocate work between adjudicative and legislative decision-making processes.[40]

From a horizontal, as opposed to vertical, perspective, these trade-off devices may be viewed as intended not to limit local autonomy, but to restrain "state interference in the affairs of other states."[41] Thus, local autonomy is on both sides of the equation, although in some instances it is represented by international institutions. "Interference arises from two basic causes, state protection of local commerce against external competition, and extra costs that result when more than one sovereign regulates or taxes the same person or transaction. The latter costs are of two kinds— multiple burdens, and conflict costs caused by inconsistent regulation."[42]

In current or static terms, trade-off devices serve as heuristics for determining when domestic regulation should be suppressed: they moderate between the domestic *(laissez-régler)* and the international on a case-by-case basis. In intertemporal terms, perhaps they serve in some cases as bridges through time from *laissez-régler* to international regulation.

This section pursues a roughly comparative methodology,[43] finding significant similarities in the texts and approaches applied in the three jurisdictions examined. Beginning with comparative cost-benefit analysis as a presumptively best alternative, this section seeks to comprehend moves to other approaches based on problems with cost-benefit analysis, and thereby also seeks to explain variations among these other approaches. These relationships cannot be drawn precisely, as there are many variables and only a small number of cases to compare, but it is hoped to suggest lines of further inquiry.

The following discussion evaluates comparative cost-benefit analysis. Subsequently, this chapter examines the European Union, WTO, and U.S. approaches to national treatment, proportionality, least trade-restrictive alternative tests, balancing tests, and cost-benefit analysis in comparative perspective.

Comparative Cost-Benefit Analysis

This subsection will develop and critique comparative cost-benefit analysis.[44] This artificial, but ideal, trade-off device serves as a benchmark for evaluation of the actual trade-off devices to be considered and compared below. It has the advantage, by definition, of maximizing the net regulatory costs and trade benefits. This subsection begins to compare trade-off devices in terms of a wider institutional cost-benefit analysis that, in addition to taking account of the ability of a trade-off device to maximize the net sum of regulatory costs and trade benefits, examines administrability, distributive concerns, moral concerns, and theoretical concerns (avoidance of interpersonal comparison of utilities). These considerations may give impetus to a retreat from comparative cost-benefit analysis to simplified or truncated, or simply different, trade-off devices, including national treatment, simple means-ends rationality testing, proportionality testing, necessity testing, and balancing: the tests actually in use. "The difficulties of balancing or 'optimization' have . . . led scholars [and, we might add, courts] to define forms of 'bounded rationality' in which various rules of thumb substitute for fully comparative weighing of alternatives."[45]

Comparative Cost-Benefit Analysis Defined
As Farber and Hudec,[46] Pearce,[47] Runge,[48] and Wils[49] have noted, it is not difficult to begin to imagine a first-best trade-off device from an economic

standpoint. The simplest cost-benefit analysis, and the one most conventionally used in the regulatory context, is static cost-benefit analysis: in the context considered here it asks, is the regulatory benefit greater than the trade detriment?[50] However, this static, single-institutional analysis is, at least in theory, insufficient, and would in theory be replaced by a more dynamic comparative approach.[51] It does not even aspire to maximize net benefits (or minimize net costs), but simply examines whether benefits exceed costs.

Domestic cost-benefit analysis has been formally implemented at least since 1981 in the United States, with varying formulations in a number of contexts in legislation[52] and regulation and through executive order,[53] in order to discipline and inform the regulatory process. The 1993 formulation modified the original 1981 formulation by recognizing that benefits and costs cannot be limited to those that may be monetized. This provision would only consider effects outside the United States indirectly, at best. A "global" cost-benefit analysis would simply add international concerns to the domestic evaluation.[54]

A further important question is which types of domestic benefits may be considered: can the benefits of protection of local industry and jobs be included on the benefit side of the equation? We ordinarily would not include such pecuniary externalities in the equation, but it is important to recognize that these considerations are critical in political contexts, and that any model that did not reflect them would have little predictive power. Furthermore, can the benefits of reelection or other benefits to politicians and bureaucrats derived from protectionism be included? A full theory would respond to these questions. These concerns might include trade concerns, but might also include, inter alia, issues of externalization and the desire for explicit or implicit cooperation with other states.[55] Of course, once global cost-benefit analysis begins to include in its calculation adverse effects of regulation on foreign persons, in the form of either non-pecuniary externalities or pecuniary externalities, some kinds of regulation will appear more costly. On the other hand, regulation that protects foreign persons or removes externalities will appear more beneficial. Environmentalists and deregulators alike would be required to accept the consequences of thinking globally and acting locally.

A comparative global perspective would compare the cost-benefit profiles of various combinations of national regulation and international discipline of national regulation in a dynamic evaluative setting. Comparative cost-benefit analysis maximizes the sum of (i) benefits of free trade plus (ii) loss of benefits of regulation. Comparative cost-benefit analysis has some unique and substantial benefits, but many faults. Of course, merely recognizing its faults is an insufficient basis for determining not to use it: assuming acceptance of the proposition that trade-off is necessary, we must find a trade-off device that is superior.

In this section, I evaluate some of the parameters by which comparative cost-benefit analysis might be compared with other trade-off devices: (i) maximization of net gains of trade and regulation, (ii) administrability, (iii) distributive concerns, (iv) moral concerns, and (v) theoretical concerns. These factors are not themselves commensurable, and so we cannot place them on a simple tote board to determine when comparative cost-benefit analysis should or should not be used. Rather, these factors must be examined and subjected to political or deliberative analysis in order to determine which trade-off device should be used in particular circumstances.

Maximization of Net Gains of Trade and Regulation
By definition, comparative cost-benefit analysis is a relentless search for the solution that results in maximum net gains of trade and regulation. As noted above, one element of such maximization involves the inclusion of global effects. The inclusion of global effects may be examined using either the rhetoric of efficiency and externalization, or the rhetoric of political legitimation. These two rhetorics are two sides of the same coin.

One of the main arguments in favor of the use of the dormant Commerce Clause in the United States has been the problem of exclusion of affected foreign parties from the political process:

> Underlying the stated rule has been the thought, often expressed in judicial opinion, that when the regulation is of such a character that its burden falls principally upon those without the state, legislative action is not likely to be subjected to those political restraints which are normally exerted on legislation where it affects adversely some interests within the state.[56]

This statement by Justice Harlan Fiske Stone reflects economic theory relating to externalities: states may be expected to seek, where possible, to impose costs on outsiders. Such externalization is often presumed inefficient because the decision makers do not take all of the costs of action into account. It is also seen as illegitimate insofar as the persons making the decisions are not the ones who will bear the full consequences of those decisions. Thus, in the Commerce Clause context, Tushnet has argued that "a national viewpoint must be inserted in the process if the real costs are to be fully considered. In a sense, national supervision is designed to guarantee that the external costs of regulation are considered by local legislatures."[57]

Externalization and Prescriptive Jurisdiction

Thus, an initial issue for any trade-off device to address is the degree of externalization: how much of the effects of a local measure are felt externally, measured in either relative (percentage of total effects) or absolute (magnitude of external effects) terms?[58] In other words, how much jurisdictional overlap exists? It is important to note that the amount of overlap depends on horizontal allocation of prescriptive jurisdiction: on how prescriptive jurisdiction is allocated among states—the subject of our discussion in Chapter 2. As shown there, it is possible in theory, but not in practice, to devise rules of prescriptive jurisdiction that would be ideal in fiscal federalism terms: that would exclude overlap. This would eliminate the externality problem discussed above and substitute a significant accounting or jurisdiction allocation problem.[59]

Levmore argues that in a specific type of externalization—cases of exploitation by one state of monopoly power to the disadvantage of outsiders—a per se rule of invalidity should apply.[60] In the case of mere "interferences" with interstate commerce, on the other hand, Levmore argues for cost-benefit analysis. He thus limits the scope of applicability of cost-benefit analysis. Levmore generalizes his exploitation-interference dichotomy by arguing that in circumstances in which externalization is greater, judicial scrutiny should be greater.[61] This is justified as a proxy for a balancing test: where externalization is greater, there is less likely to be a countervailing local benefit. However, this is not a per se rule: in some cases, cost-benefit analysis may indicate that a local regulation is justified even if most of the cost side falls on nonresidents.[62]

Implicit in Levmore's distinction is a comparative institutional analysis that prefers to leave decisions to local political processes where they are likely fully to evaluate costs as well as benefits.[63] Where the local political processes cannot be expected to reach a globally efficient position, due to the accentuated capacity to externalize, he would truncate the analysis and simply hold the state legislation invalid. To the extent, on the other hand, that costs are borne internally, by domestic consumers or others, there is less reason to expect the state political process to act inefficiently, and so a per se rule of invalidity is not appropriate.

Representation and Legitimation

As noted above, externalization and political legitimation through representation are two sides of the same coin: one in economic terms, and the other in political terms. The exclusion of foreigners argument includes—or, translated from economic into political terms, is—a claim regarding legitimacy: that the internal political process is insufficient to legitimate the application of domestic law to the disadvantage of foreigners, who, by definition, have not participated in the formal political process that led to the legislation.[64] However, the suggested remedies for this alleged illegitimacy raise other issues of legitimacy: (i) is it appropriate for central decision makers to override local decisions, and (ii) are central courts the appropriate forum to do so? These questions, which combined ask whether central courts should supervise local legislatures, raising the "government close to the people" concern of subsidiarity, recall at least part of the legitimacy problem with *Lochner*-era substantive due process.[65]

In a sense, the rejection of *Lochner*[66] is a recognition that efficiency cannot be determined in the abstract, but only by political processes.[67] This point is central to the discussion of the respective roles of courts versus legislatures. One difference between substantive due process and Commerce Clause balancing is that, as noted above, Commerce Clause balancing always includes an additional set of values that are not normally expected to be incorporated in local legislatures' deliberations.[68] The argument from representational legitimacy, like the argument from externalization, seems to have a reciprocal nature.

Administrability is an important parameter by which to critique comparative cost-benefit analysis, as comparative cost-benefit analysis entails substantial costs of administration: the costs of evaluating regulatory costs and benefits and trade costs and benefits. One way of evaluating administrability is by reference to the distinction between a standard and a rule, discussed earlier in this chapter. In this sense, comparative cost-benefit analysis is a standard, while a trade-off device like national treatment or simple means-ends rationality testing may be considered more rule-like (although in practice it too allows substantial discretion). Furthermore, national treatment and simple means-ends rationality testing are less likely to invalidate local regulation, leaving it to the political process to address inefficiencies remaining when local legislation is left standing. Therefore, administrability also implicates the choice of courts versus legislatures as institutional devices for doing trade-offs.

Proportionality, balancing, and cost-benefit analysis rebel against legal formalism, holding that mere categories are insufficient to determine rights, but that evaluative measures must be applied. Legal formalism is thus hostile to these trade-off devices. However, Sullivan counters that "standards make visible and accountable the inevitable weighing process that rules obscure."[69]

In terms of administrability, it seems that rules would be preferred to standards as a general matter. They facilitate planning by private actors, and reduce the costs of adjudication after activity has occurred. However, as discussed above, there are many detailed and situation-specific factors to consider in comparing rules with standards.

Of course, even formal rules have potentially significant costs: the exceptions, and their determination, may devour the administrability of the rule. In practice, courts may develop distinctions, exceptions, and strained interpretations in order to allow the court's vision of substantive justice to triumph over predictability and administrability.

As part of the decision whether, and what extent of, central supervision of local regulation is efficient, it is necessary to determine whether the central supervision should be effected by adjudicative or legislative institutions. While this chapter does not address the way that legislatures make trade-offs, legislation represents the default option, preferred by many, for making trade-offs. Choice of a less intrusive judicial trade-off device is consonant with an emphasis on central legislative action to make trade-offs. There are several issues that affect the choice between legislation and adjudication in this context. The first that I will address is institutional competence. Second is the dichotomy, examined above, between rules (which purport to give more control to the legislator) and standards (which purport to confer a measure of discretion to the adjudicator). Third, and most important, is the question of which institution best reflects constituent interests—best serves as a forum for the revelation of preferences. Fourth, and most sophisticated, is the question of how central adjudicative and legislative institutions work together, and how they work with local legislators.

It is a commonplace that legislatures, the consummate political branches, are best able to engage in subtle balancing and weighing of competing social interests.[70] Like other common knowledge, the origins and bases of this commonplace are often forgotten. "The competing considerations in cases involving state proprietary action often will be subtle, complex, politically charged, and difficult to assess under traditional Commerce Clause analysis. . . . The adjustment of interests in this context is better suited for Congress than this Court."[71] However, given the realist and critical insight that judicial decisions inevitably are also politically charged, and given the fact that all good adjudication of difficult cases is subtle and complex, this commonplace may be usefully subjected to further analysis. While this commonplace is suspect as a matter of bureaucratic institutional competence, it may be revalidated by virtue of the fact that legislatures provide a more direct forum for revelation of individual preferences than do courts.

Justice Antonin Scalia wondered, "I do not know what qualifies us to make . . . the ultimate (and most ineffable) judgment as to whether, given importance-level x, and effectiveness-level y, the worth of the statute is 'outweighed' by impact-on-commerce z."[72] This statement adds to our discourse in two ways. First, it frames cost-benefit analysis in something akin to Hand Formula terms. By doing so, it implicitly raises the question, if courts can balance this way in negligence cases, why can they not balance this way in interstate or international commerce cases? Second, in this statement, Scalia asks the question that this chapter must begin to address: what qualifies courts to engage in cost-benefit analysis? Academic commentators often beg the question of judicial competence to engage in balancing or cost-benefit analysis. Consider the following statement by Donald Regan:

> The [federal] court has no warrant for second-guessing the [state] legislature either about what counts as a good effect (providing the legislature is not aiming at something forbidden, which gets us back to the purpose inquiry), or about the valuation of the good effect . . . or about just how much of the good effect is actually achieved. For that matter, the court has no basis for deciding how bad is what would have to be regarded as the bad effect in a balancing analysis, namely the diversion of business.[73]

First, Regan appears to be referring to state (not federal) legislatures as the appropriate evaluators of costs and benefits. Accepting this assumption, we may consider that the state may also enter into agreements with other states in order to maximize good effects. Similarly, each individual is presumptively the best observer of his own values. However, when an individual enters society, he accepts that the things he values may be evaluated differently, and traded off differently, by others, and that it may be useful collectively to refer these questions to a court. Thus, it is plausible that a state, entering international society, would agree to accept similar institutions.

Thus, when a state enters a federation or economic integration organization, it may choose to accept that the things it values may be evaluated differently by that organization's organs. If it does not, it would not allocate power over those issues to that organization. While within the United States, this contractarian perspective may be stale, in the sense that it was more or less true in 1787, but may no longer be true today, the WTO and European Union social contracts comprise fresh examples of states giving up autonomy in exchange for reciprocal action by other states. The question Regan begs is whether or not the states have done so.

While Regan argues that "provided they do not single out foreigners, the states need not attend positively to the foreign effects of laws they adopt nor to the distribution between locals and foreigners of the benefits and burdens of those laws,"[74] there is no theoretical or empirical basis for this position. Federal governments like the United States, regional integration organizations like the European Union, and international organizations like the WTO exist not simply to police discrimination,[75] and have seen fit through both legislative and adjudicative action to enhance regulatory cooperation in more intrusive respects. Why would these entities simply leave the gains from this type of cooperation on the table? Implicit in Regan's argument, but not analytically supported, is the assumption that this cooperation should be effected by legislative bodies but not through the use of adjudicative bodies.

Certainly, individual courts seem to have fewer analytical resources at their disposal than, for example, the U.S. Congress.[76] However, if magnitude of analytical resources were the only determinant of whether courts should decide cases, there might never be any adjudication. Is the trade-off question special in a way that indicates that it should be answered legislatively rather than judicially? One important respect in which the trade-off question is special is that it is a constitutional, or meta-legislative, question: like other secondary rules, it deals with the allocation of power to legislate. Of course, in the horizontal, as opposed to vertical, federal context, courts deal with this problem frequently, under the label of "conflict of laws" or "prescriptive jurisdiction."[77] In addition, courts are frequently called upon to apply constitutional rules to invalidate legislative acts: this is what constitutional rules are for, and this is what judicial review is for.[78] Courts are required to balance and integrate multiple social values in most types of cases, including, as mentioned above, tort cases (applying the Hand Formula), choice of law decisions (applying the "modern" approach that requires balancing of multiple factors), and various types of constitutional judicial review. In each of these types of cases, courts implicitly balance or decide who balances, with or without the benefit of a legislated rule.

Courts have the ability to engage in context-specific analysis, whereas statutes are usually for general application. To the extent that rules differ from standards, the establishment of standards delegates substantial work to courts. In the U.S. dormant Commerce Clause context, "courts created the doctrine early, and undertook to monitor it, because Congress could not anticipate and provide for every conceivable impingement on interstate commerce, and the Union might not have survived if the courts had not intervened."[79] Courts have the ability to accept from legislatures a general bargain and to implement that bargain in particular cases.

Institutional Synergies: Central and Local, Legislative and Adjudicative
In the common law, property rights and liability rules developed initially through the elaboration of rules by iterative adjudication. Especially in the area of nuisance, a hybrid of property rights and liability, judicial balancing is the rule, at least in the United States. It is open to legislatures to override or supplement common law rules, and this happens often, given the fact that in domestic society we have well-developed legislative capacity. The same is true in the U.S. federal system, and in the European Union's common market: adjudication works together with legislation, and legislation intercedes where adjudication is determined by the legislature to produce an inadequate outcome. The European Union provides a vivid example of this type of interaction.[80] There are also interactions and synergies between adjudicative decision making and legislative decision making in the U.S. system.[81]

Redish and Nugent argue that state statutes within the United States should be excluded from judicial review under the dormant Commerce Clause because Congress can legislatively "review" and invalidate state statutes under the Supremacy Clause, and the states "have a special ability to protect their interests through resort to the national political process."[82] This is an argument against the doctrine of implicit preemption, which allows local regulatory barriers to trade to be addressed by courts prior to the legislation of specific (and supreme) central law. The argument in favor of dormant Commerce Clause preemption is bureaucratic and political, relying on the assertion that central legislatures are constrained by time and politics so that they cannot address all of the trade barriers local legislatures might create, and need preemptive assistance from courts.

Furthermore, it is worth noting that preemption simply reverses the bureaucratic burden of seeking central legislation, as, in the dormant Commerce Clause and European Union (former) Article 30 context, judicial invalidations may generally be "reversed" legislatively.[83] Thus, Congress may eliminate any Commerce Clause problem with state legislation, and may reverse a judicial determination of invalidity of state legislation under the Commerce Clause. On the other hand, the possibility of legislative reversal may help to legitimate and embolden judicial action invalidating local laws.[84] The European Union system lacks the broad legislative capacity of the U.S. Congress, and the WTO lacks any conventional legislative capacity at all.

In each of the circumstances studied in this section—the European Union, the WTO, and the United States—the need to establish free trade has challenged local prerogatives. In fact, the expansive definition of trade or commerce in the European Union and United States has significantly eroded the notion that there is a hard core of sovereignty reserved to their components.[85] Of course, many worry both about these challenges to state sovereignty and about challenges posed by the WTO system, as it expands and deepens its coverage of issues traditionally considered part of the *domaine reservé*.[86] However, the larger threat to sovereignty seems to come from the legislative capacity of the federal government in the United States, and of the European Union institutions. This is a critical institutional difference between the United States and European Union, on the one hand, and the WTO, on the other. The dormant Commerce Clause and former Articles 30 and 36 of the Treaty of Rome provide negative integration, but there is ample legislative capacity for positive integration, assuming political will. In the WTO system, there is little realized legislative capacity, and thus it is impossible to produce the kind of pro-integration judicial-legislative dynamic that has proven so powerful in the European Union.[87]

Distributive Concerns

It is impossible to separate issues of externalization and representational legitimation from issues of distribution. I examine externalization and legitimation above from the standpoint of whether the interests of foreigners are taken into account in the decision process; here, I consider whether those who lose due to the decision finally taken are compensated for their loss. Interestingly, none of the trade-off devices considered here provide for any direct compensation.

The U.S. Commerce Clause is often justified by reference to the political utility of economic union, and to the value of avoiding the jealousies, resentment, and retaliation that might arise from state actions that harm outsiders. The European Union's goal of economic union also has political motivations, and the WTO system also seeks, perhaps less explicitly and more indirectly, to promote political harmony. These political goals may be recharacterized as problems of distributive effects: the distributive effects of local law should not be, and should not be seen to be, too adverse for a particular outside group, or for the group of outsiders as a whole.[88] Thus, even where the global costs of a local law are less than its global benefits, it is worth considering the distribution of those costs and benefits. There are several ways of rationalizing the inclusion of distributive concerns in our analysis. First, in the standard analysis, economic efficiency is compromised for the political stability that arises from a certain distribution of incomes. Second, economic efficiency is defined broadly enough to encompass non-"economic" values, such as political stability. In both cases, it is recognized that a trade-off between efficiency (in the form of maximization of net gains) and distribution is rational; the only question is whether the trade-off is one that economics can address.

Considering economic efficiency and distribution in the first sense, it is clear that one of the central issues in analysis of "trade and . . ." problems is the distributive consequences of any determination: "trade and . . ." problems arise where increased freedom of trade comes at the expense of local regulatory benefits, and conversely, local regulatory benefits give rise to costs in trade terms. The trade costs fall on outsiders, as well as local consumers, and standard public choice theory indicates that local producers will often prevail. From a practical and from a strategic standpoint, distributive consequences may stand in the way of change: state A may request that state B revise its regulation in order to ameliorate adverse trade consequences to state B, and state A may refuse because the requested revision would confer a detriment on its residents, without consideration of the relative magnitude of the detriment conferred on state B residents. This is simply one of the types of externality discussed in Chapter 1.

A state of affairs like that described above is Pareto efficient if it is impossible to improve the welfare of state B without diminishing the welfare of state A (and vice versa). Thus, assuming for a moment that it is impossible to bribe state B, the Pareto efficiency criterion will not examine the relative size of the detriments, and will accept this state of affairs, even if it could be shown that the regulatory benefit to state B is only worth $1 million while the trade detriment to state A is worth $10 million However, if representatives of state A can communicate, negotiate, and contract with state B to divide the $9 million surplus, they would be expected to do so. Thus, if transaction costs are less than the surplus, this state of affairs is not Pareto efficient, and such procurement of consent is an acceptable means of reaching Pareto efficiency.

Potential Pareto efficiency merely requires that enough surplus be generated to compensate the injured outsiders, without concerning itself with whether compensation is actually paid, or whether the transaction costs of such payment exceed the surplus generated, in which case it would not be expected that compensation would be paid. Another way of understanding potential Pareto efficiency is that it would be equivalent to Pareto efficiency, assuming a condition of zero transaction costs. In other words, a particular move is potentially Pareto superior to the status quo if its net benefits exceed those of the status quo, and is potentially Pareto efficient if its net benefits exceed those generated by any other conceivable structure.[89]

Potential Pareto efficiency assumes away transaction costs and the problem of distribution, but reaches a potentially higher aggregate net benefit, and assumes that transactions will occur to reach that higher aggregate net benefit. For this reason, potential Pareto efficiency is often an unsatisfactory policy tool: it cannot be assumed that a potential Pareto-efficient state of affairs will be reached, due to the actual existence of transaction costs. Thus, a tribunal applying cost-benefit analysis would be well advised to consider the potential for redistributive transactions between the principals, and the distributive consequences of its decision. Potential Pareto efficiency is often eschewed by liberal economists because it allows policy changes to be justified without regard to their distributive consequences: a regulatory change that benefits the rich more than it harms the poor would be validated under potential Pareto efficiency, but invalidated under Pareto efficiency analysis.

In the real world, redistributive payoffs may be direct and in cash, but more frequently, especially in the international context, they will take the form of formal or informal, diffuse or narrow, reciprocity. Often, redistributive payoffs are agreed on and then required pursuant to law or other institutional arrangements. For example, agreement to legislate by majority vote, as in the European Union, may be viewed as an institutional structure for an unspecified, and only partially anticipated, series of transactions.[90] Agreement to a particular trade-off device to be applied by an adjudicative tribunal may be viewed similarly. Sometimes you will be disciplined, and sometimes I will be disciplined: we will receive roughly equivalent payoffs, and even if in the fullness of time yours turns out to be larger, the present value of mine is larger than what I would have received without such agreement. This is the type of Harsanyian stochastic symmetry discussed in Chapter 3 in connection with CIL, and in Chapter 5 in connection with the formation of organizations.

Potential Pareto efficiency is an armchair mechanism for striking hypothetical bargains. The armchair analyst speculates as to what people want and calculates a bargain that they might enter into to maximize the aggregate preferences of the participants. Therefore, potential Pareto efficiency has two problems. First, we have little basis for confidence that its speculated preferences are correct. Second, its phantom compensation raises the specter of adverse distributive effects.

Moral Concerns; Commensurability

Coincident with the rise of cost-benefit analysis in environmental and other regulatory areas, and its use and misuse[91] to restrain such regulation, has developed a critical literature, suggesting problems with cost-benefit analysis.[92] This literature has criticized cost-benefit analysis both in theory and in practice. Some of the practical critiques of cost-benefit analysis as used are clearly correct. For example, cost-benefit analysis that considers only regulatory costs, or only monetary costs and benefits, is simply ignorant. The more serious theoretical critiques, of the more thoughtful form of cost-benefit analysis, argue that this cost-benefit analysis relies on commensuration, which is (i) morally deficient and (ii) theoretically objectionable as it involves interpersonal comparisons of utility.[93]

Most of us seem to engage in this type of cost-benefit analysis in our individual decisions, trading off one moral principle against another, or morality against the achievement of other goals. Where we might otherwise consider a moral tenet to be a side constraint, a more parsimonious theory, with greater explanatory power, might consider a moral tenet a preference.[94]

The evaluation of costs and benefits of collective decisions is a political act, but is also probably a useful analytical step in understanding the consequences of the proposed decision. What role does monetization serve? Different endowments and different preferences make it impossible in the real world to use money to engage in interpersonal comparison of utilities. However, in a zero transaction costs world, one in which potential Pareto efficiency is the same as ordinary Pareto efficiency, an infinite series of costless transactions would result in each of us maximizing his or her own utilities, and the prices at which these transactions took place (if we used money) would be good indicators of our utility functions. This is why the fundamental theorem of welfare economics chooses market transactions as the best engine of welfare: the zero transaction cost market results in perfect revelation of utility. Thus there may be low transaction cost circumstances, perhaps where there are highly liquid markets, in which market valuation in money terms is a (relatively) good indicator of utility. Furthermore, to be selected as a tool of analysis, monetary evaluation need not be a perfect indicator of utility or method of arraying information. It need only be a better indicator than the alternatives. And so, we turn to comparative institutional analysis: what structure allows us to make social decisions that best reflect our collective individual preferences?

Conventional cost-benefit analysis seeks to reduce all costs and benefits to monetary terms, so that they will be comparable mathematically. It does so using a "willingness to pay" criterion for benefits.[95] For example, it is thought possible to deduce the willingness of individuals to pay for cleaner air by analyzing the price differentials for housing in locations with high air quality versus locations with low air quality.[96]

Cost-benefit analysis in the context discussed here necessarily involves the comparison of differently denominated values, such as free trade versus environmental protection.[97] None of these values, including the market-type values of free trade and competition, are easily monetized.[98] However, this only means that they cannot easily be compared in formal mathematical terms along a single dimension; it does not mean that they cannot be compared at all: apples are red, oranges contain more acid, both are somewhat spherical but with different distinctive shapes, and so on. Each of these qualities may be quantified, but their quantification cannot be combined, except arbitrarily. Perhaps the integration of multiple policies, and less formal analysis that compares without mathematics, is the domain of law and politics, rather than of mathematical economics. If it is, law still has much to learn from economics.

Moreover, the act of choice is an act of either explicit or implicit commensuration. That is, our trade-off decisions may be analyzed as circumstances of revelation of preferences, and combined with the trade-off decisions of others to provide information about relative "prices." This does not mean, however, that it is incumbent on *courts or legislatures* to commensurate in particular circumstances: whether they should do so is a separate question. It is a question of comparative institutional analysis. Nor does it mean that we must monetize: it may not assist clarity of analysis to do so.

> The application of the potential Pareto superiority criterion requires some metric of comparison to make sense of the requirement of full compensation, but neither that criterion nor the commitment to subjective criteria for the evaluation of personal welfare entail selecting money (or wealth) as the metric. Money is an appealing metric (or unit of account) for economists because it is the medium of exchange and therefore is the convenient denominator for comparing interpersonal exchange values of events or options.[99]

It is impossible directly to translate the values of local regulatory autonomy into monetary terms. Indirect market methods,[100] contingent valuation methods,[101] "real options" methods, and the development of a liquid market for barter of regulatory jurisdiction[102] may provide rough guides to conversion. Where there is no monetized market that may reveal valuation of particular regulatory or trade measures, the only available test of the Pareto efficiency or potential Pareto efficiency of a particular outcome is whether it is accepted by the parties involved.[103]

Theoretical Concerns: Avoidance of Interpersonal Comparison of Utility

Even if it were possible to monetize all values, interpersonal comparison of utility, using money as a reference or not, would still raise difficult theoretical problems. Despite its widespread use in law and economics, the concept of potential Pareto efficiency is criticized by some economists, because it entails the theoretical problem of interpersonal comparison of utility.[104] In our context, it does so by juxtaposing the costs (and benefits) incurred by state A with those incurred by state B, and purporting to compare them. This requires not only that the costs be measured in comparable terms (here, money), but also that a monetary unit be a valid reflection of utility for each individual involved.

Finally, it would seem useful to imagine the problem of comparative cost-benefit analysis as a problem of institutions. When an individual engages in decision making, she may commensurate between her own values on a relatively consistent and rational basis, and engage only in *intra*personal comparison of utility. When and to the extent that she enters society and shares decision-making authority, she agrees on structures that will allow her input into the relevant social unit's decisions, presumably reflecting to a satisfactory extent her values. While Arrow showed that preferences cannot be aggregated in this sense, again,[105] people seem to form institutions to do so. They can mandate those institutions to make decisions based on a gestalt or on "deliberative judgment," or they can mandate those institutions to monetize. Either way, the institutions will commensurate; either way they will engage in interpersonal comparison of utility. The choice of method will depend on an evaluation of which method provides the best decisions at the lowest cost.

Comparison of Actual Trade-Off Devices

I continue the evaluation of comparative cost-benefit analysis by examining the alternatives extant in the same terms by which I evaluated comparative cost-benefit analysis, albeit more briefly. The trade-off devices examined here, other than comparative cost-benefit analysis, are in use, to varying extents, in varying combinations, and with varying effect, in the three jurisdictions considered here.

Each of the tests mentioned above has been judicially cultivated on relatively stark textual bases, at least at first. They have met with political acquiescence and in some cases political approval, but have suffered attacks alleging illegitimacy on varying grounds, including the lack of a textual basis.[106]

Thus, even if legislatures or framers of constitutions and treaties did not intend to mandate these trade-off analyses, judges invented them. They did so not necessarily to increase their bureaucratic power, but in order to fill a gap that required filling in order to decide cases: the gap in clarity of allocation of competences between the center and the periphery. Only in a limited number of areas are *all* local impediments to free trade invalidated; only in a limited number of areas are local actions *invulnerable* to central judicial review. In these clear areas, allocation of authority along the vertical axis requires little judicial analysis, but only cursory categorization. However, in other areas, notably the field where the majority of problems involving local initiatives that impede free trade are located, the local initiatives are neither always prohibited nor always permitted. The devices described below are judicially created devices to discriminate between those to be prohibited and those to be permitted.

Of course, saying that these devices lack strong textual foundation and are judicially created is not to say that the language of the texts on which they are based is unimportant, or that their judicial creation was somehow illegitimate. However, it is fair to say that these texts serve only as a starting point of analysis. In the case of the U.S. Constitution and the Treaty of Rome, it was recognized by the relevant judicial bodies that in order to create a common market, local laws would need to be disciplined. In the United States, federal legislation was from an early point available to discipline local laws, but the preemption doctrine significantly enhanced protection from localism:

> I do not think the United States would come to an end if we lost our power to declare an Act of Congress void. I do think the Union would be imperiled if we could not make that declaration as to the laws of the several States. For one in my place sees how often a local policy prevails with those who are not trained to national views and how often action is taken that embodies what the Commerce Clause was to end.[107]

In the European Union, central legislation by majority vote was not and is not always possible, putting more pressure on judicial supervision of local law. The ECJ "did not receive the power to declare the law of a Member State void. . . . but went as far as it could to reach the same practical outcome."[108] Nor did the WTO receive the power to declare the law of a member state void, or even perhaps to require a member state to change its law, but it does have the power in effect to declare a member state law in violation of WTO law.

The Move from Comparative Cost-Benefit Analysis
I began with the proposition that comparative cost-benefit analysis unqualifiedly maximizes the net sum of gains from trade and gains from reg-

ulation. However, at least as a trade-off device, comparative cost-benefit analysis experiences real problems of administrability, and raises distributive, moral, and theoretical concerns. A comparison of other trade-off devices with comparative cost-benefit analysis in these terms might suggest that comparative cost-benefit analysis is not used because of these problems, which may be reduced, at a cost in terms of maximization of net gains, by the use of other trade-off devices. If these trade-off devices are chosen accurately with social welfare in mind, we may presume that the cost in terms of maximization is less than the gains in terms of addressing distributive, moral, and theoretical concerns.

However, it may be that our capacity to optimize social welfare is limited by institutional constraints, including transaction costs and strategic behavior. It may be that we as a global society have not yet developed institutional solutions that facilitate greater use of comparative cost-benefit analysis—that we have not extended the Pareto frontier as far as we might by institutional innovation. With greater evaluation and institutional innovation, it may be that comparative cost-benefit analysis will play a greater role in international decision making.

For many commentators and judges, simple national treatment is the appropriate fallback position. However, national treatment, in the absence of explicit discrimination or evidence of intentional unjustified discrimination, may suffer from some of the same problems as comparative cost-benefit analysis. Furthermore, there seem to be significant instances where discipline is worthwhile in the absence of explicit discrimination or evidence of intentional discrimination. Simple means-ends rationality testing adds little to the depth of scrutiny provided by national treatment. Proportionality testing is quite similar to cost-benefit analysis, with a greater margin of deference, and consequently provides some of the same benefits and is susceptible to some of the same problems as cost-benefit analysis.

Necessity testing (defined as a search for the least trade restrictive alternative reasonably available) seems overbroad and underinclusive, but nevertheless is frequently used. Necessity testing subject to the "reasonably available" qualification applied in WTO law operates on two parameters: trade cost and regulatory cost. However, it declines to include regulatory benefit in its analysis. It accepts a degree of inaccuracy in exchange for the benefits of avoiding the greatest moral and theoretical concerns that may come of evaluating and comparing the benefits of domestic regulation.

Balancing, as a fuzzy or less formal cost-benefit analysis or comparative cost-benefit analysis, seems to have some real benefits, including the avoidance of attempts to commensurate in mathematical terms. Where balancing includes considerations of whether a less restrictive alternative exists, it incorporates some of the benefits of necessity testing with a "reasonably available" qualification: a requirement that the less restrictive alternative be reasonably available.

All of the trade-off devices considered here have distributive problems: they all make binary decisions that may leave costs on outsiders. This can be rationalized on a broad stochastic symmetry basis: in a community, sometimes I lose and sometimes you lose. On the other hand, this problem of distribution—of compensation to losers—may be reduced by referring the decision to the political process.

In this connection, the political process—the legislature in particular—may be viewed as a specialized institution for the transfer of value, especially under conditions of incommensurability. Courts may transfer more difficult problems to the legislature simply by declining to settle them, or by settling them in an unsatisfactory way (particularly where not to decide is to decide). In this way, use of a device such as national treatment that declines to discipline a range of local legislation that seems inefficient may be justified as a referral of the linked tasks of interpersonal comparison of utility and distribution to the legislature. It is in this sense that those who argue for national treatment as the main trade-off device can be correct. Of course, this argument for national treatment is admissible only where the legislature is available to act; this is not widely the case in the pre–Single European Act history of the European Union, and is not the case at all in the present days of the WTO.

However, necessity testing subject to a "reasonably available" qualification seems to provide some of the same benefits as national treatment, with greater ability to maximize net gains from trade and regulation, while avoiding the greatest problems of administrability, moral concerns, and theoretical concerns. Moreover, necessity testing subject to a "reasonably available" qualification accepts more responsibility for the adjudicator than does national treatment, standing ready to fill gaps in legislative capability. This fact may support the use of necessity testing subject to a "reasonably available" qualification in the WTO context.

One might then argue that national treatment is appropriate for circumstances where a well-developed legislative capacity exists. And indeed, in the United States, the basic rule seems to be national treatment, with other tests serving as mere proxies for or adjuncts to national treatment. Conversely, a basic rule of necessity testing subject to a "reasonably available" qualification seems more appropriate where central legislative capacity is more limited, such as in the WTO.

Table 7.3 summarizes the comparison of the trade-off devices described above.

Trade-Offs, Institutional Choice, and Subsidiarity

We can consider the trade-off devices reviewed in this section as dynamic devices or heuristics for allocation of jurisdiction: as dynamic components of constitutions. In this sense, they respond to the horizontal and vertical allocation of authority problems described in Chapters 2 and 5. First, to which level of governance should responsibility be assigned? Second, is there a way in which this power can be fragmented, so that the portion that is more valuable at the local level is enjoyed there, while the portion that is more valuable at the central level is assigned to the central level? These questions are critical to the economics of federalism, which addresses the utility of congruence between effects and governance, and would seek to establish governmental units based on such congruence, subject to the costs of fragmentation of authority. It is essential to recognize that each trade-off device serves as a heuristic to allocate authority in particularistic, fact-specific ways over time, and thus may provide a more complex solution to the level of authority problem than a simple static and/or broad allocation, such as is expected to be found in constitutions.[109]

This section has argued that while comparative cost-benefit analysis can help us to choose institutions and, as applied by courts, may provide solutions to "trade and . . ." problems that maximize the net benefits of trade and regulation, comparative cost-benefit analysis has limitations. These limitations are intrinsic to comparative cost-benefit analysis, but also are dependent on the particular institutional structure in which the decisions are made. Various simplified or truncated devices, and various institutional fora, for making these trade-offs may be indicated in different factual contexts. "Social scientists have concluded from their studies that decision-making shortcuts are appropriate for relatively unimportant decisions, and fuller optimization is worth the time for major ones."[110] In addition, it is clear that courts or dispute resolution tribunals may not be the best place

Table 7.3 Summary of analysis

	Maximization	Administrability	Moral Concerns	Theoretical Concerns
National treatment	No direct maximization	Good in theory, but it flows into other tests	Often refers difficult decisions to legislature	Not raised until it flows into other tests
Necessity testing subject to a "reasonably available" qualification	Minimizes only the trade cost and cost of regulation parameters	Problem	Reduced due to abstention from from assessment of regulatory benefits	Reduced due to abstention assessment of regulatory benefits
Proportionality	Balancing with a margin of deference	Larger problem	Significant as it seeks to commensurate between values	Significant as it seeks to engage in interpersonal comparison of utility
Balancing/cost-benefit analysis	Nondynamic; therefore, limited maximization	Larger problem	Significant as it seeks to commensurate between values	Significant as it seeks to engage in interpersonal comparison of utility
Comparative cost-benefit analysis	Full maximization	Largest problem	Significant as it seeks to commensurate between values	Significant as it seeks to engage in interpersonal comparison of utility

to engage in comparative cost-benefit analysis; rather, the redistributive question always raised by potential Pareto efficiency is seen as the natural province of legislatures. Finally, legislatures overcome the problems of interpersonal comparison of utility insofar as they are places where preferences are revealed and collated directly.

The question of which preferences to express at a lower level and which to express at a higher level is the question at the core of subsidiarity analysis.[111] Just as each of our decisions is made through cost-benefit analysis, this section has argued that the choice of level would be made most accurately by cost-benefit analysis. However, this point is only one input in the choice of trade-off device, which includes as other real-world inputs costs of administration and error and distributive legitimacy, as well as problems of commensuration and interpersonal comparison of utility.

It is well to repeat that comparative cost-benefit analysis is inevitably political, and is never neutral. How could it be different, given that it seeks to bring together diverse preferences? Thus, it is important to approach comparative cost-benefit analysis with modesty, and to recognize that comparative cost-benefit analysis when performed by courts must be justified by the costs of using other preference revelation mechanisms like politics or markets, and will often be subject to being second-guessed by such mechanisms.

Finally, it may be worthwhile to suggest some testable hypotheses for further research. A new institutional economics theoretical perspective might yield a hypothesis that where political transaction costs are low for the production of central legislation, the political system would be used to make trade-offs of the kind discussed here. Thus, in circumstances of low political transaction costs, a narrow national treatment rule would be sufficient, referring the more difficult decisions to political decision making. On the other hand, in circumstances of high political transaction costs, it may become more attractive to accept trade-off decisions made by courts, suggesting a necessity test, balancing test, cost-benefit analysis, or comparative cost-benefit analysis. It is incumbent upon society to make trade-offs: the only question is which institutional mechanism should be used.

In order to test this hypothesis, it would be necessary to examine particular circumstances to understand the move from national treatment to proportionality testing or balancing and, sometimes, back again. For instance, can we explain the 1993 *Keck and Mithouard* decision of the ECJ, retrenching its supervision over national measures, in these terms?

The line of argument might point out that prior to the legislation of the Single European Act, sclerotic legislative capacity gave impetus to the ECJ's development of the *Cassis de Dijon* line of jurisprudence, in order judicially to make the trade-off decisions that could not be made legislatively except at high transaction costs. The Single European Act facilitated central legislation, diminishing this motivation for ECJ action. On the other hand, the growth of judicial discretion to balance in the WTO system may be interpreted as a reaction to the inability to legislate easily in that context. Again, decisions must be made, and national treatment alone seems to leave too much on the table. Anecdotes such as these could be reviewed with precision and grouped together, to determine whether this hypothesis may be used to guide the drafting and use of trade-off devices in particular circumstances.

Private Rights of Action

A debate has developed regarding the role of private parties in international law dispute resolution. At stake in this debate is control over the dispute resolution mechanism: whether it is controlled by states or whether it should be controlled by private persons. The focus of this debate is the WTO, and also international investment treaties like NAFTA. This debate has centered on issues of transparency and the right of private parties to submit amicus briefs. Some commentators have argued for the application of private rights of action to international trade law rules. While this section focuses on private rights of action in connection with WTO law, its methodology is applicable in other areas.

This section elaborates some considerations for use in evaluating the role of private parties in international law dispute settlement. Of course, there are a number of different ways that private persons might participate in international law dispute settlement, including rights to observe, rights to submit amicus briefs, and direct rights to bring lawsuits. In this section, I focus on private rights to bring lawsuits, although the considerations I adduce may be applied to other modes of private participation. There are also many different types of private persons, with varying interests, ranging from corporations whose interests are injured, to NGOs that are suing to protect a perceived public interest. Given these variations, and the varying preferences of states in terms of level of enforcement and other values, it is not surprising that negotiators would reach varying conclusions regarding the appropriate types of private participation in varying areas of international law.

Thus, this section suggests that the scope and character of private participation in different fields of international law–based dispute settlement (either in domestic courts or in international tribunals) would be expected to vary depending on how the more specific normative considerations discussed in this section are implicated in particular fields, and in connection with particular legal rules. It is therefore necessary to engage in case-specific analysis of the utility of private rights to participate in the context of particular legal rules, rather than a wholesale approach to private participation. Indeed, in certain areas, such as TRIPS, the WTO Agreement on Government Procurement, and NAFTA Chapter 11, private parties are required to be accorded varying rights to commence lawsuits, either within the domestic legal system or in an international legal system. In other areas, such as anti-dumping and anti-subsidies law, private parties are permitted under international law to be accorded private rights of action.

Natural law, human rights, democracy, or conventional claims regarding legitimacy are ultimately unsatisfying as bases for supporting individual participation in international law dispute settlement. In this section, we develop a set of normative considerations by which to evaluate private party participation and particular structures of private party participation. These normative considerations are adapted from two literatures that have developed in other contexts: (i) the political science literature analyzing the role of the ECJ in European integration,[112] and (ii) the law and economics literature analyzing private rights of action and public enforcement within U.S. domestic law.[113]

As with any comparative institutional analysis, the normative considerations I adduce cannot be applied directly to any particular body of law, but may form the basis for a research program to consider the effects of increased private party participation in a particular field of dispute settlement.

Litigation has two critical roles in governance.[114] As we examine the normative implications of varying modes of private participation, it is important to distinguish these modes. First, litigation is a locus where enforcement occurs ("litigation as enforcement"), and law is made formally binding. In connection with litigation as enforcement, our central question is whether states should relinquish to private actors the decision to make law binding. Here, we have a conflict between law and diplomacy. It is also a conflict between an exchange or contractual model of international law in which the maintenance of the balance of concessions between states is central,[115] and a public interest model of international law in which compliance with rules is important, even if there is a more attractive solution between the complaining state and the responding state.

Second, especially where legislation or new treaty making is difficult, litigation produces new law ("litigation as legislation"), where the incomplete instructions of treaty writers or legislators are filled in by judges, as discussed earlier in this chapter. Control over litigation entails a degree of control over the types of law that is made. WTO litigants like the U.S. Trade Representative (USTR) or the European Commission carefully and strategically select their arguments based on a long-term view of their overall perspective on what the rules *should* be. Each individual case has jurisprudential externalities that a private litigant may not take into account. Thus, the allocation of this legislative facility—whether to states or to private persons—is an important parameter in determining the scope of private rights of participation.

Furthermore, we must recognize that states accept treaty commitments as a package, including the applicable institutional arrangements, such as private access to dispute settlement. Thus, the choice of level and type of private access will have an effect on the type of commitments states will seek and make. Very simply, if international law becomes more inexorably binding due to private rights of action, states may determine to make fewer commitments, or less onerous commitments, or may determine to revisit the commitments they have made.[116] They may also determine to accord less legislative authority to the dispute settlement process, and provide more specific treaty rules, rather than general standards for further elaboration through dispute settlement. Furthermore, at this particular historical moment in the WTO context, with a recently "hardened" WTO legal regime by virtue of the 1994 change from consensus adoption to reverse consensus for panel and Appellate Body reports, some may question whether the international community is ready to digest increased "legalization" of the WTO.

It is best to avoid conclusory assertions of the rightness, fairness, democracy, or legitimacy of private participation in WTO dispute settlement. Private participation in dispute settlement should not be determined by natural law assertions, for the market is constructed, and the property, contract, and trading rights allocated to individuals are determined, not by natural law but by politics, hopefully informed by comparative institutional analysis. The right to litigate should be understood as a component of individual rights in the same way.

This analysis proceeds from a particular positivist concept of law. This concept is contractarian and does not accept the a priori goodness—the natural law credentials—of any particular law,[117] especially in the WTO legal system (as opposed to certain areas of human rights, criminal law, etc.). It is this concept that allows a detached, laissez-faire view of binding-ness and enforcement. Private participation in dispute settlement would, as an increment to public participation, increase the bindingness and enforcement of law.

Just as there is nothing natural about the market, there is nothing natural about private rights of action: they are not the natural state of the law.[118] Once we reject the assumption that there are identifiable and agreed-on natural law rights in international trade, which require particular (positive law!) remedies,[119] and once we understand each right and its quality as a function of the type of remedies available to realize the right, it is easy to conclude that these rights have no necessarily entailed remedies or rights of action.

As will be explained in more detail below, one might expect increased private rights to result in increased bindingness of a particular legal rule: increased effects on state behavior. However, in order to know from a natural law standpoint that this would be a good thing, it would be necessary to take a position on the consistency with natural law of the positive international law expected to be buttressed by private participation. To provide a brief example, the European Union's regulations concerning hormones in beef were definitively found illegal under WTO law, but the lack of domestic legal effect of WTO law permitted the European Union the flexibility to avoid compliance. Some would argue that this is a good thing. Within the trade context, Hudec has suggested that where the substantive law is suspect, "there is no reason to believe that the substantive function performed by courts is likely to move the content of policy in a more liberal direction."[120]

Nor are private rights of action necessarily consistent with the free market, human rights, or other nongovernmental spheres. Rather, and not purely as an imaginary exercise, we could describe private rights of action that would suppress market activity, or that would suppress political rights such as free speech. The law and economics literature of standing, a component of private rights of action, suggests that private rights, if too greatly dispersed, may impede market transactions. It is well understood that private rights to sue for libel may, depending on their formulation, excessively suppress free speech. Because of these problems with the natural law perspective, I take an agnostic view of private rights to participate and seek to understand their benefits and costs in particular circumstances. I conclude by recommending context-specific analysis of the utility of private rights to participate in the context of particular legal rules, rather than a wholesale approach to private participation.

Indeed, proponents of private participation of environmental or human rights NGOs in international trade dispute settlement must find a way to distinguish their proposals from, for example, support for corporate claims under Chapter 11 of NAFTA.[121] After all, Chapter 11 protects private property from certain kinds of state action, and thus is arguably consistent with natural rights. One response may be that it is not the private rights of action under Chapter 11 that raise problems, but the substantive rules and the way they have been interpreted.[122] This may be so, but it illustrates the point made above: that it is fallacious to argue on a natural law basis for broad application of private rights of action, because we lack confidence that all substantive rules will turn out to be beneficial.[123]

This section provides an instrumentalist way of evaluating the costs and benefits of these design choices. The argument that private participation in litigation enhances the "democracy" of the litigation proves too much, as private participants may be either the Friends of the Earth or Exxon, and neither has the democratic credentials per se of a democratic state, although each may be understood to perform an important social function within a liberal state. While there are different types of contribution to democracy, and NGOs and business firms can contribute their voices to a civic dialog that legitimates government in important ways,[124] neither they nor their arguments have further claims to democratic legitimacy.[125]

In other words, for example, it takes a particular view of the qualities of national democracy to place the views of an NGO on a par with those of elected governments. Perhaps the greatest reason is that (we assume that) national elected governments integrate a number of values, including those of free trade as well as those of the environment, while an NGO would be expected to be more unidimensional in its perspective. Even a public choice critic of national governments, concerned about interest group domination, must admit that an NGO is itself an interest group. Thus, giving environmental NGOs, for example, unimpeded access would also give environmental concerns an unmoderated voice, in which they are not required to compete and compromise with other concerns, at least at the national level.[126]

The argument that it is not (or not just) democracy that these rights contribute, but legitimacy, also proves too much. While transparency is often aligned with legitimacy, disproportionate influence by private persons operating outside the state may also be aligned with illegitimacy. Indeed, references to "democracy" and "legitimacy" often lack analytical content, and are red herrings,[127] because all of these types of decisions have claims to democratic and legitimacy-producing credentials—the real question is how well do the institutions we have do, compared to alternatives, in satisfying individual concerns.

New Legal Orders and Old

As we consider private participation in international dispute settlement, it must be recognized that this question is but a component of a larger question about the quality (or substantive rules) and quantity (or relative bindingness) of international law. Law, like any other social institution, must be understood as an institution that constrains the free play of politics or the market. This is the insight of John Jackson's dichotomy between legalism and pragmatism, or law and politics, in international trade.[128] One need not accept, descriptively or normatively, a modernist progression from politics to law in order to accept that private participation will tend to make the relevant international law more, rather than less, binding.

Let us consider the question of whether there should be private rights of action for individuals under WTO law. WTO law has a contractual character among states—it is therefore up to states to decide, as a design parameter, the degree of private participation in its enforcement, as part of the parties' decision, inter alia, about how binding they wish their obligations to be.[129] If one begins with a Lockean, natural rights–based view of WTO law, one arrives at different conclusions.[130] Petersmann sees private rights to sue as constituting a bulwark against government excess, and infringement of rights.[131]

Some may look to the European Union as a model for the international legal system more generally, or for the WTO. Certainly, private rights to sue have been central to the legal development of the European internal market. *Van Gend en Loos*, the landmark ECJ case finding certain European Community laws to have direct effect, announced that the European Community constituted "a new legal order . . . for the benefit of which states have limited their sovereign rights . . . and the subjects of which comprise not only Member States but their nationals."[132] In the WTO panel decision concerning Section 301 of the U.S. Trade Act of 1974, the panel took an intermediate approach, stating that the WTO is not such a new legal order, but enunciating the concept of "indirect effect," whereby international legal obligations are interpreted in a teleological way to support individual trading rights.[133]

> Many of the benefits to Members which are meant to flow as a result of the acceptance of various disciplines under the GATT/WTO depend on the activity of individual economic operators in the national and global market places. The purpose of many of these disciplines, indeed one of the primary objects of the GATT/WTO as a whole, is to produce certain market conditions which would allow this individual activity to flourish.[134]

While this type of indirect effect,[135] if it is more widely adopted, may give *states* broadened rights, in respect of measures that may "chill" the activities of private persons, it gives *private persons* no particular rights to sue on their own behalf, or to participate in litigation. Thus, this interpretive approach is interstitial.

Furthermore, insofar as the teleological approach embodied in this concept of "indirect effect" assumes a purpose to provide enhanced predictability to private persons, it may inappropriately ignore other goals, such as predictability or flexibility for states. As the panel report concedes, every state's legal system provides the capacity for threat; the panel's approach places a burden on states, when they legislate, to avoid not just violations but also threats.[136]

From the broadest perspective, of course, law is law, and it is intended to bind at some level. However, the structure of adjudication and remedies can have dramatic effects on the binding nature of law. The degree of binding effect is a design feature, with potential instrumental value, but not with intrinsic value.

The New Institutional Economics of Private Rights of Action: Factors for Use in Cost-Benefit Analysis

In the prior section, I rejected a normative perspective on private rights of action at the WTO, and in international law generally, based on natural law or "stakeholder" arguments. In this section, I construct an alternative set of normative considerations for use as a basis for determining the utility of private rights of action in international law. I focus on the WTO, as the WTO has a substantial mandatory dispute settlement mechanism, unlike most other areas of international law. The normative perspective summarized in this section draws from prior work in this field, as well as from literature regarding the law and economics of private participation in dispute settlement. I also refer to the political science literature of the role of private persons in litigation under European Union law.[137] These literatures can only be examined briefly here. Furthermore, the analysis presented in this section suggests that specific rules or areas might be treated differently from others: that wholesale grants of private rights may not be the best approach. I have not engaged in extensive analysis of the way that these factors apply to the question of private rights of action in any specific area of WTO dispute settlement.

Much of the law and economics literature is concerned with the relationship between, or comparative effectiveness of, private litigation and public enforcement in the domestic sphere. A private right of action—belonging to individuals or groups—before the WTO would be analogous to domestic private litigation. The most direct parallel to public enforcement in the international trade system would be an "attorney-general" capacity assigned to the WTO secretariat, similar to that assigned to the European Commission under former Article 169 (now 226) of the Treaty of Rome.[138] A complete comparative institutional analysis would assess not only the costs and benefits of private litigation and state-to-state litigation, but also those occasioned by public enforcement versus private enforcement.[139] I will focus on a comparison between truly private litigation and state-to-state litigation.

Although many of the insights of the domestic law and economics literature apply to the international context, there are some relevant differences between the domestic and international arenas. Much of the law and economics literature begins from the reverse perspective of our concern: it asks when private litigation should be supplemented by public enforcement, rather than why public enforcement should be supplemented by private rights. In addition, there is a "levels" difference between our concern and that of this domestically oriented literature. That is, in an "international" system, private enforcement *is* state enforcement: if the rights are for states, then enforcement by states is "private" in that sense.

Perhaps the closer analogy for our purposes relates to the possibility of derivative causes of action for shareholders of corporations. Under what circumstances should corporations have an exclusive right to represent the firm's interests, and under what circumstances should individual share-holders be permitted to bring derivative lawsuits in the "right" of the corporation? If we think of international trade law rights as the rights of the state, our question is when and to what extent individuals should have "derivative" rights.

During the past fifteen years, political scientists, and some lawyers, have developed a fascinating cross-disciplinary social scientific debate regarding the role of the ECJ in European integration.[140] The ECJ has played a leading role in developing negative integration—legal interpretations of the Treaty of Rome that discipline member state regulation that impedes trade—as well as in "constitutionalizing" the Treaty of Rome.[141] These scholars have included, for example, Karen Alter,[142] James Caporaso,[143] Geoffrey Garrett,[144] Walter Mattli, Anne-Marie Slaughter, and Alec Stone Sweet. One facet of this research examines the role of litigation by private individuals in economic integration in the European Union. Again, while the WTO is by no means the European Union, it may be interesting to see what lines of inquiry may be drawn from this literature to shed light on the problem of private parties in WTO dispute settlement.

The next part of this section reviews the central question in determining the utility of private rights of action, which is not made explicit in the prior literature. This question asks whether the right to sue, if allocated to a particular individual or government, would exclude affected parties from decision making in significant ways that are not justified by transaction cost or other countervailing concerns. The remainder of this section examines and compares the various more specific costs and benefits of private rights of action before the WTO, as opposed to the present state-to-state dispute resolution system. While this discussion is WTO specific, similar considerations would apply in evaluating private rights of action in other contexts.

Normative Individualism, Subsidiarity, Public Choice, and Externalities
Of course, a humanist or normative individualist perspective asserts that the only purpose of law is to benefit individuals: private parties. But this perspective cannot prejudge the institutional design question as to how best to benefit individuals. Representative government exists precisely because we (a collective of individuals) do not always wish individuals to have a direct role in decision making, for a variety of reasons.

On the other hand, a perspective of subsidiarity, based on normative individualism, holds that the state should act only where it can provide greater benefit to individuals than their individual action. Although we must recognize that the principle of subsidiarity has been applied more to decisions regarding the vertical locus of substantive rules than those regarding the vertical locus of authority to litigate, it seems equally applicable to the latter. Authority to litigate is valuable in public policy terms because of its legislative character, either with respect to a particular case or with respect to a group of cases.

When and in what ways should the state act as an intermediary, or filter, for its citizens in bringing international litigation at the WTO, or in interstate dispute resolution more generally?[145] When is individual action in the form of transnational dispute resolution superior? What kind of individual action, or participation in state action, is optimal? It is important to relate this question to the broader question of allocation of authority in the international legal system. The scope of private rights of action is itself subsidiary but complementary to the primary questions of the scope of state *legislative* authority and the scope of WTO *legislative* or *treaty* authority, as well as to the question of the scope of state authority to litigate. However, especially at the WTO, dispute settlement is a very important subsidiary governance device. Between rounds, and arguably at other times as well, dispute settlement is the primary governance device.

As we consider the value of state intermediation, we must address the public choice perspective. The interests of states are not perfectly aligned with those of individual citizens. When we speak of states here, we are simply referring to the actions of governments, and are not assuming that the expressed interests of any government are aligned with the public interest. Even from a public interest perspective, states may decline to bring cases that individuals wish to be brought, and states may bring cases that some individuals regret.[146] Would private party participation in dispute settlement accentuate or ameliorate this problem? The potential lack of alignment between the public interest and state interests brings added force to, and actually is a basis for, the subsidiarity perspective: given the inaccuracies of governmental representation of individuals, it may be better to allow individuals to represent themselves, all other things being equal. The public choice perspective must operate at an additional level: that of the international organization.[147] Would private party participation in dispute settlement ameliorate the problem of representativeness—the democratic deficit—of the WTO?

Conversely, the interests of individuals are not perfectly aligned with those of other individuals, and we often use the state where the state can deal with these externalities better than private arrangements. Thus, we might also ask whether individuals, operating individually, will act in the interest of society as a whole, at either the national or international level.[148] Therefore, one of the parameters that we must pay careful attention to is the extent to which a claim in litigation is one in which individuals represent and affect only themselves, or whether, on the other hand, the claim involves externalities.[149] A claim will involve externalities in the sense that a successful claim will have effects on others beyond the specific concerns of the plaintiff and defendant.[150] Litigation may have both negative externalities and positive externalities. In turn, this parameter will depend on how the particular rights are constructed and their purpose.

Indeed, the central normative question associated with private rights to participate in WTO litigation is one of governmental accountability and responsiveness.[151] How can individual access to litigation be structured to maximize the ability of government (including executive, legislative, and judicial components) to respond to individual preferences? Or will the relevant individual preferences be maximized through individual action? Where there are no externalities,[152] it is more likely, depending on transaction costs, that we would find that individuals should be in charge of enforcing their own rights before courts. However, where there are externalities, it may be that these can best be addressed by collective decisions about litigation through a governmental or other bureaucratic process.[153] It is necessary to engage in comparative institutional analysis.

This normative concern would suggest that where substantial externalities exist, a regime of espousal would serve best to allow states to determine whether the social benefits exceed social costs. However, much depends on the magnitude of the externalities, and the social costs of internalizing them. Transparency would not seem to raise substantial problems in the case of externalities, assuming that the externalities are understood domestically and seen as meriting a regulatory response. Furthermore, where the right seems to belong to private persons, truly private rights would seem to raise fewer concerns here than NGO standing and private rights, assuming that the truly private rights are carefully tailored to minimize externalities.

Efficient Breach
Some political science literature and legal scholarship assume that law enforcement is like being thin and rich: you can never have too much. However, as suggested in Chapter 4, this perspective is derived from a

particular type of, and concept of, law. Other law and economics literature recognizes that optimal enforcement does not equal maximum enforcement, but enforcement balanced to reflect social costs and benefits.

If we consider trade law to be more like contract than like an array of *jus cogens* norms, we might accept a theory of "efficient breach,"[154] to the effect that there may be circumstances where compliance with the law is too costly. This concept may be anticipated by the parties and incorporated in their treaty or contract, as in GATT's escape clause, or it may be supplied by courts as an implicit term. Where the gain from breach exceeds the harm from breach, it is in society's interest to encourage breach, which in economic terms is a "first-best" outcome.

Diplomatic Transactions

A state-to-state dispute resolution system has the advantage of discretion in allowing greater room for persuasion and negotiation. Private rights of action would take control away from states in a number of areas.[155] Accordingly, informal accommodation between states through persuasion and negotiation would be constrained.

If multiple persons have rights to litigate regarding the same matter, then settlement or diplomatic compromise will be impeded.[156] If states share access to dispute settlement with private parties, states lose control over the enforcement of the right, and therefore lose the ability to negotiate a settlement with another state.

> When standing is granted to an open or amorphous class, by definition it will be impossible to contract with all class members. Because exchange is infeasible, the right will be inalienable. An open class frustrates contracting, and a frustration of contracting is the underlying cause of all common access resources and the resulting dissipation of value.[157]

The dissipation in value comes from a failure to allocate resources to their highest valued uses—in our case, it comes from an inability of states to effect transactions in authority. Holderness explains that rules that limit standing under the common law of contracts and nuisance have the benefit of promoting exchange. Potential third-party beneficiaries, or persons who are harmed by nuisance but are not landowners, or whose property was not physically invaded, did not have standing to sue at common law. "Therefore, if it is more valuable to create the physical interference than to enjoy quiet, the person wishing to produce the nuisance can purchase the right from the owners of the land that has been physically invaded."[158]

Thus, if we understand international diplomacy as negotiation over the allocation of authority, it may be impeded under certain transaction cost profiles by cloudy allocations of authority, including expansive private rights of litigation.[159] It would be possible for states to overcome this concern, simply by changing the law to foreclose private rights of action, or to effect the desired diplomatic transaction through a change in the law. However, given the difficulty of changing international law, such formal means of effecting transactions have substantial transaction costs. Increased private rights of action would effectively prevent *informal* accommodation.

Flexibility of commitments, allowing easier negotiation, may be useful where circumstances may change. While treaties may be difficult to amend, diplomatic deference, combined with unhindered domestic legislation, may allow states to exercise flexibility.[160] Flexibility of this type may play a role in promoting negotiation of stronger commitments. On the other hand, of course, flexibility of this type may reduce the value of commitments, as states would have reduced incentives to comply. These reduced incentives to comply would arise from the fact that, as compared to a circumstance of direct effect, the domestic legal system would not be held "hostage" to compliance with international legal obligations.

Choice of Disputes for Litigation

While governments may validly or inappropriately select disputes for diplomatic reasons,[161] they may also select disputes for litigation for reasons of avoidance of "wrong" cases, or to avoid the possible development of undesirable (to them) legal rules. They may choose disputes in a way designed to develop a particular type of jurisprudence. Private parties may not have these incentives, and may not forbear in the same way.

One of the reasons that especially NGO private plaintiffs have been eager to bring public interest litigation in other contexts is to force issues onto the agenda where legislatures declined to act. However, granting this power to NGO private plaintiffs, or to any private plaintiffs, might be seen as a usurpation of the legislative right of inertia,[162] raising issues of the proper relative roles of dispute settlement and diplomacy.[163]

This problem is accentuated in the international sphere, as compared to the domestic arena. In the domestic arena, legislation is an everyday occurrence. However, in the international legal system, "legislation"—whether treaty revision or custom—is an unusual and difficult activity. This imbalance between adjudication and dispute resolution means that control of the adjudication agenda is even more important, as "legislative reversal" is less available. On the other hand, it might be argued that given the difficulty of legislation, greater possibility for adjudication is needed. This might be considered an imbalance similar to that experienced during the "eurosclerosis" years of the European Union, prior to the enhancement of legislative capacity in 1987 pursuant to the Single European Act.[164]

A complex of political and economic circumstances led to the Single European Act, and we cannot expect the advent of effective majority voting in the WTO[165] or elsewhere in international law anytime soon. However, it is worth noting the effects of weak legislative capacity on dispute resolution. To the extent there is strong social demand for "new" law, dispute resolution may be subjected to pressure to respond. Stone Sweet and Caporaso find a relationship between increasing trade and increasing preliminary references under former Article 177 of the Treaty of Rome, as well as increasing European Union regulation.[166] Thus, increased standing, like the capacity for preliminary references in the Treaty of Rome, might be one way to satisfy this demand.

Governmental Control of Arguments versus Private Control of Arguments

We may separate the right to commence a lawsuit, allowing control of the agenda of litigation, with the right to make and have considered arguments, allowing control of the intellectual agenda of litigation (except to the extent that a panel or the Appellate Body may adopt reasoning that the parties have not argued). Both the European Commission and the USTR have exercised care to assert certain types of arguments, and avoid certain other types of arguments, in an effort to foster a desirable set of precedents. Private persons, whether as litigants or as amici, might not have the same types of cross-sectoral or society-wide concerns, and might not have similar longer-term time horizons, and therefore might make different decisions about the arguments they would make. Governments that expect to be both complainants and respondents from time to time have a different perspective. There may be trade-offs between the current case and future cases.[167] This is another category of externality.

Agency Capture

One important, and broad, area of potential bias is agency capture: the concept in political science that administrative agencies tend to develop biases toward their regulatory clients.[168] Capture is predicated on the application of the rational choice assumption of economic analysis to politics, resulting in the theoretical proposition that agency personnel seek to maximize their own utility. Rational regulators will maximize a combination of their own authority and position, and their career opportunities outside government service. These forces are argued to cause regulators to favor more organized interests, often business interests,[169] over other interests, including environmental or consumer interests. In particular, regulatory enforcement may be subject to capture.

Judicial review of agency action has been suggested as an antidote to agency capture.[170] In our context, this concept would have two possible implications. At a more domestic level, it suggests that judicial review of USTR[171] or European Commission[172] decisions to litigate cases at the WTO would be useful to ameliorate any effects of capture. At the international level, where the WTO has little by way of "administrative" capacity (although this appears to be a growing phenomenon), there seems little need for judicial review of agency action.

Capture is the potential result of the discretion that is essential to a cooperative approach to enforcement, which characterizes state-to-state dispute resolution in general, and WTO dispute resolution in particular. We might think of discretionary nonenforcement by states as a form of capture of the enforcement process: states, as regulators in the WTO state-to-state system, fail to bring claims, to enforce the law fully. We might also think of the influence exerted by domestic producers on the choice by states of WTO cases as a type of capture.

Preventing Global Capture: Collusion by States against Citizens

There is a further negative perspective on this type of diplomatic flexibility. States may collude with one another to decline to enforce their rights, in a tit-for-tat relaxation of international trade rules, to the detriment of private parties and the world trading system.[173] There are two ways of considering this. From a public interest standpoint, assuming that the rules the states are evading are beneficial, this is detrimental. However, from a public choice standpoint, presumably the states are acting to maximize their joint value at any point in time. As discussed above, much depends on whether it is the rights of states that are sought to be maximized or the rights of individuals. Assuming that states exist for valid reasons, some rights will "belong" to states and some will "belong" to individuals.

Thus, private rights of action may be especially useful where one believes that states—or, more particularly, governments of states—are making sweetheart deals to get around the rules in disregard of the public interest.

Dispersed Standing as a Commitment Device: "It's beyond My Control"

Conversely, the inability to engage in future transactions may be accepted as a commitment device, in order to assure compliance with a particular norm. Here, of course, the discretion being transferred is prosecutorial discretion. And it applies in cases where the bound state would act as plaintiff, rather than defendant. This kind of commitment might result in greater levels of deterrence, promoting compliance by the potential respondent: if I precommit myself to punish you for violation, without any hope of forbearance, you are less likely to breach. This kind of commitment might alternatively provide reassurances to domestic constituencies, as an inducement to them to ratify a trade agreement.

Collective Commitment

By analogy to contract theory, we might suppose that freedom of states to modify their bilateral commitments without the impediments of private access to dispute settlement would be beneficial (at least to states): based on changes in the world or in their preferences, states could change their agreements. However, "contrary to traditional wisdom, the parties to a contract may be better off if the law enables them to tie their hands, or ties their hands for them, in a way that prevents them from taking advantage of certain *ex post* profitable modification opportunities."[174]

Thus, private rights of action could serve as a kind of collective commitment, in the sense of a commitment not to seek, or give, diplomatic forbearance.[175] In addition to reasons for excluding modification based on moral hazard, Jolls suggests that the parties' preferences may change over time, and that they may, through contract, desire to hold themselves to their initial preferences. This concept is even less problematic in the context of the state, with clearly varying preferences, than in the case of individuals, where at least theoretically we assume static preferences. Thus, by providing greater rights to private litigants, it is possible for a state to bind itself to maintain the preferences, or at least the rights and obligations, it had when it executed a trade agreement.[176] This approach dovetails with the "constitutional" perspective on trade agreements, in the sense that, like a constitution, the trade agreement, buttressed by private rights of action, may bind the state despite later changes in its preferences.[177] Like humans, states may place a greater priority on present consumption, or present political gain, at any particular point in time, than on future benefits.

Commitment in Two-Level Games

In our circumstance, if we think of international agreements as two-level games,[178] we have two "contracts": one among states and the other between the citizens and/or parliaments of those states and their executives. With respect to the latter contract, moral hazard may exist, and we may think of the potential settlement of trade disputes as a method for modification of international agreements. By providing greater rights to private litigants, the possibility of these modifications, which may be *ex ante* suboptimal, may be excluded. It is in this sense that we might find that private rights of action are related to domestic ratification of international agreements. That is, where an international agreement requires ratification (here, let us say by a legislature), how does the legislature bind the executive to enforce its rights under that agreement? The executive may not have desired to have those rights in the first place. Private rights of action act as commitment devices binding the executive not to act itself, but to accept strong enforcement by others.

This is similar to the explanation some have suggested for Section 301 of the U.S. Trade Act of 1974, and especially for Super 301: Congress predicates acceptance of trade agreements on some access for individuals, and some requirements for the executive to self-initiate enforcement activity. Within the United States, the more protectionist Congress has more generally used its power to create private rights of action to constrain the often more free trade–oriented executive. Under the Commerce Clause of the Constitution, Congress has broad and, in theory, exclusive authority over commerce "with foreign nations," but it is the president who negotiates and signs agreements, and executes statutes. Therefore, Congress finds it must delegate authority to the president, but uses private individuals with appropriate interests, and the courts, to ensure that the president carries out Congress' wishes in accordance with the statutory delegation.[179]

Incentives and the Optimal Quantity of Litigation

In international litigation, relating to international legal rights, where the rights exist "for" states, states could be expected to have the level of incentives to litigate most close to optimal[180] in order to enforce the rights for which they bargained. Under a law and economics analysis, the incentives for individuals and groups in a private litigation system to sue may be misaligned with the socially optimal incentive.[181] That is, in particular circumstances, private parties may have a socially inadequate motive to prosecute liable parties, resulting in underenforcement, or they may have too much of an incentive, resulting in overenforcement. Of course, as discussed further below, defining the optimal level of enforcement not only would be difficult but also depends on the perspective of the assessor.

Landes and Posner have argued that private parties have an incentive to overlitigate.[182] "Laws are written in an over-inclusive way and private party enforcement would lead to fuller enforcement of those laws, without a check on enforcer discretion. There may be an efficient level of violation, such that we do not want overly vigorous enforcement of the law."[183] Thus, Posner states that "discretionary nonenforcement is a technique by which the costs of overinclusion can be reduced without a corresponding increase in underinclusion (loopholes)."[184] Of course, this perspective assumes the ability of the prosecutor to discriminate accurately.

In general, a role for advocacy groups motivated by ideology could exaggerate any tendency for an existing private system toward overenforcement. The ideological motivation will raise the incentive to ideological plaintiffs to increase enforcement activity. Although advocacy groups are motivated primarily by ideology, monetary incentives and costs also will shape their actions, and may do so in ways that are not socially optimal. For example, groups may choose the cases that are easiest to win, or that will generate the most publicity. In addition, increases or decreases in cost could affect the willingness and ability of NGOs to bring suit, because of the limited resources available to them. This cost sensitivity may not only determine the volume of suits, but also lead groups to file under certain laws and not others, or to file against certain defendants and not others.[185]

Regardless of whether or not private party enforcement would lead to overenforcement, there are three major implications of the analysis of private party incentives. First, the successful operation of a private litigation system depends on the nature and precision of the incentives for private action, and these incentives may simply not result in the desired level of enforcement and may be subject to various, unanticipated misincentives. Second, even more than private enforcement motivated by monetary reward, there is no mechanism to control the level of the incentive for ideological plaintiffs to bring suit, so there is no control over the aggregate level of enforcement activity. Finally, coordination between actors in this system will be limited, resulting in duplicated effort and in lack of a strategic approach to enforcement.

Of course, in the trade context, the foregoing analysis of the adequacy of private incentives depends on an assumption that the government enforcement of WTO law is, on its own, approximately equal to an optimum level. Increased private rights to commence suit at the WTO would obviously result in greatly increased litigation at the WTO. Similarly, it is obvious that private rights of action to bring claims based on WTO law in domestic courts would result in increased WTO-law litigation. Once it is determined whether there is currently more than or less than the socially optimal level of litigation at the WTO, it would be a rather simple matter to construct impediments or incentives to reach the optimal level. The problem is in identifying the optimal level of litigation. In order to calculate the socially optimal level of litigation, it would be necessary to know the following:

(i) The level of net damage caused by breach of the law. In trade, as opposed to certain domestic law areas, such as tort, it is extremely difficult to calculate the cost of breach. The cost is not simply the lost trade volume, but also, in our public choice model, the political costs associated with adverse publicity, lost jobs, reduced campaign contributions, and so on. Moreover, in this type of model it would be appropriate to subtract from the costs to the complainant the benefits to the respondent.

(ii) The potential value in establishing a legal precedent.

(iii) The costs of litigation.

Because of the difficulty of operationalizing this model, it is not likely to be particularly informative as to whether to increase access to WTO litigation. However, it might be that policy makers would at some point in time determine that there is insufficient WTO litigation, and would thereupon seek to increase access.

To the extent that policy makers find that greater enforcement and/or integration would be desirable, this vector would argue for an increase in rights of commencement in order to increase litigation.

Informational Advantages of Private Litigants

Some literature divides surveillance between centralized (government-effected) "police patrols" and decentralized (private person–effected) "fire alarms."[186] A "fire alarm" system allows the concrete concerns of private parties to be the basis for action. "Fire alarm oversight tends to be particularistic . . . it arguably emphasizes the interests of individuals and interest groups more than the public at large."[187] Sevilla finds that most GATT-WTO complaints from 1948 to 1996 were particularistic in nature—they arose from private parties' concerns, rather than from systemic issues.[188] This could suggest that private parties are best situated to pursue these claims. But it also suggests that they already do so through a system that excludes formal private rights of action. The real question here is the counterfactual: what claims are not being brought?

Economic analysis of the role of private parties in dispute resolution may support the conclusion that a fire alarm system is superior to police patrols: private parties possess more information about the harm caused to them.[189] This does not necessarily translate into a factor in favor of private access to dispute settlement, as there are various institutional alternatives for use in harvesting this information. The United States Section 301 or European Union Trade Barriers Regulation process may be understood this way. The analytical question is: Which structure provides this information most efficiently? Private party incentives would lead them to bring their harm to the attention of their state, as readily as they would bring their harm directly to a court, all other things being equal. However, where private party harm is sufficiently dispersed, no single private party may have sufficient incentives to act. Thus, there may well be circumstances where state or other intermediary action is needed, including the possibility for class actions or other claim-aggregating devices.

But are there circumstances where this factor leads to a conclusion that private rights to commence litigation are needed? Sevilla finds in GATT-WTO disputes that "private producers are expected to target most often those countries where the greatest amount of trade is at stake in terms of value and volume."[190] Within the European Union context, Stone Sweet and Caporaso have developed data suggesting that private persons, if permitted to select cases to bring, will disproportionately target barriers to large markets compared to smaller markets.[191] They find that in the free movement of goods area, "accusations of German non-compliance dominate EC litigation."[192] Thus, private party choice of litigation may be aligned more closely with public interest goals—the reduction of larger trade barriers—instead of public choice goals. As noted above, of course, much depends on the alignment of the relevant law with the public interest.

Protectionist and Other Bias

It may be that the public choice–based bias of trade policy in favor of domestic producer interests would be accentuated by increased private access. That is, if it is expected that producer interests would be able to organize for litigation more effectively than consumer interests, we would expect a litigation bias in favor of producer interests. On the other hand, it might be argued that the executive has already been captured by producer interests, and any reduction of the monopoly enjoyed by the executive would diminish the producer bias. Within the U.S. public law litigation system, as well as within the European Union, it has been suggested that formal access to dispute resolution is disproportionately useful to wealthier interests.[193] This may help to explain developing country resistance to private party access.

It is worthy of note that domestic producers already have substantial private rights in important areas of "administered protectionism": dumping and subsidies law. These private rights are not required by WTO law, but are permitted under WTO law. These private rights may be juxtaposed with the relative paucity of private rights for lawsuits to protect consumer interests, or foreign producer interests. Perhaps this is evidence that there is capacity for selection of areas in which to accord individuals private rights.

Most proponents of private rights envision vertical (citizen suing his own state) or upwardly sloping diagonal (citizen suing other state) suits. Vertical suits would ordinarily enfranchise domestic consumer interests (assuming, for a moment, that producer interests are already enfranchised by anti-dumping and countervailing duties law), and therefore would be biased toward liberalism. Upwardly sloping diagonal suits would ordinarily attack foreign import barriers, and would therefore also be biased toward liberalism. Thus, these types of private rights would increase exports.

Of course, much of the discussion of private rights in WTO litigation has been prompted by the efforts of environmental and other advocates of "nontrade" concerns to participate in WTO litigation. Presumably these advocates feel that their participation would enhance the position of these "nontrade" concerns in WTO litigation. It is possible that they are in error: that they would be more effective if they used their resources to lobby domestic governments instead of litigating at the WTO.

If the reason these advocates seek greater access in WTO litigation is that they have lost the lobbying game in domestic governments, they need a reason to believe they will be more successful in the WTO litigation context. That is, if business interests have overwhelmed them in domestic politics, why would they not overwhelm them in WTO litigation? Thus, it is not clear that greater access would have a bias in favor of nonbusiness interests. NGOs may even have bureaucratic reasons, in terms of their fundraising or other motivations, to focus on the WTO instead of national governments.

It is worth noting that greater access would be expected to create a bias in favor of complainants, and against respondents, simply because of the greater resources available for complaints. This bias might be countervailed, to a limited extent, by assistance provided to respondents by amicus briefs taking their side.

Legitimacy

Earlier in this section, I rejected "legitimacy" as a broader basis for more conclusory assertions of private rights to participate in dispute settlement. However, legitimacy may play a more limited, but important, role in determinations to provide these rights. At the core of the civic republican insight is individual participation in the processes of government, for the purpose of satisfying individuals with the outcome, whether it is their desired outcome or not. Legitimacy, if not a conclusory assertion, must relate to satisfaction of individual preferences, or acceptance by individuals of the governmental process that satisfied or denied their preferences. In this sense, private rights to participate could enhance legitimacy and thus would be desirable. It is important to stress, however, that this factor seems appropriate as one of a number of factors.

Obviously, transparency is an important component of legitimacy. The capacity to be heard through amicus briefs would also contribute. The degree to which legitimacy is contributed by the ability to commence litigation depends to some extent on the extent of externalities: on the extent to which private plaintiffs are not viewed as imposing adverse externalities on the rest of society.

Conclusion

It is obvious that the normative considerations listed above cannot comprise anything approaching a formal model. However, it is hoped that they will provide a checklist of considerations, with some degree of analytical detail, for use in considering proposals for expanding private rights in international dispute settlement. These normative considerations exist at the level of cost-benefit analysis, rather than at the level of natural rights or natural law.

According to institutional economics theory, and subsidiarity, states have rights in international society because they may achieve more of what individuals desire than the individual constituents may achieve acting separately. While this may not always be true in practice, and while it may not be operational as a positive theory, it seems attractive as a normative approach. It suggests that before transferring rights from states to individuals, we investigate the benefits that might flow from each institutional structure, and the costs, including transaction costs. The operational problem with this theory has important practical consequences: our best preference revelation device for determining whether individuals are getting more or less of what they want, imperfect as it is, is the state.

So, arguments to the state about the types of private participation it should authorize are useful, but it is difficult for analysts to know when the state has it wrong and when it has it right. Analysts can help most by illuminating the different costs and benefits and ensuring their consideration.

Nonetheless, given this case-by-case cost-benefit analysis approach, it appears that negotiated rules of intermediated domestic effect, whereby specific treaty provisions are used in particular cases to require domestic rights of action, provide a good basis for beginning to approach private rights of action. In many cases, the costs, in terms of diminished political flexibility and other systemic factors, will outweigh the benefits of private rights of action. These systemic factors include the need for relatively cooperative enforcement and flexible adjustment and response on the part of states. Normative concerns for participation and voice could be met through more indirect participation, such as submission of amicus briefs or rights to observe, which we have not addressed directly here.

When states desire to provide private parties with rights in connection with litigation, they know how to do so. We have many instances of intermediated domestic effect. Why is it that private parties have substantial rights in connection with anti-dumping and anti-subsidies actions—with foreign mercantilist action—and such modest rights against domestic protectionist actions? Both in the United States and in the European Union, the question of domestic effect seems increasingly to be taken over by legislatures, as opposed to courts. This phenomenon is consistent with increasing intermediated domestic effect.

We also know that states seem to have developed acceptable, if not appropriate, ways to approve trade treaty commitments. Trade law litigation would seem to have similar, although perhaps attenuated, importance. After all, its role is the interpretation and application of treaty commitments. Therefore, it is worth comparing the role of private persons in formulating and approving the treaty commitments themselves, with their role in litigation.

It is worth recognizing the strategic perspective. NGO private plaintiffs and truly private plaintiffs are, first of all, strategic litigants. They seek the best forum for the outcome they desire. When the NGO loses in the domestic legislative forum, and in the domestic judicial forum, it naturally seeks an international forum. It will continue to seek fora until it wins. From the institutional design standpoint, the question is whether it is a failure of subsidiarity to provide an external forum when the matter is adequately addressed, procedurally, in domestic fora. Whether the matter is adequately addressed depends on consideration of the degree to which appropriate opportunities for voice are provided. This voice should exist at the appropriate decision-making level. If decisions about the U.S. approach to a particular trade matter are best made at the U.S. domestic level, it would seem inappropriate to provide an opportunity to negate those decisions at the international level. If the U.S. voice is but one voice in the international trade community, it may be unfair to others to give those who participated in the formulation of the U.S. voice an opportunity to speak in the international trade community.

Finally, if allocation of authority in litigation is concerned with allocation of authority in society more generally, then the institutional economics and subsidiarity perspective expressed at the beginning of this chapter is important. It suggests that the real question is not about who or which values are to be empowered, but about who will decide. Litigation is a form of governance, related to legislation. Control over litigation is a form of governance, and should be informed by these analytical perspectives.

Afterword

IS INTERNATIONAL LEGAL ANALYSIS so different from domestic legal analysis? This book suggests that they are similar enough to make the tools of law and economics, developed for use largely in the domestic context, and largely in the United States, valuable for the study of international law. Some characterize the international legal system as not law at all, or as so different as to frustrate any analogical reasoning due to its "horizontal" nature, which refers to the fact that there is no overarching sovereign in international society. Yet, as suggested at the beginning of this book, the international legal context can assist us in casting aside our unexamined assumptions about domestic law. For we might argue that domestic law, like international law, begins in a horizontal Hobbesian context. The difference is one of degree, not of category, as domestic law has developed institutions of greater capacity, and concentrated authority.

Indeed, considering the argument for the potential binding nature of customary international law expressed in Chapter 3, based, inter alia, on frequency and linkage of transactions, we might understand the domestic legal system as simply providing greater frequency and more highly articulated linkage than that developed in the international legal system. So, is contract really so different from treaty? If I violate a contract that is enforceable in a Massachusetts court, a court can order me to pay damages or perhaps to perform what I promised to perform. This may be understood as a linkage structure. If I do not pay or perform, as ordered, I will be subjected to additional penalties that may be separate from the promised performance. In effect, the community authorizes and enforces reciprocity.

No, it does not have to be eye-for-eye or tooth-for-tooth reciprocity—it is the reciprocity that was provided as a default term of the relationship I entered into. In the international legal setting, the community also may authorize and enforce reciprocity, but may do so more or less formally.[1] Is the degree of formality really the basis for distinction?

Can the dense institutional infrastructure of developed states be compared with the diaphanous institutional infrastructure of international law? Chapters 3 and 4 have suggested that linkage and repetition may support a rule of binding customary international law, as well as *pacta sunt servanda*. Once we establish the binding character of international law, in a social science sense, then there really are few limits on the possible utility of international law. From that institutional capability, we may derive a supposition that the reason we see few international legal institutions and rules is either because (i) they are not desirable, or (ii) there are still strategic or transaction cost obstacles to their formation. This work is intended to map the international legal system of secondary rules, in order to begin to evaluate the strategic and transaction cost obstacles to formation. The obvious practical implication is that where these obstacles may be overcome through institutional change, states may establish all the international legal rules that are desirable.

Of course, we say that the state has a monopoly on the use of force. However, this argument is neither completely true nor necessarily a significant distinction. Certainly, when the United Nations Security Council authorizes the use of force, the monopoly character of its use of force is unimportant. At that moment, the Security Council and the states acting under its authorization become like police, and the target state becomes like a criminal. The criminal can still use force—there is no real monopoly on the use of force. Rather, there is a monopoly on the legitimate use of force. Furthermore, law can and does have extensive effects without the use of force, both in the municipal and in the international setting.

This work has arbitraged and adapted from law and economics theory applied to municipal law issues a set of plausible understandings of international prescriptive jurisdiction, customary international law, treaty, international organization, and international adjudication. These understandings are linked, forming a coherent (albeit incomplete) whole. The coherence is derived from a coherent rationalist methodology that posits a theory of state behavior relating to international law. This theory is marginalist insofar as it does not idealistically assume that all states comply with all international law all the time. Rather, it accepts, descriptively and normatively, that violation of law is a part of social life.

This theory serves as a call to empiricism. While this theoretical structure seems plausible, as it is a theory of rational behavior under constraint, it simplifies. Theory serves as a simplification, and as a source of hypotheses to see if this simplification retains predictive value. Only through empirical work can we know whether a theory is useful.

Notes

Index

Notes

1. Introduction

1. Leading texts include RICHARD A. POSNER, ECONOMIC ANALYSIS OF LAW (7th ed. 2007); ROBERT COOTER & THOMAS ULEN, LAW AND ECONOMICS (4th ed. 2003); STEVEN SHAVELL, FOUNDATIONS OF ECONOMIC ANALYSIS OF LAW (2004).

2. *See, e.g.,* Russell B. Korobkin & Thomas S. Ulen, *Law and Behavioral Science: Removing the Rationality Assumption from Law and Economics,* 88 CALIF. L. REV. 1051 (2000).

3. *See* Robert Cooter, *Law and Unified Social Theory,* 22 J. L. & SOC. 50 (1995); Richard A. Posner, *The Decline of Law as an Autonomous Discipline: 1962–1987,* 100 HARV. L. REV. 761 (1987).

4. John Maynard Keynes, *Introduction to Cambridge Economic Handbooks,* in CAMBRIDGE ECONOMIC HANDBOOK: MONEY v (D. H. Robertson, ed. 1921).

5. For the classic work in qualitative political science methodology, *see* GARY KING, ROBERT O. KEOHANE, & SIDNEY VERBA, DESIGNING SOCIAL INQUIRY: SCIENTIFIC INFERENCE IN QUALITATIVE RESEARCH (1994). *See also* HENRY E. BRADY & DAVID COLLIER, RETHINKING SOCIAL INQUIRY: DIVERSE TOOLS, SHARED STANDARDS (2005). For an introduction to econometrics in law, *see* Alan O. Sykes, *An Introduction to Regression Analysis,* in CHICAGO LECTURES IN LAW & ECONOMICS 1 (Eric Posner, ed. 2000).

6. Attributed to Immanuel Kant. *See* http://en.wikiquote.org/wiki/Immanuel_Kant.

7. John MAYNARD KEYNES, GENERAL THEORY OF EMPLOYMENT, INTEREST AND MONEY 383 (1936).

8. There are a number of works applying economic analysis to international law. For surveys, *see* Jeffrey L. Dunoff & Joel P. Trachtman, *The Law and Economics of International Law,* 24 YALE J. INT'L L. 1 (1999); Alan O. Sykes, *The Economics of Public International Law,* University of Chicago Law and Economics Olin Working Paper No. 216 (2004), available at http://papers.ssrn.com/sol3/papers.cfm?abstract_id=564383.

9. "The most fundamental unit of analysis in economic organization theory is the *transaction*—the transfer of goods or services from one individual to another." PAUL MILGROM & JOHN ROBERTS, ECONOMICS, ORGANIZATION AND MANAGEMENT 21 (1992).

10. KENNETH N. WALTZ, THEORY OF INTERNATIONAL POLITICS 90 (1979).

11. Robert O. Keohane, *Institutional Theory and the Realist Challenge after the Cold War,* in NEOREALISM AND NEOLIBERALISM 269, 271 (David A. Baldwin, ed. 1993) ("Institutionalist theory assumes that states are the principal actors in world politics and that they behave on the basis of their conceptions of their own self-interests"). Liberal institutionalist theory seeks to understand the sources of state preferences. *See* Andrew Moravcsik, *Taking Preferences Seriously: A Liberal Theory of International Politics,* 51 INT'L ORG. 513 (1997).

12. ROBERT O. KEOHANE, AFTER HEGEMONY: COOPERATION AND DISCORD IN THE WORLD POLITICAL ECONOMY 83 (1984).

13. In fact, the contractarian model is more easily applicable to the international system than to the domestic, as the international system has more viable exit options.

14. Keohane, *supra* note 12, at 83.

15. For an analysis of spillovers of public goods, and the consequent market for agreement constraining or facilitating spillovers, *see* SCOTT BARRETT, WHY COOPERATE (2007); Albert Breton, *Public Goods and the Stability of Federalism,* 23 KYKLOS 882 (1970).

16. For the property rights example, *see* ROBERT COOTER & THOMAS ULEN, LAW AND ECONOMICS 82–84 (1999).

17. *See* Robert O. Keohane, *Reciprocity in International Relations,* 40 INT'L ORG. 1 (1986).

18. *But see* Jacques Leboeuf, *The Economics of Federalism and the Proper Scope of the Federal Commerce Power,* 31 SAN DIEGO L. REV. 555 (1994) (arguing that externalization is the appropriate touchstone).

19. To a realist lawyer, this is a strange formulation: if the harm can be done with impunity, the property rights bundle must not include the relevant stick. This leads us to recognize that the entire concept of externality begs the question of legal rights. Therefore, arguments that we should design legal rights to internalize externalities are circular.

20. *See* Joel P. Trachtman, *Externalities and Extraterritoriality: The Law and Economics of Prescriptive Jurisdiction,* in COMPARATIVE ASPECTS OF INTERNATIONAL LAW (Jagdeep Bhandari & Alan O. Sykes, eds. 1998) (analogizing rules of prescriptive jurisdiction in international society to rules of property in domestic society).

21. Harold Demsetz, *Toward a Theory of Property Rights,* 57 AM. ECON. REV. PAPERS AND PROCEEDINGS 347, 350 (1967). It is also plausible to expect that the costs of establishing and enforcing property rights would decline, and the benefits would increase, as population density increases. Greater functional economic integration would presumably yield similar results in the international arena.

22. Keohane, *supra* note 17, at 18.

23. For a summary of the Coase theorem and references to further literature, *see* Robert D. Cooter, *The Coase Theorem,* in THE NEW PALGRAVE: A DICTIONARY OF ECONOMICS 457, 457–60 (1987). *See also* Elizabeth Hoffman & Matthew Spitzer, *The Coase Theorem: Some Experimental Tests,* 25 J. L. & ECON. 73 (1982); Robert D. Cooter, *The Cost of Coase,* 11 J. LEG. STUD. 1 (1982).

24. *See* Barrett, *supra* note 15; PROVIDING GLOBAL PUBLIC GOODS: MANAGING GLOBALIZATION (Inge Kaul et al. eds., 2003).

25. The dividing line between externalities, on the one hand, and uncaptured economies of scale, on the other hand, is not clear. Network externalities arise when the value of adopting a certain measure depends on how many others adopt the same measure: standards for telephone systems are an example.

26. Of course, the fact that it is efficient to regulate activity from a global perspective does not mean that only one regulator should exist; rather, it is a problem of contracting and establishing the most efficient institutional structure in response to technical or contextual factors. A similar caveat applies with respect to "economies of scope."

27. *See* Joel P. Trachtman, *International Regulatory Competition, Externalization and Jurisdiction,* 34 HARV. INT'L L.J. 47 (1993).

28. *See* J. Panzar & R. Willig, *Economies of Scope,* 71 AM. ECON. REV. 268 (1981).

29. *See* Kenneth Arrow, *Economic Welfare and the Allocation of Research for Invention,* in THE RATE AND DIRECTION OF INVENTIVE ACTIVITY (R. Nelson, ed. 1981). All of these economies may be related to the phenomenon of "spillover" often considered in connection with neofunctional approaches to international integration. ERNST HAAS, BEYOND THE NATION STATE 48 (1964).

30. *See* Benjamin Klein, *Contracting Costs and Residual Claims: The Separation of Ownership and Control,* 26 J. L. & ECON. 367, 373 (1983) ("Coase

mistakenly made a sharp distinction between intrafirm and interfirm transactions, claiming that while the latter represented market contracts the former represented planned direction").

31. In this context, discretion means residual discretion to be exercised in the future. This formulation can be further refined. Through decentralization within the firm, the amount of individual discretion within the firm may be made to equal the amount of discretion an individual might retain outside the firm. Thus, the continuum has two parameters. The first parameter is the degree of integration *into* the firm (or other integration structure, including contract). The second parameter is the degree of centralization *within* the firm.

32. ALBERT O. HIRSCHMAN, EXIT, VOICE AND LOYALTY: RESPONSES TO DECLINE IN FIRMS, ORGANIZATIONS AND STATES (1970). *See* Joseph Weiler's use of this dichotomy to analyze European constitutionalization in Weiler, *The Transformation of Europe,* 100 YALE L.J. 2403 (1991).

33. It is important to define the term "institution" for our purposes. The term is meant here to include (i) formal organizational institutions such as legislative, executive, and judicial bodies and the organizations they comprise; (ii) formal rules from constitutional rules down to normal legislation; and (iii) informal (nonlegal) institutions composed of organizations or rules that lack legal effect. A more elegant definition is provided by Douglass North: "institutions are the humanly devised constraints that structure human interaction." Douglass C. North, *Economic Performance through Time,* 84 AM. ECON. REV. 360 (1994). Some authors distinguish "institutions" from "organizations." *See, e.g.,* Elias L. Khalil, *Organizations versus Institutions,* 151 J. INST. & THEO. ECON 445 (1995); DOUGLASS C. NORTH, INSTITUTIONS, INSTITUTIONAL CHANGE AND ECONOMIC PERFORMANCE (1990). North refers to the need to distinguish the rules from the players. However, the rules are the players insofar as a firm, qua set of rules, competes with another firm. The distinction is in large part one of point of view: from the point of view of the market, each firm is a player. From the point of view of the employee, the firm is a set of rules.

34. This maximization hypothesis is congruent with the minimization hypothesis posited by new institutional economics scholars in respect to institutions more generally. "Institutions will be chosen that minimize total costs, the sum of transformation and transaction costs, given the level of output." Douglass C. North & John J. Wallis, *Integrating Institutional Change and Technical Change,* 150 J. INST. & THEO. ECON. 609 (1994). "Economizing takes place with reference to the sum of production and transaction costs, whence tradeoff in this respect must be recognized." OLIVER E. WILLIAMSON, THE ECONOMIC INSTITUTIONS OF CAPITALISM 22 (1985).

35. For the leading legal work on comparative institutional analysis, *see* NEIL KOMESAR, IMPERFECT ALTERNATIVES (1994).

36. For example, the public choice analysis of politics systematically applies economic analysis to exchanges of value in the political system, and outside the normal monetized market for private goods.

37. *See* VIVIANA A. ZEILIZER, THE SOCIAL MEANING OF MONEY (1994); Cass R. Sunstein, *Behavioral Analysis of Law,* 64 U. CHI. L. REV. 1175, 1192 (1997) (arguing that money is no more fungible than other values); Herbert Hovenkamp, *The Limits of Preference-Based Legal Policy,* 89 NW. U. L. REV. 4 (1994).

38. *See* JAMES M. BUCHANAN, EXPLORATIONS INTO CONSTITUTIONAL ECONOMICS 31 (1989): "I suggest that we cease and desist in any attempts to model man, *either* in his market *or* in his public choice behavior, as seeking exclusively or even predominantly to maximize the value of his net wealth. I suggest that we restrict ourselves methodologically to the more limited model of *Homo economicus,* one that allows the argument for economic value to enter the individual utility function, in market or in public choice behavior, but to enter as only one among several arguments, and not necessarily as the critical influencing factor in many cases."

39. While rationalist international relations theory does not attempt to explain these preferences, liberal institutionalism recognizes the need to get inside the "billiard ball" and understand how state preferences are formed and expressed. *See* Alexander Wendt, *The State as Person in International Theory,* 30 REV. INT'L STUD. 289 (2004).

40. For a summary of the theories, *see* PAUL MILGROM & JOHN ROBERTS, ECONOMICS, ORGANIZATION & MANAGEMENT 126–65 (1992).

41. Moravcsik, *supra* note 11, at 481. Moravcsik points out that it is necessary to examine domestic politics to understand how state preferences are formed, and in order to examine strategic interaction among states.

42. Milgrom & Roberts, *supra* note 40, at 596.

43. KENNETH ARROW, SOCIAL CHOICE AND INDIVIDUAL VALUES (1951).

44. "Those who prefer to conduct inquiry into the relationships among classes, states, and other organizations as such, and without attempts to reduce analysis to the individuals who participate, do not, in my view, pass muster as social scientists in any useful sense of the term." Buchanan, *supra* note 38, at 47.

45. *Id.* at 39.

46. James G. March & Johan P. Olsen, *The New Institutionalism: Organizational Factors in Political Life,* 78 AM. POLIT. SCI. REV. 734, 739 (1984) (citations omitted).

47. *See* Kenneth W. Abbott, *Trust but Verify: The Production of Information in Arms Control Agreements and Other International Agreements,* 26 CORN. INT'L L.J. 1 (1993).

48. *See, e.g.,* Oren Bar-Gill & Chaim Fershtman, *Law and Preferences,* 20 J. L. ECON. & ORG. 331 (2004).

49. *See* Anthony T. Kronman, *Contract Law and the State of Nature,* 1 J. L. ECON. & ORG 5 (1985) (discussing the use of nonlegal enforcement devices in contract): "The existence of the state and its enforcement machinery make[s] it unnecessary, one might think, to rely on any of those devices which in a state of nature are the only source of transactional security. But the most casual observations are enough to suggest that this is not the case."

50. For law and economics–based analyses of specific substantive legal rules, *see, e.g.,* Alan O. Sykes & Eric Posner, *Optimal War and Jus Ad Bellum,* University of Chicago Law and Economics Olin Working Paper No. 211 (April 2004), available at http://papers.ssrn.com/sol3/papers.cfm?abstract_id= 546104; Joel P. Trachtman, *Global Cyberterrorism, Jurisdiction, and International Organization,* in THE LAW AND ECONOMICS OF CYBERSECURITY (Mark Grady & Francesco Parisi, eds. 2005); Jeffrey L. Dunoff & Joel P. Trachtman, *Law and Economics of Humanitarian Law Violations in Armed Conflict,* 93 AM. J. INT'L L. 394 (1999); Oona Hathaway, *Do Human Rights Treaties Make a Difference?* 111 YALE L. J. 1935 (2002); Abbott, *supra* note 47.

2. Jurisdiction

1. For important distinctions between international and domestic choice of law, *see* Albert Ehrenzweig, *Interstate and International Conflict Law: A Plea for Separation,* 41 MINN. L. REV. 717 (1957).

2. I have approached this topic in preliminary ways in the following three articles. Joel P. Trachtman, *Externalities and Extraterritoriality: The Law and Economics of Prescriptive Jurisdiction,* in COMPARATIVE ASPECTS OF INTERNATIONAL LAW (Jagdeep Bhandari & Alan O. Sykes, eds. 1998) [hereinafter, *Externalities*]; *Conflict of Laws and Accuracy in the Allocation of Government Responsibility,* 26 VAND. J. TRANSNAT'L L. 1 (1994) [hereinafter, *Conflict of Laws*]; *Economic Analysis of Prescriptive Jurisdiction and Choice of Law,* 42 VA. J. INT'L L. 1 (2001) [hereinafter, *Prescriptive Jurisdiction*].

3. This proposition is not new, although it is not universally accepted. William Baxter said of Brainerd Currie, "As his own analysis effectively shows, the process of resolving choice cases is necessarily one of allocating spheres of legal control among states." William F. Baxter, *Choice of Law and the Federal System,* 16 STAN. L. REV. 1, 22 (1963). This chapter assumes that questions of scope of prescriptive jurisdiction for "public law" and questions of

choice of law for "private law" have much in common, and may not be distinguished along traditional lines. *See, e.g.,* Hartford Fire Ins. Co. v. California, 509 U.S. 764, 821 (Scalia, J., dissenting) (1993); United States v. Aluminum Co. of America, 148 F.2d 416, 443 (2d Cir. 1945). *See* Larry Kramer, *Vestiges of Beale: Extraterritorial Application of American Law,* 1991 SUP. CT. REV. 179; Lea Brilmayer, *The Extraterritorial Application of American Law: A Methodological and Constitutional Appraisal,* 50 LAW & CONTEMP. PROBS. 11 (1987-III). *See also* Russell J. Weintraub, *The Extraterritorial Application of Antitrust and Securities Laws: An Inquiry into the Utility of a 'Choice-of-Law' Approach,* 70 TEX. L. REV. 1799 (1992) (arguing for different treatment); Harold G. Maier, *Extraterritorial Jurisdiction at a Crossroads: An Intersection between Public and Private International Law,* 76 AM. J. INT'L L. 280 (1982). On prescriptive jurisdiction, *see, e.g.,* RESTATEMENT (THIRD) OF FOREIGN RELATIONS LAW § 401 (1987) [hereinafter, RESTATEMENT THIRD], distinguishing prescriptive jurisdiction, on the one hand, from judicial or enforcement jurisdiction. Prescriptive jurisdiction is the state's power "to make its law applicable to the activities, relations, or status of persons, or the interests of persons in things, whether by legislation, by executive act or order, by administrative rule or regulation, or by determination of a court."

4. *See, e.g.,* Gerhard Kegel, *Fundamental Approaches,* in III ENCYCLOPEDIA OF COMPARATIVE LAW, PRIVATE INTERNATIONAL LAW (K. Lipstein, ed. 1987); Friedrich Juenger, *Governmental Interests—Real and Spurious—in Multistate Disputes,* 21 U.C. DAVIS L. REV. 515 (1988).

5. *See, e.g.,* Baxter, *supra* note 3; Michael E. Solimine, *An Economic and Empirical Analysis of Choice of Law,* 24 GA. L. REV. 49 (1989); RICHARD POSNER, THE ECONOMIC ANALYSIS OF LAW 645–46 (1998); Larry E. Ribstein, *Choosing Law by Contract,* 18 J. CORP. L. 247, 263 (1993); Francisco Parisi and Larry E. Ribstein, *Choice of Law,* I THE NEW PALGRAVE DICTIONARY OF ECONOMICS AND THE LAW 236 (1998); Francisco Parisi & Erin O'Hara, *Conflict of Laws,* I THE NEW PALGRAVE DICTIONARY OF ECONOMICS AND THE LAW (1998); Andrew Guzman, *Choice of Law: New Foundations,* 90 GEO. L.J. 971 (2002); William H. Allen & Erin A. O'Hara, *Second Generation Law and Economics of Conflict of Laws: Baxter's Comparative Impairment and Beyond,* 51 STAN. L. REV. 1011 (1999); Erin O'Hara & Larry E. Ribstein, *From Politics to Efficiency in Choice of Law,* 67 U. CHI. L. REV. 1151 (2000) [hereinafter, *From Politics to Efficiency*]; Michael J. Whincop, *Conflicts in the Cathedral: Towards a Theory of Property Rights in Private International Law,* 50 U. TORONTO L.J. 41 (2000); MICHAEL J. WHINCOP & MARY KEYES, POLICY AND PRAGMATISM IN THE CONFLICT OF LAWS (2000); Horatia Muir Watt, *Choice of Law in Integrated and Interconnected*

Markets: A Matter of Political Economy, 9 COLUM. J. EUR. L. 383 (2003). For a perceptive review of the literature, *see* Ralf Michaels, *Two Economists, Three Opinions? Economic Models for Private International Law: Cross-Border Torts as an Example,* working paper (2006).

6. JAMES M. BUCHANAN, EXPLORATIONS INTO CONSTITUTIONAL ECONOMICS 24–25 (1989). *See generally* GEOFFREY BRENNAN & JAMES M. BUCHANAN, THE REASON OF RULES: CONSTITUTIONAL POLITICAL ECONOMY (1985).

7. When speaking of states, this book uses the term "preferences" despite the fact that methodological individualism identifies preferences as uniquely the prerogative of individuals. I do so to avoid referring to state interests, which Currie defined to include the interstate engagement of state policies.

8. By "mandatory," I mean law that is not subject to waiver by contract. In economic theory, this would generally be law that is intended to protect third parties (noncontracting parties) from externalities. It may also be intended to protect contracting parties who suffer from strategic or information problems that prevent them from making a rational choice. *See* Guzman, *supra* note 5. I include the latter circumstances in "externalities" here for convenience of exposition. There may be different degrees of "mandatoriness," however, beginning with default rules that occasion costs in order to be modified. In addition, we might say that even mandatory law may be avoided by certain types of permissible mobility. For example, parties may change the structure of their transaction, or change the jurisdiction in which they transact, in order to avoid what is otherwise mandatory law. So, we must recognize that there are degrees of "mandatoriness," best measured by the level of costs occasioned in order to avoid the application of law.

9. Harold Demsetz, *Toward a Theory of Property Rights,* 57 AM. ECON. REV. PAPERS AND PROCEEDINGS 348 (1967) (emphasis added); *see also* ANDREAS A. PAPANDREOU, EXTERNALITY AND INSTITUTIONS (1994); Henry N. Butler & Jonathan R. Macey, *Externalities and the Matching Principle: The Case for Reallocating Environmental Regulatory Authority,* 14 YALE L. & POL'Y REV. 23, 33 (1996); Daniel C. Esty, *Toward Optimal Environmental Governance,* 74 N.Y.U. L. REV. 1495 (1999).

10. Butler & Macey, *supra* note 9, emphasize Pigouvian internalization, but also recognize certain of its limitations.

11. RONALD COASE, THE FIRM, THE MARKET AND THE LAW 95–185 (1988), incorporating and commenting upon earlier work, including Coase's seminal articles: *The Nature of the Firm,* 4 ECONOMICA 386 (1937); and *The Problem of Social Cost,* 3 J. L. & ECON. 1 (1960). *See also* Ronald Coase, *The Nature of the Firm: Influence,* 4 J. L. ECON. & ORG. 33, 33 (1988); NEIL KOMESAR, IMPERFECT ALTERNATIVES (1994); Buchanan, *supra* note 6;

Oliver Williamson, *Public and Private Bureaucracies: A Transaction Cost Economics Perspective*, 15 J. L. Econ. & Org. 306 (1999).

12. Brennan & Buchanan, *supra* note 6.

13. It should be understood that "property rights" in this context refers to the full range of legal entitlements in the Calabresi and Melamed sense. Guido Calabresi & A. Douglas Melamed, *Property Rules, Liability Rules, and Inalienability: One View of the Cathedral*, 85 Harv. L. Rev. 1089 (1972).

14. To make this analogy more apparent, we may consider the example of jurisdiction to tax: states each demand a share of the international tax base, and to some extent this tax base is a *res nullius*, but to some extent it is regulated according to bilateral tax treaties and customary international fiscal principles.

15. *See* Gunnar Schuster, *Extraterritoriality of Securities Laws: An Economic Analysis of Jurisdictional Conflicts*, 26 L. & Pol'y Int'l Bus. 165 (1995); John Conybeare, *International Organization and the Theory of Property Rights*, 34 Int'l Org. 307 (1980). *See also* Kenneth Abbott, *Modern International Relations Theory: A Prospectus for International Lawyers*, 14 Yale J. Int'l L. 335, 393 (1989); Duncan Snidal, *Public Goods, Property Rights and Political Organizations*, 23 Int'l Stud. Q. 532 (1979).

16. The rules versus standards question also arises in connection with actions of decentralized decision makers. For example, in the international system, national courts may use rules or standards to determine choice of law, and in the U.S. system, state courts may do likewise, to the extent not restricted under international law or to the extent not restricted by federal law, respectively. This chapter examines this question in connection with its discussion of autonomous lawmaking in this field. The rules versus standards question, of course, is not new. *See, e.g.,* Willis Reese, *Choice of Law: Rules or Approach?* 57 Cornell L. Rev. 315 (1972). For a description of the use of rules and standards in the United States and Europe, *see* Mathias Reimann, *Savigny's Triumph? Choice of Law in Contracts Cases at the Close of the Twentieth Century*, 39 Va. J. Int'l L. 571, 583–88 (1999). This chapter uses some law and economics–based understandings of the relationship between rules and standards.

17. *See* Anthony T. Kronman, *Contract Law and the State of Nature*, 1 J. L. Econ. & Org. 5, 9 (1985) (analogizing international society to the pre–property rights state of nature).

18. For applications of property rights theory to international jurisdiction over the seas, *see* Charles Biblowit, *International Law and the Allocation of Property Rights in Common Resources*, 4 New York Int'l L. Rev. 77 (1991); R. D. Eckert, The Enclosure of Ocean Resources: Economics and the Law of the Sea (1979).

19. *The Case of the S.S. Lotus (Fr. v. Turk.),* 1927 P.C.I.J. (Ser. A) No. 10, at 19: "Far from laying down a general prohibition to the effect that States may not extend the application of their laws and the jurisdiction of their courts to persons, property and acts outside their territory, [international law] leaves them in this respect a wide measure of discretion which is only limited in certain cases by prohibitive rules; as regards other cases, every State remains free to adopt the principle which it regards as best and most suitable."

20. This is what Paul Stephan calls a "snatch and grab constitution." Paul Stephan, *Choice of Law and Its Consequences: Constitutions for International Transactions,* 26 BROOKLYN J. INT'L. L. 211 (2000).

21. For a discussion of common property regimes, *see* Carol M. Rose, *From Local to Global Commons: Private Property, Common Property, and Hybrid Property Regimes: Expanding the Choices for the Global Commons: Comparing Newfangled Tradable Allowance Schemes to Old-Fashioned Common Property Regimes,* 10 DUKE ENV. L. & POL'Y F. 45 (1999).

22. There are many references. From different ends of the choice of law spectrum, *see, e.g.,* Friedrich K. Juenger, *A Third Conflicts Restatement?* 75 IND. L.J. 403 (2000) (cataloging the incoherence of choice of law). Baxter, *supra* note 3, at 1 (observing that "the deficiencies of present choice-of-law rules are attributable in large part to a lack of foundation on intelligible normative criteria"). *See also* Trachtman, *Conflict of Laws, supra* note 2; Trachtman, *Extraterritoriality, supra* note 2.

23. *See, e.g.,* Andreas F. Lowenfeld, *Public Law in the International Arena: Conflict of Laws, International Law, and Some Suggestions for Their Interaction,* 163 RECUEIL DES COURS 311, 335 (1979-II): "The governmental interests of which Currie and his followers speak in the private law contexts are nearly all imaginary: governments (as contrasted with courts) do not really care about whether the driver of an automobile is liable to a passenger." While Lowenfeld's general point is correct, the example he gives may not be: there may be a significant public policy expressed through such rules of liability. The important point is that private law is often facultative, and engages little state interest, especially at the interjurisdictional margins. Liability rules may engage little state interest as *ex post* determinants of responsibility, but may engage significant state interest as *ex ante* sources of incentives for particular action.

24. *See* ELINOR OSTROM, GOVERNING THE COMMONS: THE EVOLUTION OF INSTITUTIONS FOR COLLECTIVE ACTION (1990); B. C. Field, *The Evolution of Property Rights,* 42 KYKLOS 319 (1989); Thomas W. Merrill, *Trespass, Nuisance, and the Costs of Determining Property Rights,* 14 J. LEG. STUD. 13 (1985); R. S. Hartman, *A Note on Externalities and the Placement of Property Rights: An Alternative Formulation to the Standard Pigouvian Results,*

2 Int'l. Rev. L. & Econ. 111 (1982); John Umbeck, *Might Makes Rights: A Theory of the Formation and Initial Distribution of Property Rights,* 19 Econ. Inq. 38 (1981); David Ault & Gilbert Rutman, *The Development of Independent Rights to Property in Tribal Africa,* 22 J. Law & Econ. 183 (1979); John Umbeck, *A Theory of Contract Choice and the California Gold Rush,* 20 J. Law & Econ. 163 (1977); Terry L. Anderson & Peter J. Hill, *The Evolution of Property Rights: A Study of the American West,* 18 J. Law & Econ. 163 (1975); Demsetz, *supra* note 9.

25. *See* Garrett Hardin, *The Tragedy of the Commons,* 162 Science 124 (1968); Rose, *supra* note 21, at 47.

26. On the possibility that customary international law of allocation of prescriptive jurisdiction would arise, see Chapter 3.

27. *See* Michael A. Heller, *The Tragedy of the Anticommons: Property in the Transition from Marx to Markets,* 111 Harv. L. Rev. 621 (1998). *See also* James M. Buchanan & Yong J. Yoon, *Symmetric Tragedies: Commons and Anticommons,* 43 J. L. & Econ. 1 (2000).

28. Interestingly, in the domestic circumstance, the anticommons model can be deployed as an argument against national regulation. In the international context, it can be deployed as an argument in favor of national regulation (and against claims of other states to constrain national regulation).

29. *See, e.g.,* Kenneth Arrow, Social Choice and Individual Values (1951); Buchanan, *supra* note 6. For a statement of a similar perspective in the conflicts setting, *see* Kegel, *supra* note 4, at 180.

30. In Chapter 7, I discuss the criticism of private rights of action based on the concern that they may impair the exercise of preferences articulated through the state.

31. Facultative law is law that is intentionally, and formally, optional. It is intended to provide a degree of uniformity and a default rule, assuming the parties do not contract out of it. For example, in most common law systems, most rules of contract interpretation and construction are facultative. On the other hand, rules regarding capacity to enter into contracts are generally mandatory. In tort, we must distinguish between circumstances where there is an opportunity to contract with the victim, in which case some rules may be effectively facultative, and circumstances in which no contract is feasible, where the rules are effectively mandatory. We would expect little governmental interest to be engaged by facultative law, but the fact that legal rules have been legislated is indication that there is some value to establishing coordination, usually by virtue of a default rule.

32. Mandatory law, sometimes identified with "public law," also includes many types of regulatory law, such as competition or antitrust law, most securities regulation, and practically all criminal law. In regulatory theory, a necessary

but not sufficient condition for mandatory law exists where the regulated person does not absorb all of the effects, adverse or beneficial, of his or her action. We generally think of public law as also being appropriate in circumstances where the parties do not have an opportunity to contract, but information asymmetries or other bargaining problems may make mandatory regulation appropriate even in market circumstances.

33. BRAINERD CURRIE, SELECTED ESSAYS ON THE CONFLICT OF LAWS 621 (1963). Currie defined "government interest" to *include* consideration of this type of attenuation or, to put it positively, to include the level of governmental concern: "An 'interest' as we use the term is the product of (a) a governmental policy and (b) the concurrent existence of an appropriate relationship between the state having the policy and the transaction, the parties, or the litigation."

34. Here, we simply refer to the debate over whether courts may divine governmental policies and, hence, governmental interests. *See, e.g.*, Lea Brilmayer, *Interest Analysis and the Myth of Legislative Intent*, 78 MICH. L. REV. 392, 430 (1980). For a guide to this debate, *see* Herma Hill Kay, *A Defense of Currie's Governmental Interest Analysis*, 215 RECUEIL DES COURS 117–33 (1990).

35. Some would argue that even this question is illegitimate, at least when asked by a judge as opposed to a legislature. *See* Louise Weinberg, *Against Comity*, 80 GEO. L.J. 53, 55 (1991) (arguing that a forum should not depart from its own law).

36. The inconsistency may be simply that one state's law requires some action that the other state's law does not. Even though the subject person could comply with the former requirement, it may impose costs that the latter state determined, implicitly or explicitly, that its persons should not be required to bear. Thus, it may adversely affect the ability of the latter state to achieve its *negative* regulatory goals. There is no particular reason to value *prohibitive* regulatory goals more highly than *permissive* ones. *See* Trachtman, *Extraterritoriality, supra* note 2, at 671, 679; Jeffery Atik, *Extraterritoriality, Regulatory Conflicts and the "Horizontal Dormant Commerce Clause,"* 94 AM. SOC'Y INT'L L. PROC. 83 (2000); Guzman, *supra* note 5. This is why Guzman is correct to point out the substantial policy problem raised by *Hartford Fire Insurance Co. v. California*, 509 U.S. 764 (1993) (holding that only where foreign law prohibits compliance with U.S. law should a U.S. court engage in a comity analysis).

37. *See* Currie, *supra* note 33, at 48, 117, 181–82. In the context of two "interested" states, Currie made the following statement: "I can only repeat that no satisfactory solution can possibly be evolved by means of the resources of conflict-of-laws law. This does not mean that the problem cannot be

solved. It cannot be solved by any effort, judicial or legislative, however brilliant in its conception, on the part of a single state acting alone; and conflict-of-laws law, strictly speaking, is found only in the laws of individual states. . . . It is possible, however, that the conflict may be resolved by agreement between the states concerned, and it is clear that it can be resolved by higher governmental authority." Currie, *supra* note 33, at 117. *See also* Kay, *supra* note 34. In the prescriptive jurisdiction context, the authors of the *Restatement (Third) of Foreign Relations Law* came to a similar conclusion. *See* RESTATEMENT (THIRD) OF THE FOREIGN RELATIONS LAW OF THE UNITED STATES § 403 (1987).

38. Currie, *supra* note 33, at 368–70. This difference in treatment is based on the institutional differences between the interstate system and the international system.

39. *See* ARTHUR VON MEHREN & DONALD TRAUTMAN, THE LAW OF MULTISTATE PROBLEMS (1965).

40. *See* Trachtman, *Externalities, supra* note 2.

41. *See* Dan L. Burk, *Muddy Rules for Cyberspace,* 21 CARDOZO L. REV. 121, 162 (1999).

42. Currie stated, "I can find no place in conflict-of-laws analysis for a calculus of private interests. By the time the interstate plane is reached the resolution of conflicting private interests has been achieved; it is subsumed in the statement of the laws of the respective states." Currie, *supra* note 33, at 610.

43. *See* John Merryman, *The Public Law–Private Law Distinction in European and American Law,* 17 J. PUB. L. 3, 13 (1968). *See also* Kegel, *supra* note 4, at 3–19.

44. We return to this issue in our discussion of private rights of action in connection with violations of international law in Chapter 7.

45. The issue here is no less than the choice between the state and the market as mechanisms for preference revelation. My assumption is that sometimes individuals choose the state to express their preferences. *See* NEIL KOMESAR, IMPERFECT ALTERNATIVES (1994); CHARLES WOLF, MARKETS OR GOVERNMENTS: CHOOSING BETWEEN IMPERFECT ALTERNATIVES (1988).

46. *See* Guzman, *supra* note 5, at 14, seeming to assume that all effects on individuals are effects on their market-expressed preferences rather than their governmentally expressed preferences. *See also* Ribstein, *supra* note 5; Parisi & Ribstein, *supra* note 5 (focusing on contractual choice of law and stating, "It is not clear why a state should have an overriding 'interest' vis-a-vis the express and informed choice of the contracting parties"). Perhaps the clearest statement is in O'Hara & Ribstein, *From Politics to Efficiency, supra* note 5, at 1152.

47. Note 11, *supra*.

48. Autonomous law and customary international law are addressed in greater detail in Chapter 3.

49. *See* Robert C. Ellickson, *The Case for Coase and against Coaseanism*, 99 YALE L.J. 611 (1989).

50. RICHARD POSNER, THE ECONOMICS OF JUSTICE 71 (1983) (citation omitted). *See also* Posner, *supra* note 5, at 51–72; Carolyn Woj, *Property Rights Disputes: Current Fallacies and a New Approach*, 14 J. LEG. STUD. 411 (1985).

51. It is worth noting that the effects test as actually asserted and applied by the United States is different: it only seeks to determine whether some adverse effects exist in the United States and does not explicitly compare effects in the affected jurisdictions. *See* RESTATEMENT THIRD, *supra* note 3.

52. Of course, it is essential to keep in mind that the initial allocation is analogous to property law in the domestic sphere and that exchanges of property, or in this case exchanges of prescriptive jurisdiction, will take place and may well be efficient. Because of the structure of international society, the same instruments as are used for the initial allocation—often treaties—could be used for the subsequent transactions. This is analogous to a primitive or other horizontal legal system.

53. Of course, the affected state might resort to diplomacy or to retaliation, and thereby indirectly exercise authority. Thus, the instability is not necessarily absolute, but relative, depending on the transaction costs incurred to resort to diplomacy or retaliation, as the case may be.

54. *See* ROBERT C. ELLICKSON, ORDER WITHOUT LAW 72–76 (1991) (ranchers allocating the cost of fencing on common boundaries between their properties pro rata in rough accordance with the number of head of cattle that each keeps on his side).

55. *See* Baxter, *supra* note 3. *See also* Antoine Pillet, *Theorie Continentale des Conflits de Lois*, 2 RECUEIL DES COURS 447, 466–71 (1924).

56. *See* Luther L. McDougal III, *Comprehensive Interest Analysis versus Reformulated Governmental Interest Analysis: An Appraisal in the Context of Choice-of-Law Problems Concerning Contributory and Comparative Negligence*, 26 U.C.L.A. L. REV. 439 (1979).

57. Given the perspective of this chapter, it seems odd that states would reject, as illegitimate, an effects test. This book does not purport to offer an explanation, but some conjectures may be offered. First, as noted elsewhere in this chapter, cross-border effects have not been substantial enough, and effects-based prescription has not been valuable enough, to justify an assertion of jurisdiction. As the rise of regulation has occurred at different rates in different places, the status quo is asserted to favor those

states that do not regulate. Second, and perhaps more interestingly, the public international law of state responsibility has remained available, applying an "effects" test, to provide a public international law claim—a state-to-state claim—under circumstances where one state harms another in a way that violates international legal obligations. If this latter conjecture is valid, it would be interesting to analyze the reason for restricting these claims to the public international law system. The question becomes, in part, one of direct effect: can domestic courts deal with these claims? See Chapter 7.

58. On the other hand, the European Union and Germany have active antitrust laws and apply their laws in ways that may be viewed as "extraterritorial." *See* Joined Cases 89, 104, 114, 116, 117 & 125–29/85, A. Åhlstrom Oaskeyhtio v. Commission, 1988 E.C.R. 5193, 4 Common Mkt. Rep. (CCH) ¶ 14,491 (1988); James J. Friedberg, *The Convergence of Law in an Era of Political Integration: The Wood Pulp Case and the Alcoa Effects Doctrine,* 52 U. PITT. L. REV. 289 (1991); David J. Gerber, *The Extraterritorial Application of the German Antitrust Laws,* 77 AM. J. INT'L L. 756 (1983).

59. *See* Atik, *supra* note 36.

60. Coase, *supra* note 11, at 96.

61. *See, e.g.,* John Hart Ely, *Choice of Law and the State's Interest in Protecting Its Own,* 23 WM. & MARY L. REV. 173 (1981).

62. *See* Ian Ayres & Eric Talley, *Solomonic Bargaining: Dividing a Legal Entitlement to Facilitate Coasean Trade,* 104 YALE L.J. 1027, 1033 (1995); David D. Haddock et al., *An Ordinary Economic Rationale for Extraordinary Legal Sanctions,* 78 CAL. L. REV. 1, 13–17 (1990).

63. For a useful summary and critique of the literature, *see* Louis Kaplow & Steven Shavell, *Property Rules versus Liability Rules: An Economic Analysis,* 109 HARV. L. REV. 713 (1996).

64. *See* Ayres & Talley, *supra* note 62. *See also* Ian Ayres & J. M. Balkin, *Legal Entitlements as Auctions: Property Rules, Liability Rules, and Beyond,* 106 YALE L.J. 703 (1996). Ayres and Talley, and Kaplow and Shavell, argue that where information is asymmetric, property rules may not necessarily produce the most efficient result, even though transaction costs are low. Kaplow & Shavell, *supra* note 63; Louis Kaplow & Steven Shavell, *Do Liability Rules Facilitate Bargaining? A Reply to Ayres and Talley,* 105 YALE L.J. 221 (1995). *See also* Ian Ayres & Eric Talley, *Distinguishing between Consensual and Nonconsensual Advantages of Liability Rules,* 105 YALE L.J. 235 (1995).

65. *See* Thomas Merrill & Henry Smith, *Optimal Standardization in the Law of Property: The* Numerus Clausus *Principle,* 110 YALE L.J. 1 (2000).

66. Thus, Calabresi and Melamed summarize Calabresi's work as follows: "in the absence of certainty as to who [the cheapest cost avoider] is, the costs

should be put on the party or activity which can with the lowest transaction costs act in the market to correct an error in entitlements by inducing the party who can avoid social costs most cheaply to do so." Calabresi & Melamed, *supra* note 13, at 1097.

67. GUIDO CALABRESI, THE COSTS OF ACCIDENTS: A LEGAL AND ECONOMIC ANALYSIS 135–52 (1970); Calabresi & Melamed, *supra* note 13; Guido Calabresi, *Transaction Costs, Resource Allocation and Liability Rules—a Comment,* 11 J. L. & ECON. 67, 72 (1968).

68. *See* the discussion above.

69. In formulating this strategy in the liability context, Calabresi would find the "best briber" by considering the person's (x) awareness of the risk, (y) access to knowledge of possible persons to whom to reallocate, and (z) need to use coercion and ability to use coercion to address freeloaders. Calabresi, *supra* note 67, at 150–52.

70. *See* Judge Posner's opinion in *Kaczmarek v. Allied Chemical Corp.,* 836 F.2d 1055, 1058 (7th Cir. 1988): "the tort law of the state where the accident occurs is likely to be the law most closely attuned to conditions in the state affecting safety, such as climate, terrain, and attitudes toward safety." *See also* Posner, *supra* note 5, at 646. For an argument in the securities sector that regulatory expertise should be a critical factor in allocation of regulatory authority, *see* Merritt B. Fox, *Securities Disclosure in a Globalizing Market: Who Should Regulate Whom,* 95 MICH. L. REV. 2498 (1997).

71. *See* Roberta Romano, *Law as a Product: Some Pieces of the Incorporation Puzzle,* 1 J. L. ECON. & ORG. 225 (1985).

72. One example might be drawn from the perspective of the U.S. Securities and Exchange Commission (SEC). In discussions of allocation of regulatory authority, the SEC has been extremely reluctant to cede authority to other regulators. It might be argued that the SEC's position is supported by its leading position and extensive experience in securities regulation, compared to that of other securities regulators. For a discussion of the SEC's approach to allocation of regulatory authority, *see* Joel P. Trachtman, *Recent Initiatives in International Financial Regulation and Goals of Competitiveness, Effectiveness, Consistency and Cooperation,* 11 NORTHWESTERN J. INT'L L. & BUS. 101 (1991).

73. *See* Robert Leflar, *Choice-Influencing Considerations in Conflicts Law,* 41 N.Y.U.L. REV. 267 (1966); Robert Leflar, *Conflicts Law: More Choice-Influencing Considerations,* 54 CAL. L. REV. 1584, 1586–88 (1966); ROBERT LEFLAR, LUTHER MCDOUGAL, & ROBERT FELIX, AMERICAN CONFLICTS LAW 279, 298 (4th ed. 1986).

74. *See* Kegel, *supra* note 4.

75. Posner, *supra* note 5, at 58.

76. Merrill, *supra* note 24, at 25.

77. *See* Posner, *supra* note 5, at 70; Calabresi & Melamed, *supra* note 13.

78. *See* Demsetz, *supra* note 9 (clear property rights reduce dissipation of resources in conflicts and bullying). On the other hand, clear property rights may be costly where they are inconsistent with effects and private information prevents reallocative transactions. In these cases, "muddy" property rights may provide incentives for negotiation toward efficient reallocation. *See* Jason Scott Johnston, *Bargaining under Rules Versus Standards,* 11 J. L. ECON. & ORG. 256 (1995); Ayres & Talley, *supra* note 62; Richard Epstein, *Holdouts, Externalities and the Single Owner: One More Salute to Ronald Coase,* 36 J. L. & ECON. 553 (1993). This possibility is discussed below.

79. Clifford Holderness, *A Legal Foundation for Exchange,* 14 J. LEG. STUD. 321 (1985); Merrill, *supra* note 24. *See also* Carol Rose, *Crystals and Mud in Property Law,* 40 STAN. L. REV. 577 (1988) (arguing that sometimes imprecise or incomplete "muddy" approaches are appropriate even in cases of low transaction costs).

80. An example of this is the area of international taxation, in which territorial source is the "primary" basis for fiscal jurisdiction, but is often compromised in favor of nationality-based jurisdiction in tax treaties.

81. Posner, *supra* note 5, at 70.

82. *See* Johnston, *supra* note 78.

83. Posner, *supra* note 5, at 70 (suggesting that the common law doctrine of nuisance, with its standard of reasonableness, may provide incentives for negotiation of the low-cost solution or, alternatively, litigation).

84. *See* Merrill, *supra* note 24, at 26.

85. Epstein, *supra* note 78. *See also* Posner, *supra* note 5, at 69; George J. Mailath & Andrew Postlewaite, *Asymmetric Information Bargaining Problems with Many Agents,* 57 REV. ECON. STUD. 351 (1990).

86. It might be asserted that the WTO serves this purpose, combining mandatory jurisdiction with justiciable standards, albeit ones that were not designed specifically with horizontal jurisdictional disputes in mind. Recent WTO jurisprudence—notably in the *Shrimp* case and in the *Gambling* case—finds the WTO Appellate Body insisting on negotiations between states as a requirement for establishing a defense under the exceptional provisions of Article XX of GATT. *United States—Import Prohibition of Certain Shrimp and Shrimp Products,* WT/DS58/AB/R, adopted 6 November 1998; *United States—Gambling Services,* WT/DS285/AB/R, adopted 20 April 2005. These cases can certainly be understood in jurisdictional terms. *See* Joel P. Trachtman, *Regulatory Jurisdiction and the WTO,* 10 J. INT'L ECON. L. 1093 (2007).

87. Public international litigation, such as before the International Court of Justice (ICJ), is still an unusual method of resolution of disputes between

states, although it has become a frequently used means of settling boundary disputes. *See, e.g., Maritime Delimitation in the Area between Greenland and Jan Mayen (Den. v. Nor.),* 1993 ICJ Rep. 38. In order for litigation to become a viable alternative method of reallocation, it will be necessary to improve the mechanisms for international dispute resolution, in terms of their availability and binding nature. Since the *Lotus* case, international litigation has not played a significant role in determining the allocation of prescriptive jurisdiction. However, litigation is quite frequent in the WTO setting, and may have important prescriptive jurisdiction ramifications.

88. *See* Ellickson, *supra* note 54.

89. *See, e.g.,* Joel P. Trachtman, *The Domain of WTO Dispute Resolution,* 40 HARV. INT'L L.J. 333 (1999); Robert D. Cooter & Tom Ginsburg, *Comparative Judicial Discretion: An Empirical Test of Economic Models,* 16 INT'L REV. L. & ECON. 295 (1996).

90. RESTATEMENT OF THE LAW: CONFLICT OF LAWS (1934). *See also* JOSEPH H. BEALE, A TREATISE ON THE CONFLICT OF LAWS (1935). For an argument to the effect that the First Restatement provides a large measure of efficiency, *see* Erin O'Hara & Larry E. Ribstein, *Interest Groups, Contracts and Interest Analysis,* 48 MERCER L. REV. 765 (1997).

91. Brainerd Currie, *Married Women's Contracts: A Study in Conflict-of-Laws Method,* 25 U. CHI. L. REV. 227, 242–44 (1958).

92. *See, e.g.,* O'Hara & Ribstein, *From Politics to Efficiency, supra* note 5; O'Hara & Ribstein, *supra* note 90.

93. *See, e.g.,* 11 U.S.C. §§ 1507 (requiring courts to engage in a balancing analysis in connection with certain assistance to foreign bankruptcy proceedings); Foreign Trade Antitrust Improvements Act of 1982, 15 U.S.C. § 6a (providing for analysis of domestic effects as a basis for jurisdiction) (interpreted in Hoffmann-La Roche v. Empagran, 542 U.S. 155 (2004)).

94. *See* Weinberg, *supra* note 35.

95. For the first application of this literature to choice of law, *see* Parisi & O'Hara, *supra* note 5, at 391–94.

96. For an introduction to the rules versus standards discussion in law and economics, *see* Louis Kaplow, *General Characteristics of Rules,* in ENCYCLOPEDIA OF LAW AND ECONOMICS (B. Bouckaert & G. De Geest, eds. 1998); Louis Kaplow, *Rules versus Standards: An Economic Analysis,* 42 DUKE L.J. 557 (1992). *See also* Cass R. Sunstein, *Problems with Rules,* 83 CAL. L. REV. 955 (1995).

97. *Supra* note 11.

98. *See* Oliver Hart, *Incomplete Contracts and the Theory of the Firm,* in OLIVER E. WILLIAMSON & SIDNEY G. WINTER, THE NATURE OF THE FIRM (1993).

99. *See, e.g.,* Frank H. Easterbrook, *Federalism and European Business Law,* 14 INT'L REV. L. & ECON. 125, 129 (1994). *See also* Alan O. Sykes, *Externalities in Open Economy Antitrust and Their Implications for International Competition Policy,* 23 HARV. J. L. PUB. POL. 89 (1999).

100. *Supra* note 11.

101. *See* Joel R. Paul, *Comity in International Law,* 32 HARV. INT'L L.J. 1 (1991); Maier, *supra* note 3.

102. *See, e.g.,* William S. Dodge, *Extraterritoriality and Conflict-of-Laws Theory: An Argument for Judicial Unilateralism,* 39 HARV. INT'L L.J. 101 (1998). Dodge suggests that courts do not have the requisite competence to engage in multilateralism. *Id.* at 105–6.

103. Ellickson, *supra* note 54, at 52–64.

104. Herbert A. Simon, *Organizations and Markets* 5 J. ECON. PERSP. 25, 29 (1991).

105. *See* note 11, *supra.*

106. OLIVER E. WILLIAMSON, THE ECONOMIC INSTITUTIONS OF CAPITALISM 42 (1985).

107. *Id.* at 85–86.

108. *Id.* at 90.

109. 15 U.S.C. § 6a. *See* Hoffmann-La Roche v. Empagran, 542 U.S. 155 (2004).

110. Albert Breton, Alberto Cassone, & Angela Fraschini, *Decentralization and Subsidiarity: Toward a Theoretical Reconciliation,* 19 U. PA. J. INT'L ECON. L. 1, 43 (1998).

111. *See* Joel P. Trachtman, *Regulatory Competition and Regulatory Jurisdiction,* 3 J. INT'L ECON. L. 331 (2000) [hereinafter, *Regulatory Competition*].

112. Roberta Romano, *Empowering Investors: A Market Approach to Securities Regulation,* 107 YALE L.J. 2359, 2367 (1998). *But see* Merritt B. Fox, *Retaining Mandatory Disclosure: Why Issuer Choice Is Not Investor Empowerment,* 85 VA. L. REV. 1335 (1999); Joel P. Trachtman, *Regulatory Competition and Regulatory Jurisdiction in Securities Regulation,* in REGULATORY COMPETITION AND ECONOMIC INTEGRATION: COMPARATIVE PERSPECTIVES (Daniel Esty & Damien Gerardin, eds. 2001). [hereinafter, REGULATORY COMPETITION IN SECURITIES REGULATION].

113. Stephen J. Choi & Andrew T. Guzman, *Portable Reciprocity: Rethinking the International Reach of Securities Regulation,* 71 S. CAL. L. REV. 903 (1998).

114. *Supra* note 5.

115. *Id.*

116. *See, e.g.,* Robert P. Inman & Daniel L. Rubinfeld, *The Political Economy of Federalism, in* PERSPECTIVES ON PUBLIC CHOICE: A HANDBOOK 73, 85 (Dennis C. Mueller, ed. 1997). After stating that current empirical evidence is

suggestive that competitive local governments can provide an efficient level of congestible (local) public goods, Inman and Rubinfeld offer the following caveat: "What is not assured is the efficient allocation of public goods with significant spillovers. In this case, a subsidy is needed to internalize the externalities. But any such policy to control interjurisdictional spillovers would require the agreement of the competitive city-states. For such agreements we must look to more encompassing political institutions. In Madison's compound republic this is the representative central government." *Id.*, at 86.

117. The *locus classicus* is Charles Tiebout, *A Pure Theory of Local Expenditures,* 64 J. POLIT. ECON. 416 (1956). There is a vast literature, both theoretical and empirical, on the Tiebout model. For a review of some of the literature, *see* William W. Bratton & Joseph A. McCahery, *The New Economics of Jurisdictional Competition: Devolutionary Federalism in a Second-Best World,* 86 GEO. L.J. 201 (1997).

118. "Thus, we know that in a vacuum, a feather and a cannonball will fall at the same speed if dropped from the same height. But if one woodenly applied this law of gravity in trying to predict whether the feather or the cannonball would hit the ground first if dropped from the Empire State Building, the results would be ludicrous." John J. Donohue, *Some Thoughts on Law and Economics and the General Theory of the Second Best,* 73 CHICAGO-KENT L. REV. 257, 263 (1998).

119. Adapted from Robert P. Inman & Daniel L. Rubinfeld, *The Political Economy of Federalism, supra* note 116. *See also* Bratton & McCahery, *supra* note 117.

120. Edward M. Gramlich, *Cooperation and Competition in Public Welfare Policies,* 6 J. POLICY ANALYSIS & MGT. 417 (1987). *See also* Albert Breton, *The Existence and Stability of Interjurisdictional Competition,* in COMPETITION AMONG STATES AND LOCAL GOVERNMENTS (Daphne A. Kenyon & John Kincaid, eds. 1991).

121. Breton, *supra* note 120, at 43.

122. *Id.* at 51.

123. *Id.* at 49.

124. *Id.* at 51–52 (emphasis added).

125. ALBERT BRETON, COMPETITIVE GOVERNMENTS 249 (1996).

126. Bratton & McCahery, *supra* note 117.

127. Michael Skapinker, *EU Sets Out Objections to Boeing Merger,* Fin. Times, May 23, 1997.

128. *See* Andre Fiebig, *The Extraterritorial Application of the European Merger Control Regulation,* 5 COLUM. J. EUR. L. 79 (1999).

129. Council Regulation (EEC) No. 4064/89 of 21 December 1989 on the control of concentrations between undertakings, 1989 O.J. (L 257) 14, as

amended by Council Regulation (EC) No. 1310/97, 1997 O.J. (L 180) 1
[hereinafter, the Merger Regulation]. The Merger Regulation has been
superseded by Council Regulation (EC) No. 139/2004 of 20 January 2004
on the control of concentrations between undertakings, which has similar
characteristics.

130. Often, their perspectives are similar. *See ICPAC Gets Briefing on Conflicts, Remedies Involving Multijurisdictional Merger Reviews,* Antitrust &
Trade Reg. Rep. (BNA) No. 75, at 520 (November 5, 1998). See also
Adam Cohen & Mary Jacoby, *EU's Kroes Puts Antitrust Stance in Line
with U.S.,* Wall St. J., September 26, 2005, A17.

131. Commission Decision of 97/816, 1997 O.J. (L 336) 17–19.

132. Daniel K. Tarullo, *Norms and Institutions in Global Competition Policy,* 94
A.J.I.L 478, 479 (2000). *See also* Eleanor M. Fox, *National Law, Global Mar-
kets and Hartford: Eyes Wide Shut,* 68 ANTITRUST L.J. 73 (2000); Andrew
Guzman, *Is International Antitrust Possible,* 73 N.Y.U. L. REV. 1501 (1998).

133. International Antitrust Enforcement: Hearings on S521–48 before the
Subcommittee on Antitrust, Business Rights, and Competition Committee on the Judiciary United States Senate (1998) (statement of Joel I.
Klein, assistant attorney general, Antitrust Division, U.S. Department of
Justice). *See* Agreement on the Application of Positive Comity Principles
in the Enforcement of Their Competition Laws, June 4, 1998, U.S.-EC,
37 I.L.M. 1070 (1998).

134. Hoffmann-La Roche v. Empagran, 542 U.S. 155 (2004).

135. *See* Joel P. Trachtman, *Accounting Standards and Trade Disciplines: Ir-
reconcilable Differences?* 31 J. WORLD TRADE 63 (1997).

136. Romano, *supra* note 112; Choi & Guzman, *supra* note 113. *But see* Fox,
supra note 112; Trachtman, *supra* note 112.

137. Fox, *supra* note 112.

138. Bratton & McCahery, *supra* note 117.

139. *See* LEE J. ALSTON, THRÁINN EGGERTSSON, & DOUGLASS C. NORTH, EM-
PIRICAL STUDIES IN INSTITUTIONAL CHANGE (1996); Howard A. Shelanski
& Peter G. Klein, *Empirical Research in Transaction Cost Economics: A
Review and Assessment,* 11 J. L. ECON. & ORG. 335 (1995).

3. Customary International Law

1. This chapter is based on George Norman & Joel P. Trachtman, *The Customary International Law Game,* 99 AM. J. INT'L L. 541 (2005), which
contains a formal appendix showing the model described here.

2. *See, e.g.,* Mark A. Chinen, *Afterword,* 23 MICH. J. INT'L L. 201 (2001);
Mark A. Chinen, *Game Theory and Customary International Law: A*

Response to Professors Goldsmith and Posner, 23 Mich. J. Int'l L. 143
(2001); Vincy Fon & Francesco Parisi, *Customary Law and Articulation
Theories: An Economic Analysis,* George Mason L. & Econ. Res. Paper
No. 02–24 (2002), available at http://papers.ssrn.com/sol3/papers.cfm
?abstract_id=335220; Jack L. Goldsmith & Eric A. Posner, *Further
Thoughts on Customary International Law,* 23 Mich. J. Int'l L. 191
(2001); Jack L. Goldsmith & Eric A. Posner, *A Theory of Customary International Law,* 66 U. Chi. L. Rev. 1113 (1999) [hereinafter, *A Theory
of CIL*]; Andrew T. Guzman, *A Compliance-Based Theory of International Law,* 90 Cal. L. Rev. 1823 (2002); Francesco Parisi, *The Formation of Customary Law,* George Mason L. & Econ. Res. Paper No.
01–06 (2001), available at http://papers.ssrn.com/sol3/papers.cfm
?abstract_id=262032; Edward T. Swaine, *Rational Custom,* 52 Duke L.J.
559 (2002); Pierre-Hugues Verdier, *Cooperative States: International
Relations, State Responsibility and the Problem of Custom,* 42 Va. J.
Int'l L. 839 (2002).

3. The leading article here is Goldsmith & Posner, *A Theory of CIL, supra*
    note 2. This work is now incorporated in Jack L. Goldsmith & Eric A.
    Posner, The Limits of International Law (2005). For a self-described
    "traditionalist's" response, see Detlev F. Vagts, *International Relations
    Looks at Customary International Law: A Traditionalist's Defence,* 15 Eur.
    J. Int'l L. 1031 (2004).
4. *See* Vagts, *supra* note 3 (critiquing the use of examples in Goldsmith &
    Posner, *A Theory of CIL*).
5. By "self-interest," I mean merely to refer to maximization of preferences,
    which can, among other things, be other-regarding or altruistic.
6. *See* the quote from Waltz at Chapter 1, note 10, *supra.*
7. See the cautions expressed in Goldsmith & Posner, *A Theory of CIL, supra*
    note 2, and the broader treatment in Duncan Snidal, *The Game Theory of
    International Politics, in* Cooperation under Anarchy (Kenneth A. Oye
    ed., 1986).
8. While it may be argued that the game theory that I use, initially developed
    in the context of analysis of individual behavior, cannot be applied to state
    behavior, it should be noted that game theory has been applied to the be-
    havior of firms, as well as to that of states. For an argument regarding the
    adaptation of these types of models to international law, see Jeffrey L.
    Dunoff & Joel P. Trachtman, *The Law and Economics of International
    Law,* 24 Yale J. Int'l L. 1 (1999).
9. "Commons problems" are circumstances where persons share a particular
    resource, where one person's use of the resource may reduce the amount
    of the resource available to others, and where conservation of the resource

may increase the amount of the resource available to all. A fishery may, in this context, present a commons problem. "Public goods"—for example, the light of a lighthouse—are goods that are available to all and that can be used by one person without diminishing its availability to others. "Network goods" involve circumstances where wider use of the same good makes that good more valuable to all. Standards often have this characteristic.

10. An "equilibrium" is a strategic setting in which no player has an incentive to change its strategy given that the other players do not change their strategies. It is assumed that each player correctly perceives the strategic constraints under which it operates, and acts rationally in response to those constraints. A "stable equilibrium" is simply an equilibrium in which the players' strategies remain stable—no player has an incentive to deviate from the equilibrium. By "efficiency," we refer to Pareto efficiency, meaning that no player may be made better off without some player being made worse off. No equilibrium is necessarily efficient. In fact, the equilibrium outcome of the prisoner's dilemma is generally inefficient.

11. RESTATEMENT (THIRD) OF THE FOREIGN RELATIONS LAW OF THE UNITED STATES § 102 (1987).

12. Maurice H. Mendelson, *The Formation of Customary International Law*, 272 RECUEIL DES COURS 155, 268–93 (1998).

13. Goldsmith & Posner, *A Theory of CIL, supra* note 2, at 1130.

14. ROBERT C. ELLICKSON, ORDER WITHOUT LAW 72–76 (1991).

15. One might argue, however, that the general legal system serves as a background framework that supports the farmers' social norms. For example, the rules against violence impose constraints on the types of sanctions that farmers can impose on one another for noncompliance with a social norm.

16. *See* ERIC A. POSNER, LAW AND SOCIAL NORMS (2000); Richard H. McAdams, *Signaling Discount Rates: Law, Norms, and Economic Methodology*, 110 YALE L.J. 625 (2001).

17. For an example of this type of speculation comparing domestic custom to international custom, see Mendelson, *supra* note 12, at 165–68. *See also* ANTHONY A. D'AMATO, THE CONCEPT OF CUSTOM IN INTERNATIONAL LAW (1971).

18. *See, e.g.,* ROBERT O. KEOHANE, INTERNATIONAL INSTITUTIONS AND STATE POWER: ESSAYS IN INTERNATIONAL RELATIONS THEORY (1989).

19. *See, e.g.,* STEPHEN D. KRASNER, INTERNATIONAL REGIMES (1983).

20. *See, e.g.,* Stephan Haggard & Beth A. Simmons, *Theories of International Regimes*, 41 INT'L ORG. 491 (1987).

21. Duncan Snidal, *Political Economy and International Institutions,* 16 Int'l Rev. L. & Econ. 121, 124 (1996).

22. While there is no state at the global level, there is an international legal and organizational order, which is quite a bit more fragmented than most nation-states.

23. I add this qualification because one might argue that the CIL and conventional international law framework, as it exists, is comparable to a municipal state or, at least, to its constitution.

24. Robert C. Ellickson, *The Evolution of Social Norms: A Perspective from the Legal Academy, in* Social Norms 35 (Michael Hechter & Karl-Dieter Opp, eds. 2001). Note that Ellickson assumes multilateral, as opposed to bilateral, retaliation.

25. *See* Harold Hongju Koh, *Why Do Nations Obey International Law?* 106 Yale L.J. 2599 (1997) (reviewing Abram Chayes & Antonia Handler Chayes, The New Sovereignty: Compliance with International Regulatory Agreements (1995)). This internalization may be desirable under certain circumstances and may be developed as a tool for enforcing CIL. That is, states may persuade one another to use their domestic legal systems as a means of bringing about compliance with particular international legal obligations.

26. *See* Robert Cooter, *Expressive Law and Economics,* 27 J. Legal Stud. 585 (1998).

27. Robert Cooter, *Do Good Laws Make Good Citizens? An Economic Analysis of Internalized Norms,* 86 Va. L. Rev. 1577 (2000); Robert Cooter, *Models of Morality in Law and Economics: Self-Control and Self-Improvement for the "Bad Man" of Holmes,* 78 B.U. L. Rev. 903, 911–12 (1998); Jon Elster, The Cement of Society: A Study of Social Order (1989). Basu refers to these as "preference-changing norms." *See* Kaushik Basu, *Social Norms and the Law,* 3 The New Palgrave Dictionary of Economics and the Law 477 (1998).

28. *See* Paul G. Mahoney & Chris William Sanchirico, *Norms, Repeated Games, and the Role of Law,* 91 Cal. L. Rev. 1281, 1284 (2003). Mahoney and Sanchirico explain the state of the social norms literature with respect to the multilateral prisoner's dilemma. They explain that the objection to these models is that third-party enforcement is not individually rational; the players lack incentives to retaliate.

29. *Id.* at 1284 n.12 (citing works by Ellickson, Katz, McAdams, and Posner).

30. There is disagreement between institutionalists and "realists," who claim that states' interests in international relations are characterized by a search for gains relative to other states, rather than absolute gains. Realists reject the possibility of cooperation where it results in relative gains to a competi-

tor. *See* Marc L. Busch & Eric R. Reinhardt, *Nice Strategies in a World of Relative Gains: The Problem of Cooperation under Anarchy*, 37 J. CONFLICT RESOL. 427 (1993); Robert Powell, *Absolute and Relative Gains in International Relations Theory*, 85 AM. POL. SCI. REV. 1303 (1991); Duncan Snidal, *Relative Gains and the Pattern of International Cooperation*, 85 AM. POL. SCI. REV. 701 (1991).

31. See the special Summer 2000 issue of *International Organization* devoted to the phenomenon of "legalization," 54 INT'L ORG. 385 (2000).

32. *See* Kenneth W. Abbott & Duncan Snidal, *Hard and Soft Law in International Governance*, 54 INT'L ORG. 421 (2000); John K. Setear, *Treaties, Custom, Iteration, and Public Choice* (2004), available at http://ssrn.com/abstract =492604 (arguing that custom is more attractive to executive branches). To the extent that CIL is less detailed—less specific—than treaty norms, it is amenable to a rules-versus-standards type of analysis. *See* Chapter 7.

33. For a useful analysis of the "fit" of other games, including "battle of the sexes" and "stag hunt," see Swaine, *supra* note 2. *See also* Fiona McGillivray & Alastair Smith, *Trust and Cooperation through Agent-Specific Punishments*, 54 INT'L ORG. 809, 810 (2000) (noting that the prisoner's dilemma is often used to model international cooperation).

34. At another level of complexity, it would be possible to model the game of forming a CIL rule as separate from enforcement. *See* James D. Fearon, *Bargaining, Enforcement, and International Cooperation*, 52 INT'L ORG. 269 (1998) (separating the bargaining problem, modeled as a coordination game, from the enforcement problem, modeled as a prisoner's dilemma); Stephen D. Krasner, *Global Communications and National Power: Life on the Pareto Frontier*, 43 WORLD POL. 336 (1991) (arguing that many international issues are better modeled as coordination games). Fearon's two-stage approach may be more appropriate to the treaty context than to the custom context.

35. For a discussion of the use of coordination games to model certain types of international contexts, see Barbara Koremenos, Charles Lipson, & Duncan Snidal, *The Rational Design of International Institutions*, 55 INT'L ORG. 761, 774 (2001); and Duncan Snidal, *Coordination versus Prisoners' Dilemma: Implications for International Cooperation and Regimes*, 79 AM. POL. SCI. REV. 923 (1985).

36. *See* Guzman, *supra* note 2.

37. STEPHEN MARTIN, ADVANCED INDUSTRIAL ECONOMICS 98 (1993).

38. Each of the prisoners will always confess, and each will receive a longer sentence than if neither confessed. In this case, bilateral defection leads to an inefficient outcome. And since, under the game's payoff structure, each party is better off defecting, no matter what the other party does, the outcome is a

"Nash equilibrium"—a set of "strategies such that each player's strategy is an optimal response to the other players' strategies." DREW FUDENBERG & JEAN TIROLE, GAME THEORY 11 (1991).

39. This is a "Nash equilibrium." *Id.* at 11.

40. This is a subgame-perfect equilibrium. "A *subgame perfect equilibrium* is a strategy profile that induces a Nash equilibrium in every subgame." M. J. OSBORNE, AN INTRODUCTION TO GAME THEORY 166 (2004).

41. Elinor Ostrom, *Collective Action and the Evolution of Social Norms*, 14 J. ECON. PERSP. 137, 138 (2000).

42. *See* ROBERT AXELROD, THE EVOLUTION OF COOPERATION (1984). Evolutionary games are designed to compare the success of different strategies when played by a population of individuals in repeated play against other strategies.

43. In the language of game theory, it is not "subgame perfect." *See* OSBORNE, *supra* note 40, at 444–46.

44. *Id.* at 444.

45. *See supra* note 38.

46. Scott Barrett, *A Theory of Full International Cooperation*, 11 J. THEORETICAL POL. 519 (1999); SCOTT BARRETT, ENVIRONMENT AND STATECRAFT: THE STRATEGY OF ENVIRONMENTAL TREATY-MAKING (2003).

47. *See, e.g.,* Joseph Farrell & Eric Maskin, *Renegotiation in Repeated Games*, 1 GAMES & ECON. BEHAV. 327 (1989); FUDENBERG & TIROLE, *supra* note 38, at 174.

48. Indeed, this argument is not uncommon in international law discourse. *See, e.g.,* Scott M. Sullivan, *Changing the Premise of International Legal Remedies: The Unfounded Adoption of Assurances and Guarantees of Non-repetition*, 7 U.C.L.A. J. INT'L L. & FOREIGN AFF. 265 (2002–2003).

49. While a precise definition of "renegotiation-proof" has not yet been agreed upon in game theory literature, the treatment by Farrell and Maskin is worth considering. They define a "weakly renegotiation-proof" (WRP) equilibrium for an infinitely repeated game to be a subgame-perfect equilibrium strategy profile that is not Pareto-dominated by any other subgame-perfect strategy profile. Using this definition, the grim trigger strategy profile described above is not WRP, since after defection the payoffs to cooperation Pareto-dominate those of punishment. *See* Farrell & Maskin, *supra* note 47.

50. *See* FUDENBERG & TIROLE, *supra* note 38, at 179–82. "Penance" is sometimes referred to as "getting even." *See* ROGER B. MYERSON, GAME THEORY: ANALYSIS OF CONFLICT 326–27 (1991).

51. That is, it is both subgame perfect and weakly renegotiation-proof. FUDENBERG & TIROLE, *supra* note 38, at 180 (citing Farrell & Maskin, *supra* note

47); Eric van Damme, *Renegotiation-Proof Equilibria in Repeated Prisoners' Dilemma*, 47 J. ECON. THEORY 206 (1989).

52. FUDENBERG & TIROLE, *supra* note 38, at 180. See also the "defect for deviate" strategy proposed by Mahoney and Sanchirico, *supra* note 28, at 1296.

53. Articles on Responsibility of States for Internationally Wrongful Acts, *in* Report of the International Law Commission [ILC] on the Work of Its Fifty-third Session, UN GAOR, 56th Sess., Supp. No. 10, at 43, UN Doc. A/56/10 (2001), *available at* www.un.org/law/ilc [hereinafter, Articles on State Responsibility]. Rather than expressing international law per se, these articles are an attempt to codify existing custom. *See* Chorzow Factory Case (Pol. v. Ger.), 1928 PCIJ (ser. A) Nos. 7, 9, 17, 19 (concerning obligation to make reparations).

54. *See* David J. Bederman, *Counterintuiting Countermeasures*, 96 AM. J. INT'L L. 817 (2002).

55. FUDENBERG & TIROLE, *supra* note 38, at 112.

56. MYERSON, *supra* note 50, at 371.

57. The first law of welfare economics suggests that under perfect competition, the outcome of market transactions is Pareto optimal. DAVID M. KREPS, A COURSE IN MICROECONOMIC THEORY 200 (1990).

58. The Coase theorem states that where transaction costs are zero, parties will bargain (costlessly) to achieve an efficient allocation. *See* Ronald H. Coase, *The Problem of Social Cost*, 3 J. L. & ECON. 1 (1960).

59. PAUL MILGROM & JOHN ROBERTS, ECONOMICS, ORGANIZATION AND MANAGEMENT 24 (1992).

60. A Pareto improvement is one that makes at least one person better off without making anyone worse off.

61. *See supra* note 9 and accompanying text.

62. While our model deals with games in which information is available to all, Parisi develops the Harsanyian concept of stochastic symmetry and role reversibility: the longer the shadow of the future, the less any one state can be certain of the way in which it will be affected by a particular rule. *See* Parisi, *supra* note 2. "Articulations that are made prior to unveiling of conflicting contingencies can be analogized to rules chosen under a Harsanyian veil of uncertainty." *Id.* at 19. *See also* Robert O. Keohane, *The Demand for International Regimes*, 36 INT'L ORG. 325 (1982). Harsanyi's concept of stochastic symmetry refers to the idea that parties may enter into an agreement where they are unsure—under a veil of uncertainty—as to precisely how the agreement will affect their particular interests. They can see that the agreement is an overall improvement, and are assumed to be willing to take a chance as to how that welfare improvement is distributed.

63. *See* Lisa L. Martin, *The Rational State Choice of Multilateralism, in* MULTI-LATERALISM MATTERS: THE THEORY AND PRAXIS OF AN INSTITUTIONAL FORM 91, 99 (John Gerard Ruggie, ed. 1993) (suggesting techniques, including delegation as in the UN Security Council, for reducing the effective number of players).

64. Oscar Schachter, *New Custom: Power,* Opinio Juris, *and Contrary Practice, in* THEORY OF INTERNATIONAL LAW AT THE THRESHOLD OF THE 21ST CENTURY: ESSAYS IN HONOUR OF KRZYSZTOF SKUBISZEWSKI 531, 536–37 (Jerzy Makarczyk, ed. 1996); *see also* Mendelson, *supra* note 12, at 194, 215, 225 (in the past, "civilized" states were considered sufficient, and the applicable group of states did not need to be geographically constrained).

65. *See Asylum (Colom. v. Peru),* 1950 ICJ REP. 266 (November 20); *Right of Passage over Indian Territory (Port. v. India),* 1960 ICJ REP. 6 (April 12). *Cf.* MALCOLM N. SHAW, INTERNATIONAL LAW 72–73 (4th ed. 1997); Edward T. Swaine, *The Local Law of Global Antitrust,* 43 WM. & MARY L. REV. 627, 706–25 (2001). ICJ reports are available at http://www.icj-cij.org.

66. Goldsmith & Posner, *A Theory of CIL, supra* note 2, at 1132.

67. *Id.*

68. MANCUR OLSON JR., THE LOGIC OF COLLECTIVE ACTION: PUBLIC GOODS AND THE THEORY OF GROUPS 2 (1965); *see also* Kenneth A. Oye, *Explaining Cooperation under Anarchy: Hypotheses and Strategies, in* COOPERATION UNDER ANARCHY, *supra* note 7, at 1.

69. OLSON, *supra* note 68, at 48.

70. RUSSELL HARDIN, COLLECTIVE ACTION 43 (1982).

71. *See* Arthur Lupia & Gisela Sin, *Which Public Goods Are Endangered? How Evolving Communication Technologies Affect the Logic of Collective Action,* 117 PUBLIC CHOICE 315 (2003); Ronald B. Mitchell, *Sources of Transparency: Information Systems in International Regimes,* 42 INT'L STUD. Q. 109 (1998).

72. Oye, *supra* note 68, at 18–19.

73. *See* Samuel Bowles & Herbert Gintis, *The Moral Economy of Communities: Structured Populations and the Evolution of Pro-social Norms,* 19 EVOLUTION & HUM. BEHAV. 3, 11–14 (1997).

74. Michihiro Kandori, *Social Norms and Community Enforcement,* 59 REV. ECON. STUD. 63 (1992).

75. *Id.*

76. Paul R. Milgrom, Douglass C. North, & Barry R. Weingast, *The Role of Institutions in the Revival of Trade: The Law Merchant, Private Judges and the Champagne Fairs,* 2 ECON. & POL. 1, 3 (1990). Note that these authors are suggesting that information may compensate for infrequency of bilateral interaction.

77. *Id.* at 8.
78. *Id.* at 15.
79. A "discount factor" is a mathematical factor structured to reflect the degree of patience of a player. It represents the present value today of a payoff in a future period.
80. *See* MYERSON, *supra* note 50, at 308–69.
81. FUDENBERG & TIROLE, *supra* note 38, at 111.
82. *Id.*
83. *Id.* at 150 (referring to the Folk theorem).
84. Drew Fudenberg & Eric Maskin, *The Folk Theorem in Repeated Games with Discounting or with Incomplete Information,* 54 ECONOMETRICA 533 (1986).
85. *See* KEOHANE, *supra* note 18, at 91; Ernst Haas, *Why Collaborate? Issue Linkage and International Regimes* 32 WORLD POL. 357 (1980); Michael D. McGinnis, *Issue Linkage and the Evolution of International Cooperation,* 30 J. CONFLICT RESOL. 141 (1986); Robert D. Tollison & Andrew D. Willett, *An Economic Theory of Mutually Advantageous Issue Linkage in International Negotiations,* 33 INT'L ORG. 425 (1979). McGinnis shows formally that in a prisoner's dilemma "multisupergame," players may adopt strategies that create linkages across time and games, providing opportunities for cooperation, whereas cooperation would not be possible for isolated games.
86. *See* Giancarlo Spagnolo, *Issue Linkage, Credible Delegation, and Policy Cooperation,* Center for Econ. Pol'y Res. Discussion Paper No. 2778 (2001), available at http://ssrn.com/abstract=269364.
87. *See, e.g.,* B. Douglas Bernheim & Michael D. Whinston, *Multimarket Contact and Collusive Behavior,* 21 RAND J. ECON. 1 (1990); Corwin D. Edwards, *Conglomerate Bigness as a Source of Power, in* BUSINESS CONCENTRATION AND PRICE POLICY 331 (1955); Hitoshi Matsushima, *Multimarket Contact, Imperfect Monitoring, and Implicit Collusion,* 98 J. ECON. THEORY 158 (2001); Giancarlo Spagnolo, *On Interdependent Supergames: Multimarket Contact, Concavity and Collusion,* 89 J. ECON. THEORY 127 (1999).
88. Spagnolo, *supra* note 87, at 128.
89. Spagnolo, *supra* note 87, at 133.
90. *See* Guzman, *supra* note 2, at 1869–70; Snidal, *supra* note 35, at 923, 939.
91. *See supra* note 85.
92. Matsushima, *supra* note 87, at 164–65.
93. *See* Koremenos et al., *supra* note 35, at 764–65.
94. George W. Downs & Michael A. Jones, *Reputation, Compliance, and International Law,* 31 J. LEGAL STUD. 95, 101 (2002) (suggesting that

reputation varies by field of activity, and that this segmentation reduces the effects of reputation).

95. *See* Anne-Marie Slaughter, *The Real New World Order,* 76 FOREIGN AFF. 183 (1997).

96. Milgrom et al., *supra* note 76, at 1.

97. *Trail Smelter Case (U.S. v. Can.),* 3 R.I.A.A. 1905 (1938 & 1941). The principle of *sic utere tuo* was included as Principle 21 of the Stockholm Declaration, UN Conference on the Human Environment, Stockholm Declaration, June 16, 1972, UN Doc. A/CONF.48/14, 11 ILM 1416 (1972). *See also* Principle 2 of the 1992 Rio Declaration on Environment and Development, June 14, 1992, UN Doc. A/CONF.151/5/Rev.1, 31 ILM 874 (1992).

98. *See also* International Liability for Injurious Consequences Arising out of Acts Not Prohibited by International Law, *in* Report of the International Law Commission on the Work of Its Fifty-fifth Session, UN GAOR, 58th Sess., Supp. No. 10, at 103, UN Doc. A/58/10 (2003), available at http://www.un.org/law/ilc/.

99. *See* note 24, *supra.*

100. Mark W. Zacher, *The Territorial Integrity Norm: International Boundaries and the Use of Force,* 55 INT'L ORG. 215 (2001). This norm does not prevent states from exercising influence over policy within other states.

101. Grim trigger is not necessarily tougher than penance. While in some cases grim trigger will provide a greater incentive to cooperate than penance, the opposite will be true if the gain for defection when the other state cooperates is less than the gain for defection when the other state defects.

102. The International Court of Justice has recognized that even the protection of diplomats has an important multilateral dimension. *See United States Diplomatic and Consular Staff in Tehran (U.S. v. Iran),* 1980 ICJ REP. 3, para. 92 (May 24). In that case, the ICJ made the following statement: "In recalling yet again the extreme importance of the principles of law [protection of diplomats] which it is called upon to apply in the present case, the Court considers it to be its duty to draw the attention of the entire international community, of which Iran itself has been a member since time immemorial, to the irreparable harm that may be caused by events of the kind now before the Court. Such events cannot fail to undermine the edifice of law carefully constructed by mankind over a period of centuries, the maintenance of which is vital for the security and well-being of the complex international community of the present day, to which it is more essential than ever that the rules developed to ensure the ordered progress of relations between its members should be constantly and scrupulously respected."

103. *See, e.g.,* Robert Pahre, *Multilateral Cooperation in an Iterated Prisoner's Dilemma,* 38 J. CONFLICT RESOL. 326 (1994); Snidal, *supra* note 35, at 929.

104. For a discussion of global public goods, *see* PROVIDING GLOBAL PUBLIC GOODS: MANAGING GLOBALIZATION (Inge Kaul et al., eds. 2003).

105. Other areas of international law (for example, relating to sovereignty and diplomatic protection) may exhibit network effects, which may arise simply from efficiencies due to consistency of arrangements. For a relevant analysis in the corporate law field, see Michael Klausner, *Corporations, Corporate Law, and Networks of Contracts,* 81 VA. L. REV. 757 (1995).

106. The classic reference on this last point is Bernheim & Whinston, *supra* note 87.

107. Chinen, *Game Theory and Customary International Law, supra* note 2, at 154.

108. *See* Komesar, *supra* note 35; HERVÉ MOULIN, COOPERATIVE MICROECONOMICS: A GAME-THEORETIC INTRODUCTION (1995).

109. *See* Chapter 7.

110. Goldsmith & Posner, *A Theory of CIL, supra* note 2, at 1131–33.

111. D'AMATO, *supra* note 17, at 66.

112. It is worth noting the relationship of this proposition to the first formulation of Kant's categorical imperative: "Act only on that maxim through which you can at the same time will that it should become a universal law." IMMANUEL KANT, GROUNDWORK OF THE METAPHYSICS OF MORALS 31 (Mary Gregor, trans. & ed. 1998) (1785).

113. *See Military and Paramilitary Activities in and against Nicaragua (Nicar. v. U.S.),* 1986 ICJ REP. 14, para. 207 (June 27) ("Reliance by a State on a novel right, or an unprecedented exception to the principle, might if shared in principle by other States, tend towards a modification of customary international law").

114. "At the initial stage of the development of the custom, it is sufficient that the States concerned regard the practice as what the Court . . . referred to as 'potentially norm-creating', as conforming to a rule which either already exists or is a useful and desirable rule which should exist." Hugh Thirlway, *The Law and Procedure of the International Court of Justice 1960–1989 (Part Two),* 1990 BRIT. Y.B. INT'L L. 1, 43 (citing North Sea Continental Shelf (FRG/Den.; FRG/Neth.), 1969 ICJ REP. 3, 42 (February 20)). *See* MYRES MCDOUGAL ET AL., STUDIES IN WORLD PUBLIC ORDER 773–74 (1960); Mendelson, *supra* note 12; Swaine, *supra* note 2, at 615 (suggesting that states that initiate a custom might be analogized to offerors in a contractual setting, and that this conditional obligation is consistent with *opinio juris*); *see also* D'AMATO, *supra* note 17, at 73–102.

115. *See* Parisi, *supra* note 2, at 18 (describing "articulation theories" of CIL in these terms).

116. Comm. on Formation of Customary (Gen.) Int'l Law, Int'l Law Ass'n, Final Report: Statement of Principles Applicable to the Formation of General Customary International Law §1(i) (2000) (*citing* Mendelson, *supra* note 12, at 399), available at http://www.ila-hq.org/pdf/CustomaryLaw.pdf.

117. Goldsmith & Posner, *A Theory of CIL*, *supra* note 2, at 1115.

118. *See* Keohane, *supra* note 17.

119. *But see* Swaine, *supra* note 2 (raising concerns regarding Goldsmith and Posner's perspective on CIL doctrine).

120. *Cf.* Guzman, *supra* note 2, at 1875 (asserting that Goldsmith and Posner's claim that CIL does not affect state behavior goes beyond what the evidence suggests).

121. For some criticism of Goldsmith and Posner's description of CIL doctrine, *see* Vagts, *supra* note 3.

122. Goldsmith & Posner, *A Theory of CIL*, *supra* note 2, at 1157.

123. *See, e.g.,* Shaw, *supra* note 65, at 69.

124. *See* Anne-Marie Slaughter, *International Law in a World of Liberal States*, 6 Eur. J. Int'l L. 503 (1995).

125. *See* Slaughter, *supra* note 95.

126. This chapter does not by any means challenge the theory that law can affect behavior by modifying preferences. It merely presents a theory that does not depend on modifying preferences.

127. *See* Swaine, *supra* note 2, at 618 ("states do not, in fact, interact solely with respect to one rule or the other, and it is also possible to understand their interaction with respect both to an individual rule and to the system of customary international law").

4. Treaty

1. *See* Robert E. Scott & Paul B. Stephan, The Limits of Leviathan: Contract Theory and The Enforcement of International Law (2006).

2. For example, a 1996 WTO Appellate Body Report stated, "The WTO Agreement is a treaty—the international equivalent of a contract." *Japan—Taxes on Alcoholic Beverages*, WT/DS8/AB/R (October 4, 1996) at 15. The U.S. Supreme Court has likewise long noted this analogy. *See Trans World Airlines, Inc. v. Franklin Mint Corp.*, 466 U.S. 243, 253 (1984) (treaty is in the nature of a contract between states); *Fong Yue Ting v. United States*, 149 U.S. 698, 720 (1893) (same); *Chae Chan Ping v. United States*, 130 U.S. 581, 600 (1889) (the *Chinese Exclusion Case*) (same).

3. H. W. Malkin, *Reservations to Multilateral Conventions*, 7 BRIT. Y.B. INT'L L. 141 (1926). *See also* MARK JANIS, INTERNATIONAL LAW 9 ("However styled, [treaties] are in the first place essentially contracts between states").

4. *See* Vienna Convention, Art. 36; *Free Zones of Upper Savoy and the District of Gex (Fr. v. Switz.)*, P.C.I.J., ser. A/B, No. 46.

5. PHILIP C. JESSUP, A MODERN LAW OF NATIONS 124 (1949).

6. MARK JANIS & JOHN NOYES, INTERNATIONAL LAW 39 (2001).

7. *See, e.g.*, EVANGELOS RAFTOPOULOS, THE INADEQUACY OF THE CONTRACTUAL ANALOGY IN THE LAW OF TREATIES (1990); SHABTAI ROSENNE, DEVELOPMENTS IN THE LAW OF TREATIES 1945–1986 at 128 (1989) (analogy between treaty and contract is "simply false").

8. In their analysis of treaty, Jack Goldsmith and Eric Posner analogize treaty to a nonbinding letter of intent. Jack L. Goldsmith & Eric A. Posner, *International Agreements: A Rational Choice Approach*, 44 VA. J. INT'L L. 113, 114, 118 (2003).

9. For an excellent review in the environmental context, *see* SCOTT BARRETT, ENVIRONMENT AND STATECRAFT: THE STRATEGY OF ENVIRONMENTAL TREATY-MAKING (2003).

10. *See* ABRAM CHAYES & ANTONIA HANDLER CHAYES, THE NEW SOVEREIGNTY: COMPLIANCE WITH INTERNATIONAL REGULATORY AGREEMENTS (1995) (arguing that specificity enhances compliance).

11. Goldsmith and Posner argue that this is the primary purpose of treaty, and of nonlegal international agreements. Goldsmith & Posner, *supra* note 8, at 118.

12. *See* John K. Setear, *Treaties, Custom, Iteration, and Public Choice* (2004), available at http://ssrn.com/abstract=492604.

13. *But see* Edward T. Swaine, *Rational Custom*, 52 DUKE L.J. 559, 574 (2002) (suggesting that international law is best understood as noncooperative); Duncan Snidal, *Rational Choice and International Relations*, in THE HANDBOOK OF INTERNATIONAL RELATIONS 73, 77 (Walter Carlsnaes et al., eds. 2002) ("non-cooperative game-theoretic models are the predominant approach").

14. *See generally* HERVÉ MOULIN, COOPERATIVE MICROECONOMICS: A GAME-THEORETIC INTRODUCTION (1995). It is important to note that cooperative games are not by any means necessarily correlated with the production of a "cooperative outcome," as it has come to be known in the literature. Rather, the cooperative nature of a game is dependent simply on the availability of communication and binding agreement.

15. *See, e.g.*, John F. Nash, *Two-Person Cooperative Games*, 21 ECONOMETRICA 128 (1953).

16. *See* Daniel G. Arce M. & Todd Sandler, *A Cooperative Game Theory of Noncontiguous Allies*, 3 J. PUB. ECON. THEORY 391 (2001); Todd Sandler,

Alliance Formation, Alliance Expansion and the Core, 19 J. CONFL. RES. 43 (1999).

17. *See* BARRETT, ENVIRONMENT AND STATECRAFT, *supra* note 9, at 197.

18. This discussion draws substantially from the standard description of the basic structure of a cooperative game in Arce & Sandler, *supra* note 16.

19. DUNCAN LUCE & HOWARD RAIFFA, GAMES AND DECISIONS (1957).

20. *See* RICHARD E. BENEDICK, OZONE DIPLOMACY (1991)

21. Arce & Sandler, *supra* note 16, at 394.

22. Moulin, *supra* note 14, at 15.

23. *Id.* at 731.

24. *Id.*

25. Jane Black, Maurice D. Levi, & David de Meza, *Creating a Good Atmosphere: Minimum Participation for Tackling the "Greenhouse Effect,"* 60 ECONOMICA 281 (1993).

26. *Id.,* at 200.

27. Adapted from Todd Sandler, *Treaties: Strategic Considerations,* 2008 ILL. L. REV. 155.

28. *See* Michael Rauscher, *International Environmental Negotiations Are Chicken Games,* available at http://folk.uio.no/ninalill/konferanse/ MichaelR.pdf.

29. Adapted from STEVEN J. BRAMS & D. MARC KILGOUR, GAME THEORY AND NATIONAL SECURITY 41 (1998).

30. It seems reasonable, at least as a simplifying assumption, to elide the distinction between signature and adherence, as signature brings certain obligations, including obligations to seek ratification. States often address this problem by providing that the treaty will not come into force for any state until a minimum number of states have ratified.

31. Sandler, *supra* note 27.

32. *Id.*

33. Todd Sandler, *Collective versus Unilateral Responses to Terrorism,* 124 PUB. CHOICE 75 (2005).

34. Sandler, *supra* note 27.

35. Articles on Responsibility of States for Internationally Wrongful Acts, *in* Report of the International Law Commission [ILC] on the Work of Its Fifty-third Session, UN GAOR, 56th Sess., Supp. No. 10, at 43, UN Doc. A/56/10 (2001), available at www.un.org/law/ilc [hereinafter, Articles on State Responsibility].

36. See, e.g., *British Claims in the Spanish Zone of Morocco,* UNRIAA, vol. II, p. 615 (1925); *Religious Property Expropriated by Portugal,* UNRIAA, vol. I, p. 7 (1920); *Walter Fletcher Smith,* UNRIAA, vol. II, p. 913 (1927), at p. 918; *Heirs of Lebas de Courmont,* UNRIAA, vol. XIII, p. 761 (1957), at p. 764.

37. *See* Guido Calabresi & A. Douglas Melamed, *Property Rules, Liability Rules, and Inalienability: One View of the Cathedral,* 85 HARV. L. REV. 1089, 1090 (1972).

38. Article 30 of the Draft Articles on State Responsibility.

39. Text of the Draft Articles with Commentaries Thereto, in Report of the International Law Commission, Fifty-third Session, U.N. GAOR, 56th Sess., Supp. No. 10, at 59–365, U.N. Doc. A/56/10 p. 357 (2001) [hereinafter, Commentaries].

40. Christine Gray, *Types of Remedies in ICJ Cases: Lessons for the WTO, in* IMPROVING WTO DISPUTE SETTLEMENT PROCEDURES 401, 404 (Friedl Weiss, ed. 2000).

41. *Factory at Chorzów, Merits,* 1928, P.C.I.J. Series A, No. 17, p. 48.

42. Article 35.

43. See generally E. ZOLLER, PEACETIME UNILATERAL REMEDIES: AN ANALYSIS OF COUNTERMEASURES (1984); O. Y. ELAGAB, THE LEGALITY OF NON-FORCIBLE COUNTER-MEASURES IN INTERNATIONAL LAW (1988).

44. Countermeasures are distinguished from retorsion by virtue of the fact that countermeasures would be illegal if they were not taken in response to a prior wrongful act by the target state. Article 49.

45. Understanding on Rules and Procedures Governing the Settlement of Disputes, April 15, 1994, Marrakesh Agreement Establishing the World Trade Organization, Annex 2, Art. 22.3, 33 I.L.M. 1125, 1226 (1994); THE LEGAL TEXTS: THE RESULTS OF THE URUGUAY ROUND OF MULTILATERAL TRADE NEGOTIATIONS 370–71 (1999).

46. Commentary to Chapter II, para. 9, p. 328.

47. *See* Warren F. Schwartz & Alan O. Sykes, *The Economic Structure of Renegotiation and Dispute Resolution in the World Trade Organization,* 31 J. LEGAL STUD. 179 (2002) (arguing that limitation on retaliation was the main purpose of the innovations in the DSU).

48. *See* Andrew Guzman, *International Law: A Compliance-Based Theory,* 90 CAL. L. REV. 1823 (2002).

49. For analyses of the role of reputation, sometimes referred to in this literature as "international obligation," *see* Shannon K. Mitchell, *GATT, Dispute Settlement and Cooperation: A Note,* 9 ECONOMICS AND POLITICS 87 (1997); Dan Kovenock & Marie Thursby, *GATT, Dispute Settlement and Cooperation,* 4 ECONOMICS AND POLITICS 151 (1992).

50. *See, e.g.,* the sources cited in Chapter 3, notes 85–87.

51. Paul R. Milgrom, Douglass C. North, & Barry R. Weingast, *The Role of Institutions in the Revival of Trade: The Law Merchant, Private Judges and the Champagne Fairs,* 2 ECON. & POL. 1, 3 (1990).

52. Giovanni Maggi, *The Role of Multilateral Institutions in International Trade Cooperation,* 89 AM. ECON. REV. 190 (1999).

53. *Supra* note 49.

54. Chad P. Bown, *On the Economic Success of GATT/WTO Dispute Settlement*, 86 REV. ECON. & STATS. 811 (2004).

55. *See, e.g.,* John H. Barton, *The Economic Basis of Damages in Breach of Contract*, 1 J. LEGAL STUD. 277 (1972); Robert L. Birmingham, *Breach of Contract, Damage Measures and Economic Efficiency*, 24 RUTGERS L. REV. 273 (1970); Calabresi & Melamed, *supra* note 37, at 1092–93; Ian Ayres & Eric Talley, *Solomonic Bargaining: Dividing a Legal Entitlement to Facilitate Coasian Trade*, 104 YALE L. J. 1027, 1036–72 (1995); Louis Kaplow & Steven Shavell, *Property Rules versus Liability Rules: An Economic Analysis*, 109 HARV. L. REV. 713, 715 (1996).

56. *See* STEVEN SHAVELL, FOUNDATIONS OF ECONOMIC ANALYSIS OF LAW 305 (2004).

57. Hence, the caveat that "it is important to avoid a court-centered view when discussing in general the consequences of breaches of international law." Christine Gray, *Is There an International Law of Remedies?* 56 BRIT. Y.B. INT'L L. 25, 31 (1985).

58. *But see* Setear, *supra* note 12 (discussion of international legal doctrine and international relations theory on rules of release and rules of remediation that apply in the event of treaty breach).

59. In the terminology employed by Calabresi and Melamed, under property rules, property can be sold, but only if the owner is willing to give up the entitlement and the recipient is willing to accept it. Under a liability rule, others may take an entitlement by, for example, destroying it in an accident, but then must compensate the owner at a rate determined by a governmental body.

60. Daniel Friedmann, *The Efficient Breach Fallacy*, 18 J. LEGAL STUD. 1 (1989); Thomas S. Ulen, *The Efficiency of Specific Performance: Toward a Unified Theory of Contract Remedies*, 83 MICH. L. REV. 341 (1984).

61. Perhaps this explains some of the concerns over the "democracy deficit" in the WTO, the European Union, and other international bodies: these bodies are increasingly making the sorts of trade-offs that are frequently made by national governments, but many question whether these bodies can appropriately make such decisions without greater democratic representation.

62. It also appears that efficient breach is a more attractive concept to those from a common law background than to those from a civil law background. Ruben Kraiem, *Leaving Money on the Table: Contract Practice in a Low-Trust Environment*, 42 COLUM. J. TRANSNAT'L L. 715, n.50 (2004).

63. MICHAEL AKEHURST, A MODERN INTRODUCTION TO INTERNATIONAL LAW 25 (6th ed. 1987).

64. *See* Barbara Koremenos, *Contracting around International Uncertainty,* 99 AM. POL. SCI. REV. 549–65 (2005).

65. Alan O. Sykes, *Protectionism as a "Safeguard": A Positive Analysis of the GATT "Escape Clause" with Normative Speculations,* 58 U. CHI. L. REV. 255 (1991). *See also* Warren F. Schwartz & Alan O. Sykes, *The Economic Structure of Renegotiation and Dispute Resolution in the World Trade Organization,* 31 J. LEG. STUD. 179 (2002).

66. In fact, as noted above, efficient breach exists in GATT in two respects. First, the escape clause provides for a type of efficient breach, available in limited circumstances. Sykes, *supra* note 65. Second, as described in the text, the dispute resolution features of WTO law allow for compensation for breach.

67. However, it is clear that this efficient breach, although permitted, is disfavored: "neither compensation nor the suspension of concessions or other obligations is preferred to full implementation of a recommendation to bring a measure into conformity with the covered agreements." DSU Art. 22:1. The argument that the DSU creates a strong preference for changing the offending measure over compensation is developed in John H. Jackson, *The WTO Dispute Settlement Understanding—Misunderstandings on the Nature of Legal Obligation,* 91 AM. J. INT'L L. 60 (1997); John H. Jackson, *International Law Status of WTO Dispute Settlement Reports: Obligation to Comply or Option to "Buy Out"?* 98 AM. J. INT'L L. 109 (2004).

68. Actually, firms, too, are imperfect mediators of individual interests, as shown by the study of corporate law over the past fifty years. This raises the question, in connection with contracts entered into by firms and damages or penalties assessed against firms, whether a nonwelfarist approach to damages would be desirable in order to respond to the representational defects of the firm.

69. Article 31 refers to the ordinary meaning in the context of, and in light of, the object and purpose of the treaty. While these are obviously outside the text, and while Article 32 allows further reference outside the text, the main reference remains the text and its ordinary meaning in this context and light.

70. RICHARD A. POSNER, ECONOMIC ANALYSIS OF LAW 251–61 (4th ed. 1992).

71. For an argument that statutory interpretation should follow the precepts of contract interpretation, *see* Frank Easterbrook, *The Supreme Court, 1983 Term—Foreword: The Court and the Economic System,* 98 HARV. L. REV. 4 (1984).

72. For an argument that this is the proper role of judicial review of statutes, *see* Jonathan Macey, *Promoting Public-Regarding Legislation through Statutory Interpretation,* 86 COLUM. L. REV. 223 (1986).

73. On the domestic level, law and economics scholars have taken widely divergent positions regarding the implications of the public choice model of legislation for the judicial construction of statutes. *See, e.g.,* Frank Easterbrook, *Statutes' Domains,* 50 U. CHI. L. REV. 533 (1983); Richard A. Posner, *Legal Formalism, Legal Realism, and the Interpretation of Statutes and the Constitution,* 37 CASE W. RES. L. REV. 179 (1986); Macey, *supra* note 72.

5. International Organization

1. The new institutional economics (NIE) is best seen as within the paradigm of neoclassical economics, but adds transaction cost analysis, game theory, and other analytical techniques to the model used by neoclassical economics. It thus constitutes a more accurate model for use with institutional or organizational analysis. Neoclassical economics is often criticized by NIE adherents as being single institutional: as focusing only on the price system as an institution for economic organization. NIE adds analysis of firms and other organizations, and is thus multi-institutional, and importantly, can engage in comparative institutional analysis. *See, e.g.,* NEIL KOMESAR, IMPERFECT ALTERNATIVES (1994); THRAIN EGGERTSSON, ECONOMIC BEHAVIOR AND INSTITUTIONS: PRINCIPLES OF NEO-INSTITUTIONAL ECONOMICS (1990); Bruno Frey, *Institutions Matter: The Comparative Analysis of Institutions* 34 EUR. ECON. REV. 443 (1990); Steven Medema, *Discourse and the Institutional Approach to Law and Economics,* 2 J. ECON. ISSUES 417 (1989); Douglass North, *Institutions, Transaction Costs and Economic Growth* 25 ECON. INQUIRY 419 (1987); Douglass North, *The New Institutional Economics,* 142 J. INST. & THEO. ECON. 230 (1986); Werner Pommerehne, *The Empirical Relevance of Comparative Institutional Analysis,* 34 EUR. ECON. R. 458 (1990); Oliver Williamson, *Comparative Economic Organization: The Analysis of Discrete Structural Alternatives,* 36 ADMIN. SCI. Q. 219 (1994); Ronald Coase, *The New Institutional Economics,* 140 J. INST. & THEO. ECON. 229 (1984).
2. *See, e.g.,* STEPHEN MARTIN, ADVANCED INDUSTRIAL ECONOMICS (1993); JEAN TIROLE, THE THEORY OF INDUSTRIAL ORGANIZATION (1988); *or* PAUL MILGROM & JOHN ROBERTS, ECONOMICS, ORGANIZATION AND MANAGEMENT (1992).
3. Charles P. Kindleberger, *International Public Goods without International Government,* 76 AM. ECON. REV. 1 (1986) (citations omitted).
4. Robert O. Keohane, *The Demand for International Regimes,* 36 INT'L ORG. 325 (1982). *See also* ROBERT O. KEOHANE, AFTER HEGEMONY: COOPERATION AND DISCORD IN THE WORLD POLITICAL ECONOMY 83 (1984); ROBERT O. KEOHANE, INTERNATIONAL INSTITUTIONS AND STATE POWER: ESSAYS IN INTERNATIONAL RELATIONS THEORY (1989).

5. These papers are included in RONALD COASE, THE FIRM, THE MARKET AND THE LAW (1988).

6. *Id.,* at 6.

7. Jason Scott Johnston, *The Influence of The Nature of the Firm on the Theory of Corporate Law,* 18 J. CORP. L. 213, 216 (1993). One is tempted to add the following: "This type of messy mixture of empirical and normative judgments is familiar fare for lawyers, much as it may dissatisfy social scientists." Daniel A. Farber, *Positive Theory as Normative Critique,* 68 S. CAL. L. REV. 1565 (1995).

8. This point is illustrated in the account of the allocation of powers to the European Community in Joseph Weiler, *The Transformation of Europe,* 100 YALE L.J. 2403 (1991). *See also* Williamson, *supra* note 1, at 219 ("The paper unifies two hitherto disjunct areas of institutional economics—the institutional environment and the institutions of governance—by treating the institutional environment as a locus of parameters, changes in which parameters bring about shifts in the comparative costs of governance").

9. For a critical perspective, *see* Herbert A. Simon, *Organizations and Markets,* 5 J. ECON. PERSP. 25, 29 (1991).

10. *See* Richard Posner, *The New Institutional Economics Meets Law and Economics,* 149 J. INSTITUTIONAL & THEO. ECON. 73 (1993). The economics of organization and more particularly the theory of the firm comprise one area of inquiry for law and economics.

11. OLIVER E. WILLIAMSON, THE ECONOMIC INSTITUTIONS OF CAPITALISM 277 (1985).

12. Johnston, *supra* note 7.

13. *See, e.g.,* Farber, *supra* note 7, at 1582; William N. Eskridge Jr. & Philip P. Frickey, *Foreword: Law as Equilibrium,* 108 HARV. L. REV. 26 (1994).

14. *See, e.g., Symposium on New Institutional Economics: Bounded Rationality and the Analysis of State and Society,* 150 J. INST. & THEO. ECON. (1994); JOSEPH E. STIGLITZ, THE ECONOMIC ROLE OF THE STATE (1989); Barry R. Weingast & William J. Marshall, *The Industrial Organization of Congress; or, Why Legislatures, like Firms, Are Not Organized as Markets,* 96 J. POLIT. ECON. 132 (1988) (examining internal organization of legislatures); Terry M. Moe, *The New Economics of Organization,* 28 AM. J. POLIT. SCI. 739 (1984); Gary J. Miller & Terry M. Moe, *The Positive Theory of Hierarchies, in* POLITICAL SCIENCE: THE SCIENCE OF POLITICS (Herbert F. Weisberg, ed. 1986); Jean-Jacques Laffont & Jean Tirole, *The Politics of Government Decision Making: Regulatory Institutions,* 6 J. L. ECON. & ORG. 1 (1990); Jean Tirole, *Hierarchies and Bureaucracies: On the Role of Collusion in Organizations,* 2 J. L. ECON. & ORG. 181 (1986).

15. *See* Beth V. Yarbrough & Robert M. Yarbrough, *Dispute Settlement in International Trade: Regionalism and Procedural Coordination, in* THE

POLITICAL ECONOMY OF REGIONALISM (Edward Mansfield & Helen Milner, eds. 1996); Beth V. Yarbrough & Robert M. Yarbrough, *International Institutions and the New Economics of Organization*, 44 INT'L ORG. 235 (1990); Paul R. Milgrom, Douglass C. North, & Barry R. Weingast, *The Role of Institutions in the Revival of Trade: The Law Merchant, Private Judges, and the Champagne Fairs*, 2 ECON. & POL. 1 (1990).

16. *See* Johnston's description of Coase's theory of the firm as offering a "progressive research program" in corporation law. Johnston, *supra* note 7, at 218. The progressive research program (in the Lakatosian sense) that this methodology offers in international organizations is similar: it provides both complexity and rationality. *See Imre Lakatos, Falsification and the Methodology of Scientific Research Programmes, in* CRITICISM AND THE GROWTH OF KNOWLEDGE 91 (Imre Lakatos & Alan Musgrave, eds. 1970). Johnston points out that prior scholarship had obscured the complexity of policy issues, and that the prior legal realist tradition failed to provide a theory of behavior. Coase's theory of the firm both embraced complexity and satisfied the scholar's need for rationality.

17. These costs are not easy to value, and thus do not fit neatly into neoclassical models.

18. *See, e.g.,* David A. Lake, *Anarchy, Hierarchy, and the Variety of International Relations*, 50 INT'L ORG. 1 (1996) (applying industrial organization concepts to security alliances).

19. *See* Duncan Snidal, *Political Economy and International Institutions*, 16 INT'L REV. L. & ECON. 121 (1996); Thomas Bernauer, *International Financing of Environmental Protection: Lessons from Efforts to Protect the River Rhine against Chloride Pollution*, 3 ENVIRONMENTAL POL. 369 (1995).

20. For examples of recent political science literature focusing on international organizations, *see* Barbara Koremenos, Charles Lipson, & Duncan Snidal, *The Rational Design of International Institutions*, 55:4 INT'L ORG. 761, 767 (2001); Kenneth Abbott, Robert Keohane, Andrew Moravcsik, Anne-Marie Slaughter, & Duncan Snidal, *The Concept of Legalization*, 54:3 INT'L ORG. 401 (2000). On the other hand, the tendency of international lawyers to emphasize the formal has been criticized: "contemporary public international lawyers have developed a highly formalistic and exclusively technical legal positivist approach to international relations," neglecting "the great issues of American foreign policy and world affairs." FRANCIS BOYLE, WORLD POLITICS AND INTERNATIONAL LAW 59 (1985), as quoted by Kenneth W. Abbott, *Modern International Relations Theory: A Prospectus for International Lawyers*, 14 YALE J. INT'L L. 335, 336 (1989).

21. *But see, e.g.,* MILES KAHLER, INTERNATIONAL INSTITUTIONS AND THE POLITICAL ECONOMY OF INTEGRATION (1995).

22. J. Martin Rochester, *The Rise and Fall of International Organization as a Field of Study,* 40 INT'L ORG. 777, 784 (1986). *See also* ORAN R. YOUNG, IN-TERNATIONAL COOPERATION: BUILDING REGIMES FOR NATURAL RESOURCES AND THE ENVIRONMENT 207 (1989): "Political scientists steeped in the power-oriented perspectives of realism or trained in the empirical method-ologies of behavioralism tend to dismiss any emphasis on the role of institu-tions as a vestige of the discredited ideas of the formal, legal, institutional school of thought. Yet other students of politics as well as most lawyers (who typically make a living by devising, interpreting, and refining institu-tional arrangements) cannot imagine treating institutions as anything but central determinants of collective behavior."

23. Duncan Snidal, *Political Economy and International Institutions,* 16 INT'L REV. L. & ECON. 121 (1996). *See also* DELEGATION AND AGENCY IN INTER-NATIONAL ORGANIZATIONS (Darren G. Hawkins, David A. Lake, Daniel J. Nielson, & Michael J. Tierney, eds., 2006); INTERNATIONAL INSTITUTIONS: AN INTERNATIONAL ORGANIZATION READER (Lisa L. Martin & Beth A. Sim-mons, eds., 2001).

24. *Id.* at 780–87. *See, e.g.,* ERNST HAAS, BEYOND THE NATION-STATE (1964).

25. For a full description of the realist perspective, *see id.* "Realism is the an-tithesis of legalism." Anne-Marie Burley & Walter Mattli, *Europe before the Court: A Political Theory of Legal Integration,* 47 INT'L ORG. 41, 48 (1993). *See also* the description of this separation as one between law and political science in Harold Hongju Koh, *Transnational Legal Process,* 75 NEB. L. REV. 181, 191 (1996). *Id.* at 20 (citations omitted). Of course, many realists see some role for law and institutions. *See* KENNETH N. WALTZ, THEORY OF INTERNATIONAL POLITICS 114 (1979), who accepts that "world politics, although not formally organized, is not entirely without institutions and orderly procedures." *But see* Susan Strange, *Cave! Hic Dragones: A Critique of Regime Analysis,* 36 INT'L ORG. 479, 487 (1982) ("All those in-ternational arrangements dignified by the label regime are only too easily upset when either the balance of bargaining power or the perception of na-tional interest (or both together) change among those states who negotiate them").

26. *See* STEPHEN D. KRASNER, INTERNATIONAL REGIMES (1983). *See also* the review of this literature in Marc A. Levy, Oran R. Young, & Michael Zurn, *The Study of International Regimes,* 1 EUR. J. INT'L REL. 267 (1995); BETH V. YARBROUGH & ROBERT M. YARBROUGH, COOPERATION AND GOVERNANCE IN INTERNATIONAL TRADE: THE STRATEGIC ORGANIZATIONAL APPROACH 49–67 (1992). *See also* ROBERT ELLICKSON, ORDER WITHOUT LAW (1992) (describing how cattle ranchers in Shasta County, California, devise what we might call "regimes" outside of or inconsistent with law).

27. Keohane's neoliberal institutionalism has neorealist assumptions. "Drawing on analogies from economics rather than politics, he offered a neo-realist explanation for the endurance and importance of international institutions that was consistent with neo-realist assumptions." Anne-Marie Burley, *Law and the Liberal Paradigm in International Relations Theory,* 1992 PROC. ANN. MTG. AM. SOC. INT'L L. 180 (1992).

28. Keohane, *The Demand for International Regimes, supra* note 4, at 30–46.

29. *See* Abbott, *supra* note 20, at 339 ("None of the prevailing definitions [of regimes], moreover, is congruent with the usual descriptive categories of [international law], such as customary rules, conventional rules and international organizations").

30. Burley, *supra* note 27, at 182.

31. *See* KEOHANE, INTERNATIONAL INSTITUTIONS AND STATE POWER, *supra* note 4, at 1–20, 158–79.

32. *See, e.g.,* Yarbrough & Yarbrough, *supra* note 26, at 65 ("The enforcement powers of GATT or any other body against a sovereign state are, in a legal sense, almost nonexistent. Without legal enforcement, a strong arbitrator is necessary for cooperation. The arbitration required for successful multilateral agreements is unlikely without a hegemon to act as a supporter of international institutions such as the GATT"). From this perspective, the formal institution becomes a mere guise for power, an instrument through which the hegemon acts. *See also* James E. Alt & Lisa L. Martin, *Contracting and the Possibility of Multilateral Enforcement,* 150 J. INST. & THEO. ECON. 265 (1994): "In a Realist framework, institutions have no power to bind states or even significantly change the constraints in which they operate. . . . Hegemonic stability theory would predict that institutions will only be stable and effective as long as the distribution of power underlying their construction remains stable." *Id.* at 265–66.

33. James G. March & Johan P. Olsen, *The New Institutionalism: Organizational Factors in Political Life,* 78 AM. POLIT. SCI. REV. 734, 739 (1984). *See also* Andrew Moravcsik, *Taking Preferences Seriously: A Liberal Theory of International Politics,* 51 INT'L ORG. 513 (1997); Stephen D. Krasner, *Structural Causes and Regime Consequences: Regimes as Intervening Variables,* 36 INT'L ORG. 185, 189 (1982) (power and interest as most prominent causal variables, moderated by regimes).

34. "Ruthless egoism does the trick by itself." Burley & Mattli, *supra* note 25, at 54. The focus on interests is consistent with neofunctionalism. "The process of community formation is dominated by nationally constituted groups with specific interests and aims, willing and able to adjust their aspirations by turning to supranational means when this course appears profitable." ERNST HAAS, THE UNITING OF EUROPE xiv (1958), *quoted in id.,* at 55.

35. For an analysis of the incompleteness of the constraint in the domestic sphere, *see* Ellickson, *supra* note 26.
36. *See* Arild Underdal, *The Concept of Regime "Effectiveness,"* 27 NORD. J. INT'L STUD. 227 (1992). On efficient breach in international law, *see* Chapter 4.
37. The realist contention that international relations take place in an anarchic setting is based on the relatively horizontal nature of the international legal system: the lack of an "ultimate" source of enforcement authority. *See* the interesting analysis in Emerson M. S. Niou & Peter C. Ordeshook, *"Less Filling, Tastes Great": The Realist-Neoliberal Debate,* 46 WORLD POL. 209, 222 (1994). Niou and Ordeshook point out that in the domestic constitutional system, there is no "ultimate" source of enforcement authority: there is no answer to the problem of what happens when the president and Congress disagree in the United States. Niou and Ordeshook find that "at least at the constitutional level, then, a state is in principle no less anarchic than an international system in the sense that the enforcement of constitutional agreements must be endogenous." *Id.* They conclude that realists "must explain why they believe that coordination can more readily be achieved at one level of social interaction than at another." *Id.* at 223–24.
38. Beth Yarbrough and Robert Yarbrough, writing together, constitute an important exception. *See, e.g.,* Yarbrough & Yarbrough, *International Institutions and the New Economics of Organization, supra* note 15, at 243.
39. *See, e.g.,* Waltz, *supra* note 25. *See also* John J. Mearsheimer, *The False Promise of International Institutions,* 19 INT'L SEC. 5 (1994) ("My central conclusion is that institutions have minimal influence on state behavior").
40. *See, e.g.,* KEOHANE, AFTER HEGEMONY, *supra* note 4. *See also* Robert Keohane & Lisa Martin, *Delegation to International Organizations* (unpublished manuscript dated August 1994), who state that the new institutionalism "has taken the study of institutions out of a ghetto of international relations research—the study of formal international organizations such as the United Nations—to point out the broad significance of sets of rules, or 'international regimes,' that affect the behavior of states." In the latter work, Keohane and Martin develop a theory of why states delegate formal authority to formal organizations.
41. *See* Krasner, *supra* note 33; *see also* Waltz, *supra* note 25, chaps. 5 and 6.
42. "For regime theorists, the most interesting thing about an international regime is not necessarily the presence of a governing treaty. As a consequence, they pay less attention than international lawyers do to the formalities of the treaty process, treaty language, or negotiating history." Abram Chayes & Antonia Handler Chayes, *Compliance without Enforce-*

ment: State Behavior under Regulatory Treaties, 1991 NEGOTIATION J. 311, 312 (1991). *But see* ORAN R. YOUNG, INTERNATIONAL COOPERATION: BUILDING REGIMES FOR NATURAL RESOURCES AND THE ENVIRONMENT 58–80 (1989).

43. *See* Ronald H. Coase, *The Institutional Structure of Production,* 82 AM. ECON. REV. 713, 714 (1992).

44. For a description of this literature, and of the transition in economic analysis, *see* Ronald J. Gilson, *Corporate Governance and Economic Efficiency: When Do Institutions Matter?* 74 WASH. U. L. Q. 327 (1996).

45. *See* Oliver Williamson, *Economic Institutions: Spontaneous and Intentional Governance,* 7 J. L. ECON. & ORG. 159 (1991).

46. *See* Charles Lipson, *Why Are Some International Agreements Informal?* 45 INT'L ORG. 495 (1991).

47. Robert H. Mnookin & Lewis Kornhauer, *Bargaining in the Shadow of the Law: The Case of Divorce,* 88 YALE L.J. 950 (1979).

48. *But see* Rudolf Richter, *The Louvre Accord from the Viewpoint of the New Institutional Economics,* 145 J. INST. & THEO. ECON. 704 (1989).

49. *See, e.g.,* THE POLITICAL ECONOMY OF INTERNATIONAL ORGANIZATIONS (Roland Vaubel & Thomas D. Willett, eds. 1991).

50. *But see* Yarbrough & Yarbrough, *supra* note 15.

51. Keohane, *The Demand for International Regimes, supra* note 4, at 335.

52. Frey, *supra* note 1, at 445. *See also* ERNST-ULRICH PETERSMANN, CONSTITUTIONAL FUNCTIONS AND CONSTITUTIONAL PROBLEMS OF INTERNATIONAL ECONOMIC LAW 6 (1991).

53. While welfare economics may be viewed as a "theory of market failure," the field of public choice may be viewed as a "theory of government failure" that offsets the "theory of market failure." JAMES M. BUCHANAN, EXPLORATIONS INTO CONSTITUTIONAL ECONOMICS 24–25 (1989).

54. *See* Hendrik Spruyt, *Institutional Selection in International Relations: State Anarchy as Order,* 48 INT'L ORG. 527 (1994).

55. *See* Michael Jensen & William Meckling, *Theory of the Firm: Managerial Behavior, Agency Costs and Capital Structure,* 3 J. FINANCIAL ECON. 305 (1976).

56. *See supra* note 11. Williamson and North have developed this insight from the standpoint of NIE. *See, e.g.,* Williamson, *supra* note 11; Oliver E. Williamson, *Comparative Economic Organization: The Analysis of Discrete Structural Alternatives,* 36 ADMIN. SCI. Q. 269 (1991); Oliver Williamson, *Transaction Cost Economics, in* HANDBOOK OF INDUSTRIAL ORGANIZATION 136–82 (Richard Schmalensee & Robert Willig, eds. 1989); Douglass North, *Economic Performance through Time,* 84 AM. ECON. REV. 359 (1994); Douglass North, *The New Institutional Economics,* 142 J. THEO. &

INST. ECON. 230 (1986); Douglass North, *Institutions*, 5 J. ECON. PERSPEC-
TIVES 97 (1991).

57. *See* Douglass C. North & John J. Wallis, *Integrating Institutional Change
and Technical Change*, 150 J. INST. & THEO. ECON. 609, 622 (1994) (arguing that "institutions do not exist to minimize transaction costs. Rational
economic actors wish to reduce costs at all margins"). The transaction
cost–minimizing position is not to transact at all, and thus to incur deadweight losses. Wherever the deadweight losses are greater than the transaction costs, this is a mistake.

58. *See* Coase, *supra* note 5, at 15. Coase has often been misinterpreted to
argue that policy should be formed as though transaction costs are zero.
However, transaction costs are never zero and are rarely insignificant. *See*
Komesar, *supra* note 1, at 109–11, *citing* Robert Ellickson, *The Case for
Coase and against "Coaseanism,"* 99 YALE L.J. 611 (1989).

59. Komesar, *supra* note 1.

60. Williamson, *supra* note 11, at 36.

61. Komesar, *supra* note 1.

62. For a summary and reference to further literature, *see* Robert D. Cooter,
The Coase Theorem, in THE NEW PALGRAVE: A DICTIONARY OF ECONOMICS
457, 457–60 (1987). *See also* Elizabeth Hoffman & Matthew Spitzer, *The
Coase Theorem: Some Experimental Tests*, 25 J. L. & ECON. 73 (1982);
Robert D. Cooter, *The Cost of Coase*, 11 J. LEG. STUD. 1 (1982).

63. Coase, *supra* note 5, at 85–185.

64. Another way of stating the Coase theorem, which formulation has been
cited with approval by Coase, is that under conditions of zero transaction
costs, "private and social costs will be equal." Coase, *supra* note 5, at 174,
citing GEORGE STIGLER, THEORY OF PRICE at 113 (1966).

65. *See* EGGERTSSON, *supra* note 1, at 13: "Theoretically, only one set of rules
will maximize the wealth of a nation. It can be argued that, in the absence
of transaction costs, eventually such a set of rules will evolve. Although a
shift from a relatively inefficient structure of rights to a more efficient set
will involve losers as well as winners, the gains are greater than the losses.
Therefore, the winners will compensate the losers and still be better off
than before."

66. John Conybeare, *International Organization and the Theory of Property
Rights*, 34 INT'L ORG. 307 (1980).

67. *See* Robert Cooter, *The Cost of Coase*, 11 J. LEGAL STUD. 1 (1982); Varouj
A. Aivazian & Jeffrey L. Callen, *The Coase Theorem and the Empty Core*,
24 J. L. & ECON. 175 (1981).

68. *See* Stephen D. Krasner, *Global Communications and National Power: Life
on the Pareto Frontier*, 43 WORLD POL. 336, 340 (1991) ("the problem is

not how to get to the Pareto frontier, but which point along it will be chosen"); Geoffrey Garrett, *International Cooperation and Institutional Choice: The European Community's Internal Market*, 46 INT'L ORG. 533, 541 (1992).

69. Garrett, *supra* note 68, at 541.

70. GEOFFREY BRENNAN & JAMES M. BUCHANAN, THE REASON OF RULES: CONSTITUTIONAL POLITICAL ECONOMY 28–32 (1985). *See also* James M. Buchanan, *The Domain of Constitutional Economics*, 1 CONST. POL. ECON. 1 (1990).

71. Brennan & Buchanan, *supra* note 70, at 29.

72. *Id.*

73. For a thoughtful exegesis of the contractarian view, and its cosmopolitan, individual-centered perspective, *see* Buchanan, *supra* note 70. Buchanan defines the research program, in the Lakatosian sense, of constitutional economics as having its foundation in "methodological individualism." "Unless those who would be participants in the scientific dialogue [of constitutional economics] are willing to locate the exercise in the choice calculus of individuals, *qua* individuals, there can be no departure from the starting gate." *Id.* at 13.

74. Brennan & Buchanan, *supra* note 70, at 6 ("the rules that constrain sociopolitical interactions—the economic and political relationships among persons—must be evaluated ultimately in terms of their capacity to promote the separate purposes of all persons in the polity").

75. *See* Bruno S. Frey & Beat Gygi, *International Organizations from the Constitutional Point of View, in* THE POLITICAL ECONOMY OF INTERNATIONAL ORGANIZATIONS 65 (Roland Vaubel & Thomas D. Willett, eds. 1991); AMARTYA K. SEN, COLLECTIVE CHOICE AND SOCIAL WELFARE (1979).

76. *See, e.g.*, FRANK H. EASTERBROOK & DANIEL R. FISCHEL, THE ECONOMIC STRUCTURE OF CORPORATE LAW (1991).

77. Frey & Gygi, *supra* note 75.

78. *See* Spruyt, *supra* note 54, at 532 ("Most notably, the absence of a clear medium of exchange—that is, the absence of profit making as an evaluative mechanism of the rationale of such association—makes comparisons problematic").

79. *See* Barry R. Weingast, *The Political Institutions of Representative Government*, Working Paper in Political Science P-89–14, Hoover Institution, Stanford University (1989) at 2. Weingast argues that "while the specific forms of transaction problems found in legislatures differ from those in markets, the general lessons of the new economics of organizations hold. Institutions are necessary to mitigate these problems in order for the gains from exchange to be captured."

80. Frey & Gygi, *supra* note 75, at 58, 60, *citing* Brennan & Buchanan, *supra* note 70.

81. Frey & Gygi, *supra* note 75, at 62.

82. *Id.* at 64.

83. Robert D. Cooter, *The Best Right Laws: Value Foundations of the Economic Analysis of Law,* 64 NOTRE DAME L. REV. 817, 822 (1989). This ship's carpenter metaphor seems attractive, yet it fails to capture the complex interaction between components. *See* JOHN D. STERMAN, BUSINESS DYNAMICS: SYSTEMS THINKING AND MODELING FOR A COMPLEX WORLD (2000).

84. *See* the analysis and citations in Gilson, *supra* note 44. *See also* Mark J. Roe, *Chaos and Evolution in Law and Economics,* 109 HARV. L. REV. 641 (1996).

85. *See* Oliver E. Williamson, *The Evolving Science of Organization,* 149 J. INST. & THEO. ECON. 36 (1993).

86. *See* Roland Vaubel, *A Public Choice View of International Organization, in* THE POLITICAL ECONOMY OF INTERNATIONAL ORGANIZATIONS 33 (Roland Vaubel and Thomas D. Willett, eds. 1991).

87. Abbott and Snidal refer to the possibility of "laundering" policies through IEOs, as a way that domestic governments, or components thereof, may avoid responsibility for unpopular policies. Kenneth W. Abbott & Duncan Snidal, *Hard and Soft Law in International Governance,* 54 INT'L ORG. 421 (2000).

88. Vaubel, *supra* note 86, at 39.

89. *See* Joel P. Trachtman, *Unilateralism, Bilateralism, Regionalism, Multilateralism and Functionalism: A Comparison with Reference to Securities Regulation,* 4 TRANSNAT'L L. & CONTEMP. PROBS. 69 (1994).

90. *See* ALAN O. SYKES, PRODUCT STANDARDS FOR INTERNATIONALLY INTEGRATED GOODS MARKETS 10–11 (1995) (arguing that the effects of technical barriers to trade are difficult to measure).

91. Williamson, *supra* note 11, at 282: "The analysis here focuses entirely on transaction costs: neither the revenue consequences nor the production cost savings that result from asset specialization are included."

92. *Id.* at 277.

93. *See* Benjamin Klein, R. A. Crawford, & A. A. Alchian, *Vertical Integration, Appropriable Rents, and the Competitive Contracting Process,* 21 J. L. & ECON. 297 (1978). Klein, Crawford, and Alchian considered asset specificity only one explanation of vertical integration. Ronald Coase has challenged the factual accuracy of this example. Ronald H. Coase, *The Acquisition of Fisher Body by General Motors,* 43 J. L. & ECON. 15 (2000). However, the example is useful as a parable, regardless of its veracity.

94. Williamson, *supra* note 11, at 42.

95. For example, under Art. 1 of GATT.

96. Williamson, *supra* note 11, at 34.

97. *See* Ellickson, *supra* note 26. *See also* ROBERT AXELROD, THE EVOLUTION OF COOPERATION (1984),

98. Richter, *supra* note 48, at 705.

99. Williamson, *supra* note 11, at 52–61. *See also* Milgrom & Roberts, *supra* note 2, at 30–33.

100. Williamson, *supra* note 11, at 52–61.

101. *Id.,* at 90.

102. *Id.,* at 277–80.

103. *Id.* at 85–86.

104. *Id.*

105. *See* FREDERIC KIRGIS, INTERNATIONAL ORGANIZATIONS (1993); D. W. BOWETT, THE LAW OF INTERNATIONAL INSTITUTIONS (1982).

106. John E. Noyes, *The Functions of Compromissory Clauses in U.S. Treaties,* 34 VA. J. INT'L L. 831 (1994).

107. *General Agreement on Tariffs and Trade: Dispute Settlement Panel Report on United States Restrictions on Imports of Tuna,* 30 I.L.M. 1594 (1991).

108. *General Agreement on Tariffs and Trade: Dispute Settlement Panel Report on United States Restrictions on Imports of Tuna,* 33 I.L.M. 839 (1994).

109. *See, e.g.,* Jeffrey L. Dunoff, *Institutional Misfits: The GATT, the ICJ and Trade-Environment Disputes,* 15 MICH. J. INT'L L. 1042 (1994). In the *Shrimp* case, the Appellate Body found that international environmental rules could supplement the GATT contract in particular interpretative ways. Appellate Body Report, *United States—Import Prohibition of Certain Shrimp and Shrimp Products—Recourse to Article 21.5 of the DSU by Malaysia,* WT/DS58/AB/RW; and Appellate Body Report, *US— Shrimp,* WT/DS58/AB/R. *See* Chapters 6 and 7.

110. Milgrom, North, & Weingast, *supra* note 15, at 19. The synergistic model that establishes institutions necessary to facilitate private sanctions "appears to have been structured to support trade in a way that minimizes transaction costs, or at least incurs costs only in categories that are indispensable to any system that relies on boycotts and [private] sanctions." *Id.*

111. Armen Alchian & Harold Demsetz, *Production, Information Costs, and Economic Organization,* 62 AM. ECON. REV. 777 (1972).

112. *See, e.g.,* Michael Jensen & William Meckling, *Theory of the Firm: Managerial Behavior, Agency Costs and Ownership Structure,* 3 J. FINANCIAL ECON. 305 (1976); Alchian & Demsetz, *supra* note 111; Eugene Fama, *Agency Problems and the Theory of the Firm,* 88 J. POLIT. ECON. 288 (1980).

113. Simon, *supra* note 9, at 29.
114. *Id.* at 41–42.
115. *Id.* at 42.
116. Milgrom & Roberts, *supra* note 2, at 113.
117. *Id.* at 548.
118. *See* GARY MILLER, MANAGERIAL DILEMMAS: THE POLITICAL ECONOMY OF HIERARCHY (1992) (in complex environments, delegation is necessary to compete).
119. Milgrom & Roberts, *supra* note 2, at 114.
120. At present, foreign and security policy for the European Union are subject to a rule of unanimity. Most internal market issues, on the other hand, are subject to majority voting.
121. Horizontal federalism may also be motivated by a desire to provide "checks and balances." There are various game-theoretic and public choice reasons why checks and balances may be appropriate.
122. *See* Richard Epstein, *Holdouts, Externalities and the Single Owner: One More Salute to Ronald Coase,* 36 J. L. & ECON. 553 (1993).
123. *See* Lisa L. Martin, *Heterogeneity, Linkage and Commons Problems,* 6 J. THEO. POL. 473, 488 (1994).
124. *Id.* at 489.
125. "Qualified" majority voting is a type of weighted majority voting used for certain types of decisions in the European Union.
126. *See* Stephen Zamora, *Voting in International Economic Organizations,* 74 AM. J. INT'L L. 566, 571–75 (1980). Zamora notes that "under traditional international law, as exemplified by early diplomatic conferences, two basic truths controlled the question of voting: every state had an equal voice in international proceedings (the doctrine of sovereign equality of states), and no state could be bound without its consent (the rule of unanimity)." *Id.* at 571.
127. Frank H. Easterbrook & Daniel R. Fischel, *Voting in Corporate Law,* 26 J. L. & ECON. 395, 405 (1983).
128. *See* Robert D. Tollison & Thomas D. Willett, *Institutional Mechanisms for Dealing with International Externalities, in* THE LAW OF THE SEA: U.S. INTERESTS AND ALTERNATIVES, 77, 82 (Ryan C. Amacher and Richard J. Sweeney, eds. 1976).
129. Williamson, *supra* note 11, at 133–35.
130. *See* Milgrom, North, & Weingast, *supra* note 15.
131. Williamson, *supra* note 11, at 387–88.
132. For a law and economics approach to comparative institutional analysis, *see* Nicholas Mercuro, *Toward a Comparative Institutional Approach to the Study of Law and Economics, in* LAW AND ECONOMICS (Nicholas Mercuro, ed. 1989). *See also* Edward L. Rubin, *Institutional Analysis and*

the New Legal Process, 1995 Wis. L. Rev. 463 (1995) (reviewing Komesar, *supra* note 1).

133. *See, e.g.* Bruno S. Frey, *Institutions Matter: The Comparative Analysis of Institutions,* 34 Eur. Econ. Rev. 443 (1990); Eric Stein, *Uses, Misuses—and Nonuses of Comparative Law,* 72 Nw. U. L. Rev. 198 (1977). *See also* Franklin Zimring & Gordon Hawkins, Deterrence: The Legal Threat in Crime Control, 263–70 (1973) (discussing "natural experiments"); Arend Lijphart, *Comparative Politics and the Comparative Method,* 65 Am. Pol. Sci. Rev. 682 (1971).

134. Mauro Cappelletti, Monica Seccombe, & Joseph Weiler, Integration through Law: Europe and the American Federal Experience 5 (Vol. 1, Bk. 1 1986) (citations omitted). *See also* Alberta M. Sbragia, *Thinking about the European Future: The Uses of Comparison, in* Euro-Politics: Institutions and Policymaking in the "New" European Community (Alberta M. Sbragia, ed. 1992)

135. *See, e.g.,* Ugo Mattei, *Efficiency in Legal Transplants: An Essay in Comparative Law and Economics,* 14 Int'l Rev. L. & Econ. 3 (1994) (examining comparative law and economics as a positive discipline, but recognizing the possibility of a normative comparative law and economics).

136. *See* Daniel Farber & Robert Hudec, *Free Trade and the Regulatory State: A GATT's-Eye View of the Dormant Commerce Clause,* 47 Vand. L. Rev. 1401 (1994).

137. Lijphart, *supra* note 133, at 689.

138. *See, e.g.,* the symposium on "megaorganizations," considering inter alia ancient Rome; Tokugawa, Japan; and multinational corporations in comparative perspective, in 151 J. Inst. & Theo. Econ. 703 (1995).

139. *See, e.g.,* Simeon Djankov, Edward Glaeser, Rafael La Porta, Florencio Lopez-de-Silanes, & Andrei Shleifer, The New Comparative Economics (2003); Daron Acemoglu, Simon Johnson, & James Robinson, *The Colonial Origins of Comparative Development: An Empirical Investigation,* 91 Am. Econ. Rev. 1369 (2001); Rafael La Porta, Florencio Lopez-de-Silanes, Andrei Shleifer, & Robert Vishny, *Investor Protection and Corporate Governance,* 58 J. Financial Econ. 3 (2000); Rafael La Porta, Florencio Lopez-de-Silanes, Andrei Shleifer, & Robert W. Vishny, *Law and Finance,* 106 J. Pol. Econ. 113 (1998).

140. Rubin, *supra* note 132, at 471.

141. Komesar, *supra* note 1, at 109.

142. James M. Buchanan & Gordon Tullock, The Calculus of Consent: Logical Foundations of Constitutional Democracy (1962).

143. *See* Robert O. Keohane & Stanley Hoffmann, The New European Community: Decision Making and Institutional Change (1991);

Weiler, *supra* note 8; Bernard Steunenberg, *Decision Making under Different Institutional Arrangements: Legislation by the European Community,* 150 J. INST. & THEO. ECON. 642 (1994).

144. Treaty Establishing the European Economic Community, March 25, 1957, 1973 Gr. Brit. T.S. No. 1 (Cmd.5179_II) 298 U.N.T.S. 3 (1958), as amended by Single European Act, O.J. L 169/1 (1987), [1987] 2 C.M.L.R. 741 [hereinafter, SEA]. The Treaty of Rome has subsequently been amended further.

145. *See* George A. Bermann, *The Single European Act: A New Constitution for the Community?* 27 COLUM. J. TRANSNAT'L L. 529 (1989). *See also* Fritz W. Scharpf, *The Joint-Decision Trap: Lessons from German Federalism and European Integration,* 66 PUB. ADMIN. 239 (1988).

146. For a game-theoretic analysis of these modifications, *see* Robert Cooter & Josef Drexl, *The Logic of Power in the Emerging European Constitution: Game Theory and the Division of Powers,* 14 INT'L REV. L. & ECON. 307 (1994).

147. *See* COMMISSION OF THE EUROPEAN COMMUNITIES, RESEARCH ON THE COST OF NON-EUROPE (1988). *See also* Jean Waelbroeck, *1992: Are the Figures Right? Reflections of a Thirty Per Cent Policy Maker,* in THE COMPLETION OF THE INTERNAL MARKET (Horst Siebert, ed. 1990); Anton Bakhoven, *An Alternative Assessment of the Macro-Economic Effects of "Europe 1992,"* in THE COMPLETION OF THE INTERNAL MARKET (Horst Siebert, ed. 1990).

148. *See* Ellickson, *supra* note 26.

149. Koenrad Lenaerts, *The Role of the Court of Justice of the European Community: Some Thoughts about the Interaction between Judges and Politicians,* 1992 U. CHIC. LEG. FORUM. 93 (1992).

150. *See, e.g.,* original Arts. 169, 170, 173, 175, and 177 of the Treaty of Rome.

151. *See, e.g.,* original Arts. 189, 235, and 236 of the Treaty of Rome.

152. *See* Anthony L. Teasdale, *The Life and Death of the Luxembourg Compromise,* 31 J. COMM. MKT. STUDS. 567 (1993).

153. *Id.* at 568.

154. *See* W. Nicoll, *The Luxembourg Compromise,* 23 J. COMM. MKT. STUDS. 35 (1984) (reprinting the French text of the Luxembourg Compromise).

155. Teasdale, *supra* note 152, at 571.

156. *See* Weingast & Marshall, *supra* note 14. Weingast and Marshall argue that the committee system in the U.S. Congress exists due to the problem of enforcing political bargains in a legislature that votes issue by issue: the problem of noncontemporaneous benefit flows. *See also* Bruno S. Frey, *The Public Choice View of International Political Economy,* in THE POLITICAL ECONOMY OF INTERNATIONAL ORGANIZATIONS 65 (Roland Vaubel and Thomas D. Willett, eds. 1991).

157. Abbott & Snidal, *supra* note 87.

158. Another name for "laundering" is the "democracy deficit."

159. Yarbrough & Yarbrough, *supra* note 26, at 96.

160. *See* JEAN DE RUYT, L'ACTE UNIQUE EUROPEEN 112–19, 255–58 (1989).

161. Andrew Moravcsik, *Negotiating the Single European Act: National Interests and Conventional Statecraft in the European Community,* 45 INT'L ORG. 19 (1991). *See also* David R. Cameron, *The 1992 Initiative: Causes and Consequences, in* EURO-POLITICS: INSTITUTIONS AND POLICYMAKING IN THE "NEW" EUROPEAN COMMUNITY (Alberta M. Sbragia, ed. 1991).

162. Teasdale, *supra* note 152, at 573.

163. Michael Calingaert, THE 1992 CHALLENGE FROM EUROPE: DEVELOPMENT OF THE EUROPEAN COMMUNITY'S INTERNAL MARKET 11 (1988).

164. Robert O. Keohane & Stanley Hoffmann, *Institutional Change in Europe in the 1980s, in* ROBERT O. KEOHANE & STANLEY HOFFMANN, THE NEW EUROPEAN COMMUNITY: DECISION MAKING AND INSTITUTIONAL CHANGE 17 (1991).

165. *See* Joseph H. H. Weiler, *The Future of the European Community in the Light of the American Federal Experience, in* TWO HUNDRED YEARS OF U.S. CONSTITUTION AND THIRTY YEARS OF EEC TREATY 49, 56 (Koen Lenaerts, ed. 1988).

166. *See* William Diebold Jr., *The End of the ITO, in* ESSAYS IN INTERNATIONAL FINANCE 19 (International Finance Section of the Department of Economics and Social Institutions in Princeton University, ed. 1952) (arguing that fear of defection was one of the critical factors in the United States' rejection of the proposed International Trade Organization).

167. This suggestion differs somewhat from the perspective of some of the "legalization" literature, which argues that it is more difficult for states to make stronger commitments. However, this is only half of the picture: while mandatory dispute settlement may make it more difficult for the obligor to agree, it makes it more attractive for the obligee to accept the obligor's promise. Thus, just as borrowers, *ex ante*, prefer enforceable contracts in order to reduce the cost of borrowing, states prefer at least the availability of enforceable treaties to enhance their ability to make commitments, and to get valuable consideration for their commitments.

168. Again, with the possibility of countervailing "regulatory deadweight losses" due to international constraints on national regulatory decisions, in the areas of subsidies, environment, intellectual property, and so on.

169. *See, e.g.,* Andreas F. Lowenfeld, *Remedies along with Rights: Institutional Reform in the New GATT,* 88 AM. J. INT'L L. 477 (1994); G. Richard Shell,

Trade Legalism and International Relations Theory: An Analysis of the World Trade Organization, 44 DUKE L.J. 829 (1995); Michael K. Young, *Dispute Resolution in the Uruguay Round: Lawyers Triumph over Diplomats,* 29 INT'L LAW. 389 (1995); Miguel Montana i Mora, *A GATT with Teeth: Law Wins over Politics in the Resolution of International Trade Disputes,* 31 COLUM. J. TRANSNAT'L L. 103 (1993).

170. In the Omnibus Trade and Competitiveness Act of 1988, the United States expressed as its first trade-negotiating objective "to provide for more effective and expeditious dispute settlement." Omnibus Trade and Competitiveness Act of 1988, Pub. L. No. 100–418, § 1101(b)(1), 102 Stat. 1107 (codified at 19 U.S.C. § 2901(b)(1) (1988)). *But see* Ernst-Ulrich Petersmann, *Uruguay Round Negotiations 1986–1991,* in ERNST-ULRICH PETERSMANN & MEINHARD HILF, THE NEW GATT ROUND OF MULTILATERAL TRADE NEGOTIATIONS: LEGAL AND ECONOMIC PROBLEMS 555 (1991) (arguing that this was not a significant problem).

171. ROBERT E. HUDEC, ENFORCING INTERNATIONAL TRADE LAW: THE EVOLUTION OF THE MODERN GATT LEGAL SYSTEM 286 (1993). *See also* William J. Davey, *Dispute Settlement in GATT,* 11 FORDHAM INT'L L.J. 51 (1987).

172. DSU, Art. 16(4). Automatic adoption can be blocked either by consensus or, for a panel report, by an appeal.

173. TERENCE P. STEWART, THE GATT URUGUAY ROUND: A NEGOTIATING HISTORY (1986–1992) 58–61 (1993). *See also* JOHN CROOME, RESHAPING THE WORLD TRADING SYSTEM: A HISTORY OF THE URUGUAY ROUND 149 (1995).

174. *Id.*

175. ERNEST H. PREEG, TRADERS IN A BRAVE NEW WORLD: THE URUGUAY ROUND AND THE FUTURE OF THE INTERNATIONAL TRADING SYSTEM 78 (1995).

176. *See* Ernst-Ulrich Petersmann, *The Dispute Settlement System of the World Trade Organization and the Evolution of the GATT Dispute Settlement System since 1948,* 31 COMM. MKT. L. REV. 1157, 1216 (1994).

177. *See* Williamson, *supra* note 11, at 390–93.

178. Yarbrough & Yarbrough, *supra* note 26, at 115, referring to Williamson, *supra* note 11, at 204–5.

179. Kirk Monteverde & David Teece, *Supplier Switching Costs and Vertical Integration in the Automobile Industry,* 13 BELL J. ECON. 206 (1982).

6. Interfunctional Linkage and Fragmentation

1. Lawyers may answer positive questions about laws and institutions for linkage that already exist: for example, *whether* and *how* trade rules and

environmental rules are presently combined at the WTO. That has been done in many analyses and in decisions of panels and the Appellate Body at the WTO. *See, e.g.,* Joel Trachtman, Book Review: *Conflict of Norms in Public International Law: How WTO Law Relates to Other Rules of International Law. By Joost Pauwelyn,* 98 AM. J. INT'L L. 855 (2004). It is not the subject of this chapter.

2. *See* Appellate Body Report, *European Communities—Conditions for the Granting of Tariff Preferences to Developing Countries,* WT/DS246/AB/R, April 7, 2004 (describing limits on this type of linkage in the context of the Generalized System of Preferences).

3. Trachtman, *supra* note 1. *See also Appellate Body Decision: Mexico—Soft Drinks,* WT/DS308/AB/R, March 6, 2006 (WTO panels and the Appellate Body are not authorized to interpret other international law for application as law).

4. North American Free Trade Agreement, December 8, 1992, art. 104, 32 I.L.M. 289, 297–98 (1993).

5. *See Thailand—Restrictions on Importation of and Internal Taxes on Cigarettes,* November 7, 1990, DS10/R, 37 B.I.S.D. 200.

6. For a discussion of the relationship between the WTO and the IMF, *see* Frieder Roessler, *Domestic Policy Objectives and the Multilateral Trade Order: Lessons from the Past,* in THE WTO AS AN INTERNATIONAL ORGANIZATION (Anne O. Krueger, ed. 1998).

7. *See* Giancarlo Spagnolo, *Issue Linkage, Credible Delegation, and Policy Cooperation,* Center for Economic Policy Research Discussion Paper No. 2778 (May 2001).

8. *See* Andrew T. Guzman, *International Antitrust and the WTO: The Lesson from Intellectual Property,* 42 VA. J. INT'L L. 933 (2003); Michael P. Ryan, *The Function-Specific and Linkage-Bargain Diplomacy of International Intellectual Property Lawmaking,* 19 U. PA. J. INT'L ECON. L. 535 (1998).

9. JAMES M. BUCHANAN & GORDON TULLOCK, THE CALCULUS OF CONSENT 153 (1962).

10. *See* Kenneth E. Scott, *The Dual Banking System: A Model of Competition in Regulation,* 30 STAN. L. REV. 1 (1977); Henry N. Butler & Jonathan R. Macey, *The Myth of Competition in the Dual Banking System,* 73 CORNELL L. REV. 677 (1988).

11. *See* Henry N. Butler & Jonathan R. Macey, *Externalities and the Matching Principle: The Case for Reallocating Environmental Regulatory Authority,* 14 YALE L. & POL'Y REV. 23, 33 (1996); Daniel C. Esty, *Toward Optimal Environmental Governance,* 74 N.Y.U. L. REV. 1495 (1999).

7. International Adjudication

1. *See* Chapter 5. *See also* James D. Fearon, *Bargaining, Enforcement, and International Cooperation*, 52 INT'L ORG. 269 (1998); Alan O. Sykes, *Protectionism as a "Safeguard": A Positive Analysis of the GATT "Escape Clause" with Normative Speculations*, 58 U. CHI. L. REV. 255 (1991).

2. By "enforceable," I mean not just enforceability in a court of law, but also enforceability through informal means. Of course, there are many examples of unenforceable agreements, and they have purposes. But if they are neither formally nor informally enforceable, they have no direct effect on the parties, but may be designed for political theater: to impress domestic constituencies or other onlookers.

3. For an analysis of the role of dispute resolution in enforcing trade treaties, *see* Warren F. Schwartz & Alan O. Sykes, *The Economic Structure of Renegotiation and Dispute Resolution in the World Trade Organization*, 31 J. LEGAL STUD. 179 (2002).

4. Note the importance ascribed to the Rome Agreement to create an international criminal court. Rome Statute of the International Criminal Court, U.N. Doc. A/CONF.183/9 (1998), *reprinted in* 37 I.L.M. 1002 (1998).

5. *See, e.g.,* MARTIN SHAPIRO, COURTS 28–32 (1981); Michael Wells, *French and American Judicial Opinions*, 19 YALE J. INT'L L. 81, 92 (1994).

6. Art. 10 of the Agreement Establishing the World Trade Organization.

7. *See* Contribution by Chile and the United States, Negotiations on Improvements and Clarifications of the Dispute Settlement Understanding on Improving Flexibility and Member Control in WTO Dispute Settlement, TN/DS/W/28, 23 December 2002.

8. *See* Richard H. Steinberg, *Judicial Law-Making at the WTO: Discursive, Constitutional, and Political Constraints*, 98 AM. J. INTL L. 247 (2004).

9. *See, e.g.,* Robert Cooter & Josef Drexl, *The Logic of Power in the Emerging European Constitution: Game Theory and the Division of Powers*, 14 INT'L REV. L. & ECON. 307 (1994).

10. Gillian K. Hadfield, *Weighing the Value of Vagueness: An Economic Perspective on Precision in the Law*, 82 CAL. L. REV. 541, 547 (1994). *See also* Ian Ayres & Robert Gertner, *Strategic Contractual Inefficiency and the Optimal Choice of Legal Rules*, 101 YALE L.J. 729 (1992).

11. H. L. A. HART, THE CONCEPT OF LAW, chap. VII (2d ed. 1994).

12. *See* Gillian K. Hadfield, *Weighing the Value of Vagueness: An Economic Perspective on Precision in the Law*, 82 CAL. L. REV. 541, 550 (1994), *citing* Linda R. Cohen & Roger G. Noll, *How to Vote, Whether to Vote: Strategies for Voting and Abstaining on Congressional Role Calls*, 13 POL. BEHAV. 97 (1991).

13. Kenneth W. Abbott & Duncan Snidal, *Why States Act through Formal International Organizations*, 42 J. CONFLICT RESOL. 3 (1998).

14. For this use of the terms "primary predictability" and "secondary predictability," *see* William F. Baxter, *Choice of Law and the Federal System*, 16 STAN. L. REV. 1, 3 (1963).

15. *See* Louis Kaplow, *General Characteristics of Rules*, in ENCYCLOPEDIA OF LAW AND ECONOMICS (B. Bouckaert & G. De Geest, eds. 1998); Louis Kaplow, *Rules versus Standards: An Economic Analysis*, 42 DUKE L.J. 557 (1992).

16. *See, e.g.,* John Ferejohn & Barry Weingast, *A Positive Theory of Statutory Interpretation*, 12 INT'L REV. L. & ECON. 263 (1992). *See also* Cass R. Sunstein, *Problems with Rules*, 83 CAL. L. REV. 955, 973 (1995).

17. Cooter & Drexl, *supra* note 9.

18. Jason Scott Johnston, *Bargaining under Rules versus Standards*, 11 J. L. ECON. & ORG. 256 (1995).

19. *Id.* (citations omitted).

20. *See also* Carol Rose, *Crystals and Mud in Property Law*, 40 STAN. L. REV. 577 (1988).

21. Johnston, *supra* note 18, at 257.

22. *Id.* at 272.

23. Appellate Body Report, *European Communities—Measures Affecting Asbestos and Asbestos-Containing Products*, WT/DS135/AB/R, adopted April 5, 2001, at para. 100.

24. Appellate Body Report, *United States—Import Prohibition of Certain Shrimp and Shrimp Products—Recourse to Article 21.5 of the DSU by Malaysia*, WT/DS58/AB/RW; Appellate Body Report, *US—Shrimp*, WT/DS58/AB/R,

25. Appellate Body Report, *Korea—Measures Affecting Imports of Fresh, Chilled and Frozen Beef ("Korea—Various Measures on Beef")*, WT/DS161/AB/R and WT/DS169/AB/R, adopted January 10, 2001.

26. Decision on Trade and Environment, April 14, 1994, WTO Agreement, Annex 1C [hereinafter, Decision on Trade and Environment].

27. World Trade Organization, Report (1996) of the Committee on Trade and Environment, WTO Doc. WT/CTE/W/40 (November 7, 1996) [hereinafter, 1996 CTE Report]. *See* Steve Charnovitz, *A Critical Guide to the WTO's Report on Trade and Environment*, 14 ARIZ. J. INT'L & COMP. LAW 341 (1997).

28. Singapore Ministerial Declaration, adopted December 13, 1996, 36 I.L.M. 218, 224, para. 16 (1997).

29. 1996 CTE Report, *supra* note 27, at 14.

30. NICHOLAS EMILIOU, THE PRINCIPLE OF PROPORTIONALITY IN EUROPEAN LAW: A COMPARATIVE STUDY 6 (1996). A wider definition of proportionality

developed in the European Union context includes three tests: (i) proportionality sensu stricto, (ii) a least trade restrictive alternative test, and (iii) a simple means-ends rationality test. This chapter will consider only the narrower type of proportionality.

31. *See* Michael E. Smith, *State Discriminations against Interstate Commerce,* 74 Cal. L. Rev. 1203, 1205 (1979) ("the Justices take all relevant circumstances into account and render judgment according to their overall sense of the advantages and disadvantages of upholding the regulation"). At their most precise, balancing tests are the same as cost-benefit analyses. *See* Earl M. Maltz, *How Much Regulation Is Too Much—An Examination of Commerce Clause Jurisprudence,* 50 Geo. Wash. L. Rev. 47, 59–60 (1981).

32. "If we had a way of quantifying all the appropriate inputs, and a way of comparing them, and a theory that told us how to do so, we would not call it balancing. Rather, it would be called something like 'deriving the most cost-effective solution,' or just 'solving the problem.'" Stephen E. Gottlieb, *The Paradox of Balancing Significant Interests,* 45 Hastings L.J. 825, 839 (1994). *See also* T. Alexander Aleinikoff, *Constitutional Law in the Age of Balancing,* 96 Yale L.J. 943, 1002–4 (1987).

33. For more general and technical treatment of cost-benefit analysis, *see, e.g.,* Cost-Benefit Analysis: Legal, Philosophical and Economic Perspectives (Matthew D. Adler & Eric A. Posner, eds. 2001); Peter S. Menell & Richard B. Stewart, Environmental Law and Policy 81–160 (1994); D. Pearce & C. Nash, The Social Appraisal of Projects: A Text in Cost-Benefit Analysis (1981); R. Tresch, Public Finance: A Normative Theory (1981); Edith Stokey & Richard Zeckhauser, A Primer for Policy Analysis (1978); E. J. Mishan, Cost-Benefit Analysis (1976); H. Raiffa, Decision Analysis (1968).

34. It is common to distinguish between negative integration, by virtue of invalidating local rules that burden commerce, and positive integration, by virtue of central legislation that preempts or supersedes the local law.

35. Daniel Farber & Robert Hudec, *Free Trade and the Regulatory State: A GATT's-Eye View of the Dormant Commerce Clause,* 47 Vand. L. Rev. 1401, 1402 (1994).

36. Ernst-Ulrich Petersmann, Constitutional Functions and Constitutional Problems of International Economic Law 210–21 (1991); *see also* Jan Tumlir, *Need for an Open Multilateral Trading System,* 6 World Econ. 393, 406 (1983).

37. Edmund Kitch, *Regulation and the American Common Market, in* Regulation, Federalism and Interstate Commerce 13–14 (A. Dan Tarlock, ed. 1981). *But see* Mancur Olson, *The Principle of Fiscal Equivalence: The Division of Responsibilities among Different Levels of Government,*

59 Am. Econ. Rev. 479, 480–81 (1969) (explaining why simple bargaining is insufficient to achieve Pareto optimality under circumstances of positive transaction costs). *See also* Robert P. Inman & Daniel L. Rubinfeld, *A Federalist Fiscal Constitution for an Imperfect World, in* Federalism: Studies in History, Law and Policy (Harry N. Scheiber, ed. 1988).

38. Douglass C. North, *An Economist's Perspective on the American Common Market, in* Regulation, Federalism and Interstate Commerce 78 (A. Dan Tarlock, ed. 1981).

39. *Id. See also* Chapter 5.

40. "If the Contracting Parties were to decide to permit [environmental] trade measures . . . it would be preferable for them to do so not by interpreting Article XX, but by amending or supplementing the provisions of the General Agreement." *United States—Restrictions on Imports of Tuna,* 39 B.I.S.D. 155, 204, para. 6.3 (1993), reprinted in 30 I.L.M. 1594 (1991).

41. Richard B. Collins, *Economic Union as a Constitutional Value,* 63 N.Y.U. L. Rev. 43, 109 (1988). In this regard, the problem can be viewed as having a reciprocal nature in the Coasean sense.

42. Farber & Hudec, *supra* note 35, at 1402.

43. *See* Arend Lijphart, *Comparative Politics and the Comparative Method,* 65 Am. Pol. Sci. Rev. 682 (1971).

44. Cost-benefit analysis may be static: considering the costs and benefits of a single alternative and considering whether the benefits exceed, or otherwise justify, the costs. On the other hand, cost-benefit analysis may be comparative or dynamic: identifying a series of alternatives and choosing the alternative that provides the greatest net benefits or the smallest net costs. For a description of cost-benefit analysis in a comparative mode, *see, e.g.,* James T. Campden, Benefit, Cost, and Beyond: The Political Economy of Benefit-Cost Analysis 22 (1986).

45. Gottlieb, *supra* note 32, at 855, citing James G. March, Decisions and Organizations 3, 12–14 (1988).

46. Farber & Hudec, *supra* note 35, at 1417: "A cost-benefit analysis would insure that the rules were optimal, and also that regulators had taken regulatory burdens on outsiders into account." Farber and Hudec argue that courts avoid cost-benefit analysis because of its Lochnerian implications, and turn to a search for intent. The search for intent often turns into a search for proxies for intent. However, the search for proxies leads back toward more inchoate balancing tests. We thus vacillate between formalism and realism.

47. David Pearce, *The Greening of the GATT: Some Economic Considerations, in* Trade & the Environment: The Search for Balance 20 (James Cameron, Paul Demaret, & Damien Geradin, eds. 1994).

48. C. Ford Runge, Freer Trade, Protected Environment, at 32, 85 (1994).

49. Wouter P. J. Wils, *The Search for the Rule in Article 30 EEC: Much Ado about Nothing*, 1993 Euro. L. Rev. 475 (1993). *See also* Saul Levmore, *Interstate Exploitation and Judicial Intervention* 69 Va. L. Rev. 563, 574 (1983) (arguing for use of cost-benefit analysis in cases of "interferences," and invalidation in cases of "exploitations" under the U.S. Commerce Clause).

50. *See also* Farber & Hudec, *supra* note 35, at 1405: "In a community consisting of several smaller units of government (a United States consisting of individual states, or a GATT consisting of individual nations), the ultimate question is whether the gain of the regulation for insiders outweighs the harm it causes to outsiders" (footnote omitted).

51. *See* Wils, *supra* note 49, at 478–79. Wils establishes a first-best balancing test between "valued regulatory effects" and "anti-integrationist effects," then shows how under former Art. 30 of the Treaty of Rome, the ECJ has retreated from and advanced to such a test.

52. *See, e.g.,* the Unfunded Mandates Reform Act of 1995, Pub. L. No. 104–4, 109 Stat. 48, 2 U.S.C. § 1501.

53. Executive Order No. 12,866 establishes a requirement of cost-benefit analysis. 3 C.F.R. 638 (1994). *See also* the well-known Reagan era predecessor, Executive Order No. 12,291, 3 C.F.R. 127 (1981).

54. Cost-benefit analysis must "include all costs and all benefits of a programme, no matter to whosoever they accrue, over as long a period as is pertinent and practicable." H. E. Klarman, *Application of Cost Benefit Analysis to Health Services*, 4 Int'l J. Health Serv. 326 (1974). *But see* the Unfunded Mandates Reform Act, *supra* note 52, §§ 202, 205 (excluding effects on foreign governments, and perhaps implicitly including only U.S. private sector effects); Economic Analysis of Federal Regulations under Executive Order 12866, a report dated January 11, 1996, prepared by an interagency group convened by the Administrator of the Office of Information and Regulatory Affairs of the Office of Management and Budget, available at http://www.whitehouse.gov/WH/EOP/OMB/html/miscdoc/riaguide.html#select. This report makes the following statement on international effects: "Regulations limiting imports—whether through direct prohibitions or fees, or indirectly through an adverse differential effect on foreign producers or consumers relative to domestic producers and consumers—raise special analytical issues. The economic loss to the United States from limiting imports should be reflected in the net benefit estimate. However, a benefit-cost analysis will generally not be able to measure the potential U.S. loss from the threat of future retaliation by

foreign governments. This threat should then be treated as a qualitative cost." *See* Philip Jones & John Cullis, *Legitimate and Illegitimate Transfers: Dealing with "Political" Cost-Benefit Analysis,* 16 INT'L REV. L. & ECON. 247 (1996).

55. This fact indicates the need for greater functional integration in international society: while the WTO system is concerned with trade matters, and its cost-benefit analysis would not address for example international environmental benefits, it is necessary to include all costs and all benefits in an integrated analysis.

56. South Carolina State Highway Department v. Barnwell Bros., Inc., 303 U.S. 177, 185 n.2 (1938) (citations omitted).

57. Mark Tushnet, *Rethinking the Dormant Commerce Clause,* 1979 WISC. L. REV. 125, 143 (1979).

58. For a review of the economics of externalization, *see* Maureen L. Cropper & Wallace E. Oates, *Environmental Economics: A Survey,* 30 J. ECON. LIT. 675, 677 (1992).

59. *See* Richard Epstein, *Holdouts, Externalities and the Single Owner: One More Salute to Ronald Coase,* 36 J. LAW & ECON. 553 (1993).

60. Levmore, *supra* note 49, at 567. *See also* Frank H. Easterbrook, *Antitrust and the Economics of Federalism,* 26 J. L. & ECON. 23 (1983).

61. Levmore, *supra* note 49, at 610 ("In examining local regulations, courts should be more suspicious of those imposing substantial costs out-of-state than those placing costs primarily within the legislating jurisdiction").

62. Of course, this leaves open a significant distributive issue. *See* Jacques Leboeuf, *The Economics of Federalism and the Proper Scope of the Federal Commerce Power,* 31 SAN DIEGO L. REV. 555 (1994).

63. *See also id.;* Tushnet, *supra* note 57, at 132–33.

64. Regan refers to this argument as the *Carolene Products* theory of the dormant Commerce Clause. Donald Regan, *The Supreme Court and State Protectionism: Making Sense of the Dormant Commerce Clause,* 84 MICH. L. REV. 1091, 1103 (1986): "The central idea of [this theory] is that the courts should supervise state economic regulation in order to guarantee that out-of-state interests, which are unrepresented in the legislature that produced the regulation, are fairly treated." *See also id.* at 1160–67; United States v. Carolene Products Co., 304 U.S. 144 (1938), and especially n.4 thereof, which suggests a process or representation basis for judicial review. For a proponent of this theory, *see* Tushnet, *supra* note 57. *See also* LEA BRILMAYER, CONFLICT OF LAWS: FOUNDATIONS AND FUTURE DIRECTIONS 206 (1991) (arguing against the application of one state's laws to impose costs on persons not part of its political community).

65. *Lochner v. New York*, 198 U.S. 45 (1905). Justice Rufus Peckham's majority opinion in *Lochner* speaks of a means-ends rationality-type review. 198 U.S. at 57–58. Tushnet draws the parallel between substantive due process and Commerce Clause balancing. Tushnet, *supra* note 57, at 143–50.

66. *West Coast Hotel Co. v. Parrish*, 300 U.S. 379 (1937).

67. However, *Lochner* might be resurrected by the recognition that adjudication too is a political process, or at least the exercise of power delegated from the political process.

68. There is, however, an argument that local legislatures would consider "global" values in order to induce reciprocity, or as a matter of specific agreements (subject to the Compacts Clause, U.S. Const., Art. 1, § 10, within the United States) between local governments. *See* the discussion of unilateralism versus multilateralism in Chapter 2.

69. Kathleen Sullivan, *The Supreme Court, 1991 Term Foreword: The Justices of Rules and Standards*, 106 HARV. L. REV. 24, 67 (1992).

70. *But see* the social choice critique of collective decision making.

71. *Reeves, Inc. v. Stake*, 447 U.S. 429, 439 (1980).

72. *CTS Corp. v. Dynamics Corp. of America*, 481 U.S. 69, 95 (Scalia, J., concurring in part and in judgment) (1987). *See* Sullivan, *supra* note 69, at 84 (Scalia would "deconstitutionalize issues and remit to politics"). *See also* Eric J. Segall, *Justice Scalia, Critical Legal Studies, and the Rule of Law*, 62 GEO. WASH. L. REV. 991, 1012 (1994).

73. Regan, *supra* note 64, at 1131.

74. *Id.* at 1165. Regan himself is not completely comfortable with this proposition, suggesting that "interstate comity should prevent a state from passing a law which it knows will impose large costs out-of-state and which secures only a trivial local benefit." *Id.* at 1167. This is a thread that, if pulled, would unravel the rest of Regan's argument, for what is comity but a kind of meta-law, and what is this formulation but a proportionality test? Regan stipulates suggestively but delphically that this comity "should not be judicially enforced in the present context." *Id.* For a defense of Regan's position, *see* Donald Regan, *What Are Trade Agreements For? — Two Conflicting Stories Told by Economists, With a Lesson for Lawyers*, 9:4 J. INT'L ECON. L. 951 (2006).

75. As shown below, anti-discrimination rules are unstable, and shade into proportionality testing, necessity testing, balancing, and perhaps cost-benefit analysis in a way that renders untenable the argument that "simple" anti-discrimination is sufficient.

76. The conventional argument based on judicial competence is framed as follows: "The judiciary has less access to relevant information than does Congress, which can marshall its committee and agency resources to hold hearings and engage in debate before deciding the matter at hand. While this can

be said of any decision of the judiciary, it is of particular import in dormant commerce clause cases because the decision made under the dormant commerce clause is essentially a legislative determination." Martin H. Redish & Shane V. Nugent, *The Dormant Commerce Clause and the Constitutional Balance of Federalism,* 1987 DUKE L.J. 569, 594 (1987). While the first quoted sentence is no doubt true, its relevance is rebutted by the first clause of the second quoted sentence. More importantly, the second clause of the second quoted sentence does no more than beg the relevant question.

77. *See* Chapter 2.

78. *But see* Louis Henkin, *Infallibility under Law: Constitutional Balancing,* 78 COLUM. L. REV. 1022, 1041 (1978), arguing that in the Commerce Clause context, courts "weigh, not constitutional values which have been specially committed to their care, but economic, social, and political data, and they make projections that are normally committed to legislatures and that have presumably been weighed by a state legislature beforehand."

79. *Id.* at 1041 (citations omitted).

80. *See* Kalypso Nicolaidis, *Comment, in* ALAN O. SYKES, PRODUCT STANDARDS FOR INTERNATIONALLY INTEGRATED GOODS MARKETS 143–46 (1995). *See also* Koen Lenaerts, *Two Hundred Years of U.S. Constitution and Thirty Years of EEC Treaty—Outlook for a Comparison,* in TWO HUNDRED YEARS OF U.S. CONSTITUTION AND THIRTY YEARS OF EEC TREATY: OUTLOOK FOR A COMPARISON 17 (Koen Lenaerts, ed. 1988). Lenaerts views the years from 1957 to 1987 as the European Union's "confederal" period, during which unanimity was required for action, resulting in less than satisfactory progress.

81. Professor Henkin points out that "early intervention by the courts, of course, permitted Congress to avoid addressing problems and issues, and may have deterred Congress also from assigning them to regulatory agencies. In fact, the courts have become a kind of regulatory agency applying doctrine that they create and develop, but that is ultimately under congressional control." Henkin, *supra* note 78, at 1041.

82. Redish & Nugent, *supra* note 76, at 594. "Given their origin as negative judicial inferences from a constitutional grant of power to Congress, the Supreme Court's doctrinal limitations on state interference are always subject to congressional revision." LAURENCE H. TRIBE, AMERICAN CONSTITUTIONAL LAW 403 (1988) (citations omitted). *See Whitfield v. Ohio,* 297 U.S. 431, 440 (1936); *in re Rahrer,* 140 U.S. 545, 561 (1891).

83. That is, Congress may authorize the states to take action that would otherwise be preempted. *Prudential Insurance Co. v. Benjamin,* 328 U.S. 408 (1946); *Western & Southern Life Ins. Co. v. State Board of Equalization,* 451 U.S. 648, 658 (1981). *See* Levmore, *supra* note 49, at 567 (arguing that

the Court should base its review of state statutes on the Commerce Clause, rather than other, less reversible, grounds).

84. *See* Tribe, *supra* note 82, at 404.

85. As to the European Community, *see* Koen Lenaerts, *Constitutionalism and the Many Faces of Federalism,* 38 AM. J. COMP. L. 205 (1990); Renaud Dehousse, *Integration v. Regulation? On the Dynamics of Regulation in the European Community,* 30 J. COMMON MKT. STUD. 383 (1992). For an interesting dialogue on this issue, *see* Theodor Schilling, *The Autonomy of the Community Legal Order: An Analysis of Possible Foundations,* 37 HARV. INT'L L.J. 389 (1996); and the response in J. H. H. Weiler & Ulrich R. Haltern, *The Autonomy of the Legal Order: Through the Looking Glass,* 37 HARV. INT'L L.J. 411 (1996). As to the United States, *see* the discussion of cumulative effects on interstate commerce in Tribe, *supra* note 82, at 310–11.

86. *See, e.g.,* Lenaerts, *supra* note 85, at 220 (1990) ("There simply is no nucleus of sovereignty that the Member States can invoke, as such, against the Community"); *Garcia v. San Antonio Metropolitan Transit Authority,* 469 U.S. 528, 552 (1985) ("In short, the Framers chose to rely on a federal system in which special restraints on federal power over the States inhered principally in the workings of the National Government itself, rather than in discrete limitations on the objects of federal authority"). *In Gonzales v. Raich,* 545 U.S. 1 (2005); *United States v. Morrison,* 529 U.S. 598 (2000); *Seminole Tribe v. Florida,* 517 U.S. 44 (1996); *United States v. Lopez,* 514 U.S. 549 (1995); and *New York v. United States,* 505 U.S. 144 (1992), the Supreme Court has shown at least some willingness judicially to circumscribe federal power.

87. *See* Joseph Weiler, *The Transformation of Europe,* 100 YALE L.J. 2403 (1991).

88. *See* Michael T. Maloney, Robert E. McCormick, & Robert D. Tollison, *Economic Regulation, Competitive Governments, and Specialized Resources,* 27 J. L. & ECON. 329, 330 (1984) ("Economic regulation will be less costly for vote-maximizing regulators to supply where the primary costs of cartelization are borne by consumers in foreign jurisdictions").

89. *See* Gregory C. Keating, *Reasonableness and Rationality in Negligence Theory,* 48 STAN. L. REV. 311, 333 (1996).

90. *See generally* GEOFFREY BRENNAN & JAMES M. BUCHANAN, THE REASON OF RULES: CONSTITUTIONAL POLITICAL ECONOMY 28–32 (1985).

91. See Richard L. Revesz & Laura Lowenstein, *Anti-Regulation under the Guise of Rational Regulation: The Bush Administration's Approaches to Valuing Human Lives in Environmental Cost-Benefit Analyses,* working paper (March 12, 2004), available at http://papers.ssrn.com/paper.taf? abstract_id=556721.

92. Potential Pareto efficiency and cost-benefit analysis are criticized by critical legal studies scholars as being indeterminate for two main reasons. First, wealth effects result in preferences that vary depending on the distributive effects of the legal rule at issue, rendering preference-based policy making circular. Second, the value of regulation to individuals varies depending on whether they are asked to pay to avoid a harm or asked how much they would accept to incur a harm: the offer and asking price disparity. *See, e.g.,* MARK KELMAN, A GUIDE TO CRITICAL LEGAL STUDIES 142–50 (1987). On the willingness to pay versus willingness to accept pricing problem, *see, e.g.,* Elizabeth Hoffman & Matthew L. Spitzer, *Willingness to Pay vs. Willingness to Accept: Legal and Economic Implications,* 71 WASH. U. L.Q. 59 (1993).

93. For an analytical survey of the normative critiques, *see* Jane B. Baron & Jeffrey L. Dunoff, *Against Market Rationality: Moral Critiques of Economic Analysis in Legal Theory,* 17 CARD. L. REV. 431 (1996). *See also* FRANK ACKERMAN & LISA HENZERLING, PRICELESS (2004).

94. *See* IRVING L. JANIS & LEON MANN, DECISION MAKING: A PSYCHOLOGICAL ANALYSIS OF CONFLICT, CHOICE, AND COMMITMENT, chap. 6 (1977). *But see* Paul Milgrom, *Is Sympathy an Economic Value? Philosophy, Economics, and the Contingent Valuation Method, in* CONTINGENT VALUATION: A CRITICAL ASSESSMENT (Jerry A. Hausman, ed. 1993).

95. *See* Peter A. Diamond & Jerry A. Hausman, *On Contingent Valuation Measurement of Nonuse Values, in* CONTINGENT VALUATION: A CRITICAL ASSESSMENT 21–23 (Jerry A. Hausman, ed. 1993) (exploring the distinction between willingness to pay and willingness to accept).

96. Robert W. Hahn & John A. Hird, *The Costs and Benefits of Regulation: Review and Synthesis,* 8 YALE J. REG. 233, 242 (1990).

97. *See, e.g.,* Tushnet, *supra* note 57, at 144–45; Baron & Dunoff, *supra* note 93.

98. *See* Cass R. Sunstein, *Incommensurability and Valuation in Law,* 92 MICH. L. REV. 779 (1994).

99. Keating, *supra* note 89, at 311, n.83, citing Armen A. Alchian, *Cost, in* 3 INTERNATIONAL ENCYCLOPEDIA OF THE SOCIAL SCIENCES 404, 405 (David L. Sills, ed. 1968).

100. Indirect market methods "exploit the relationships between environmental quality and various marketed goods." Maureen L. Cropper & Wallace E. Oates, *Environmental Economics: A Survey,* 30 J. ECON. LIT. 675, 677 (1992).

101. Contingent valuation involves direct survey questioning regarding valuation of environment. *See, e.g.,* W. Michael Hannemann, *Valuing the Environment through Contingent Valuation,* 8 J. ECON. PERSP. 19 (1994); Note, *"Ask a Silly Question . . .": Contingent Valuation of Natural Re-*

source Damages, 105 HARV. L. REV. 1981 (1992); Robert C. Mitchell & Richard T. Carson, USING SURVEYS TO VALUE PUBLIC GOODS: THE CONTINGENT VALUATION METHOD 65 (1989); CONTINGENT VALUATION: A CRITICAL ASSESSMENT (Jerry A. Hausman, ed. 1993).

102. This might be something like a system of tradeable pollution permits. See Cropper & Oates, supra note 100, at 682–92.

103. See Bruno S. Frey & Beat Gygi, International Organizations from the Constitutional Point of View, in THE POLITICAL ECONOMY OF INTERNATIONAL ORGANIZATIONS 64 (Roland Vaubel and Thomas D. Willett, eds. 1991). See also Brennan & Buchanan, supra note 90.

104. See, e.g., INTERPERSONAL COMPARISONS OF WELL-BEING (Jon Elster & John E. Roemer, eds. 1991).

105. See, e.g., KENNETH J. ARROW, SOCIAL CHOICE AND INDIVIDUAL VALUE (1963). For a criticism of this perspective, see Herbert Hovenkamp, Arrow's Theorem: Ordinalism and Republican Government, 75 IOWA L. REV. 949 (1990).

106. See Farber & Hudec, supra note 35, at 1408–9, and sources cited therein.

107. OLIVER WENDELL HOLMES, COLLECTED LEGAL PAPERS 295–96 (1920).

108. Lenaerts, supra note 85, at 256.

109. See Eugene D. Cross, Pre-Emption of Member State Law in the European Economic Community: A Framework for Analysis, 29 COMM. MKT. L. REV. 447 (1992).

110. Helmut Jungermann, The Two Camps on Rationality, in JUDGMENT AND DECISION MAKING: AN INTERDISCIPLINARY READER 627, 633 (Hal R. Arkes & Kenneth R. Hammond, eds. 1986)

111. Dehousse has pointed out the "dual subsidiarity" at work in the European Union: "subsidiarity with respect to the [European Union's] main raison d'être, namely market integration, and subsidiarity with respect to national regulatory policies." Dehousse, supra note 85, at 388.

112. See, e.g., Walter Mattli & Anne-Marie Slaughter, Revisiting the European Court of Justice, 52 INT'L ORG. 177 (1998).

113. It is well understood that the telos and the expected destiny of each of these other entities—the United States and the European Union—are, at least at this moment and for the foreseeable future, different from one another and from that of the WTO or other international law. However, the predicate for comparison is difference. The purpose of this comparison is neither to suggest that institutions should be borrowed from one context to the other, nor to assume that other conditions are the same in these contexts. Rather, it is to examine how particular institutional components have worked in one jurisdiction, to begin to understand how these components

would operate in another. For a discussion of the methodology of comparative institutional analysis, *see* Chapter 5.

114. *See* MARTIN SHAPIRO, COURTS: A COMPARATIVE AND POLITICAL ANALYSIS (1981).

115. It will be recalled that it was this exchange model, and its flexibility, that formed the rationale for the ECJ to deny direct effect to GATT within the European Community in the *International Fruit* case, as well as in subsequent jurisprudence. In *International Fruit,* Case 21–24/72 [1972] E.C.R. 1219, the GATT rules were found insufficiently unconditional, precisely because states had the ability to bargain around the rules, or otherwise escape their application. The implication of this decision was that if the rules became more firm, and more unconditional, they would qualify for direct effect. My point is the converse: that to the extent that states intended this law to be conditional, or flexible, it would frustrate states' intent to rigidify it by giving this law direct effect.

116. *See* Meinhard Hilf, *The Role of National Courts in International Trade Relations,* 18 MICH. J. INT'L L. 321, 354 (1997).

117. *See* Edwin D. Dickinson, *Changing Concepts and the Doctrine of Incorporation,* 26 AM. J. INT'L L. 239, 251 (1932).

118. For an opposing perspective, see Pierre Pescatore, *The Doctrine of "Direct Effect": An Infant Disease of Community Law,* 8 EUR. L. REV. 155, 167 (1983).

119. Alfred Rubin suggests that while natural law rights may exist, they are not necessarily appropriate for, or amenable to, application in positive law fora. ALFRED P. RUBIN, ETHICS AND AUTHORITY IN INTERNATIONAL LAW (1997).

120. Robert E. Hudec, *The Role of Judicial Review in Preserving Liberal Trade Policies,* in NATIONAL CONSTITUTIONS AND INTERNATIONAL ECONOMIC LAW 503, 514 (Meinhard Hilf & Ernst-Ulrich Petersmann, eds. 1993).

121. It is not enough to argue that the NGOs are on the side of right, while the corporations are wrong. First, NGOs have their own political biases, and may well not be defenders of right. *See* Clifford Bob, *Merchants of Morality,* Foreign Policy, March–April 2002. Second, in a market economy, corporations play a legitimate role, despite the fact that there was nothing natural about laissez-faire. Thus, the advocacy of neither NGOs nor profit-seeking corporations is presumptively illegitimate.

122. Note that the Free Trade Commission issued Clarifications Related to NAFTA Chapter 11 on July 31, 2001. These clarifications were intended to reduce the potential scope of national measures that could give rise to responsibility.

123. *See* Laurence Helfer's essay in Mark A. Pollack, Martin Shapiro, Karen J. Alter, & Laurence R. Helfer, *Do the Lessons of EU Legal Integration "Travel"?* 13 ECSA REV. 2 (2000).

124. *See* Mark Seidenfeld, *A Civic Republican Justification for the Bureau-cratic State,* 105 HARV. L. REV. 1512 (1992).

125. *See* Curtis A. Bradley, *The Costs of International Human Rights Litiga-tion,* 2 CHI. J. INT'L L. 457, 460 (2001); Peter J. Spiro, *New Global Poten-tates: Nongovernmental Organizations and the "Unregulated" Marketplace,* 18 CARDOZA L. REV. 957 (1996); John R. Bolton, *Should We Take Global Governance Seriously?* 1 CHI. J. INT'L L. 205, 217 (2000) ("Civil society's 'second bite at the apple' [in addition to their domestic ef-forts] raises profoundly troubling questions of democratic theory that its advocates have almost entirely elided"). Dunoff argues that the demo-cratic legitimacy of NGOs is irrelevant, if their arguments are sound. Jef-frey L. Dunoff, *The Misguided Debate over NGO Participation at the WTO,* 1 J. INT'L ECON. L. 433, 439 (1998).

126. Alter and Vargas find that the narrower the interest group's mandate, the more likely it is to use a litigation strategy, while interest groups with broader mandates are less likely to use litigation, because these broad-based interest groups have competing objectives. Karen Alter & Jeannette Vargas, *Explaining Variation in the Use of European Litigation Strategies: EC Law and UK Gender Equality Policy,* 33 COMP. POL. STUDS. 452 (June 2000).

127. *See* Robert E. Hudec, *"Circumventing Democracy": The Political Moral-ity of Trade Negotiations,* 25 N.Y.U. J. INT'L L. & POL. 311 (1993).

128. JOHN H. JACKSON, THE WORLD TRADING SYSTEM 109–11 (2nd ed. 1997).

129. *Id.* at 113; Joel P. Trachtman, *Bananas, Direct Effect and Compliance,* 10 EUR. J. INT'L L. 655 (1999); Kenneth W. Abbott & Duncan Snidal, *Hard and Soft Law in International Governance,* 54 INT'L ORG. 421, 423 (2000): "International actors often deliberately choose softer forms of le-galization as superior institutional arrangements." The role of private par-ties contributes to a determination of whether a particular legal norm is "hard" or "soft," or more accurately, where the norm appears on a contin-uum between hard and soft.

130. Ernst-Ulrich Petersmann, *Constitutionalism and International Organiza-tions,* 17 NORTHW. J. INT'L L. & BUS. 398, 421 (1997). See *also* ERNST-ULRICH PETERSMANN, CONSTITUTIONAL FUNCTIONS AND CONSTITUTIONAL PROBLEMS OF INTERNATIONAL ECONOMIC LAW (1991); Matt Schaefer, *Are Private Remedies in Domestic Courts Essential for International Trade Agreements to Perform Constitutional Functions with Respect to Sub-Federal Governments?* 17 NORTHW. J. INT'L L. & BUS. 609 (1997); John O. McGinnis & Mark L. Movsesian, *The World Trade Constitution,* 114 HARV. L. REV. 512 (2000).

131. *See* Petersmann, *supra* note 130. For a similar perspective in the U.S. domestic sphere, *see* RICHARD EPSTEIN, BARGAINING WITH THE STATE 216–17 (1993) (suggesting broad standing for citizen challenges to laws on

constitutional grounds). For a cogent criticism, *see* Robert L. Howse & Kalypso Nicolaidis, *Legitimacy and Global Governance: Why Constitutionalizing the WTO Is a Step Too Far*, in EFFICIENCY, EQUITY AND LEGITIMACY: THE MULTILATERAL TRADING SYSTEM AT THE MILLENNIUM 236–39 (Robert B. Porter, Pierre Sauvé, Arvind Subramanian, & Americo Beviglia Zampetti, eds. 2001).

132. Case 26/92, *N.V. Algemene Transp. and Expeditie Onderneming Van Gend en Loos v. Nederslandse Administratie der Belastingen*, 1963 E.C.R. 1, 12., [1963] C.M.L.R. 105.

133. WTO Panel Report, *United States—Sections 301–310 of the Trade Act of 1974*, WT/DS152/R (December 19, 1999) [hereinafter, Section 301 Panel Report].

134. *Section 301* Panel Report, para. 7.73.

135. *Section 301* Panel Report, para. 7.78. This type of "indirect effect" is different from that found in ECJ jurisprudence, whereby domestic legislation is required to be interpreted insofar as possible in conformity with European Union law.

136. *See Section 301* Panel Report, para. 7.62 and note 673.

137. *See* Mark A. Pollack, Martin Shapiro, Karen J. Alter, & Laurence R. Helfer, *Do the Lessons of EU Legal Integration "Travel"?* 13 ECSA REV. 2 (2000) (considering in a series of brief essays "whether the study of EU legal integration has yielded generalizable hypotheses or lessons which might inform the study of other domestic or international legal systems").

138. Individuals may be viewed as allies of this attorney-general function, but only as an approximation, and only to the extent that these individual private interests are aligned with international public interests.

139. For such an analysis, see Philip M. Moremen, *Private Rights of Action in International Law*, unpublished Ph.D. dissertation, Fletcher School of Law and Diplomacy, Tufts University (2005).

140. For a review of this literature, see Slaughter & Mattli, *supra* note 112.

141. Eric Stein, *Lawyers, Judges, and the Making of a Transnational Constitution*, 75 AM. J. INT'L L. 1 (1981); Weiler, *supra* note 87; Koen Lenaerts, *Constitutionalism and the Many Faces of Federalism*, 38 AM. J. COMP. L. 205 (1990).

142. *E.g.*, Karen J. Alter, *The European Union's Legal System and Domestic Policy: Spillover or Backlash*, 54 INT'L ORG. 489 (2000).

143. *E.g.*, Alec Stone Sweet & James A. Caporaso, *From Free Trade to Supranational Polity: The European Court and Integration*, in EUROPEAN INTEGRATION AND SUPRANATIONAL GOVERNANCE (W. Sandholtz & A. Stone Sweet, eds. 1998).

144. *E.g.,* Geoffrey Garrett, Daniel Keleman, & Heiner Schulz, *The European Court of Justice, National Governments, and Legal Integration in the European Union,* 52 INT'L ORG. 149 (1998).

145. *See* Robert O. Keohane, Andrew Moravcsik, & Anne-Marie Slaughter, *Legalized Dispute Resolution: Interstate and Transnational,* 54 INT'L ORG. 457 (2000).

146. *See* Panel Discussion, *Is the WTO Dispute Settlement Mechanism Responsive to the Needs of the Traders? Would a System of Direct Action by Private Parties Yield Better Results?* 32 J. WORLD TRADE 148 (1998) (especially remarks of William J. Davey). Gary Horlick refers to the "glass-house problem" (people who live in glass houses should not throw stones), whereby states decline to bring cases in the knowledge that they could be subjected to similar criticism. *Id.* at 151. At that time, Horlick pointed out that there were no cases under the Subsidies Agreement during the first three years of the WTO. He states, "Visibly governments have refused to pull the trigger on many valid subsidy complaints under the Subsidies Agreement because they feel vulnerable themselves." Since that time, there have been a number of subsidies cases, with some perhaps displaying a retaliatory motive.

147. *See* Paul B. Stephan, *Accountability and International Lawmaking: Rules, Rents and Legitimacy,* 17 NORTHW. J. INT'L L. & BUS. 681 (1996); THE POLITICAL ECONOMY OF INTERNATIONAL ORGANIZATIONS (Roland Vaubel and Thomas D. Willett, eds. 1991).

148. *See* Steven Shavell, *The Fundamental Divergence between the Private and Social Motive to Use the Legal System,* 26 J. LEGAL STUD. 1, 1 (1997) ("the privately determined level of litigation can either be socially excessive or inadequate and may call for corrective social policies").

149. *See* Jeffrey Waincymer, *Transparency of Dispute Settlement within the World Trade Organization,* 24 MELB. U. L. REV. 797, 833 (2000).

150. Interestingly, this depends in part on the extent to which tribunals follow precedent: to the extent that a rule in a single case may determine the outcome of other cases, there are greater externalities, either positive or negative. In fact, if one assumes that precedents are useful to others, because they develop efficient rules, because they deter violations by others, or simply because they allow greater predictability, then the very fact of concluded litigation may provide positive externalities. *See* Robert D. Cooter & Daniel L. Rubinfeld, *Economic Analysis of Legal Disputes and Their Resolution,* 27 J. ECON. LIT. 1067, 1092–93 (1989).

151. *See* Philip M. Nichols, *Extension of Standing in World Trade Organization Disputes to Nongovernment Parties,* 17 U. PA. J. INT'L ECON. L. 295, 310–12 (1996) (emphasizing the domestic representativeness component

of the arguments for private participation). Nichols critiques G. Richard Shell, *Trade Legalism and International Relations Theory: An Analysis of the World Trade Organization*, 44 DUKE L.J. 829, 911–13 (1995); Shell responds in G. Richard Shell, *The Trade Stakeholders Model and Participation by Nonstate Parties in the World Trade Organization*, 17 U. PA. J. INT'L ECON. L. 359 (1996). Steve Charnovitz also responded to Nichols. Steve Charnovitz, *Participation of Nongovernmental Organizations in the World Trade Organization*, 17 U. PA. J. INT'L ECON. L. 331, 342 (1996). For Nichols's sur-rebuttals, see Philip M. Nichols, *Realism, Liberalism, Values, and the World Trade Organization*, 17 U. PA. J. INT'L ECON. L. 851 (1996); and Philip M. Nichols, *Two Snowflakes Are Alike: Assumptions Made in the Debate over Standing before World Trade Organization Dispute Settlement Boards*, 24 FORDHAM INT'L L.J. 427 (2000).

152. Including in externalities cost savings available from economies of scale, as well as savings that may arise from avoiding costly strategic problems.

153. *See* Panel Discussion, *supra* note 146, remarks of Professor Eleanor Fox, at 159.

154. *See* Chapter 4. *See also* Alan O. Sykes, *Protectionism as a "Safeguard": A Positive Analysis of the GATT "Escape Clause" with Normative Speculations*, 58 U. CHI. L. REV. 255 (1991). *See also* Warren F. Schwartz & Alan O. Sykes, *The Economic Structure of Renegotiation and Dispute Resolution in the World Trade Organization*, 31 J. LEGAL STUD. 179 (2002).

155. The one-voice argument is important in a number of areas of U.S. jurisprudence, including the Commerce Clause, the asserted exclusive foreign affairs power, the Act of State doctrine, and the Alien Tort Claims Act.

156. *See* Clifford G. Holderness, *Standing, in* 3 NEW PALGRAVE DICTIONARY OF ECONOMICS AND THE LAW 505, 508 (1998); Michael C. Jensen, William H. Meckling, & Clifford G. Holderness, *Analysis of Alternative Standing Doctrines*, 6 INT'L REV. L. & ECON. 205 (1986).

157. Holderness, *supra* note 156, at 506. In the international setting, we might understand this problem as that of an anticommons, in which multiple persons have the right to exclude others from access to a resource. *See* Michael A. Heller, *The Tragedy of the Anticommons: Property in the Transition from Marx to Markets*, 111 HARV. L. REV. 621 (1998). *See also* James M. Buchanan & Yong J. Yoon, *Symmetric Tragedies: Commons and Anticommons*, 43 J. L. & ECON. 1 (2000). In some respects, due to the lack of clarity of international legal rules allocating authority, the international system is both a commons and an anticommons.

158. Holderness, *supra* note 156, at 507. *See also* Ronald Coase, *The Problem of Social Cost*, 3 J. L. & ECON. 1 (1960).

159. For a discussion of the "property-like" aspects of jurisdiction, or governmental authority, and of its implications for allocation of authority, *see* Chapter 2. As discussed there, there are certain transaction cost circumstances in which cloudy property rights might actually promote exchange.

160. John H. Jackson & Alan O. Sykes, *Questions and Comparisons, in* IMPLEMENTING THE URUGUAY ROUND 457, 462 (John H. Jackson & Alan O. Sykes, eds. 1997). For a broader analysis of the value of flexibility to permit "efficient breach" in the context of the GATT escape clause, see Sykes, *supra* note 154.

161. Alan O. Sykes, *Public versus Private Enforcement of International Economic Law: Standing and Remedy,* 34 J. LEGAL STUD. 631 (2005).

162. *See id.*

163. *See* Frieder Roessler, *Are the Judicial Organs of the World Trade Organization Overburdened? in* EFFICIENCY, EQUITY, LEGITIMACY: THE MULTILATERAL TRADING SYSTEM AT THE MILLENNIUM 308 (Roger B. Porter, Pierre Sauvé, Arvind Subramanian, & Americo Beviglia Zampetti, eds. 2001) (arguing that "institutional balance" in the WTO requires a degree of deference by dispute settlement to the political organs of the WTO).

164. *See* Chapter 5; Weiler, *supra* note 87.

165. While the WTO Charter provides for majority voting, these provisions are generally not used.

166. Stone Sweet & Caporaso, *supra* note 143.

167. Steve Charnovitz, *Participation of Nongovernmental Organizations in the World Trade Organization,* 17 U. PA. J. INT'L ECON. L. 331, 353 (1996).

168. *See generally* JERRY L. MASHAW, GREED, CHAOS, AND GOVERNANCE: USING PUBLIC CHOICE TO IMPROVE PUBLIC LAW 118–19, 140–42 (1997). It is not clear to what extent "agency capture" is an important phenomenon. *See* Ian Ayres & John Braithwaite, *Tripartism: Regulatory Capture and Empowerment,* 16 LAW & SOC. INQUIRY 435, 436 (1991) ("capture has not seemed to be theoretically or empirically fertile to many sociologists and political scientists working in the regulation literature"); Jonathan R. Macey, *Transaction Costs and the Normative Elements of the Public Choice Model: An Application to Constitutional Theory,* 74 VA. L. REV. 471, 513 (1988).

169. *See* MANCUR OLSON, THE LOGIC OF COLLECTIVE ACTION (1964).

170. *See* Richard B. Stewart, *The Reformation of American Administrative Law,* 88 HARV. L. REV. 1669 (1975).

171. *See* Erwin P. Eichmann & Gary N. Horlick, *Political Questions in International Trade: Judicial Review of Section 301,* 10 MICH. J. INT'L L. 735 (1989).

172. *See* Case 191/82, *Fediol v. Commission,* 1983 E.C.R. 2913, 2936, [1984] 3 C.M.L.R. 244, 268 (1983).

173. *See* Petersmann, *Constitutionalism and International Organizations, supra* note 130, at 285; Carlos A. Ball, *The Making of a Transnational Capitalist Society: The Court of Justice, Social Policy, and Individual Rights under the European Communities Legal Order,* 37 HARV. INT'L L.J. 307 (1996).

174. Christine Jolls, *Contracts as Bilateral Commitments: A New Perspective on Contract Modification,* 26 J. LEGAL STUDS. 203 (1997) (citations omitted).

175. Moremen, *supra* note 139, at 47.

176. It has been suggested that Mexico, and Canada as well, entered into NAFTA at least in part to "lock in" domestic economic reforms. *See* Jonathan Schlefer, *What Price Economic Growth: North American Free Trade Agreement,* The Atlantic, December 1992, at 113. Similar suggestions have been made with respect to China's accession to the WTO.

177. *See* Petersmann, *Constitutionalism and International Organizations, supra* note 130.

178. *See* Robert D. Putnam, *Diplomacy and Domestic Politics: The Logic of Two-Level Games,* 42 INT'L ORG. 427 (1988); ROBERT D. PUTNAM, DOUBLE-EDGED DIPLOMACY: INTERNATIONAL BARGAINING AND DOMESTIC POLITICS (Peter B. Evans, Harold K. Jacobson, & Robert D. Putnam, eds. 1993).

179. This model of private rights of action is contentious. In *Lujan v. Defenders of Wildlife,* 504 U.S. 555, 571–78 (1992), Justice Scalia rejected congressional authority to vest standing in private persons in order to supervise agency action. In an earlier case, Justice Sandra Day O'Connor had stated that this supervision is the purpose of standing doctrine. *Allen v. Wright,* 468 U.S. 737, 760 (1984).

180. There might be a number of reasons why they would not be optimal. For example, the weak remedies in WTO litigation would serve as an artificial disincentive to litigation by states.

181. Shavell, *supra* note 148. *See also* Mark A. Cohen, *Monitoring and Enforcement of Environmental Policy, in* THE INTERNATIONAL YEARBOOK OF ENVIRONMENTAL AND RESOURCE ECONOMICS 1999/2000 44 (Henk Folmer & Tom Tietenberg, eds. 1999).

182. William Landes & Richard A. Posner, *The Private Enforcement of Law,* 4 J. LEGAL STUD. 1 (1975).

183. Moremen, *supra* note 139, at 35, citing Landes & Posner, *supra* note 182.

184. Richard A. Posner, ECONOMIC ANALYSIS OF LAW 660 (5th ed. 1998).

185. Cohen, *supra* note 181, at 44. In the 1980s, many more citizen suits were filed under the Clean Water Act than under other federal statutes. Jeffrey G. Miller, *Citizen Suits: Private Enforcement of Federal Pollution Control Laws* (1987), citing Environmental Law Institute, *Citizen Suits: An*

Analysis of Citizen Enforcement Actions under EPA-Administered Statutes, at III-4, -5, -9, -10 (1994); Michael Greve, *The Private Enforcement of Environmental Law,* 65 TUL. L. REV. 339, 352 (1990). This is probably because the Act requires polluters to submit detailed monitoring reports, available to the public, which necessarily disclose pollution violations. Citizens can then use these reports as the basis for their claims, significantly reducing the cost of bringing suit. *See* also Jeremy A. Rabkin, *The Secret Life of the Private Attorney General,* 61 L. & CONTEMP. PROBS. 179, 190–92 (1998).

186. *See* Matthew D. McCubbins & Thomas Schwartz, *Congressional Oversight Overlooked: Police Patrols versus Fire Alarms,* 28 AM. POL. SCI. REV. 165 (1984); Kal Raustiala, *Police Patrols and Fire Alarms in the NAAEC,* 26 LOY. L.A. INT'L & COMP. L. REV. 489 (2004); Christina R. Sevilla, *A Political Economy Model of GATT/WTO Trade Complaints,* working paper (1996). Sevilla considers WTO committees such as the Trade Policy Review Mechanism as the equivalent of "police patrols," while dispute settlement complaints brought by private persons are the equivalent of "fire alarms."

187. McCubbins & Schwartz, *supra* note 186, at 172.

188. Sevilla, *supra* note 186, at 16.

189. *See* Steven Shavell, *The Optimal Structure of Law Enforcement,* 36 J. L. & ECON. 255, 267 (1993).

190. Sevilla, *supra* note 186, at 32.

191. Caporaso & Stone Sweet, *supra* note 143, at 115, 120, table 4.4.

192. *Id.* at 120.

193. LISA CONANT, JUSTICE CONTAINED: LAW AND POLITICS IN THE EUROPEAN UNION (2002).

Afterword

1. In the WTO setting, for example, the community formally authorizes retaliation, but does not itself enforce reciprocity.

Index